THE GLOBAL REPUBLIC

THE GLOBAL REPUBLIC

· ·

*America's Inadvertent Rise
to World Power*

FRANK NINKOVICH

THE UNIVERSITY OF CHICAGO PRESS
Chicago and London

FRANK NINKOVICH is professor emeritus of history at St. John's University, New York. He is the author of many books, including *Modernity and Power* and *The Wilsonian Century*, both also published by University of Chicago Press. His most recent book is *Global Dawn: The Cultural Foundation of American Internationalism*.

The University of Chicago Press, Chicago 60637
The University of Chicago Press, Ltd., London
© 2014 by Frank Ninkovich
All rights reserved. Published 2014.
Printed in the United States of America

23 22 21 20 19 18 17 16 15 14   1 2 3 4 5

ISBN-13: 978-0-226-16473-1 (cloth)
ISBN-13: 978-0-226-17333-7 (e-book)
DOI: 10.7208/chicago/9780226173337.001.0001

Library of Congress Cataloging-in-Publication Data

Ninkovich, Frank A., 1944– author.
  The global republic : America's inadvertent rise to world power / Frank Ninkovich.
    pages cm
  Includes bibliographical references and index.
  ISBN 978-0-226-16473-1 (cloth : alk. paper) — ISBN 978-0-226-17333-7 (e-book)
1. United States—Foreign relations—20th century. 2. Exceptionalism—United States. 3. Globalization. I. Title.
  E744.N543 2014
  327.73009′04—dc23

2014004076

To Akira Iriye
For turning on the lights
and allowing me to see

CONTENTS

ACKNOWLEDGMENTS

This is a book that just happened, with little conscious planning, at a point in my scholarly life when I believed that the writing of books was behind me. In retrospect, however, it is obvious that more than a few of its key ideas have been gestating for at least a decade. Most of the points raised in chapter 3 about the discontinuities of American policy in the 1890s were first made in a paper delivered at the University of Konstanz at a conference on imperialism and the civilizing mission in September 2003. Much of chapter 4 has been borrowed from a presentation at the Wilson Center in Washington in October 2006 and a complementary paper delivered at the Sorbonne in January 2008. Parts of the concluding section of chapter 9 are based on an essay, "Paradigms Lost: The Cultural Turn and the Internationalization of American Diplomatic History," written for a Festschrift for Detlef Junker. Some of the arguments about the importance of the cultural background were previously tried out in a paper on culture and anti-imperialism for a conference on American anti-imperialism that met in Oxford in 2011. A revised version of this paper will be published in a Festschrift, edited by Robert David Johnson, in celebration of Akira Iriye's eightieth birthday. Complete references to the published versions of these papers can be found in appropriate locations in the endnotes.

Writing is a lonely business, but doing history is more communal and collaborative than it might seem at first glance. Without the contributions of a host of scholars, it would have been impossible to undertake this work. Some have been acknowledged in the notes, which I had intended to keep to a minimum, but most have gone unnamed. For those who contributed in a hands-on fashion, thanks are due to Doug Mitchell, executive editor of the University of Chicago Press, who was receptive to taking on what in years past would have been an "over the transom" manuscript from an author who was too lazy to negotiate a contract beforehand. I am extremely fortunate to have had him as an editor in a relationship that goes back more than two decades. Tim Mennel, who took over the project from Doug, has earned my respect and gratitude, not only for shepherding the manuscript through the review process, but for going well beyond the call in expertly helping to rewrite portions of the introduction. I should also mention two anonymous, and no doubt ill-paid, reviewers who treated the manuscript with undeserved generosity. Their comments, positive and negative, were extremely helpful. Mark Reschke, who copyedited the manuscript, saved me from numerous errors of style and substance. Copyediting is demanding but indispensable work that deserves more recognition than it typically receives.

As always, my wife Carol has been an indispensable source of support and understanding for a project that required frequent and often prolonged disappearances into the study that often produced no obvious results.

No book is perfect. And while I am aware of some points on which the book is likely to be criticized, and to which I would be able to respond, there are certain to be shortcomings that have eluded me. None of this absolves me from its errors of style and substance, all of which are my own.

This book is dedicated to Akira Iriye, who was my mentor at the University of Chicago in the 1970s and has continued to provide me with advice and support throughout my life as a scholar. This is the second book that I have dedicated to him, the first being what one critic benevolently described as a "workmanlike" effort. I would like to think that this volume is more worthy of being dedicated to Akira. But even if it is, it cannot begin to repay the debt that I owe to him.

INTRODUCTION

This book is a conceptual history of the relationship between globalization and American foreign policy. The abridged version of the story begins in the 1890s when the United States adopted the first of a nearly unbroken succession of globalization-oriented policies and continues through a series of challenges and crises that led, by the end of the twentieth century, to an unprecedented position of global hegemony. In the opening stages of this journey, the United States was in the position of having to adapt to globalization; at midpoint, it became its savior; and as the twenty-first century dawned, the nation was again subordinating itself to a more powerful version of globalization that it had taken great pains to nurture. But whatever the precise relationship at any point in time, throughout this period America's rise to world power was intimately related to the tortuous advance of the globalization process.

With its numerous plot twists and dramatic qualities, this is, by any measure, an extraordinary tale. But it is also the story of a modern foreign policy approach that introduced an unprecedented sweep and complexity to the way that international relations were conceived and carried out. Conspicuously absent from my account, however, is a stock plot device often found in histories of US foreign relations: exceptionalist beliefs. In contrast to a widely held view, a key assertion of this book is that America's climb to global preeminence was *not* animated from the moment of the nation's birth by a deep sense of historical mission, which, if allowed full expression in foreign affairs, was supposed to lead the world to peace, prosperity, and democracy. The stimulus for the nation's ascent to dizzying heights of power, far from emanating from within, was in-

1

stead of external origin, an inadvertent consequence of the need to keep up with a fast-changing globalizing world that was filled with promise and peril.

I would have preferred to avoid entirely the fraught topic of American exceptionalism were it not for the fact that its tenacious staying power stood in the way of telling the story that I have in mind. Doing so requires that I show that exceptionalism was not doing work in foreign policy at the birth of the nation or in various key episodes of its foreign policy history, which is why I have chosen to start my story in 1776 rather than a century later. However, the chief purpose of the book is not to debunk exceptionalism but, more productively, to make a case for global developments as the source of motivation for policies that led to America's ascendancy. Accordingly, following the preliminary removal of obstructions like Manifest Destiny, once under way this intellectual journey will not stop to visit roadside diversions like the crusading impulse, the cultural urge to refashion the world in America's self-image, secular utopianism, or the alleged tendency of Americans to allow their domestic ideology or popular pressures to dictate their approach to foreign relations.

After one sets aside the idea that a deeply rooted universalizing impulse in the national character has been at work since 1776, it becomes easier to recognize the disruptive impact of the first wave of globalization that inundated the world in the nineteenth century. Whereas a story that plays up ideas inherited from the Founding Fathers would emphasize continuity, my narrative highlights an ideological break in which the nation's initial localist outlook on foreign relations was severed from its eighteenth-century republican roots and reoriented in a global direction. The process of breaking away from the past began after the Civil War in the Gilded Age, an era when a new and enduring appreciation of the nation's place in the world took its place as a prominent feature of the wider culture. Those were the years in which Americans came to appreciate the degree to which the breakneck conversion of their pastoral land into an industrial society was the result of irresistible global forces that had come into being independently of American initiative. Like all other nations overrun by globalization, the United States had been in no position to stave off its enormous power.

Cosmopolitan Americans of the day were acutely aware that the United States was becoming an integral part of an emergent international society. Such people realized that one of the principal implications of membership in this planetary process was that the United States was losing its distinctiveness vis-à-vis Europe, that is, it was actually becoming *less* exceptional. But here is the twist: The turn to political globalism that was to make US foreign policy factually unique was grounded in the growing appreciation of the benefits that came from the nation's membership in a global society whose inhabitants were coming to resemble one another in some fundamental ways. Over time, the importance of membership in this society would grow to the point that its good health came to be considered a vital interest. Thus it was the absence of an exceptionalist impulse as commonly understood that made possible the unfolding of this story line.

Early on, this growing alignment with global trends was neatly fitted into a tradition of isolation from the politics of Europe that dated back to the early days of the republic. But foreign policy broke radically new ground around the time of World War II with the adoption of a muscular globalist stance that, as I plan to argue, made US foreign policy unique in world history. Before that critical point was reached, the main concern of American diplomacy had been to integrate the nation into the worldwide societal network through various forms of cooperation. But when that global web was being ripped apart in the late 1930s, the United States decided first to intervene and then to preserve and revitalize international society throughout the period known as the Cold War. Though this foreign policy revolution was sparked by the events of the 1930s, the necessary cultural fuel was already being produced in the late nineteenth century. Put another way, the trajectory of US foreign relations was redirected by international social history—by external happenings—though that is not to suggest that it was an inevitable consequence of global pressures.

More often than not, this connection with globalization was not explicitly articulated or foregrounded in foreign policy discussions. Once its novelty had worn off, the awareness of globalization was internalized and left to work unobtrusively behind the scenes, not unlike a computer's operating system. Because of this taken-for-granted quality, I will refer to the various processes that are lumped together under the rubric of globalization as "the background." The idea of a background will be used in two related senses, the social and the cultural. Society as a background entity has been well explored by sociologists (with the notable exception of its international dimension), while the task of investigating the cultural background has fallen to social theorists and philosophers. For the most part, I refer to the societal background as international society or global society. In one way or another, a concern with international society was a basic component underlying American foreign policy from the late nineteenth century to the present day. Later chapters will shift to a discussion of the role played by the unanticipated appearance of a global cultural background that foreshadowed the transformation of a global society into a global community, a development that was crucial to resolving the Cold War.

This focus on international society gave the history of US foreign relations a creative uniqueness that set it apart from nations that tended to robotically repeat the same old mantras of power. It led the United States to break with assumptions and practices that had been staples of foreign policy for so long that they seemed to enjoy the status of historical laws; in the process, the means and ends of foreign policy were rewritten in a uniquely modern idiom that emphasized the preservation and nurture of a global society. The novel features of this new approach had less to do with a belief in spreading the American dream than with keeping it alive; less with imposing American values on the world than with preserving a way of life that developed countries already enjoyed; less with power politics than with the social conditions that made "great power" status possible in the first place; less with inner drives than with novel external threats; and less with local or regional interests than with global concerns. As great individuals often emerge from great crises, so too with nations.

Of course, whether or not the events I discuss were unique depends on how sharply they stand out in a comparison with the careers of other noteworthy powers. A convincing demonstration of this thesis would have required a lengthy excursion into comparative history and taken me far beyond the limited ambitions of this book, so I will only venture the hypothesis here that a diligent search of the historical record would fail to turn up anything like America's behavior in the twentieth century. With a nod to the historical mind-set that tends to see nothing new under the sun, one can always find some similarities, for example, by comparing the United States to the classical Roman republic, Periclean Athens, or imperial Britain. Fascinating (though ultimately incongruous) affinities with the present can be uncovered in the study of many distant historical phenomena. But history, and especially modern history, is also about novelty and discontinuity, and, especially in recent centuries, radical discontinuity.

A word of caution is in order here because making a claim for the singularity of American policy brings with it a danger of drawing too much attention to national peculiarities at the expense of an appreciation of the globalized age in which we happen to live. Treating American foreign policy as a great departure makes sense only when one sees it in the context of the profound rupture that first revealed itself in the nineteenth century as it became clear what the Industrial Revolution was doing to the world. The history of US foreign relations is closely tied to the growing appreciation of that literally earth-shaking historical transition. While many experts in foreign relations continue to talk about power relationships as if they were historical constants, I have long been persuaded that international relations in the latter-day world have diverged profoundly from traditional patterns.

No one disputes that the industrial way of life is radically novel. This comports with our understanding of the major transitions that humankind has passed through since the emergence of *Homo sapiens* as a species: the passage from hunter-gather Paleolithic existence to an agricultural style of life, which was the foundation of early civilizations, and the shift from an agricultural society to the industrial system that lies at the heart of modern civilization. If societies have changed so radically as a result of these upheavals, why not international relations as well? To me it is obvious that no serious overview of US foreign relations can afford to ignore the most important development of modern world history. US foreign policy was unique, as I hope to show, but its journey could not have been undertaken without being situated in this new global environment.

Notwithstanding my belief in the groundbreaking features of American policy, I have refrained from calling it exceptional. My characterization of American foreign relations, with 1940 as the point of no return, will emphasize the historical singularity of policies whose formulation,

implementation, and consequences were prompted by an unprecedented commitment to maintaining an international society that had
developed independently of American initiative. American exceptionalism, by contrast, suggests a redemptive compulsion to export American
views and values to an unreformed world.

By focusing on the relationship with international society, my goal is to
bring closer together two disciplinary approaches, the sociocultural and
the political, that have tended to go their separate ways without demonstrating much appreciation of what the other has to offer. Unfortunately,
the path I have chosen to travel toward this destination bypasses many
important social and political elements of US foreign relations. Portray-
ing the decisions to act as the bulwark of world society in such general
terms runs the risk of making it appear that policies evolved smoothly
and naturally when in reality they were the result of problematic personal and political choices by those who believed in international society, often in the face of determined opposition from many others who
did not. The political side of my story will pass over many important
debates, within the government and in the private sector, which had an
important bearing on what happened. Nongovernmental relations, already the subject of an enormous literature, will be neglected to an even
greater extent. Doing history in this way is akin to simplifying fractions
in math, where the general relationship is clarified by throwing out most
of the vital particulars.

In extenuation, this book was conceived as a conceptual history that
focuses on the influence of foundational worldviews or axioms that
straddle the line between culture and ideology. By conceptual, I mean
that it proceeds from a single overarching idea—America's response to
globalization—that works itself out in complicated ways that would only
be obscured in a fact-laden narrative history of US foreign relations.
Structuring the account in this way was a calculated decision on my
part. For that reason, I am keenly aware that this book oversimplifies a
history whose intricacies many skillful historians have taken great pains
to explore. But had I done otherwise the pace of the argument would
have slowed to an unproductive crawl. Thus, making sense of my story
requires that the reader be familiar, at least in broad outline, with the history of US foreign relations. Those who crave an in-depth understanding

of excluded events and themes will have to look elsewhere to the work of historians who have mined the documents and archival sources with a thoroughness that I could never hope to equal.

But that in turn points to the virtues of my account. Regrettably, one downside of scholarly productiveness is that our stockpile of data is now so vast that it threatens to overtax our ways of processing it. We are, according to one historian, "snowed under by an avalanche of information, much of it unassimilable into a coherent national narrative."[1] But while facts may rule in history, interpretation continues to reign as sovereign. If only to impose order and coherence on an unruly realm of facts, a reliance on interpretation is unavoidable. Hence this book is probably best viewed as another way of telling the story—and, one hopes, a better way than the interpretive schemas currently in use. However, to identify it as an interpretation, or a history stingy with the facts, does not mean that it is factitious, for it is fully consistent with the details that other historians work with—more so, actually, because it incorporates more categories of facts than are found in traditional narratives of foreign relations.

Though its basic idea is quite simple, nevertheless I would maintain that it is a more complex way of framing a story that is impossibly intricate and beyond my ability, or that of any historian, to fully explain. The complexity in this case comes from trying to tie together national and global narratives, but also to connect political, social, and cultural aspects of foreign relations that have come to resemble separate and often warring disciplinary kingdoms. The point is that more convincing explanations of foreign relations require that the connections between politics and society be brought together in ways that reflect their intricate relationship in real life. I am not an absolutist when it comes to historical explanations—a historian certain of the truth is deceiving himself—but I am certain of the inexhaustible complexity of history. So while this narrative is hardly the whole story, its conceptual design makes possible a more textured account than the deceptively smooth tales that we have been telling ourselves.

....

Herewith the plan of this book. Chapter 1 looks at exceptionalism prior to the Civil War and argues that the republican ideology of the Founding Fathers provided neither means, motive, nor opportunity to create a foreign policy aimed at implementing the export of American ideals. If anything, the antebellum period saw republican ideas shrink in importance and in geographical scope vis-à-vis foreign relations. Chapter 2 introduces a development crucial to my argument, the advent of globalization. It argues that opinion elites, whose members would become the makers of foreign policy, realized that the United States would need to adapt to this powerful new global reality rather than vice versa. It also shows how the idea of exceptionalism was challenged by an awareness of America's wide-ranging inferiority to Europe. In the end, however, various schemes of accommodation to international society, all of them based on the assumption of a deep compatibility between domestic and international trends, were devised. The third chapter discusses American foreign policy at the fin de siècle in the light of this new understanding of the desirability of adaptation, the principal political expressions of which were imperialism and dollar diplomacy. The underlying theme of these precursory policies was the longing for recognition as a great power by emphasizing America's role as a senior partner in abetting the globalization process.

Chapter 4 tries to take a fresh look at Wilsonianism—the poster child for those who believe that American foreign policy is afflicted by exceptionalist idealism—by continuing to focus on international society. The thrust of the argument is that Wilsonianism, contrary to its reputation, was a freakish, ill-conceived, one-off episode in the history of US foreign relations. The signature theme of the Wilsonian project, Wilson's promotion of the League of Nations, was a historical cul-de-sac, the practical terminus of one strand of American thinking about international relations, and not an especially American strand, at that. Wilson was still a great president. But, over the long term, his most important contributions lay in other directions, none of them notably idealistic—for example, keeping alive liberal ideas such as free trade and forewarning his audiences about the threats to liberal globalization arising from revolutionary changes in warfare.

Chapter 5 addresses the 1920s, which remain an underappreciated period, especially in light of the continuing influence that this decade's policy assumptions would continue to exert on American policy through the remainder of the century and beyond. The foreign policies of this Republican decade are best understood as a continuation and amplification of policies that had been articulated immediately prior to the Great War, principally the reliance placed on international cooperation and commercial and cultural exchanges. There was one huge change, however: the United States now held the chair in the club of great powers. Undergirding the various foreign policy mutations of the decade was the axiomatic belief that international society, with the Great War behind it, was constitutionally robust and required no drastic political involvement by the United States for it to be restored to good health.

The turning point at which the United States made the choice to preserve and sustain a globalized international environment that might otherwise collapse is discussed in chapter 6. It shows that the nature of the threat facing the country in World War II was more diffuse and shot through with uncertainty than the self-assured postwar consensus would have it. Many intelligent isolationists who challenged the realist position also doubted that such a thing as international society even existed or, if it did, that it mattered very much for American security. But that did not mean that there was no threat, for an appreciation of the dangerous consequences of the collapse of international society rested on more solid empirical ground than did ill-defined and highly arguable forecasts of the military dangers facing the country. The debate was put to rest only by participation in a war whose aims were defined as the rescue and repair of the political and economic organs of a critically injured global society. In the process, the political and the social came together in unprecedented ways, ushering in an era in which the United States became not only a global power but a historically unparalleled one as well.

Chapter 7 approaches the Cold War as a singular episode in the history of foreign relations in the way it was perceived, fought, and resolved. The methodological predicament at the heart of the United States–Soviet rivalry was the impossibility of finding a political or military way of resolving the conflict. Because all conceivable power solutions led to dead ends, the most likely outcome appeared to be an indefinite continuation of the status quo. However, power did play a critical role in the Cold War, if only negatively, by averting a third world war, thus opening

9

a space for economic and cultural forces to step in and make possible what politics could not achieve. This peaceful resolution of the struggle was in marked contrast to a long history of international relations in which major transitions of power have been midwifed by war.

How ideology and culture influenced the outcome of the Cold War in ways far more important than normally conceded is the subject of chapter 8. Here, I distinguish between ideology and culture to show how background processes affected the outcome of the Cold War. Over-simplified, the argument is that government policies were ideological in nature, and hence political, even those policies that were advertised as being nonpolitical. As a result, they could have only minor impacts on the outcome of the Cold War. Only cultural processes that lay beyond the range of political manipulation, whose anatomy is briefly discussed, could do more. As it happened, the dawning of a global culture created a background that opened up the possibility of significant political change.

Chapter 9 takes up the topic of change in the international cultural background, better known as Americanization or the formation of a global culture, and argues that these nonpolitical phenomena were crucial to the resolution of the Cold War. Americanization, however, needs to be understood as a catalyst that gave new life to the globalization process and should not be mistaken for the larger process. The chapter also reintroduces individual agency as an important part of the story in the person of Mikhail Gorbachev, whose understanding of the changes in international society led him to make decisions that were crucial to ending the Cold War in a peaceful manner. This emphasis on the operation of intercultural processes raises a basic question: is the Cold War better understood in terms of conflict or as an instance of politically aided acculturation?

Chapter 10 attempts to sort out how best to explain the first two post–Cold War decades. The outlook prevailing at the time was that American exceptionalism was at its apogee. My view is that the military dominance of the United States was an institutional residue of the Cold War, that the policies of the so-called war on terror were a historical outlier, and that the social and cultural foundations of the extraordinary influence enjoyed by the United States were at any rate beginning to erode. The

war on terror was a new wrinkle without solid roots in America's historical approach to the problems of globalization. The concluding chapter
provides a conceptual wrap-up of what has been presented. The historiographical appendix is probably best seen in the physiological sense
as a vestigial organ—unnecessary for the functioning of the book yet
potentially life threatening when diseased.

For those who are indifferent to conceptual arguments, I hope that
this shorthand account will become more legible once it has been more
fully spelled out.

....

The title of this book is not meant in the sense that political scientists
sometimes use it: as a theoretical conception of the world as a republic.
For obvious reasons, the achievement of that kind of global republic
faces insuperable obstacles in any future worth worrying about. Instead,
the title is intended to suggest two complementary meanings, the more
conspicuous being the globalizing impact of the United States. But this
was a two-way process in which the United States was itself affected
by globalization. One side or another of this double-edged sword may
have cut deeper at particular times—in the late nineteenth century, it
was clearly the United States that was primarily on the receiving end of
globalization, whereas a century later it would be a major globalizing
force—but the larger point is that the process was always reciprocal, tension laden, and politically productive.

If I were younger and possessed of the same general understanding of
US foreign relations that I now enjoy, the chapters of this book would
provide the program for a life's work. But it is too late for that. Ordinarily, historical wisdom is the product of insights and information accumulated in the course a lengthy life's journey. In my case, such wisdom
as I have been able to gather consists of glimpsing a way forward for a
journey that I am unable to begin.

1 Provincial Prelude

Limiting Legacies

"We have it in our power to begin the world over again," boasted Thomas Paine in his revolutionary pamphlet *Common Sense*. By announcing that "the birthday of a new world is at hand," Paine was articulating a common assumption about the origins of American exceptionalism: that by breaking free from England the American colonists were also escaping from the grip of the past and ushering in a new era of world history. Unfortunately, his revolutionary swagger was riddled with wishful thinking, for while separation from Britain was merely difficult, securing independence from the past was impossible. For one thing, the faith in American exceptionalism did not originate in an act of self-creation, but was descended from a sense of British exceptionalism that permeated America's political consciousness long before the countdown to revolution began. In classic Burkean fashion, the political way of life of the new state grew out of a well-established tradition of colonial self-rule. Common ethnicity, British common law, the English language, religious links, literary and intellectual culture, and bonds of trade — none of these connections and affinities disappeared in 1776. Following independence and through most of the nineteenth century, these and other important features of American life would remain outliers of developments in Britain and in Europe. So deep was this legacy that more than two centuries of growing cultural distance and ethnic diversification would not eradicate it.[1] Expectations of leading others to a radically new future would prove even more unrealistic.

The past, especially the political ideology inherited from Britain, provided the cultural wherewithal that enabled Americans to conceptualize their grievances and their liberation. In this case, Britain was only the custodian for a bundle of ideas whose lineage ran from classical Greece and Rome, to Renaissance Italy, and then through the opposition English "country" Whigs, whose arguments against the crown were appropriated as the ideological vocabulary of the revolution. As is obvious from the wealth of classical references in the political discourse of the period, this deep historical legacy allowed Americans to frame their revolution and constitution making in a well-established context of principles and practices. Indeed, the kinetic energy stored in the call of the past was so strong that echoes of the republican civic creed would reverberate through the centuries following the founding.[2]

But this inherited Atlantic republicanism would also circumscribe what the new republic could hope to achieve, particularly in its foreign relations. While some of its features overlapped with elements that later were incorporated into liberal thought, others were alien to what would become the liberal sensibility, particularly the obsession with civic virtue as the core value of a republic. A virtuous citizen, in the classical sense, was expected to place the good of the community above personal desires, quite unlike the liberal commitment to individual self-fulfillment. This emphasis on the centrality of altruism, though quite useful in making the argument against a corrupt British monarch and indispensable in time of war, was a serious liability in creating the kind of humdrum world of peace and prosperity that many Americans hoped would come into being in the wake of their revolution. In its classical form, virtue had been indispensable to survival in a Greco-Roman world inhabited by carnivorous polities in which war belonged to the natural order of things. In that kind of environment, only militarily virtuous republics could hope to remain standing in the midst of violent neighbors. At best, in the classical scheme of things, republican universalism envisaged a

13

world of militant republics competing with one another to demonstrate the superiority of their brand of virtue.

Any hopes of creating a peaceful new world thus depended on the degree to which the United States was able to break with the classical past and its history of violence. In theory, this was not impossible, for the new United States was, by some key measures, the antithesis of a classical republic. The constituent ideas of republicanism, even the core belief in a virtuous altruism, were already in process of being dramatically altered under the influence of the Enlightenment and a nascent liberalism. The historian J. G. A. Pocock, widely credited with calling attention to the role of republicanism as the ideology of the American Revolution, pointed out that it was "notorious that classical republicanism was . . . transformed in the making of the Federal Constitution and the Federalist and Republican minds." The most celebrated reversal of hoary republican truths involved James Madison's abandonment of the hitherto axiomatic view of republics as territorially diminutive face-to-face civic communities. In his classic *Federalist* number 10, Madison argued ingeniously that a large republic could be stable because it could neutralize the problem of faction in national politics by confining it to the local level.[3]

In making his case, Madison jettisoned another republican axiom. Whereas the classical view held that successful republics required public spirited citizens, Madison postulated a society of self-interested individuals who possessed "different and unequal faculties of acquiring property." The influence of local men on the make, whose natural tendency was to coalesce into self-serving factions and parties, could be diluted to harmless proportions within the new republic's vast territory, thereby making room for a high-minded elite—"representatives whose enlightened views and virtuous sentiments render them superior to local prejudices and schemes of injustice"—to guide the nation. True, Madison did not do away with virtue altogether, whose most noble features would continue to reside in a quasi-aristocratic class. But whether self-interest was something that needed to be reined in or, as later liberal thought would have it, to be unleashed, the definition of virtue, which was the central concept of republicanism, was radically different in the American republic and was already en route to being hustled off the stage. Madison's innovations marked a sharp change from the Founders' view in the 1770s of a virtuous public to the more jaundiced outlook of the 1780s in which an uninhibited and unprincipled populace was thought to be dangerously prone to "licentiousness."[4]

Despite many continuing affinities with the republican past, there is little reason to doubt, therefore, as one historian has concluded, that "there was, in, fact, a chasm separating the Americans from the ancient Greeks" or that the domestic institutions of the United States were unmistakably anomalous for their day. This form of republicanism was genuinely novel, as Thomas Jefferson, in particular, never tired of repeating. "We can no longer say that there is nothing new under the sun," he wrote in 1801. "For this whole chapter in the history of man is new. The great extent of our Republic is new. Its sparse habitation is new. The mighty wave of public opinion which has rolled over it is new." And he was right, for the American Revolution was in many respects an Enlightenment project that represented a radical break not only with the monarchical past, but also with many elements of classical republicanism. Among its distinguishing characteristics was a commitment to popular sovereignty, constitutionalism, divided powers of government, and political representation via elections based on an expansive male franchise. The pointed Jeffersonian emphasis on liberating the people from the grip of government in order to pursue their individual desires marked a 180 degree conceptual reversal of classical republican theory in which the polis shaped the people. So pronounced were the differences that the new republican state, standing alone in a world of monarchical empires, stood out like a fresh flower among a family of nations overrun by weeds. By such measures, it did really seem, as Paine claimed, that "a new era for politics is struck—a new method of thinking hath arisen."[5]

However, in contrast to its creative achievements on the domestic side, American republican thinking about foreign affairs hewed more closely to British-inspired views. At first sight, these received ideas appeared to be potentially as transformative as their domestic complements, for the outlook passed on by the opposition country Whigs appeared to offer a means of escape from the cutthroat world of foreign relations in which republics had always been ensnared. The hostility of radical Whigs to the European balance of power fit nicely into the Enlightenment narrative of breaking away from a conflict-ridden past. At the same time, their emphasis on peaceful commerce distanced American republicanism from the classical fixation with war. To be sure, the new nation had more than its share of hardheaded types who saw commerce in a more cynical light, but in Alexander Hamilton's recollection, at the end of the Revolutionary War "the phantom of perpetual peace danced before the eyes of every body." The problem with this republican idealism, however, was that its own ideas placed major obstacles in the way of republicanism's spread.[6]

In the long run, the more enthusiastic among the revolutionaries believed that foreign policy difficulties would melt away following the universalization of the American model. As starry-eyed rebels everywhere tend to do, they presumed that the coming era of enlightened self-rule would attract other peoples into following the new nation's example, thus ending the conspicuous marginality of America's position as an outlier of Europe. This expectation that Americans were creating a model republic was evident prior to the Enlightenment, when John Winthrop, the first governor of Massachusetts Bay Colony, told his Puritan shipmates that "we must always consider that we shall be as a city upon a hill—the eyes of all people are upon us." The motto of the great seal, *novus ordo seculorum*—the new order of the ages—expressed a commonplace contemporary understanding of the nation's progressive historical meaning. Timothy Dwight, the president of Yale, brazenly asserted that the United States was destined to be "God's own Word," while in his inaugural address, Thomas Jefferson would call America "the world's best hope" and "a chosen country." Paine's conviction that "the cause of America is in a great measure the cause of all mankind" was well on the way to becoming a self-evident truth of America's political culture.[7]

The universal aspirations were plainly apparent, but they raised a very practical question: How, exactly, would republicanism spread? Even had the new republic desired to propagate its ideas by official means, it possessed neither the desire nor the power to forcefully promote the advance of its ideology to other parts of the globe. In the absence of a foreign policy aimed specifically at spreading revolutionary ideals, there were only two possibilities, contagion and commerce. In the short run, the only possible way for republican ideas to spread was through imitation rather than policy. However, the power of American example depended in turn upon the continued spread of the Enlightenment, an international cultural process over which the United States exercised no control, whose center lay in Europe. In its most ambitious iteration, this would involve the creation of new republics abroad, but also their eventual consolidation into a universal federal republic. Unlike imitation, which relied on the diffusion of seductive ideas, commerce appeared to hold the promise of a radical change achieved by means of social processes. Unfortunately for those who looked to a future of worldwide republican expansion, each possibility contained fatal shortcomings. In the end, formidable conceptual and practical barriers to universality, the residual influence of classical republican assumptions, and the underdeveloped state of liberal ideas presented insurmountable barriers to aspirations for republican expansion.

Jefferson, arguably the most prominent believer in America's millenarian destiny, also serves as the best example of the limited role that American foreign policy could play in fulfilling the nation's ideological ambitions. At the time, the only possible vector for the viral transmission of republicanism was revolutionary France, with whom Jefferson had developed an intense identification that was partly geopolitical and partly ideological. As one scholar put it, Jefferson "considered France as the sheet anchor of this country and its friendship as a great object," both because the Franco-American alliance had made possible independence from Great Britain and because the French Revolution had given a "coup de grâce" to the prospects of monarchy in the United States. But it was the French Revolution's incendiary potential in Europe that set Jefferson's republican glands to salivating. Though he would have preferred to see the upheaval stop in 1790 with the adoption of the mixed constitution, in an infamous 1793 letter to his chargé d'affaires he nevertheless defended the revolution's excesses up to that point. "Rather than it should have failed," he wrote, "I would have seen half the earth desolated. Were there but an Adam and Eve left in every country, left free, it would be better than as it now is."

Jefferson was clearly operating on the "if Paris sneezes . . ." hypothesis, in the hope that the success of republicanism in France would create an irresistible momentum in other lands. Should republican govern-

17

ment become established in France, he wrote to George Mason, "it will spread sooner or later all over Europe." On the other hand, if the revolution failed, "a check there would retard the revival of liberty in other countries." In 1795, shortly after retiring as secretary of state, he saw in the continuing turmoil in Holland and France the unfolding of an ineluctable process. "This ball of liberty," he predicted, "is now so well in motion that it will roll round the globe, at least the enlightened part of it, for light & liberty go together. It is our glory that we first put it into motion." Unfortunately, revolutions of this magnitude depended upon factors that were utterly beyond the control of American policy makers. If one defines a policy as instrumental governmental action whose deliberate intent is to produce an outcome B as a result of doing A, this hopeful expectation had as much influence on the trajectory of the French Revolution as cheerleaders have on the outcome of a football game.[8]

Politically, the love affair with France was exceedingly brief, as second thoughts materialized quickly when the firebrand Girondist consul Edmond-Charles Genêt, in blatant disregard of the Washington administration's policy of neutrality, began to actively recruit American privateers to prey on British shipping. Even those who would have been willing to throw in their lot with France soon tempered their enthusiasm. Jefferson, most notably, realized that his hopes had been built on a flimsy foundation. His sober reassessment marked a return to some of his more skeptical initial judgments about France's capacity for change. In 1787, for example, when serving as US minister in Paris, he wrote to Abigail Adams that "this nation is incapable of any serious effort but under the word of command." In another letter written at the same time, he feared that a revolutionary France was likely to overreach. "Should they attempt more than the established habits of the people are ripe for," he warned, "they may lose all, and retard indefinitely the ultimate object of their aim." When it came to cultural maturity, he was convinced that the French people were two centuries behind American yeomen farmers for whom self-government had become second nature.[9]

In the end, waiting for France was, like waiting for Godot, an absurdist exercise. Only after the alliance broke up in the late 1790s did Jefferson bring himself to admit that "the people of France have never been in the habit of self-government, are not yet in the habit of acknowledging that fundamental law of nature, by which alone self-government can be exercised by a society, I mean the lex majoris partis." In 1802, trying to explain away his earlier views, he exclaimed, "Who could have thought the French people incapable of [self-government]?" He would remain a lifelong Francophile, albeit much chastened in his view of what was politically possible in France. Perhaps ruing his earlier enthusiasm, in his last years he even altered his letters to suggest that he had been more consistently negative in his view of France's future. But whatever his earlier position, there is no question of his skeptical mature outlook. Thus in an 1817 letter to Lafayette, he restated a position that he had maintained when he first arrived in France: "What government she can bear, depends not on the state of science, however exalted, in a band of enlightened men, but on the condition of the general mind." For Jefferson, revolution was something that happened only to nations that had attained a certain level of enlightenment, but when and how that level was attained in each case could not be determined in advance.[10]

The weakening of revolutionary momentum was a huge disappointment, both with France and with the larger historical process. For the better part of two centuries to follow, American estimates of France would be colored by the judgment that France's potential for republicanism was severely handicapped by defects buried deep within its national character, which made for an erratic politics plagued with authoritarian temptations and regime changes. Cultural constraints were not unique to France; they severely curbed American expectations about the possibility for progress in all countries. Ultimately, the lesson learned by Americans was the one taught by Edmund Burke in his famous *Reflections on the Revolution in France*: that deep cultural traditions and habits of political conduct threw up insuperable barriers to thoroughgoing revolutionary makeovers, whether sparked from within or imposed from the outside. The practical implications of this view pointed to the need for resigned patience over the long term. In a late letter to John Adams, Jefferson predicted eventual self-government in Europe and Spanish America, but "to attain all this however rivers of blood must yet flow, and years of desolation pass over." The moral of the story? Other peoples might look to the United States for inspiration, but they would have to rely first and foremost on their own cultural resources. Thus far, the people of the United States were among the few who possessed the character traits needed to support a republic. The list of other societies on the threshold of republicanism was not long. Just as discouraging, if revolutionary contagion was unlikely in the near future, there was no sense of the mechanics of the process whereby republicanism would proliferate over the long term.[11]

Apart from imitation, the only other route to expanding republicanism lay through trade. Many Enlightenment intellectuals were already beginning to argue that trade conduced to peace and that trading nations were less prone to warlike behavior. Thinkers like Adam Smith, the French physiocrats, Voltaire, and David Hume, among others, envisioned a new international division of labor that would promote interdependence among nations. This marked an enormous advance over ancient economic views in which land was the basic source of wealth, margins over subsistence were slender, wealth was accumulated via power, and in which a generalized increase in well-being through economic growth was not part of the mental landscape. In the new enlightened view, trade made for prosperity, encouraged "the rise of politeness and learning" (Hume), and removed "destructive prejudices" and produced "gentle mores" (Montesquieu). In the words of the poet Joel Barlow, a republican internationalist, the spirit of commerce was calculated "to open an amicable intercourse between countries, to soften the horrors of war, to enlarge the field of science and speculation, and to assimilate the manners, feelings, and languages of all nations." The Model Treaty adopted in 1776 by the Continental Congress, which outlined comparatively open commercial standards while ignoring political obstacles, has been viewed by some historians as a practical attempt to promote this Enlightenment view of commerce.[12]

But enthusiasm for the utopian potential of commerce was atypical among Enlightenment republicans, who were often of two minds on the matter. Behaviorally, the new republic's attitude to trade was decidedly nonutopian. In colonial America, trade was largely viewed, as James Hutson has argued, in bilateral terms of reciprocal advantage, a perspective that dominated the commercial affairs of the early republic. As one historian put it, "Americans learned few lessons from revisionist ideas in political economy. Straight through the imperial crisis, Revolution, and the establishment of national government, American politicians used a predominantly prerevolutionary, mercantilist political economy to understand their commercial circumstances and to devise policies for them." The events of the 1780s appeared to confirm these analyses, as the United States found itself embroiled in competition over fisheries, the carrying trade, and in commercial rivalry more generally, not to mention territorial disputes at every point of the compass.[13]

Small wonder, then, that the Founders were such quick studies who understood the rules of power politics and were quick to exploit divisions among the European powers. The founding generation lived in a transatlantic world in which trade was essential to many: slaves, finished products, markets for American fish, agricultural produce, and rum were all important to the colonial economy. For that reason alone, foreign policy, to the extent that trade and relations with the Europeans were necessary, would have to be conducted according to Europe's rules rather than American preferences. Trade took place within a world of empires, which used the commonly understood selfish principles of mercantilism to grant privileges on the basis of self-interest narrowly conceived. In this world, commerce was construed as a prize or weapon. The Americans understood this full well, having used commercial extortion to good effect upon the British prior to the revolution, but when the shoe was on the other foot they were quick to recognize their weakness and to accept what was conceded to them. Jay's Treaty of 1794, negotiated when the French Revolution was at high tide, left tempers inflamed in the United States, but it was on the whole a good deal and certainly better than no deal at all. That the treaty was accepted in the end dovetailed with the realistic political economy of the time. Even if, for the sake of argument, Americans had preferred a revolutionary system of free trade, there was no way of putting it into place in a world of empires where commerce continued to be dominated by exclusionary mercantilist practices.

The extent of America's commercial network, though far-reaching, was not yet global, being limited largely to the Atlantic world in which European empires lay at the center. With the exception of the slave trade, Africa was a mercantile desert; the China trade was in its early days; and even large swaths of Europe were obscure and of little commercial interest. Probably the most important region was the Caribbean, both as a site of trade and as the anticipated locus of future commercial and perhaps territorial expansion. That was one reason why Alexander Hamilton, in two numbers of *The Federalist*, outlined a geographic scheme that would later be adopted as part of the Monroe Doctrine. It was not an idealistic position, but one that was based on a hardheaded understanding of geopolitics in which the world was conceived as being divided into four spheres—Europe, Africa, the Americas, and Asia—and in which the obvious destiny of the United States was to dominate the Americas.

Hamilton's skepticism about the irenic effects of commerce is well known, but even the idealistic Jefferson, who on occasion enthused about the benefits of releasing commerce from its shackles, was conflicted on the matter. On the negative side, the legacy of classical republicanism exerted a strong bias against international exchange. Unlike some proto-liberals who conflated commerce and peace, Jefferson long held the opposite view. Beginning with his famous apothegm in the *Notes on Virginia* ("abandon the ocean and escape war"), he would sing the same refrain for years to come. In a 1785 letter he said, "Were I to indulge my own theory, I should wish our states to practice neither commerce nor navigation, but to stand with respect to Europe precisely on the footing of China. We would thus avoid wars, and all our citizens would be husbandmen"—though he was quick to add that "this is theory only, and a theory which the servants of America are not at liberty to follow."[14] Even so, thirty years later, he was still warning that too much commerce would "bring nothing to our country but wars, debt and dilapidation."[15]

With their preindustrial outlook, Jeffersonian republicans continued to glorify yeoman farmers, living in rural face-to-face communities, against the mercantile interests. Although the Jeffersonian notion of interest centered on economic self-interest, it was the individual self-interest of the farmer and not the merchant that was paramount in his scheme. Jefferson's ambivalence about exchange harked back to classical times, when the widely admired Spartan polis minimized trade for fear of being seduced by wealth, luxury, and corruption. Even in the Athenian case, where trade was essential to empire, much of the commerce in the city was in the hands of the *metics*, resident aliens who, like the Jews in medieval Europe or the Phanariot Greeks in Ottoman Istanbul, performed functions considered beneath the dignity of leisured Athenian citizens.

The lifeworld of Americans in the era of the revolution was overwhelmingly local, and he would have preferred to keep it that way for fear that trade would have a corrupting effect. The problem, as he put it, was that "money and not morality is the principle of commerce and commercial nations." If trade was necessary, domestic commerce was far preferable to foreign transactions.[16]

Although statements of this kind suggest that Jefferson saw commerce as politically entangling and ideologically corrupting, his views were more complicated than that. A complete cutoff of trade was impractical, for even he was forced to admit that commerce was necessary, though only as a handmaiden to agriculture. For those of the Jeffersonian persuasion, trade was supplementary to agricultural activity in a premodern republic that depended primarily on open space for continued settlement as a condition of maintaining its agricultural orientation. Trade was a secondary good that in measured doses was beneficial, but in the last analysis it was something that could be sacrificed to a greater political end. It was with such reasoning that the revolutionaries had launched successful boycotts against Great Britain in the 1760s and the 1770s. The coercive benefits of limiting British access to the American market continued to loom large in the thinking in the minds of Jefferson and Madison. But while Jefferson, like Adam Smith, was not insensible to using trade as an instrument of "peaceable coercion," as a substitute for war in which mercantilist prohibitions could be met by counterprohibitions, that did not mean that trade itself, for Americans at any rate, was worth fighting over. In good classical republican fashion, for Jefferson, sacrificing trade made good sense, especially when it could be used as a weapon in contentious dealings with powers that were dependent on commerce.[17]

The spectacularly unsuccessful embargo in the run-up to the War of 1812, whose self-denying assumptions look positively weird to contemporary eyes, made all the sense in the world from the republican perspective. Because he believed the United States to be "the only monument of human rights and the sole depository of the sacred fire of freedom and self government, whence it is to be lighted up in other regions of the earth," he asked rhetorically, "to what sacrifices of interest, or commerce ought not these considerations to animate us?" For all the

23

self-inflicted pain caused by the embargo, Jefferson spied a silver lining in the form of an unintended program of import substitution avant la lettre. The stimulus to domestic manufactures provided by the embargo would reduce America's dependence on foreign producers, especially for enervating luxury goods, and thereby lessen the harmful effects of commercial entanglements. Thus, in this ironic Jeffersonian twist, a war fought on behalf of neutral rights—the unimpeded right to trade with and make money from belligerents in wartime—found its vindication in the building up of an autarchic capability. If Jefferson's decidedly anti-liberal views are any indication, assigning much weight to the influence of Adam Smith and other Enlightenment writers on commerce may be presumptuous.[18]

Nevertheless, Jefferson was also a child of the Enlightenment who was not insensible to arguments about the benefits of commerce. Although trade could be a handmaiden of corruption, entanglement, and war, its Enlightenment image was far more pleasing. Stressing its benign side, Jefferson wrote to Elbridge Gerry in 1799 that "I am for free commerce with all nations; political connection with none"—a maxim that was incoherent then and later for those who knew trade to be a catalyst for political embroilment. But while arguments about the general benefits of freer trade were on the increase since the late seventeenth century, these arguments focused primarily on the advantages to be derived from a more specialized international division of labor. Just as prominent in these discussions as the economic benefits to be derived from the un-impeded exchange of goods was the conviction that trade would expose strange peoples to each others' ideas and, in the process, spread enlightenment, almost as if trade were a way of conducting an international conversation. Thus American merchants would have the same role in spreading republican ideas as Muslim traders in Asia who had been so instrumental in spreading the Islamic faith on that continent.[19]

Trade mattered a great deal: to New England shipping interests, southern slaveholders, and others besides. As a reminder of how serious a business it was, one should recall that the original purpose of the Annapolis Convention of 1786, which led to the calling of the Constitutional Convention in Philadelphia the next year, was to address practical problems of international trade. But to this Enlightenment way of thinking, trade was merely a convenient way of meeting some basic needs and a means of cultural exchange, not a coercive instrument for creating a global society. Tellingly, intercultural understanding operated via an elite cosmopolitanism rather than at the mass level, thus constituting what one author has called "a self-serving privilege for cosmopolitans" in which knowledge and delectation of the exotic was a perquisite of the well-educated few. In the eighteenth century, no one was as yet talking of global homogenization or a global culture. Cultures would remain separate and distinctive. An appreciation of the beauty of cultural particularity was an aesthetic activity restricted to cosmopolitan types who, from their rarefied perches, were free as tourists or anthropologists to enjoy the diverse delights of the world. A reciprocal process that expanded the horizons of a small numbers of cultural connoisseurs could hardly be expected to transform entire political cultures. At bottom, the Enlightenment conception of commerce was a way of maintaining a fragmented and incoherent international system rather than a means of transforming it.[20]

As a system of ideas, compared to what would come after, this was a very weak view of economics, more poetry than social science. Enlightenment republican thought possessed no sense of economic behavior as a powerful, and perhaps decisive, autonomous social force. According to Joyce Appleby, in classical civic humanist thought "no concepts existed for analyzing a trading system that had not only moved beyond the confines of political boundaries but had created wealth essential to the conduct of politics." The situation was not yet one where "necessity, rather than a mutually beneficial exchange of services" was the primary motive behind trade. Moreover, there were, as yet, few intimations of infrastructural forces at work, of explosive productive powers operating beneath the surface that had the potential to utterly transform societies by wiping out livelihoods, entire ways of life, and the international system as well. It was known that trade bred cities, mobs, and mercantile elites—all bad things to Jeffersonians—but before the advent of revolutionary technologies like steamship transport and the telegraph and the ability to create industrial production platforms in undeveloped societies, the republican view of trade was absent any sense of its massive potential to transform entire ways of life.[21]

In its impracticality, the republican outlook on foreign affairs was to liberalism what utopian socialism would be to Marxism, which is to say that the United States was lacking in the conceptual and practical tools for a revolutionary foreign policy. Its domestic innovations, which were by far more radical, could not be translated into policies that would spread the American model abroad. The refusal of diplomats like John Adams to adopt court dress or to engage in aristocratic kowtowing was a symbolic assertion of the nation's different domestic makeup, but such posturing had little practical bite. In their misplaced hope for republican revolutions in Europe, Jeffersonians were not unlike the Bolsheviks of 1917 who counted on revolutions in the West to validate their boldness. But for a truly radical foreign policy, one needed to look no further than revolutionary and Napoleonic France, which was far more disruptive of the old order in its zeal to employ force in spreading revolutionary ideas and institutional practices. Americans had received only a small taste of French revolutionary ardor in the Genêt affair; European nations would experience its effects in more profound and enduring ways.

Enlightenment republicanism was distinctly premodern in at least one other fundamental respect: like its classical forebears, the particularism and localism of its outlook distinctly limited its geographic horizons. For classical republicans, a political morality that was closely tied to the polis was impossible to reconcile with the universalist claims of the Enlightenment. Unlike classical republics, face-to-face communities that were tightly bound to specific places, the Madisonian republic was not so restricted, but it was nevertheless a territorially limited political space. Even after Jefferson's purchase of Louisiana, the republic was essentially continental, a New World. With the addition of vast new territories to the west and south, until the middle of the nineteenth century the expansion of republicanism would mean continental expansion. And that expansion would continue to be based on local communities in which bonds of shared experience continued to unite the self-regarding individuals of whom Madison had written. The roots of community remained local, its outlook more in keeping with commonsense philosophy than with liberal notions.[22]

What could ideological universalism have meant in the eighteenth century? In the thinking of someone like Kant, perhaps, "the world itself formed a republic," as one scholar suggests, but American republicanism was still far removed from seeing the world as a community, actual or potential. There was yet no bond of shared experience, the social fact that lay at the root of republican thinking, to warrant imagining the universalization of American republican ideals. The Founding Fathers were a remarkably cosmopolitan lot who believed in the universality of science, but they were not societal universalists, nor were their fellow Americans citizens of the world. No one at the time was realistically talking about the spread of republicanism to China, Japan, or Africa. The understanding of geography was still too sketchy and the understanding of other peoples too primitive for this kind of global ambition to have taken root. American views of their fellow human beings, as everyone acknowledges, were restricted by their narrow conceptions of race, gender, and culture and by a lack of understanding about how such boundaries might be overcome. They were also restricted by the absence of a sense of the possibilities for sweeping cultural change and human integration that would come into being only in the next century. That expansion of sensibility would depend on new concepts of culture and an updated understanding of the socially revolutionizing impact of commerce and industrial technology.[23]

So, notwithstanding their extraordinary ideological inventiveness, Americans could not escape fully from the insularity of classical republicanism. Considered as a system of thought with the potential for spreading a way of life abroad, the particularistic residues of a waning republican mentality remained too strong while the universalizing potential of Enlightenment proto-liberalism was still too weak, underdeveloped both conceptually and in real-world application. The policy options were no less unfriendly to expansion. The weak Enlightenment view of trade, even if it had somehow been able to replace the mercantilist system, could not have done the trick. The United States would quickly become a great trading nation, but two-way commerce was an unsuitable vehicle for the fulfillment of unidirectional millenarian expectations. The only other conceivable means by which republicanism might spread was imitation, but cultural constraints on the adoption of democratic institutions abroad suggested little progress to come on this score in the near future. By process of elimination, that meant there was very little foreign policy significance to republican exceptionalism. Before Americans could hope to change the world, first the world would have to change, as would the American understanding of the world.

Coming Down to Earth: The Ascendancy of Local Interests before 1865

Sooner or later, all revolutions come down to earth. After 1800, once the bubble of revolutionary expectations for millennial change in Europe had been punctured, the focus of American policy shifted to more conventional concerns of war, peace, and commerce. Though that might appear to suggest that the United States became an ordinary nation, it overstates the degree to which foreign policy mattered prior to the Civil War. As the new nation rid itself of foreign threats, it enjoyed the luxury of being able to devote itself to local concerns, principally to expansion across the continent and its consequences. In this geographically bounded version of republican expansion, domestic policy drove foreign policy. The most prominent ideological counterpart of this process, a belief in the nation's Manifest Destiny, justified spreading the American way of life as a cover for appropriating and settling land and dispossessing Native Americans, all the while sidestepping an increasingly fractious debate over what the American way of life actually was.

With the American model unsuitable for overseas export, the most important determinants of American foreign policy until the onset of the Civil War were political geography and demography. With the Atlantic Ocean on one side and a continental expanse on the other inhabited by relatively powerless peoples, Americans enjoyed an unusual degree of freedom from the kinds of dangers that preoccupied the diplomats of most other nations. Changes in political geography were indispensable to creating a misconceived sense of "free security." After 1815, Europe's political horizons contracted as a consequence of the gradual breakup of the old mercantilist system, most noticeably with the disintegration of the Spanish empire in Latin America. As Europe became more inward looking, so too did the United States. With no Europe-erected barriers to stop it, a powerful wave of continental expansion became the common thread of both domestic and foreign policy. This was already evident in the dawning years of the century. As one French writer then observed,

American ambition "tends to nothing less than to devour the whole of North America, whilst Europe is unconscious of their object."[24]

Unencumbered by fear of a foreign power or by a powerful central government, American republicanism was increasingly at liberty to cater to the appetites of local and particular interests, be they freebooting individuals, ravenous economic groupings, or spread-eagling regions. Overland expansion in the nineteenth century had a number of features that might be characterized as "hard" interests, that is, objects of desire that possess compelling qualities. Most notable was the inexorable retreat of the agricultural frontier, which was sometimes seen as a peaceful process of settlement. The contrast between the advance of armies and agriculturalists was then a conventional way of describing what was going on. In Tocqueville's description, for example, Russia's military expansion was set off against American continental conquests that were "gained by the plough share," though in practice the process was far from bloodless. It was also implacable, as the unrelenting movement westward of settlers often left the government scrambling to deal with the consequences of their forward progress. Alongside the advancing farmers were trappers, cattle ranchers, miners, and traders seeking harbors on the Pacific Coast for overseas trade, all of whom added to the pressure on the government. And, lastly, there were geopolitical interests in which the further acquisition and settlement of territory was justified in the knowledge that if the United States did not claim and occupy this "Virgin Land," one of the European powers was likely to do so and establish a balance of power system in the Western hemisphere.[25]

One might question whether farming was a hard "interest." Land hunger is a metaphor that describes a sociocultural longing, not some natural urge that demands regular satisfaction. Moreover, farming for many people was a way of life determined by choice, in part out of the desire to participate in the romance and the cultural mystique of life on the land. And there is reason to question how profitable and satisfying farming was. But all interests are to some extent socially shaped, and yeoman farming in the preindustrial era was a powerfully seductive way of life that embodied the republican ideal. Farming afforded the possibility of a self-made existence that was not yet challenged by the kinds of competing life choices that an urban-industrial society would soon

29

make possible or, in many cases, necessary. For politicians, all this was irrelevant, as farmers were still numerically predominant among voters, constituting a potent interest group that would have been politically suicidal to oppose. As far as interests went, farming was as compelling an interest as one could imagine.

By the late 1840s, expansion was being justified under the banner of "Manifest Destiny." The peculiarly American flavor of this frontier advance, in which new states continued to be added to the union, was "republican expansion" of the kind envisioned by Franklin, Madison, and John Quincy Adams and the kind later celebrated by the historian Frederick Jackson Turner as the nation's defining experience. This way of putting it suggests that expansion was an expression of nationalism, when in practice it was anything but. The settlers were not propelled by Madisonian rationales, a belief in Manifest Destiny, or some peculiarly American cultural impulse, but by powerful material interests. Though the chattering classes may have talked in terms of extending the sphere of freedom, this counted for little to those on the frontier for whom acquiring land was the underlying motivation and for whom the vernacular meaning of Manifest Destiny was "This is ours." For a time, expansion appeared to be capable of providing enough elbow room to satisfy the contending interests. But the idea of expansion as a transcendent interest began to fall apart as soon as conflicting kinds of land hunger came into direct contact, at which point the idea of nation itself came into question.

The rather obvious ideological toupee covering an otherwise bald pate of expansion perhaps explains what Richard W. van Alstyne once called "the pharisiaical flavour" of American foreign policy prior to the Civil War. The moral nadir came in 1846, when President James K. Polk precipitated a war with Mexico that culminated in the nation's largest and most notorious landgrab. In addition to extending the southern boundary of Texas, where American immigrant settlers had already won independence from Mexico in 1836, Polk acquired California, Utah, Arizona, and portions of other future states. Polk was an aggressive and energetic leader, but to blame him and his supporters for foisting an ideological *Lebensraum* on the nation would be extreme, because for all his audacity Polk was a servant of some very potent domestic pressure groups. His methods, not his results, were the chief objects of controversy.[26]

The term "Manifest Destiny" was itself a tip-off that a smoke screen was being laid down. Manifest Destiny could be taken to mean that Americans were God's chosen people fulfilling a divine plan to take over and govern what came to be forty-eight contiguous states of the union. As a matter of faith, the term implied that expansion was so obviously written in the stars that it was not worth taking the trouble to justify. Thus viewed, Manifest Destiny was a slogan whose justification was to serve as a justification—in this case, to rationalize the dispossession of Native Americans, Mexicans, and anyone else who got in the way of this irrepressible movement of population. In its role as a justification, it is an excellent illustration of the concept of ideology as a belief system whose chief function was to rationalize the material interests of collective be-havior. Apart from camouflaging the base desires of people who were interested in acquiring land or wealth in other forms, its causal value was negligible. But Manifest Destiny was too superficial to be a real ideology, for ideologies are complicated systems of thought with the power to gen-erate enthusiasm in their own right. However hard one tries, it is difficult to imagine anyone being moved to action at this time solely by a belief in Manifest Destiny. *Belle parole, ma brutti fatti.*[27]

The historian Frederick Merk hit on something important when he distinguished Manifest Destiny from mission as ideological forces in American life. Far from being a national ideology that expressed funda-mental beliefs, he argued that Manifest Destiny was concocted by and for particular interests. Besides providing a source of income for some enterprising publicists, it served as cover for voracious farmers on the expanding frontier, whereas mission was something less concretely em-bedded, broader, more intellectual and abstract, more cultural, more idealistic, and a more praiseworthy expression of the national character. Whether mission as Merk defined it was laudable or as influential as he suggests is open to question, but his main point—to show Manifest Destiny in a narrow and selfish light by dispersing the idealistic fog of its rhetoric—was well taken. Considered purely as an intellectual artifact, if one is looking for a cultural compulsion that pointed to a larger global future, Manifest Destiny was clearly a deeply parochial expression of an expansionist impulse that had no relevance to the fulfillment of exceptionalist ambitions in the wider world.[28]

The superficial character of Manifest Destiny comes out more clearly when overland expansion is viewed in comparative context. To focus exclusively on the connection between overland expansion and local interests misses something deeper and more universal at work, a civilizational process whose dynamics were not uniquely American. Although Americans long subscribed to the notion of an unoccupied continent with vast amounts of Virgin Land available for the taking, it is now clear that a substantial population of Native Americans, numbering perhaps as many as ten million, was already present prior to the arrival of the European settlers. Though large numbers of Indians practiced agriculture (which gave them, according to the taxonomy of the times, the intermediate status of "barbarians"), the superior numbers, technology, weaponry, relative immunity to diseases, and organizational skills of the white settlers left no doubt about the final outcome.

Over the broad sweep of history, barbarian peoples had often posed significant threats to civilized societies, but Americans no longer took seriously the possibility of catastrophic defeat on the frontier. Writing in his notebook, Alexis de Tocqueville described the "cold selfishness and complete insensibility" of the American attitude toward Native Americans. "This world here belongs to us, they tell themselves every day; the Indian race is destined for final destruction which one cannot prevent and which it is not desirable to delay. Heaven has not made them to become civilized; it is necessary that they die." Leaders like John Quincy Adams, Henry Clay, and John Calhoun agreed that the Indians were "destined to extinction" and "not worth preserving." The result, nineteenth-century Americans believed, was foreordained, and many onlookers agreed. The pioneering geologist Charles Lyell, for example, wrote that "few future events are more certain than the speedy extermination of the Indians of North America . . . in the course of a few centuries, when these tribes will be remembered only in poetry and tradition."[29]

The plausibility of this grim verdict accords with our contemporary understanding of sweeping historical processes in which, beginning with the Neolithic revolution, hunter-gatherers receded before the advance of civilized agriculturalists. How and why this happened varied from case to case, as violence, disease, technology, trade, overhunting, enticement, acculturation, cultural ecology, and climate change played out their various influences. In this case, Native Americans were confronted by a double-barreled assault of modern agriculturalists embedded within an incipient industrial civilization. Whatever the particular combination of pressures, in the long run the net outcome was the same: the end of a premodern way of life through assimilation, displacement to the margins, and outright extinction. As Andrew Jackson explained to Congress in 1830, the government was being confronted, in his view, by "events which it cannot control." He acknowledged that "humanity has often wept over the fate of the aborigines of this country, and philanthropy has been long busily employed in devising means to avert it," but only by way of prelude to the grim conclusion that civilization's progress "has never for a moment been arrested, and one by one have many powerful tribes disappeared from the earth."[30]

It is easy to be condemnatory long after the fact—for his part in the removal of the Cherokee, Jackson has been described as "the ethnic cleanser of the first democratic age"—but it is hard to plausibly imagine how the larger outcome, by one account "the greatest demographic calamity in human history," could have been avoided. Unfortunately, morality is a helpless bystander to those historical processes that fit the Greek understanding of tragedy as something horrible that is beyond the capacity of humans to prevent. There were heartfelt objections, undeniably, but the many contemporary expressions of guilt and howls of protest at the iniquity of American behavior had little effect. Much of the outrage emanated from New England, a region where the natives had long since been pushed aside. This made it easy for cynics to dismiss such complaints as coming from people who had gotten religion only after having sinfully disposed of their own Indian problem. Morality was even less a concern to a government joined at the hip with importunate farmers and settlers whose expansionist desires it would have been unthinkable to thwart. Though the antebellum American state was a weak and limited organism, one doubts that even a stronger government could have held this movement in check. In principle, the evolution of westward movement could be steered by political means, but the basic process itself was outside of politics, even prior to politics, which meant that the spectrum of foreign policy choice was quite limited.[31]

This kind of expansion would have taken place with enormous speed and power regardless of the provenance of the settlers—so long as their origins lay in Europe—with ideology providing little more than window-dressing. As historian Michael Hunt, among others, has observed, "this process was in its origins and in its outcome wholly unexceptional." Nowhere in the world was stopping this kind of demographic steamroller a live political possibility. That is why the frontier experiences of Russia, Canada, Australia, and New Zealand, nations in South and Central American, the Boers in South Africa, not to mention many other peoples over time, were similar in broad outline. In each instance, the more modern society extended its own way of life, territorially and culturally, at the expense of less developed peoples. Given these striking similarities, one doubts that American expansion during this period, as some historians have claimed, "derived from the primordial, exceptional American commitment to liberty" or from a "secular utopianism." Instead of being attributable to a specifically American cultural impulse, it was the product of historically broader and deeper civilizational forces. It was in this sense that one writer insisted that "the triumph of Civilization over Barbarism is the only Manifest Destiny of America." Viewed in this comparative light, there was little of note that was distinctively American about Manifest Destiny.[32]

The overall process of expansion at the expense of the original inhabitants was no more reversible or preventable than the southward flow of the Mississippi, but, like the river, it could be channeled in a distinctively American fashion. In the 1830s, the US Supreme Court, that most Madisonian of federal institutions, handed down a number of important decisions that sought to domesticate a foreign policy problem and to normalize a one-sided civilizational struggle. Legally, the status of the Indians was dealt with in a contradictory fashion. Supreme Court Chief Justice John Marshall's decision in *Cherokee Nation v. Georgia*, which characterized the Cherokee as a "denominated domestic dependent nation," was a masterpiece of oxymoronic thinking that wrestled with the irreconcilable tendencies at work. Later, in *Worcester v. Georgia*, the Cherokee were defined as a "distinct community" who were subject only to federal and not state law. The treaty process was reaffirmed as a way of providing a fig leaf of sovereign equality before the law of nations. But while international law at least assumed a legal equality of states, "nation" as defined by the court in this instance was a grotesque caricature of nineteenth-century models of nationalism.

All this was clearly a legal fiction, a pretense created to deal with a situation that conventional law was incapable of addressing. Marshall was draping a legal cloak over a process that was largely beyond the reach of the law, whether national or international. Law implies legitimacy coupled with the power to coerce, but in this case the law was absolutely impotent to rein in some ungovernable social forces. Jackson's apocryphal statement, "John Marshall has made his decision, now let him enforce it," perhaps best captured the sense of inevitability that surrounded the issue. Marshall's attempt to square the circle was not entirely unsuccessful, as it did lead to a regularization of the process of expropriation and displacement, but it was ultimately a progression of events in which human choice, the law, morality, and anthropological romanticism were powerless to reverse the larger outcome. In extenuation, things might have been worse, for without such a solution Native Americans would have been left to the untender mercies of the states.[33]

Although Manifest Destiny was a justification of particular interests, in the end it was not a very coherent justification because it also masked an explosive tension between ideology and political practice. Vis-à-vis the outside world, virtue was supposed to be on display in the exemplary nature of republican institutions; but on the local level, the kowtowing to expansionist local interests had the effect of throwing those very institutions into question. Although slavery as an institution appeared to be on the verge of dying out in the early 1800s, it quickly sank deeper roots as a basic interest following the invention of the cotton gin, as the spectacular growth of the cotton economy and its attendant need for slave labor gave the institution a new life and an aggressive new ideological rationale. The "peculiar institution" was a particularistic euphemism that surfaced in the late 1820s whose intent was to distinguish southern slavery from harsher varieties found elsewhere as well as from the northern and liberal way of life more generally. Its very name constituted an explicit denial of universality and modernity. Southern ideologues took

35

pride in painting their region as being based on traditional mores, locality, codes of honor and virtue, as a society that was paternalistic, hierarchical, and proudly romantic in sensibility.

Slave owners were not a naked interest group, for they did try to dress up their interest with a corporatist conception of society and an international ideology of sorts. Their localism was embellished by a wider regional imaginary, "an American Mediterranean," which, if not exactly cosmopolitan, provided a touch of international embroidery to the ideological fabric of slavery. Although southern polemicists tried to paint the contrast with the North in black and white colors, the North was hardly an anti-South, everything that the South was not. By comparison, the North was comparatively unclothed ideologically. If the South defined itself by slavery, antislavery was not yet a northern cause. For most of the antebellum period, the universal side of the antislavery cause was being promoted chiefly by Great Britain.[34]

Ideology also showed a foreign face in the years prior to the Civil War, but its meager impact only further underscored the insubstantial role of exceptionalism in US foreign policy. Ideological issues related to overseas events did surface on a number of occasions prior to the Civil War, most notably in connection with the independence of the South American republics, the Greek rebellion, and the revolutions of 1848 in Europe, but these ideologically charged episodes generated much heat but little of practical policy consequence. As a rule, the establishment of republics abroad was welcomed, but their creation merited no serious commitment of blood and treasure. As John Quincy Adams famously defined America's position: "she goes not abroad, in search of monsters to destroy." Jefferson in 1815 had already expressed similar views. Envisioning a growth in American power, he nevertheless hoped that "our wisdom will grow with our power, and teach us, that the less we use our power, the greater it will be." Despite the conceit that these revolutions were inspired by the American example, policy consisted primarily of declarations of fellow feeling unaccompanied by political commitment.[35]

Americans showed considerable enthusiasm for the Hellenes in their rebellion against Ottoman rule, but this paled by comparison to the widespread sympathy elicited in European public opinion and the eventually decisive intervention by the continental powers in securing Greek independence. Recognizing the independence of Latin America was a gesture of republican sympathy, but diplomatic recognition is to foreign affairs what a marriage license is to Las Vegas, something to be granted quickly and without a fuss. The option of refusing to recognize monarchical or autocratic regimes was never taken very seriously. Not until the Taft and Wilson administrations would nonrecognition be inserted into the tool kit of policy options. The thwarted revolutions of 1848 were a disappointment to Americans, but the revolutionaries were even more discouraged by the absence of American aid. "Oh, that you had been a neighboring nation," exclaimed the Hungarian nationalist Lajos Kossuth, "The Old World would now be free." Out of desperation, Kossuth would later ask Americans to provide more than mere words, but his plaintive remark underscored the by now widespread understanding abroad of the constraints under which American policy operated.[36]

This record of tepid support for democratic revolutions abroad was compiled at a time when the number of republics in the world remained disappointingly small and the long-term outlook for the spread of democracy was problematic. Once achieved, Greek independence was a letdown; so too was the lack of progress toward popular rule in the other "republics" in the Western hemisphere. Most disenchanting of all to those who continued to hope for a global future for republicanism was the conservative rollback of the revolutions of 1848, which, if anything, demonstrated the long-term staying power of the anciens régimes and, worse still in the case of Napoleon III's France, their genuine popularity. In the face of such dispiriting circumstances, one would think that an ideologically motivated republic would have done more than pay lip service to the cause of expanding the sphere of liberty throughout the world, but it did not. With the exception of a few paroxysms of noisy rooting from the sidelines, there was little substantive connection between republicanism and foreign policy. Though the outlook for change abroad was discouraging, the ideological zeal of the Americans was not strong enough to impel them to create their own opportunities.[37]

The failure of the United States to do more to advance its ideas was due to the absence of two essential sources of motivation: a compelling ideology and significant interests abroad. In addition, limited cultural horizons and practical constraints severely restricted what the new republic could expect to achieve in its foreign affairs. The built-in limitations of republicanism, particularly its localist bent and its ambivalence about commerce, pretty much rendered it unfit for active service in foreign parts. Far better suited to duty closer to home, republicanism came into play principally in connection with continental expansion and an attendant surge of state making that was not exportable to the rest of the world. But even as a purely domestic phenomenon, its most prominent incarnation, Manifest Destiny, fails to pass the historical lie detector test. Hence Americanization before the Civil War was overwhelmingly a domestic process whose chief tasks were the creation of a common culture and the acculturation of successive waves of immigrants.[38]

For the first three quarters of a century of its existence, America's uniqueness as a geopolitically isolated republic was not matched by a corresponding exceptionalism in its approach to foreign relations. In the absence of a galvanizing ideology, foreign relations were reduced to the same kind of down-to-earth concerns that drove the policies of other states, only much less so, for the primary task of foreign policy — providing for national security — was so lacking in urgency that the United States was able to give free rein to expansionist local interests. The parochial nature of those interests, a changing international environment that disconnected the Western hemisphere from old-style mercantilist struggles, and the primacy of domestic politics all conduced to a foreign policy with limited horizons. Had the United States been populated predominantly by Germans, French, Russians, or Chinese, the resulting social and cultural environment would obviously have been much different, but the expansionist outcome would have been the same.

In the wake of the revolution, Americans had no way of conceptualizing much less realizing any universalist ambitions, given their lack of the ideological and material means for pursuing exceptionalist policies abroad. It was less a matter of resources that they didn't have than what they had plenty of, for the rich cultural and ideological legacy inherited from the founding generation was incapable of generating a workable vision for disseminating republicanism. But even as the attention of policy makers was trained on local affairs, the country was being swept up in a larger global movement that the revolutionary generation had not anticipated. Before long, Americans were forced to the realization that instead of changing the world, the world was changing their nation in profound ways that made the United States look more and more like other countries. As a result, any lingering expectations of transforming the world would have to take a back seat to the revolutionary impact of globalization.

2 Global Society and the Challenge to Exceptionalism

Histories of US foreign relations typically divide the post–Civil War years into a period of high isolation followed by a sudden breakthrough to world power in the Spanish-American War of 1898. When one switches to the wide-angle lens of globalization, however, a different picture comes into view in which it is the continuity between the nineteenth and twentieth centuries that strikes the eye. From this perspective, a second distinct phase of US foreign relations begins in 1865 and, with one striking interruption, lasts until 1940, the eve of the nation's participation in the Second World War. During this period, Americans developed an acute awareness of being pulled inescapably into a new world not of their making, one in which the United States was in many important respects a second-rate nation.

Because these new global processes looked to be unstoppable, adapting to them appeared to be the only realistic option. As a result, US foreign relations during this period were concerned primarily with fitting in, not standing out. The emphasis was on following a trend rather than creating one; on playing a complementary role rather than looking on from the outside or attempting to transform the world; on finding some way of reconciling the new global realities with unrealized republican expectations. Postponed during the pre–Civil War period, American exceptionalism was severely challenged and transformed in the post–Civil War era.

The Emergence of Global Society

The most important change after 1865 was a growing awareness of the worldwide diffusion of a new way of life introduced by the Industrial Revolution. The transnational face of this process, then commonly called "civilization," would come to be known a century later as globalization. In the words of historian Eric Hobsbawm, this was "the greatest transformation in human history since the remote times when men invented agriculture and metallurgy, writing, the city and the state." Civilization was a convenient abstraction for powerful forces of history that had altered seemingly everything concrete: how people lived and died, governed, worked, loved, worshipped, proselytized, traveled, and understood themselves and the world. The breakneck reshaping of the physical, social, and cultural landscapes of people's lives was still so new that that it had yet to be normalized into what would later become a ho-hum topic of history texts. Having emerged in the living memory of many Americans, awestruck comments on its impact were still quite common. · Comparing life in 1897 to the circumstances of Americans in the early days of the republic, the historian John Bach McMaster marveled at the enormous changes that had taken place. "As we to-day look back to them," he noted, "their condition of life seems so crude that it is hard to realize that they are separated from us by a hundred, not a thousand years." In 1893, the evangelical missionary Josiah Strong marveled at the change: "It is as if the earth had been, in two or three generations, reduced to a much smaller scale and set spinning on its greater speed."[1]

References to civilization during this period turned up anywhere and everywhere. Presidential addresses were sprinkled with expressions of astonishment at the all-encompassing spread of civilization—the well-deserved reputation for mediocrity earned by American presidents during these years stands in ironic counterpoint to the cosmic significance of the events that they were saluting. Magazines for the burgeoning educated middle class provided detailed information about global happenings. To a significant extent, the idea embedded itself in the thinking of both political parties, with emphases that differed only in degree. By the turn of the century, the literary imagination of Americans was also becoming global, suggesting, according to one hyperbolic interpretation, that "the shift by which the nation is replaced with the globe as the fundamental unit of human association" was well advanced. A notable example of the enlargement of geographical sensibility was the formation of the National Geographic Society in 1888 and the publication of its magazine, which would become standard attic fodder for generations to come.[2]

The most striking feature of civilization was its terraforming ability to · reshape agricultural societies throughout the world into its own modern image. In 1867, Charles Francis Adams Jr., then serving as US minister in London, pointed to the ubiquitous influence of railroads as a prime example of the inexorable nature of the change. "No power has been so great as to be able to defy the influence of the new force at work in those sixty years, and no locality so obscure as to escape it," he said. "From the most powerful of European monarchies to the most insignificant of New England villages, the revolution has been all-pervading." Technology and global markets were integrating the world functionally and transforming it structurally by creating similar ways of life in which people lived increasingly in cities, worked in factories and new professions, and participated in mass culture. Although the United States was a major contributor to this process, it was clear that the nation, without conscious intent, was being fundamentally transformed by it. Civilization was a social force, a thing in itself with emergent properties that lay beyond the reach of anyone's ability to orchestrate. One could attempt to channel the process domestically, in the way that the nation sought to cope with the displacement of Native Americans, but no thought was given at the time to actively managing a global juggernaut that had materialized willy-nilly independently of individual volition or national policy.[3]

As Adams well understood, the social changes within each society were parts of a broader shift taking place in which the United States was being incorporated into an international society. Civilization was international society in forward motion, expanding territorially and remaking the innards of individual societies as it gained momentum. For reductionist liberals convinced of the primacy of the individual, especially, it is not easy to take seriously an abstraction like society, much less the cosmic idea of international society. When sociology was in its infancy, the very idea of society was so poorly understood that pioneering scholars like Emile Durkheim and Lester Frank Ward felt compelled to make powerful arguments on its behalf. But despite their best efforts, sociology struggled to win recognition as a science of society and would continue to be plagued by doubts about its intellectual bona fides. As late as the 1980s, British Prime Minister Margaret Thatcher insisted that "there is no such thing as society." Nearly a century earlier, Woodrow Wilson, then president of Princeton University and a PhD who probably knew better, had also expressed his doubts, though less heavy-handedly. "I don't know what sociology is (laughter)," he told his audience. "Moreover, I am convinced that there isn't a man living who does (laughter and applause). Whenever a man is studying anything queer, he calls it sociology (laughter)."[4]

But even as traditional academic disciplines were suffering from cultural lag, Americans who thought seriously about international relations came to understand that the structuring powers of society operated at the international level, too, which meant that international relations could no longer be conceived of solely as political relations among states. The sea change in which the United States was caught up had the effect of shifting the attention of American observers to the commanding social forces that were driving industrial globalization. This recasting of international relations as a socioeconomic process marked a historic reversal of what one noted scholar has described as "the logic of the agrarian age, which decreed that power trumped wealth." Since at least the time of Aristotle, it had been assumed that politics was the principal agent of historical change. While the suffocating grip of the classical framework upon scientific thought had already begun to relax in the sixteenth and seventeenth centuries, it was not until the 1800s that the primacy of politics in human events came under direct challenge from thinkers who asserted the supremacy of the social over the political, thereby overturning a perspective that had held sway for millennia.[5]

One sees this new privileging of the social over the political in the rise of sociology, anthropology, and economics as distinct fields of study, in the conceptual schemes of important thinkers like Karl Marx and Herbert Spencer, and in the blossoming of liberalism and socialism as

43

ideologies. Prior to Marx and the invention of sociology, when politics was still the principal vehicle for conceptualizing social change, there was little understanding of what underlying structural forces might have meant. Whatever his shortcomings, Marx, who had early made the shift away from the political as the primary mode of historical explanation, was prescient in anticipating the course that scholarship would take in the late twentieth century.[6]

With clear definitions of society hard to come by, it is hardly surprising that there should be no canonical definitions of international society and globalization, but there were some key respects in which Americans understood the globalizing world to be a society that was created by social processes. It was clearly a functionally meaningful collectivity, a transnational structure with a growing degree of cohesion that possessed a mushrooming number of functional institutions, hierarchy, and a division of labor. Most importantly for my purposes, international society also had the ability, in addition to sustaining routine behaviors, to restructure the functioning of its component parts through compulsion. It exhibited the defining attribute of what Emile Durkheim later called a "social fact," namely, a society's possession of "the power of external coercion which it exercises or is capable of exercising over individuals." How else could it have transformed ways of life without peoples or their rulers choosing to be transformed? This power was strikingly described by Marx and Engels in *The Communist Manifesto*, where capitalist commerce compelled "all nations, on pain of extinction, to adopt the bourgeois mode of production; it compels them to introduce what it calls civilisation into their midst, i.e., to become bourgeois themselves. In one word, it creates a world after its own image." Thus viewed, the power of international society as a social force was breathtaking in scope.[7]

We accept this power to compel in sociology when we talk about social forces whose operations we do not fully comprehend—sometimes they can be identified and measured, though oftentimes not—but which we know are having a major impact, for example, the murky functioning of the market economy. This preoccupation with the social was also visible in the elaborate societal blueprints drawn up by utopian socialists like Saint-Simon, Fourier, and others. In the American context, perhaps the best example from this period is Francis Lieber, a pioneering figure of political science, who argued that the United States was better understood not from the top down as a polity but from the bottom up as a society. But such ideas were also evident at the journalistic level. According to one editor, the fascination with political history was passé. "Instead of merely recording the intrigues of courts, the succession of sovereigns, the movements of armies," he suggested that the writing of history "should rather be employed in tracing the growth of nations, the advance of arts and sciences, the spread of commerce, and the development of industry."[8]

All this is part of the ordinary meaning that sociologists give to society as a grouping that orders human relations in systematic ways that society's inhabitants have not elected to be ordered. Though at all times it was created and kept in being by individuals, it nevertheless wielded coercive force upon them. It could shape and reshape behaviors of all kinds without the knowledge or consent of those upon whom it was acting. Those who violated its conventions risked being punished for lagging behind. For individual societies, those who had yet to experience the juggernaut's impact retained their relative freedom, but this had the perverse effect of leaving them vulnerable to imperial predation from more powerful industrial states that were capable of imposing new ways of life upon them. International society did not yet possess the legal authority, monopoly of military force, or legitimacy enjoyed by states domestically, but through the agency of the industrializing states that were its main beneficiaries it nevertheless generated enormous powers of persuasion and coercion.[9]

If society was the new object of attention, the privileging of the economic as the dominant aspect of society was a basic feature of nineteenth-century liberal thought. Although economics became the dominant social science, it was not the old-style economics, for economic thinking was in the process of being transformed as well. Adam Smith's once-compelling emphasis on the mutual benefits of trade specialization and the division of labor had seen change as a matter of degree, but this framework was no longer capable of explaining the socially transformative power of the new industrial factors of production. So revolutionary were the implications of trade under the new conditions that Jefferson would have been horrified by the antiagrarian ramifications of modern commerce. If nothing else, the direction of events drove home the fact that international society operated anterior to political control, independently and at a more profound level because it had come into being with little in the way of political anticipation or encouragement. Like a poorly understood force of nature, it just happened, swallowing everything in its path, without forethought or planning.[10]

Industrial technology, or what Marx called new forces of production, received much of the credit for this unsettling reorganization of social relations. Apart from the jeremiad of the occasional technophobe or rearguard romantic, most reflections on the impact of mechanization verged perilously close to a technological utopianism. One writer, for example, believed it was "quite susceptible of proof that the moral condition of the world depends on the mechanical, and that it has advanced and will advance at equal pace with the progress of machinery." Early in the twentieth century, the young historian Charles Beard speculated that "it may be that steam and electricity are to achieve that unity of mankind which rests on the expansion of a common consciousness of rights and wrongs through the expansion of identical modes of economic activity." Who can say with without a doubt that they were wrong?[11]

As a matter of economic geography, industrial technology had made possible the consolidation of the nation-state, and it appeared to be laying the same broad social foundations for international political cohesion. But technology could only operate on a global scale within the context of a geographically expanding market structure. Raw materials, foodstuffs, and commercial goods were all traded and transported in a global marketplace, which made the world feel smaller—"visibly shrinking in the hard grip of commerce," as one writer put it. Capital became patently international and, to a lesser extent, labor also became an international commodity. If the measure of a society was functional interdependence, then the world was already a social whole. "It is impossible to depict in an adequate way the measure of dependence of our modern civilized man upon the world about him," wrote Nathaniel Shaler in 1893. "The functions of his body and mind depend curiously on objects from the end of the earth." Industrial societies were the most deeply enmeshed, but civilization was rapidly creating a web of relationships and dependencies in which all the world's inhabitants would eventually be entangled.[12] This appreciation of growing social interconnectedness would have an enormous impact on the future of internationalism.[13]

Paralleling the structural changes, the spread of civilization was extending the idea of social solidarity to encompass a global expanse. For some, these deeper attachments to distant others spotlighted, often in narrow-minded ways, the exotic and presumably inferior features of formerly unfamiliar peoples and places. But for a growing number of cosmopolitan Americans, the flood of information from abroad contributed to a growing appreciation of a common human identity. A marvelous expression of the new universalism that was emerging at this time can be found in an 1851 journal article that described commerce as "creating intimate acquaintanceship and associated interests between people of the most diverse habits, languages, laws, and customs; which in short leads all to recognize in all others of whatever kindred, tribe or tongue, not anthropophagi, nor troglodytes, nor cyclops, nor pigmies, as the ancients did, but human beings, veritable men, with senses, dimensions, affections, passions like their own." This emphasis on a common humanity in the face of radical cultural differences was infracultural; a century later, the understanding of humanity would take another step forward by moving toward the view that there existed a cultural commonality among peoples.[14]

For all but a small number of inveterate globe-trotters, this new global sensibility was mediated. With the telegraph, it was easier to expand one's sense of humanity because the senses of sight and hearing were "extended around the globe." According to one essayist, "the press has made our whole world of civilization one great lecture-room, from which no reading man can escape." The result was a marked broadening of one's geographic and cultural horizons. For instance, an early essay in the American Whig Review defined a "truly civilized" person as someone who "carries about with him the familiar feeling that he is here in a world where there are not only New Englanders, with their peculiar prejudices and institutions—not only Americans and Europeans, but Hindoos also, and Turks, and Tartars, and Chinese and Japanese, who, like his own neighbors, are all proud of their several countries, creeds and characters;

in a world, too, where there have been Jews, Greeks, Romans, Egyptians and Arabians: in short, his mind is to a certain degree a geographical and historical omnipresence."[15]

The compulsion of industrial technology and commerce to destroy customary ways of life was disturbing to some notable critics, but most observers chose to emphasize their positive role in building a new global civilization—more harmonious, prosperous, and peaceful—atop the ruins of traditional societies. Lieber's "Ode on the Sub Atlantic Telegraph" was a rhapsody on the liberating effects of this technological impulse ("commune unceasingly, exchange, increase the means of peace and culture, large and high: without this dowry modern freedom must, fevered and self-consuming, die"). The new technology-driven commerce was producing contact, from which (albeit often involuntarily) came understanding and eventually an expansion of fellow feeling. As one writer put it, "Such a spirit as this is rapidly bringing all sections and classes of mankind into sympathy with one another." Or, in Adams's description, "Increased communication, increased activity, and increased facilities of trade destroy local interests, local dialects, and local jealousies."[16]

The growing awareness that the United States had been swept up in a torrent of global change exploded many republican expectations. Like the self-confident Americans that he had studied, Tocqueville believed that other countries would come to resemble the United States and that the study of America afforded a preview of the world's future. However, this "world revolution of westernization" was so clearly not made in America that ethnocentric assumptions about the world following in America's footsteps had to be set aside or at least seriously revised. Despite its dreams of being an object of imitation, the United States was becoming more like other newly industrializing countries in a group whose clear leader was Great Britain. In a world of traditional societies, the United States had plainly been different—its unique status as an agrarian republic was characterized by a one-off equality of social condition that Tocqueville had so masterfully analyzed. But now agriculture-based societies in both western Europe and the United States were giving way to an urban industrial way of life. Thanks to globalization, the old world was no longer old and the new world no longer distinctively new. Instead, both were caught up in the process of becoming modern.[17]

Globalization was cutting the United States down to size by making it just one industrial society among others. The United States did maintain its uniqueness as a great republic and as a nation that enjoyed a historically rare absence of potential enemies. But when compared to other industrializing nations, it came up woefully short in an embarrassing number of areas. It had long been apparent that America was an outlier of European civilization, a variation thereof thanks to its historical exemption from feudalism, but the roughly parallel arrival of industrial societies severely challenged the belief in American social distinctiveness and superiority. Many observers feared that the stormy labor unrest of the post–Civil War period heralded a pauperization of formerly well-paid republican labor that would destroy the egalitarian social setting in which republicanism had flourished. The arrival of scientific naturalism and industrialization had already produced, as historian Dorothy Ross has noted, "a deep sense that America had changed" in ways that challenged traditional notions of the nation's uniqueness. As a result, talk of American exceptionalism during these years was alloyed with an uncharacteristic degree of humility and soul-searching.[18]

True, the United States possessed social dynamism, excelled at technological innovation, and enjoyed a high standard of living, but Americans were painfully aware of their country's comparative backwardness in many areas. When the word "Americanization" first surfaced in France in the late 1860s, it was as a snobbish shorthand description of a nation known for mechanical ingenuity and cultural mediocrity. Americans took pride in their technological precociousness even as many were quick to agree with snooty European critics that excellence in this area came at the expense of high culture. The nation's art, music, cuisine, and literature were not up to world standards; its cities were not very inviting places; the educational system lacked great universities and cutting-edge scholarship, most notably in science; and a crude popular culture threatened to drag all culture down to its level. Most chastening of all, American politics, once thought to be a beacon for the rest of the world, was now better known for corruption and slipshod administration. Even in countries where representative government was making progress during this period, the American republican model held little allure.

Despite some significant strides made toward addressing these short-

49

comings, the image of the United States fixed in the minds of Europeans was that of a coarse frontier society with few cultural goods worthy of export. Attempts were made during these years to introduce American baseball to the British empire, most notably through a globe-girdling tour of all-stars sponsored by the Spalding Company, but the transplant failed to take on Britons and their colonists who remained attached to cricket. The enthusiasm that greeted Buffalo Bill's Wild West spectacle abroad was a bittersweet success that played to foreign stereotypes. Though the show was wildly popular, American elite types who yearned for a less vulgar presentation of American culture grumbled about the uncouth image of their country conveyed by the show. Foreign visitors continued to come to the United States, but many of them, particularly the French, left with negative impressions, bolstered in their conviction that European high culture was clearly superior.

Overall, the nation remained a cultural importer. Americans continued to indulge their passion for European literature, largely pirated from Great Britain due to the absence of an international copyright agreement, in a period when American literature was stagnating. International tourism, which had become a well-developed industry by mid-century, was largely directed toward Europe, where well-to-do types spent many months in the so-called Grand Tour of the continent. Americans who wanted to study art received their educations in Paris while those who sought a world-class university education were forced to apply to Germany's famed universities. Johns Hopkins opened its doors in 1876 as the first American graduate school, but other colleges would not make the transition until 1890 and after. Parisian fashion ruled, as did French cuisine. Americans were quick to build symphony halls and opera houses, often in remote and unlikely locations, but the music was overwhelmingly written and performed by European, predominantly German, composers, conductors, and musicians. Making up in consumption what was lacking in cultural production, American women purchased decorative foreign artifacts for their homes. As industrialization continued its advance, the nation's nouveaux riches ransacked Europe for its art and domestic furnishings. Typically, this embarrassing cultural dependency was shrugged off as the growing pains of a young industrializer that, it was claimed, would, in due course, inevitably match or surpass Europeans in high cultural attainments.[19]

The unfulfilled expectation of a republican future was more diffi-cult to digest. Following the disappointments of the French Revolution and the false millenarian alarms of the 1820s and 1848, the unfolding of events for the remainder of the nineteenth century failed to follow the republican script drafted by the more optimistic Founders. As the Civil War came to a close and slavery no longer hobbled the nation's exceptionalist promise, some leading intellectuals looked forward to a global great awakening in which the United States, at long last, would lead the rest of the world to the promised land of republicanism. But, if anything, the tide of republican expectations began to weaken and recede. Although representative forms of government had taken root in the politics of many countries after 1865, other creeds—conservative, nationalist, radical—were attracting larger and more enthusiastic popu-lar followings. As the world drifted into these democratic doldrums, the periodic outbursts of enthusiasm prompted by revolutions abroad in the first half of the nineteenth century pretty much disappeared as a feature of American political life for more than a century to come. The belief that popular rule was the future of mankind never waned, but it was a future that was substantially deferred. With the exception perhaps of the fall of China's Qing dynasty in 1911, the enthusiasm would not be seen again until the 1980s, and then only in muted form.[20]

With the global spread of republican institutions becalmed, the politi-cally centered narrative of the revolution was displaced by a new empha-sis on the power of technology and trade to reshape societies. Although this retelling of the story celebrated the advance of human progress, the creation of a world whose societies were developing in parallel through the operation of mighty social forces was not easily reconciled with the traditional expectation that the world would imitate the American po-litical model. The new global trends that were reshaping their nation meant that Americans would have to rethink their role in the world and adjust the nation's policies, foreign and domestic, to the global realities of the new industrial way of life. What would be America's place in this new world? Would America be transformed—many suspected that it already had been changed, and not for the better—or would the United States be in a position to make over other societies in ways that reflected its founding spirit?

There was a disturbing irony in the realization that the nation that was supposed to be the agent of global transformation was instead being fundamentally reshaped by the world. The result, after 1865, was a "crisis of American exceptionalism," in which "the radical difference of America was coming to be seen as a lost illusion." The impact of this crisis in intellectual history and in literature has been well explored, but the growth of an increasingly homogeneous international society carried with it a largely overlooked foreign policy side. Intellectually, adapting to this challenging new situation required a recasting of history in which the progress of American society came to be seen as part of a larger global story of convergent development, a story in which the nation's role had yet to be sorted out. The signs of this emerging new world were everywhere, but understanding them in a way that would lead to satisfactory practical adjustment required a new outlook, a postrepublican narrative.[21]

As it turned out, Americans soon articulated a new discourse that envisioned a leading role in international society for the United States. The key was the rise of a successor ideology or worldview: liberalism. Whereas the republican vision inherited from the revolution had been well suited to the preindustrial era in which an agrarian society celebrated the collective wisdom of like-minded neighbors, the Scottish Common Sense philosophy that informed this outlook was poorly equipped to understand or appreciate the formation of an industrially driven global society. Although vestigial remnants of republicanism would have a very long half-life, and though it continued to serve as a powerful source of criticism of new departures, it was eventually supplanted by a more expansive liberal ideology as the default way of understanding the world. By 1815, in their personal behavior Americans were showing every sign of being a liberal society in which the importance of personal consumption prefigured the later advent of consumerism. But the ability to understand this change lagged behind social practice. Over time, a burgeoning liberalism, a worldview that was first given a name in Europe circa 1820, provided the ideological foundation for a new foreign policy of cooperative internationalism that would steer America to a global future. The germs of liberalism can be found in the writings of Locke and Hobbes, if not earlier, but it did not come to maturity as an ideology capable of organizing political action until the middle of the nineteenth century.[22]

Nineteenth-century liberalism possessed much greater depth, breadth, and explanatory power than its republican Common Sense precursor. Intellectually, it rested on a more powerful disciplinary base, as followers of Smith, Ricardo, Hume, and Bastiat advanced the claim that their understanding of economics constituted a universally valid science. Its economic doctrines received intellectual support in the influential evolutionist scheme of Herbert Spencer, and more powerfully still in the momentous biological theory of Charles Darwin. Darwinian thought was given a variety of social applications—it could be, and was, applied to individuals, to corporations, and to societies and cultures—but nowhere was the metaphorical fit more powerful than in the connection between biology and economics. To take one example, the "creative destruction" that Joseph Schumpeter a century later saw as the hallmark of a market economy meshed nicely with the rise and demise of species that Darwin attributed to natural selection. The establishment of anthropology in the late nineteenth century reinforced this type of thinking when it attributed the dying out of traditional societies to their inability to compete with fitter social units. Other disciplines like history and philology likewise offered evolutionist support in their own ways.[23]

More importantly, liberalism overthrew politically centered ideology as the dominant mode of social analysis in favor of economics. Liberals believed that the creation of a global society was attributable to economic forces. In their view, change was driven increasingly at the societal level by processes that differed fundamentally from the political rules that governed the family of nations. Economic forces were now so powerful that notable liberals saw them as foundational, to the degree that military power and war in international relations were demoted to lower rank while commercial and cultural relations were elevated in standing. For example, in 1853, then-Senator William H. Seward put the matter bluntly in declaring that "commerce has largely taken the place of war." In the same vein, Charles Morris wrote in 1895 that war had been "replaced by more efficient civilizing agencies. . . . Commerce, travel, and emigration have gone far to overcome national isolation, and a peaceful commingling of people has taken the place of warlike invasion." At the extreme, with politics on the verge of becoming a mere aftereffect of social precipitants, the definition of success in international relations had been reversed. Nevertheless, it was well understood that peaceful economic processes were not producing a world without power, just that the seat of power had been relocated from the political to the social field. As Seward argued, "political supremacy follows commercial ascendancy."[24]

Like Marxism, liberalism was deep. Its analyses and prescriptions covered virtually every aspect of human experience. It had important things to say about personal character and behavior, the organization of the family, racial relations, gender, politics, the economy, culture, and global geography. It could be used to structure an individual life in areas such as career, marriage, and ethics, to organize the political and economic traits of a nation, to regulate relations between individuals and societies, and it could be used as a template for organizing international society. No longer immature or beholden to the inherited limitations of the republican style of thought, liberalism was a full-blooded ideology capable of making sense of the forces that were turning the world upside down. While for some the coming of international society was an ominous upheaval, the liberal sensibility saw it as a force for human emancipation. And as part of this growing awareness of its all-encompassing impact, a liberal understanding of globalization would increasingly be relied upon to explain and justify a changing international role for the United States.

As a result of this shift, ideology and culture, which initially hindered the adoption of an outward-looking foreign policy, became more welcoming from the middle of the nineteenth century onward as more and more Americans—largely well-educated members of the middle and upper classes—began to think of the nation as an important member of an emerging international community. For the better part of a century, these cosmopolitan types would take for granted the favorable operation of globalization as the setting of international relations. This embrace of globalization was facilitated by the simultaneous rise to intellectual prominence of liberal ideas. But the transition was neither natural nor obvious. The immediate problem faced by internationalist liberals was a need to harmonize the inherited national story of republican exceptionalism with the more recent understanding of the nation's participation in an international society in which the United States did not stand out from the crowd. Eventually, their engagement with globalization provided for the first time the conceptual resources for the adoption of a universalist foreign policy in which the United States would play a distinctive role, though far more modest than the one originally envisioned in the heady years of the early republic.

Globalization as Americanization

Unlike the localist outlook built into republicanism, liberalism was a cosmopolitan creed that envisioned an end to cultural narcissism and ethnocentrism. Ironically, for a country that would later be described as having been born liberal, there was nothing distinctively American about liberalism as a creed. Virtually all the innovative liberal ideas were generated in England, "the veritable birthplace of liberalism and . . . its nineteenth-century bastion," by thinkers like Adam Smith, David Ricardo, Herbert Spencer, Richard Cobden, John Bright, and Walter Bagehot. Besides pioneering in theory, the political practice of liberalism, with the exception of suffrage, was further advanced in Europe. In Great Britain, Gladstonian liberalism made some spectacular advances from the 1860s to the 1880s, while even authoritarians like Napoleon III could lay claim to some impressive liberal achievements. In other areas, too, Americans were indebted to evolutionist thinkers in the new social sciences of history and anthropology like Henry Maine, Darwin, and E. B. Tylor, whose ideas articulated many staples of the liberal creed of the day and helped to establish the belief in the universal applicability of liberal ideas. Moreover, Whig history, the notion that history is a chronicle of freedom, was not unambiguously American, either. The fact that the pedigree of liberalism was not traceable to American ancestry only underscored the growing power of international currents of thought and behavior to shape how Americans conceptualized a fast-changing world.[25]

At first, the impressive intellectual edifice of the new liberalism had few American tenants. In the United States, doctrinal liberalism remained a minority creed that had only limited purchase on the policies of the two major political parties. Its intellectual center of gravity was located in a journal of modest circulation, the *Nation*, founded in 1865 under the editorship of the Irish-born E. L. Godkin, who promoted without letup the cardinal liberal nostrums of free trade and civil service reform. Politically, the heyday of the classical liberals was the 1870s and 1880s, when liberal republicans, pejoratively known as mugwumps, made themselves a thorn in the side of mainstream Republicans and perhaps even swung the 1884 election to Democrat Grover Cleveland. Though they succeeded in achieving civil service reform (with a huge assist from the fortuitous assassination of the newly elected president, James A. Garfield), they failed miserably on free trade. Beginning with the Civil War, low tariff policies were abandoned and, over the course of a generation, protective duties that imposed some of the highest rates in the world became deeply entrenched with the combined backing of industry and labor. Unlike Great Britain, where free trade enjoyed solid working-class support prior to the Great War, American labor was sold on protectionism as a device for propping up wages.

Mugwumps aside, mainstream American liberalism departed in some significant respects from the free trading, night-watchman state propounded by British economists. The American version of political economy, which accorded greater influence to politics, was propounded most influentially by Henry C. Carey, a self-professed but quite heterodox disciple of Adam Smith, whose ideas echoed well into the twentieth century and who for a time enjoyed a period of international renown. Long before his name fell into oblivion, one admirer predicted that "Ricardo and Malthus will be to Carey as Ptolemy to Copernicus." Even Karl Marx acknowledged Carey as the "the only American economist of importance." Carey was a nationalist who believed that the economy should be shaped so as to provide a bountiful income to American workers, in contrast to the widespread poverty being generated by a British capitalism that pursued greater aggregate wealth with little concern for social equality. The idea of class conflict is usually ascribed to the London banker David Ricardo, who saw one group's gain as another's loss, but Carey's "American system" posited a harmony of interests in which the capitalist's decreasing proportionate share of total wealth was compensated for by a growing absolute portion. Carey's economic ideas have been forgotten, but an important residue of his cultural influence remains in the widespread belief that an industrial America is or ought to be a middle-class society free of class conflict.[26]

High tariffs were the key to this harmonization of class interests. Carey distinguished between "legitimate" free trade and "bastardized" free trade, the latter being England's characteristic technique of using its degraded labor as a weapon for depressing the wages of American workingmen. Protection was a means of self-defense against the threat of wage slavery, but it was not absolute; in Carey's decentralized or "concentrated" system—that is, free from London's imperial center—there existed the possibility of legitimate or fair trade in which exchange could take place to mutual advantage between societies whose economies were complementary. This primitive model of reciprocity was something that other nations could adopt to the mutual benefit of all. "To raise the value of labour throughout the world, we need only to raise the value of our own," he wrote. Carey was relying not on the coercive force of international society—that was the British way—but on the power of the American model to evoke imitation. The US system would spread by means of a demonstration effect, through "the establishment of an empire the most extensive and magnificent the world has yet seen, based upon principles of maintaining peace itself, and strong enough to insist on the maintenance of peace by others, yet carried on without the aid of fleets, or armies, or taxes." Perhaps the best example of the internationalization of this outlook would come in the 1970s, when a group of developing nations called for "the internationalization of protectionism for less developed countries."[27]

Later generations would come to see economic nationalism as a cause of international conflict, but Carey thought otherwise, insisting instead that it would promote the peace and prosperity of all nations. As he put it, "To improve the political condition of man throughout the world, it is needed that we ourselves should remain at peace, avoid taxation for the maintenance of fleets and armies, and become rich and prosperous." In the eyes of economic nationalists, protection was not opposed to civilization; on the contrary, by promoting equal development, it was its necessary condition. His American system, Carey argued, was "the only one ever devised the tendency of which was that of ELEVATING while EQUALIZING the condition of man throughout the world." For Carey, the British system of free trade, by contrast, produced global inequality and war. Free trade was an end, not a means, which could be "successfully administered only after an apprenticeship of protection." Free traders could not have disagreed more, but for Carey the global aggressiveness of British foreign policy settled the issue.[28]

Unremarked upon but essential to Carey's nationalist argument was the assumption that a favorable world environment would allow nations to exploit high tariffs with a minimum of perturbation. The United States was an early modernizer that behaved like a late developer; it was what many Americans would criticize Japan and China for being in the twentieth century, a "free rider." At this time, Americans were members of the international community for reasons not unlike the motives of those who join a political club to take advantage of its social benefits. It was only a matter of time before other members caught on to this game and joined the roster of protectionist nations. In reply, the US tariff was "internationalized" in the 1890s with a view to expanding exports to Latin America by encouraging reciprocity deals. Ironically, for Careyites, as one historian has pointed out, all of this "depended upon the structure of British hegemony," which allowed the United States to export products to Great Britain and its colonies while maintaining its high tariff wall.[29]

So while the manifest disposition of protectionism was nationalist, its latent underside presumed a global market underwritten by Great Britain. As a result, evangelists of economic expansion like William Seward and many like-minded successors felt no need to worry about a conflict between the openness required by globalization and the political nationalism that was implicit in protectionism. Thus, for example, the high protectionist politician William McKinley felt perfectly comfortably in arguing that commercial competition was unrelated to political rivalry. After all, international society had developed out of a mercantilist world of power politics, and international trade in the late nineteenth century, the heyday of the first globalization, showed no signs of slowing down. As John Maynard Keynes would write in 1919, the international conflicts of the day "appeared to exercise almost no influence at all on the ordinary course of social and economic life, the internationalization of which was nearly complete in practice." The fact that global prosperity was increasing even as more nations jumped on the protectionist bandwagon suggested that civilization was compatible with economic nationalism.[30]

But to focus on the tariff alone overlooks the internationalist side of many economic nationalists, who felt free to invoke without embarrassment the international gold standard. In a repudiation of the views of Carey's "American school" of economics, the demonetization of silver in 1873 (the "crime of '73," in the inflationist lexicon) was a landmark in American history, as it marked the point at which the populist impulse for inflation was effectively reversed. The gold advocates, paying no mind to their nationalist tariff arguments in which they portrayed the United States as a world unto itself, agreed fully with free trade liberals when they equated a gold standard with "civilization" and suggested that bimetallic currencies were fit only for backward lands. As the *Nation* remarked in a discussion of the resumption of specie payments: "there is perhaps no higher test of civilization than a nation's mode of dealing with a question of this kind." Gold was truth, as opposed to "paper lies." Inflationists and monetary nationalists, meanwhile, tended to see the gold standard as a British contrivance that "brought the whole world perpetually in debt to her." But even those who favored the monetization of silver realized that it would require international action to create an effective bimetallic standard. With this end in view, a few international congresses were convoked in the 1880s and 1890s, albeit to no lasting effect.

In other areas, too, the United States promoted liberal policies that meshed with globalization. The country developed a huge market economy with internal free trade, remained wide open to foreign investment, and continued to be a magnet for immigration, attracting so many newcomers that a nativist backlash flared up in the late 1870s. Though foreign trade as a percentage of economic activity declined through the century—and it would continue to decline until 1950 even as America's share of world GDP rose—it increased in absolute terms, as did the conviction that it should continue to grow. In sectors such as agriculture, exports were crucial. By the end of the century, American agricultural production accounted for more than half of the grain sold throughout the world. Increasingly, American manufacturers also set their sights on expanding into foreign markets, American missionaries ringed the globe, and by the later decades of the century the United States was even exporting capital. There was a widespread sense of a world that was open for the making in a universe of expanding possibilities.

Americans who were concerned with the political implications of globalization nurtured different ideas of how the world would continue to be brought closer together. Perhaps no one better conceptualized how global integration would bring about liberty than Francis Lieber, a pioneering figure in nineteenth-century political science, human rights, and international law (who also may have coined the word "internationalism"). Lieber's ideas departed from classical republican views in some significant ways. Taking a position opposed to the elitist political perspective found in Mill's magnum opus, *On Civil Liberty and Self-Government*, Lieber minimized the historical importance of top-down contract theories of constitution making, which he called "Gallican liberty," in favor of the organic role of "Anglican" or "institutional liberty" as the true foundation of self-government. In his theory of civil society, the flourishing of freedom in the United States was embedded in associational activity, "a vast system of institutions, whose numbers support the whole, as the many pillars support the rotunda of our capitol." These autonomous social institutions—businesses, professional associations, churches, schools and other educational bodies, media, reform movements, and functional organizations—were essential to the American character. "The [American] people," Lieber once told Tocqueville, "has the Republic to the marrow of the bones."[31]

The growth of internationalism depended no less than American nationalism on the working of underlying social and cultural forces. Lieber was a free trader, but his economic views were but one part of a more sweeping belief in the "material elementary law of civilization—that of exchange." Thanks to an expansion of contact and exchange of all kinds, Lieber envisioned the growth of a global civil society that would, by virtue of its grassroots origins, be democratic in character. Besides facilitating the movement of goods back and forth, globalization allowed for the easier movement of people through travel and migration, thus making possible fruitful contacts in the form of associational activities that would create a global civil society from the bottom up, culminating eventually in the creation of international juridical and political institutions. In one of his many fields of interest, international law, he believed that conferences of experts could speed things along. All this reflected "the all-pervading law of interdependence, without which men would never have felt compelled to form society . . . this divine law of inter-dependence applies to nations quite as much as to individuals."[32]

Breaking with the earlier fixation on political imitation, he was more interested in the widespread adoption of social best practices. Just as cutting-edge technology spread quickly across borders, so too, he believed, would the dynamic institutional practices of democracy. This was not an ethnocentric conceit on Lieber's part, for democratization was but one part of a complex network of international exchange from which the United States also stood to derive enormous benefits. "To learn liberty," Lieber argued, "I believe that nations must go to America and England, as we go to Italy to study music and to have the vast world of the fine arts opened up to us, or as we go to France to study science, or to Germany that we may learn how to instruct and spread education." Less easily transferable practices such as copyright could be regulated by treaties and international law among increasingly like-minded nations. This process differed from the cosmopolitanism of the eighteenth century in that the understanding of foreign ways was not restricted to the aesthetic appreciation of a few. It was a deep social process that was essential to continued progress. "Modern civilization extends over regions, tends to make uniform, and eradicates even the physical differences of tribes and races," he contended.[33]

The German-born Lieber had imbibed early German philosophic views of nationalism (he claimed to have invented this word, too) as well as civil society. In Lieber's cosmopolitan formulation of nationalism, the world's leading nations were working side by side in pulling the rest of the globe to democratic modernity. Assigning equal weight to a plurality of nations was quite common for international liberals of the day who believed in a harmonious blending of nationalisms. One essayist's description of the progress of knowledge typified how national diversity conduced to global harmony: "There is no pure white light until seven colors blend; so to the mental illumination of humanity many hues of national genius must consent."[34]

Others, however, preferred to see the process in more narrowly national terms, which, in the American context, tended to take the form of an American-led "Anglo-Saxonization" of the world, a theme that gained wider currency as the century advanced. This more ethnocentric outlook, which also relied on commercial and cultural processes to do the bulk of the work of globalization, including the spread of English as the world's lingua franca, was visible in the thought of very different individuals like John Fiske, a Harvard historian and popularizer of evolution, and Josiah Strong, an evangelical minister. Strong, who maintained that "the civilization of all peoples is inversely as their isolation," argued that the acculturation brought about by evangelical activity and economic interaction was the most effective engine of an American-led globalization. But there was a powerful demonstration effect at work here, too, that would multiply the impact of direct contact. According to Strong, "with its resources fully developed; such numbers, homogeneous in their civilization, such a race, thrice fitted to prepare the way for the full coming of the kingdom, must, under God, control the world's future." While Strong showed little interest in Europe, it was toward the continent that Fiske directed his attention. Fiske predicted that the American model, by virtue of its superior economic competitiveness, would have a decisive impact on European history. Without the drag of militarism to hold it back, the American economy would so vastly outperform the Europeans that they would have no choice but to end their love affair with armaments and warfare. In this way would the heartland of civilization finally be civilized.[35]

Whatever their differences of emphasis, Fiske and Strong both envisioned a pacification of global society that was based on a new understanding of the relationship between society and politics. In the area that counted—socioeconomic progress—the United States was destined for supremacy, and many influential Europeans agreed. In 1900, the British journalist W. T. Stead, for example, declared that "the advent of the United States as the greatest of world-powers is the greatest political, social, and commercial phenomenon of our times." Though Strong emphasized acculturation and Fiske imitation, the common theme was that civilization was opening the door to the universalization of the American model by doing what the Europeans were doing, only better. This was a world in which the United States felt increasingly at home, a world that played to strengths that until recently Americans did not know they had.[36]

While the differences among such thinkers could be dramatic, especially the clashes between free traders and protectionists, they obscured their underlying agreement on the beneficial functioning of civilization. They agreed that international society presented the nation with a renewed opportunity to claim the exemplary status that had been promised at the founding. They had different road maps, but the presumed destination was the same in each case: an Americanized world and a globalized America. By defining the essential features of civilization as those things that the new America did best—its proven ability to unleash the dynamic forces inherent in society—they co-opted an external process as an instrumental expression of America's national personality. America had only to be itself, to continue doing what it was doing, in order to realize its promise abroad.

In the process of the nation's changeover into an industrial society in the nineteenth century, some basic precepts of the republican creed regarding the nature of international relations were supplanted by liberal ideas. These ideas were by no means uniform, but they did bear a recognizable family resemblance in their optimistic conception of how global processes would play out. In their own distinctive ways, Carey and Fiske predicted that the world would emulate America's achievements, while Lieber and Strong laid greater emphasis on the impact of international social and cultural processes. In all these schemes, the common denominator was social processes while international politics remained an afterthought—unsurprisingly so, inasmuch as the United States was a peripheral nation of little consequence to the central international issues of the day.

It would not be long, however, before internationally minded Americans came to the realization that political adaptation to global currents was necessary and desirable. Once articulated and put into practice, it was anticipated that an internationalist foreign policy would bring the nation to the forefront of the world movement. Happily, in the prevailing view, this good fortune would come at little or no cost, especially as it would not be necessary to renounce the fundamentals of political isolation.

3 Gaining Entrée: The United States Joins the Club

Until the 1890s, the prevailing view held that the United States could be an active member of international society without having to abandon the fundamentals of its isolationist foreign policy. A good example of this outlook came from Charles W. Eliot, Harvard's longest-serving president, who in 1896 drew up an inventory of America's chief contributions to civilization. His list included advances in eliminating war as a method of settling disputes, mass suffrage, religious toleration, acculturation of a vast number of immigrants, and the widespread diffusion of well-being. The only item in his list with a direct bearing on foreign policy was a reference to international arbitration and international law. Likewise indifferent to foreign policy as a means of realizing exceptionalist ambitions was the Democratic chieftain William Jennings Bryan. In a 1900 speech, Bryan praised "a republic increasing in population, in wealth, in strength and in influence, solving the problems of civilization and hastening the coming of an universal brotherhood—a republic which shakes thrones and dissolves aristocracies by its silent example and gives light and inspiration to those who sit in darkness." Though neither man was modest about America's stature, both imagined the United States performing a meaningful but nonpolitical part in moving forward a collective historical enterprise.[1]

The leitmotif of such thinkers, whether free traders or protectionists, evangelists or believers in secular redemption, was that America's role would continue to be defined by what would later be called "soft power." By the fin de siècle, global and domestic currents were coming together so nicely that one author flatly declared that "the study of American history is the study of modern history." There was no need for greater political engagement during these years because the United States enjoyed what one historian has called "free security." This unique situation, utterly alien to the experience of other great nations of the day, allowed the United States to conduct its relations with the rest of the world primarily at the commercial and cultural level. This view harmonized with a conception, in Akira Iriye's words, of a world that existed primarily as "a global civil society, as distinct from the society of nations."[2]

Nevertheless, the close identification of the United States with global trends did lead to growing political engagement by the turn of the century. This more active involvement took three overlapping forms. One was the decision to become a colonial empire following a successful war with Spain over its handling of unrest in Cuba. In an outcome that no one had anticipated at the war's outset, the United States seized the opportunity afforded by its painless military victory to replace Spain in the Philippines and Puerto Rico. A second innovation was the adoption of a quasi-imperial posture in the Caribbean region. Still another form of involvement was a turn to more globally oriented policies of great power cooperation in the administrations of Theodore Roosevelt and William Howard Taft. While the desire for colonies was a temporary enthusiasm, the entanglements in the Caribbean and Taft's dollar diplomacy were longer lasting. Often seen as the least consequential policy of the three, dollar diplomacy would continue to set a standard for future policy makers long after its initial disappointments.

None of these departures, it should be emphasized, was security driven. At this point, the growing entanglement with the world did not create new threats. If anything, the security of the United States improved after 1895 following Great Britain's naval retreat from the Western hemisphere and the subsequent acknowledgment by the great powers of America's preeminent role in the region. These policy shifts were prompted by positive expectations about the future of international relations, not by credible apprehensions of danger from abroad. American imperialism was a product of a belief in a Western civilizing mission, whereas great power cooperation offered the prospect of a leadership role for the United States that required no new political responsibilities. In both cases, America's response to globalization continued to take for granted the objective existence of a community of interests among peoples, economies, and states that was producing ever-greater collaboration on global matters.

Joining as an Empire

US imperialism, like much of the imperialist surge of the late nineteenth century, was largely a consequence of globalization. Unfortunately, among American historians this vital connection between empire and global processes has been obscured by the widely held assumption that imperialism was the product of an expansionist impulse that had become second nature to Americans. It was, in this view, only the latest expression of ingrained "habits of empire." Many of the leading imperialists clearly believed this to be true, or at least they believed that others would believe it. When arguing the case for annexation of the Philippines, for instance, Theodore Roosevelt, one of the more vociferous promoters of the nation's colonial calling, insisted that the parallels between overland expansion and imperialism were so "exact" that "we are making no new departure." In attempting to justify retention of the Philippines, other spokesmen for empire pointed so often to the experience with Native Americans as a model that American historians would later come to see imperialism as a natural extension of the nation's history. "If the arguments which have been offered . . . be just," said Henry Cabot Lodge in rebuttal to the claim that colonialism promised to be a devitalizing abandonment of tradition, "then our whole past record of expansion is a crime." Many historians have agreed with such arguments, though usually with a more negative view of the right and the wrong of the matter.[3]

The argument that empire was an expression of the nation's basic character fails to take into account the sharp discontinuities introduced by the industrial way of life, something that was generally understood at the time. For example, one writer denied what the Founding Fathers had considered indispensable when he claimed that "the experience of antiquity is of very little practical value to the present age." Another insisted that in the recent era a host of "queer and strange old notions" had been "destroyed forever." Charles Francis Adams believed that "the changes of thirty years throw deep into the shade those of thirty centuries." For one reporter, the global era sharply marked a clear-cut beginning in which radical change was the rule: "as it brings to a close events which have been in operation since nations were first formed, we may now expect the events before us to be wholly unlike any hitherto known." If history as a whole had entered a period of discontinuity, why should not this have also been true for US foreign relations?[4]

Nothing in the previous history of the United States made imperialism inevitable—indeed, anti-imperialists insisted that empire was unnatural for Americans. Nevertheless, it made good political sense for people like Roosevelt and Lodge to portray empire as the product of a natural progression, even though spinning the issue in this way masked the extent to which novel global factors had introduced powerful motives for becoming an empire that were not outgrowths of prior national experience. Whereas American foreign policy prior to the Civil War could be understood principally by reference to internal events, by the end of the century global phenomena were becoming important drivers of policy. The net result of this emphasis on internal causes, at the time and afterward, was to mask the prominence of distinctively new ideas and justifications that emanated from the outside world. The continuity argument also obscured the fact that traditional determinants of expansion had either reached their limits or been exhausted. But if one could superimpose the international picture over the domestic image at the turn of the century, the resulting overlay would make clear that the increasingly faint pattern of interest-driven expansion of the antebellum period had been completely covered over by the bold lines of a new understanding of America's place in the world.[5]

Looked at from a variety of angles, the discontinuities between interest-based expansion and policies based on global considerations make it clear that domestic causes alone were incapable of producing imperialism. The story of continental expansion was principally a tale of

a preindustrial civilizational displacement that was driven by an unap-
peasable land hunger. With overseas expansion, by contrast, there were
no settler pressures. America, as a society still open to (white) immigration, had no surplus population to serve as a pool of transplanted settlers
like those, say, who migrated to Rhodesia in order to pursue an agricultural way of life under the banner of the mother country. And even if
there had been a settler movement, there was no disease gradient of the
kind that had worked to the advantage of the acquisitive European settlers by radically depopulating Native American societies. Hawaii, with
its early missionary presence, American economic elite, and a disease-
decimated native population, was the exception that proved the rule. As
anti-imperialists were quick to point out, it was believed that the operation of climate and disease in a tropical environment would result in the
physical and moral degeneration of white men.[6]

To some, the shift to overseas expansion from an agricultural impulse
that had reached its continental limits resembles a relay race in which
the baton was handed to a powerful industrial capitalism. Unlike the
potent grassroots impulses that powered the conquest and settlement of
the continent, however, the new industrial interests saw greater opportunities for profit in fields less risky than the acquisition of an empire. The
Philippines stands high on the list of examples of how little economic
interests could matter in such decisions. As a remote Spanish colony,
the Philippine Islands had few American visitors and only a handful of
Americans resident in 1898 (there is more than a grain of truth to Ambrose Bierce's quip that war was God's way of teaching Americans geography). Even after they had been annexed, Americans had difficulty in
finding much of value to exploit. The islands turned out to be profitable
for a few businesses, as is true even for the poorest economies, but they
never became an El Dorado worthy of a gold rush. As tribute systems,
classical empires had made sure to transfer wealth to the imperial center, but a final accounting of the costs and benefits of US imperialism
supports those who argued that empire was a poor investment.

However, many imperialists would have readily conceded the point:
the real economic prize was China, with its massive population and its
potentially enormous market. But the key word is "potentially." The fact
is that American interests in China were minor and by the 1890s the

golden age of the China trade had come and gone. Admittedly, there was no shortage of big dreams, but reveries seldom inspire nations to action. In objective terms, the China trade in the 1890s represented only a small fraction of America's overall trade and was increasing no faster than commerce with other regions of the world. The best argument that the imperialists could muster at the time to connect the Philippines to the China trade was to describe the islands as an entrepôt or warehouse, though just why one needed an entrepôt to China, to which the United States already enjoyed direct access, was a question that few thought fit to ask. Once acquired, this commercial argument dropped completely out of sight as the islands became chiefly a military entrepôt for the United States.

What about the role played by other economic interests? In the case of Cuba, the casus belli in 1898, Americans had invested heavily in the island's sugar industry. But there is little evidence that investors favored war for protection of American interests in Cuba, much less for empire. For businessmen, sticking with Spain made more economic sense than casting one's lot with the potentially radical rebels. As the crisis evolved, the Spanish decision to grant local autonomy to the Cubans might well have solved the problem had greater patience been shown. Once war with Spain loomed on the horizon, Wall Street became spooked, leading Roosevelt to vent his spleen on the absence of spine among America's business types. Julius Pratt's conclusion, reached long ago, that businessmen were "either opposed or indifferent to the expansionist philosophy which had arisen since 1890," has stood the test of time.[7]

Another discontinuity: the patent inevitability of the conquest of the continent stands in stark distinction to America's unforeseen leap into imperialism. Whereas overland expansion earlier in the century resembled an irreversible force of nature, imperialism in 1898 appeared suddenly and unexpectedly. No gift of prophecy was needed early in the nineteenth century to foresee that the United States would dominate North America; the only surprise was that it did not swallow up more of it—particularly Canada. By comparison, it would have been absurd for someone in 1895 to predict that the United States would soon find itself master of the Philippines; even the imminent acquisition of Cuba, a topic that had a long history of public discussion, would have seemed a stretch. In the absence of expansionist boosterism prior to the war, such military preparations as there were took the form of academic exercises in contingency planning. Speaking a few years later about the unforeseeable sequence of events in 1898, President McKinley recalled that in 1898 "we stood on the brink of war without the people knowing it and without any preparation or effort at preparation for the impending peril."[8]

Contrasting rationales for war also merit some comment. The Mexican war was widely understood for what it was—an indecently naked land grab. Similarly, no discussion of the Indian wars at the time was complete without the inclusion of settler lust for land as an explanation of their repeated flare-ups. In the case of Cuba, however, the chief concern was for what today we would call violations of "human rights,"[9] the term used by the Republican platform of 1900 in retrospective justification. One can dispute the sincerity of this humanitarian concern, but one cannot argue that it was absent from the media. Ordinarily, this kind of sentiment would not have sufficed to plunge the nation into a war, but the weakness of Spain and a volatile domestic public opinion changed the equation. The Spanish-American War was a prime example of the new role that the press was playing in international relations through its ability to publicize the importance of events that formerly would have been safely ignored by policy makers. While a frenzied press alone was not responsible for the war or the leap to empire, our inability to convincingly show deeper causes at work of the kind that accounted for previous episodes of expansion is a major source of the continuing appeal of the "newspaper circulation war" explanation of the conflict with Spain.

But to focus on the Hearst-Pulitzer circulation war in New York is historically nearsighted. For decades prior to the 1890s, journalistic media had been doing the even more important work of making empire seem attractive. In a nonjingoistic fashion that contrasts with the drumbeat for intervention in Cuba, print magazines as well as newspapers introduced major novelties in the discourse of civilization that provided the ideological justification for empire. Three changes, in particular, merit attention: the broader global perspective that had ripened by the 1890s; the greater emphasis on civilization as a communal project; and the growing fascination with cultural difference, cultural diffusion, and deracination.

The lure of these external attractions, in combination with the absence of "deep" causes such as a threat to national security or a compelling economic interest, reinforces the point that the Spanish-American War and the decision for empire were products of a choice made in response to contingent developments abroad rather than the fruit of a fundamental impulse.

The growing appreciation of globalization introduced a new, though hardly compelling, motive for colonialism. This was evident in the marked generational discontinuity at work in the debate over empire in which the anti-imperialists were distinguished by their advanced age. Imperialism was not wholly a young person's fancy, but this generational divide does suggest that the formative experience of the younger generation was significantly different. The globalizing world in which they had come to maturity had exposed them to new ideas of empire. Without the example of European imperial expansion, it is hard to imagine empire springing forth full-blown from America's brow alone. Crudely put, this is a "monkey see, monkey do" kind of argument, but it was more sophisticated than that. Crucial to making the choice was the conviction among growing numbers of younger American leaders and educated elites that imperialism would align the nation's foreign affairs with powerful global currents.[10]

Though anti-imperialists warned of the geopolitical pitfalls that were bound to accompany a decision for empire, the nation was now more secure than it had been during the era of overland expansion. Because of the desire to avoid a balance of power in the Western Hemisphere, by the 1840s overland expansion had become closely tied to the Monroe Doctrine's warning against the introduction of a diplomacy of imperialism into the Western hemisphere. The first flare-up of American assertiveness in the 1890s resurrected this strain of American thinking, when the Venezuela boundary crisis of 1895 aroused fears that the tidal wave of European empire building would reach the Western hemisphere. But by 1898 those kinds of apprehensions had been dispelled, in large part because the great powers, despite Spain's best efforts to enlist their support, were at pains not to antagonize the Americans. Such fears were briefly revived afterward, notably in the Venezuela crisis of 1903, but Roosevelt, now president, was careful to assuage them with a very quiet and effective diplomacy. In its immediate neighborhood, the United States never had it so good, so much so that a good deal of Roosevelt's diplomacy in the Caribbean came down to dotting the i's and crossing the t's of a tacit understanding that had been reached with the Europeans in the 1890s.

Roosevelt and his wingman Lodge wanted badly to see the United States recognized as a great power, which was not as fraught with peril as their opponents seemed to think. For anti-imperialists, all sorts of dangers lurked beyond the Western hemisphere. But expansionists believed that civilization provided a pain-free way of demonstrating that the United States was equal in status to the other great civilized powers—until the headaches of empire proved otherwise. Imperialism, in this view, was not a competitive affair, but a vehicle of cooperation among the leading powers. It could be both, but the expectation was that differences could be resolved to everyone's satisfaction. As the 1890s advanced, sentiment within the United States gravitated increasingly in of favor joining an exclusive club by meeting its requirements for admission. One expression of this desire for acceptance as a member of the community of civilized great powers came from Roosevelt's friend and ally Senator Henry Cabot Lodge, who put the matter quite clearly: "The great nations are rapidly absorbing for their future expansion, and their present defense all the waste places of the earth. It is a movement which makes for civilization and the enhancement of the race. As one of the great nations of the world the United States must not fall out of the line of march." Lodge was not advocating US imperialism on this particular occasion, but statements of this sort, unlike those that stressed continuity with the past, highlighted the importance of adapting to recent dramatic events abroad. Marching in step with the others did not mean lining up at the head of the column, but it would earn the nation a greater measure of respect. As an administration spokesman confirmed, thanks to the events of 1898, "the whole world listens to the United States now."[11]

Another prominent theme associated with the expansion of international society involved the civilizing mission. Familiarity with the idea of empire had been gestating for a few decades as Americans were exposed by a multitude of media accounts to happenings in Asia, Africa, and the Pacific. The communal aspect of empire was most evident in discussions of British imperialism. Americans greatly admired the spread of Anglo-

Saxon values in Great Britain's settler colonies, but they also applauded their diffusion in India and in the African possessions. As the *New York Times* put it, "Great Britain's colonizing policy varies from that of other European countries, inasmuch as it combines what is good in them all, and, while its own interests are never forgotten, it tries according to its lights, to improve the country and the people over which the flag is displayed." Such admiration was not restricted to British expansion. Despite frequent condemnations of excessive harshness and exploitation, American commentators also approved of the imperial exploits of the French in Africa and the Russians in central Asia.[12]

Discussions of imperial expansion in the decades following the Civil War had not yet come around to asking whether the United States should become an empire, but rather whether imperialism qua imperialism was justified. The answer was usually a qualified "yes," provided that the colonial power was honestly committed to the uplift of natives who otherwise would have remained in a state of barbarism. At least through the first decade of the twentieth century, an imperialism that embraced the civilizing mission was viewed as an enlightened project. This helps to explain why Herbert Croly, the leading progressive intellectual of his day, could flatly declare that "there is no rigid objection on democratic principles to colonial expansion." When the opportunity did arise quite unexpectedly in the 1890s for the United States to demonstrate its greatness and its civilizing prowess by acquiring a colonial empire of its own, imperialism narrowly won the day in a debate that was notable for its emphasis on an American civilizing mission as a matter of global responsibility. Because the civilizing mission was an internationalist ideology, American imperialism was perceived as a contribution to a larger international project.[13]

Nowhere was the global sensibility as evident as in the new positions on race and culture change. Though it was once the fashion for historians to emphasize a strong link between imperialism and racism, it has since become clear that racist arguments were far more prevalent among anti-imperialists who were concerned to avoid the pollution of America's racial stock. By contrast, imperialists preferred to focus, albeit quite patronizingly, on uplift. While it lasted, this enthusiasm for the civilizing potential of empire marked a willingness to set aside long-standing skepticism about the ability to introduce culture change from the outside (it would subsequently return in other guises). This belief in the capacity of backward peoples to modernize points to an important feature of liberalism that was absent from republican thought: the capacity for universality. The idea of universality was already embedded in the conviction that the emerging economy was structurally global and henceforth interdependent—trade, travel, migration, and flows of ideas were impressively widespread. But the idea of a civilizing mission made universality conceptually coherent by virtue of the understanding that a world civilization would also have to be culturally inclusive in matters of race and modernizing potential.[14]

Previous justifications for the use of military power as a way of opening societies to trade, which had produced much hand-wringing among liberals, were now fortified by the grander ambition of completely transforming traditional societies. The coercive power of the Western nations, in this view, needed to be placed in the service of human emancipation and equality because without it traditional societies would stubbornly continue to obstruct progress. However questionable this connection between force and freedom, it was present. Heretofore, the idea of human equality had been restricted largely to the recognition of equality in the eye of God. But the rising belief in the fundamental equality of humankind would increasingly be conceived in a secular register. Fortunately, there was plenty of conceptual room for such a reworking, for while the nineteenth century witnessed many attempts at casting the hierarchy of race into permanent biological form, no scientific consensus was ever achieved. Racism was scientifically argued by some, but no paradigmatic science of race won the day. On the contrary, many educated types as well as scientists remained quite skeptical of the findings of the so-called science of race. And, in any case, science has rarely governed policy.

Thus the civilizing mission, which formerly had been restricted to justifying the displacement of Native American peoples, was now looked at in an expanded global context. Though both sides of the debate on empire sought to package their ideas in exceptionalist rhetoric, the global frame of reference had little to do with purely national ideals. Theodore Roosevelt, who succeeded to the presidency following McKinley's assassination in 1901, took the idea of the civilizing mission to a provoca-

75

tive extreme by insisting that "in every instance [imperial] expansion has been of benefit, not so much to the power nominally benefited, as to the whole world." Besides sowing the seeds of economic growth, he believed that imperialism also promoted global law and order. That these objectives were being achieved through violence was not a problem; quite the contrary, the use of force was believed to be a necessity—especially for TR, who believed that it was essential to psychological fitness and a vigorous national character. Happily, in this view, American power, national character, and world peace were quite compatible. In a postpresidential address, Roosevelt reaffirmed his view that peace would come to the world only through "the warlike power of a civilized people."[15]

Race was in some cases clearly less important than religion, most notably in assessments of Islamic societies whose faith was seen as an insurmountable handicap to progress. Asian societies, by contrast, which were more distant as races and civilizations from the West than the Arab Islamic world, were commonly credited with a much greater capacity for modernization. Race, on the other hand, was a more pliable notion in the usage of the day, its meaning being closer to what a century later was commonly understood as culture. The civilizing mission as applied to strange races was therefore viewed as an adventure in culture change, an idea that anticipated twentieth-century modernization projects. While the biological study of race was not very encouraging to this project, it did not hold a scientific monopoly of the topic. More congenial were new professional "sciences" of anthropology and history that postulated a common origin among human beings, followed by a long period of separation and differentiation, and a culminating reunification brought about by the integrative powers of global civilization. Hierarchy was by no means absent from this belief that history was restoring mankind to its natural wholeness—it was, in truth, essential to the imperialist project—but it was not considered to be a permanent feature of the human condition.[16]

Essential to the coherence of the liberal idea of a global civilizing mission was a view of race that was nonhierarchical in the long run. In 1898, McKinley declared that American rule over a foreign people "is always for the sake of humanity and the advancement of civilization." One could, obviously, digest such pronouncements with a sprinkling of cynicism. Nevertheless, imperialism as civilizing mission, despite its condescending and paternalistic assumptions, incorporated a more generous view of both race and culture than a xenophobic anti-imperialism because it showed greater confidence in the cultural potential of colonized peoples. By the 1890s, it was quite clear that civilization took in not only peoples of western Europe, but also Asia, Latin America, and even that most disesteemed of continents, Africa. One might wish that it had not happened this way, but when one looks backward from the standpoint of path dependency, it becomes possible to view this justification for empire as a necessary step in the later rise of an anti-imperialist sensibility. While globalization was closely tied to imperialism in the short run, over the long term its compass point would swing in the direction of anti-imperialism.[17]

Globalization made American imperialism possible, not inevitable. Despite the spectacular impression that it made at the time and long afterward (on American historians), imperialism was not a fundamental change of course because nothing pointed unequivocally to empire as a project indispensable to the national interest. There was no compelling reason for the United States to become an empire: no insistent economic interests, no settlers, no existential threat, no commanding mercantilist logic of self-sufficiency. By process of elimination alone, then, the argument on behalf of the importance of the civilizing mission, which otherwise would warrant dismissal as an ideological front for concealed interests, grows more sure-footed in proportion as other rationales lose traction. This absence of exigent causes for the turn to empire also meant that it could be abandoned readily enough once imperial governance proved to be more difficult and less satisfying than advertised. And that is exactly how it happened, as the American imperialists came late to the party and departed early (they would have left even earlier if party politics had not gotten in the way). If imperialism was supposed to provide accreditation of America's rise to world power, the decertification process that followed soon after should cast doubt on that characterization.

In the 1930s, Samuel Flagg Bemis called American imperialism a "great aberration." He was half right, for colonial empire was pretty much a clean break with the past. But he failed to discern that empire also fit, though not altogether comfortably, with the commitment to globalization that was becoming the new standard for American foreign

77

policy. Viewed in this light, the "aberration" was part of an even greater and more consequential discontinuity that would continue to gain momentum long after imperialism was abandoned. Even as the colonial calling was losing its allure, a more durable and more telling expression of America's connection to the rest of the world, focused more on hard social reality than status aspirations, was emerging in its new relationship to Europe. This rapidly evolving connection with the continent would be the central feature of US foreign policy in the coming century. It was the pursuit of cooperation among the so-called civilized powers, and not empire, that would leave a deeper and more lasting imprint on American policy.[18]

Joining through International Cooperation

Boosters of empire predicted great things, but the actual experience brought mostly frustration. A surprisingly nasty war against a Filipino independence movement, followed by the chronic headaches and inevitable missteps of colonial administration, quickly divested the civilizing mission of its glamour and opened the door to the steady growth of anti-imperialist sentiment over the coming decades. As the glow of empire dimmed, American policy reverted to an emphasis on commerce and culture, but with a big difference. Instead of continuing to take selfish advantage of a favorable international environment, after 1898 policy makers began increasingly to talk about contributing to the ongoing advance of global society as a matter of national responsibility. Whereas imperialism had been principally about joining the community of leading nations—as a secondary power, as it turned out—this new emphasis on the cooperatively managed undertaking of globalization was intended to place the United States at the head of the line of march. If successful, this new turn would have Europeans following America's example, thus reversing the previous pecking order.

. . . .

After the imperial fireworks display of 1898, policy makers turned their attention to defining the place of the United States in global society. For a nation that supposedly had joined the ranks of the great powers in

1898, there was remarkably little bluster or chest thumping. Instead, political rhetoric in the immediate aftermath of the Spanish-American War reverted to the theme of civilization that had dominated prewar thinking. On the day of his assassination, for example, McKinley made the now-obligatory reference to American greatness, promising that "by no act of ours will we assign to ourselves a subordinate rank in the family of nations." But there was nothing in his vision of national greatness to suggest a dramatic leap into world politics. If anything, McKinley sounded more like a merchant than a geopolitician. "The period of exclusiveness is past," he said, followed immediately by the assertion that "the expansion of our trade and commerce is the pressing problem." But might not trade expansion require adopting a more aggressive international profile? McKinley quickly scotched such thoughts by declaring that "commercial wars are unprofitable." None of this was new. The president had already sounded the same notes in his first inaugural address, in which, echoing the rhetoric of William Seward, he insisted that "our real eminence lies in the victories of peace, not those of war."[19]

The "globalizing of America," as one historian termed it, was not a daring entry into the competitive raceway of great power. Rather, it was more like a leisurely drive along a smooth parkway that had been paved before the war. McKinley's declaration that "isolation is no longer possible or desirable" was located in the middle of a paragraph that recited the by-now familiar indicators of globalization: the annihilation of distance, global markets, rapid and far-ranging travel, and the real-time dissemination of global news. After elaborating on the enormous changes that had taken place in the world over the previous century, he concluded that "God and man have linked the nations together. No nation can longer be indifferent to any other." It was to this global unfolding of history that American foreign policy was attuned prior to the Great War. Though the three presidencies between the Spanish-American War and the Great War are identified with ostensibly quite different foreign policy themes—empire, great power relations, and commercial/legal internationalism—a common recognition of the importance of globalization ties this period together and marks the historical point of departure for American internationalism through the remainder of the century and beyond.

It was within this framework of advancing civilization that Americans understood their country as a power—a status it had already earned in the protocols of diplomacy in 1893 when representation was elevated to the ambassadorial level. Stripped of this civilizational context, fin de siècle assertions of national greatness look rather strange from the distance of a century, for by the standards of the day "great power" was not the most apt description of America's status. Yes, the United States had acquired an empire, but it was a puny domain in comparison to the vast territorial holdings of lesser states like Belgium, Portugal, or the Netherlands. Yes, it was one of the quasi-imperial China powers—it had been since 1844—but only as a hanger-on whose status was dependent on riding the coattails of more active and influential stakeholders, particularly Great Britain. And China, for all the fascination with its future, was hardly a vital interest. Yes, the United States had a mighty new navy, but beyond its responsibility for regional defense its larger role, if any, was unclear. America's standing in European affairs was even more marginal. Only in the nearby Caribbean was the United States the dominant presence, but even there, as we shall see, greatness was closely tied to the idea of civilization.[20]

The widespread perception that the Spanish-American War had fundamentally transformed American policy is attributable in large measure to the outsize personality of McKinley's successor, the charismatic Theodore Roosevelt, who personified a newly self-confident and assertive nation. Roosevelt's skepticism about the imminent extinction of war fortified his lifelong belief in the continued indispensability of warlike virtues (which, to his mind, also paid sizable nonmilitary dividends). And yet, contradicting the common view of a man dominated by a volcanic martial instinct, firmly emblazoned in the nation's historical consciousness as the Rough Rider in the White House, Roosevelt's conduct of foreign policy was the very opposite of impetuous or violent. One of the striking ironies of his presidency is that this presumed worshipper of force was awarded a Nobel Peace Prize. Where he did bring to bear American influence and power, the field for exercising the martial virtues was always the settled global landscape of civilization, not a jungle-like world of predation. Rather than being the architect of a new global policy, Roosevelt was more like a general contractor who needed to work out the kinks in a blueprint that had already been drafted.[21]

Like many other progressives of the day, Roosevelt assumed that relations among developed nations were becoming more peaceful. In his 1905 inaugural address, he repeated what was now a platitude of American politics that "we have become a great nation"—*a* great nation, not *the* greatest nation—but he added an important qualification. Inasmuch as the United States had only recently achieved that status, he immediately added that "we must behave as beseems a people with such responsibilities." This emphasis on the responsibilities rather than the dangers of this new status was made in the vernacular language of community. It gave no indication that the newly earned greatness had thrown the United States into the midst of a violent milieu; just the opposite, it was as if the United States had moved into an exclusive gated community where it would contribute to a declining crime rate by joining a neighborhood watch organization. Rather than portending danger ahead, America's new standing as a great power would instead increase the nation's security.

Most of the world's problems, though not all, were attributed to the misconduct of a shrinking number of barbarous troublemakers. In a much-quoted letter to the diplomat Henry White, TR defined the conditions needed before peace would prevail: "If China became civilized like Japan, if the Turkish Empire were abolished, and all of uncivilized Africa and Asia held by England or France or Russia and Germany, then I believe we should be within sight of a time when a general international agreement could be made by which armies and navies could be reduced so as to meet merely the needs of internal and international police work." With the exception of China's modernization, those conditions were in fact on the verge of being met. In the 1910 Nobel lecture delivered on the occasion of his accepting the peace prize, Roosevelt went further. Without denying the existence of a "cruel and unhealthy militarism in international relationships"—a problem that was attributed to domestic pathologies rather than to inherent properties of the international system—Roosevelt went on to imagine a situation in which "those great powers honestly bent on peace would form a League of Peace, not only to keep the peace among themselves, but to prevent, by force if necessary, its being broken by others." In the mind of the Rough Rider, world peace was far more a live possibility than it would be a century later.[22]

Roosevelt accepted as a fact the new globalization, but he always distinguished the universalizing social side—what he called "the world movement"—from the political aspect, especially the diplomacy of imperialism. Because they were potentially, though not necessarily, at odds, he was at pains to find ways of harmonizing the two. His instinct was to work out a regional division of labor in which the leading "civilized powers" would relate to one another peacefully while allowing globalizing processes to work their magic. The best example of this approach was his willingness to allow Japan the equivalent of a Monroe Doctrine for Asia as its contribution to global order. There were the inevitable complications, such as the tension between Russia and Japan over Manchuria, but nothing that could not be handled through judicious power balancing and, in China, by a restrained application of the cooperative Open Door policy. Recent experience showed that imperialist squalls blew over quickly without causing major damage, as in the Fashoda crisis of 1897, Anglo-Russian tensions in Iran, and Franco-German disagreements in Morocco.

A division of labor presumes, among other things, specialization, efficiency, and an overall harmony of interests, even in cases where relations among the great power role-players are not especially cordial. As TR conceived of political geography, regional specialization made the international system functionally more effective and organically more integrated, for there was nothing in it that required the great powers to go to war. Superficially, TR's emphasis on regional domination resembled Alexander Hamilton's conception of a world divided into four separate watertight "spheres," but his assumption that the benefits of being a great power were balanced by the discharging of responsibilities on behalf of a common international good went far beyond Hamilton's mercantilist horizons in its call for self-restraint on the part of all concerned. The regional hegemon's primary interest needed to be tempered by an acknowledgment of the interests of nonlocal great powers, whereas for their part those powers needed to understand that their secondary interests were being looked after by the local kingpin. Imperialism, especially, qualified for this kind of division of labor, for the new imperialism was a secondary interest for both the European powers and for the United States. This was, in later jargon, not a zero-sum world.

Being a great power meant, first and foremost, being a local power. Reduced to practical terms, America's new "world power" status meant having a free hand in the Western hemisphere, principally in the Caribbean region, except that it was not so free. Roosevelt needed to tend to Europe's legitimate economic interests in the region in order to head off situations that otherwise had the potential for generating friction among the leading nations. "Each part of the world should be prosperous and well-policed," he confided to a British friend in 1904, which implied that the United States was the natural choice for the role of beat cop in the Caribbean. This was how the image of the United States, depending on one's perspective, became one of policing or bullying—though in the real world the two often came down to the same thing. Undoubtedly, America's newfound assertiveness, coupled with the growing preoccupation of Europe's powers with continental crises, explains much about why the United States was given the run of the hemisphere, though another way of making the point would be to describe the region as not important enough for the European powers to make a fuss over.[23]

Roosevelt's behavior in the Caribbean region has created a thick fog of skepticism that obscures our view of his internationalism, not least among Latin Americans who continue to see him as the avatar of Yanqui imperialism. While a detailed exposition is impossible here, no conceptual shoehorn is needed to force his behavior into a model of international relations in which great power cooperation was the norm. Cooperation in the Western hemisphere was contingent on the removal of the potential for European incursions—that had been the central concern of the two Venezuela crises (1895 and 1903). This was the justification used by TR in articulating his notorious "corollary" to the Monroe Doctrine, in which he defended American intervention as a way of forestalling European incursions that otherwise were likely to occur—quite legally, under existing international law—in the performance of debt collection from delinquent debtor nations in the region. That kind of involvement was unwelcome, but at the same time Roosevelt clearly sympathized with European bondholders when he invoked an "international police power" to be exercised on their behalf.[24]

Without this avowed sense of responsibility, American policy in the Caribbean region might easily have been far more domineering than it was. Even the most flagrant instance of overbearing behavior and questionable means had its principled elements. Thus Roosevelt's complicity in the scheme to get Panama to secede from Columbia as a way of gaining imperial rights to build and operate the Panama Canal was justified as a boon to civilization. America's construction of the canal was obviously in the national interest, but in his spirited defense of the acquisition of the canal zone, Roosevelt also pointed to a "universal feeling that it was our duty to the world to provide this transit in the shape of a canal." The decision by Woodrow Wilson not to grant preferential tolls for American ships was indicative of a shared conviction that the canal was an international public good, as subsequently it proved to be. Roosevelt's concern for the larger weal was demonstrated in other ways, too. His eagerness to mediate the Russo-Japanese War was based on the shared perception that the United States, with no fundamental interests at stake in east Asia, could serve as an impartial go-between. The same held true for his role as honest broker in the Algeciras talks on Morocco, which forestalled a Franco-German war and perhaps a broader European conflict.[25]

Following the tradition of classifying policy makers as realists or idealists, Roosevelt and his handpicked successor Taft are often portrayed as an ideological odd couple, with Roosevelt cast as the Martian and Taft as the Venusian. Their clash over foreign policy and their antagonistic roles in the Republican Party schism of 1912 make it appear as if their policy differences were fundamental. So strong are the contrasting colors in which they are painted that one wonders how Roosevelt could have dropped the ball so badly in hand-picking Taft to succeed him. However, in American politics, the spectrum of positions tends to be quite narrow, so that the distance between two poles is normally not as extreme as rhetoric would suggest. The Taft-Roosevelt split on foreign policy is no exception, as the overly dramatized differences between the two tend to obscure the important commonalities that had brought them together in the first place. From that perspective, Roosevelt was more than a temporal forerunner of Taft; he was also his ideological precursor.

As was all too typical of Rooseveltian wrangles, the rhetoric had a way of getting out of hand. In a letter to his son, for example, Roosevelt accused Taft of being "an incompetent fool in foreign affairs." But Taft was not the bumbling idealist that Roosevelt made him out to be or the stooge of finance capital on whom later historians would dwell. Much of his language was indistinguishable from his predecessor's. Early in 1908, he asserted that "we are a world power and cannot help it." In his first inaugural address he warned against becoming "foolish idealists," warning that "with all the nations of the world armed and prepared for war, we must be ourselves in a similar condition, in order to prevent other nations from taking advantage of us." In China and the Orient, he stressed that the nation could "maintain her interests intact and can secure respect for her just demands" only if it were understood that policy was based on more than "mere verbal protest and diplomatic note." In Latin America, Taft was not afraid to use threats or gunboat diplomacy when necessary to protect American interests. There was no mistaking the mailed fist inside the soft glove of his dollar diplomacy.[26]

The primary difference between the two men lay in the greater practical weight that Taft assigned to international society. In an era when policy makers still spoke confidently about grand historical trends, Roosevelt and Taft were both believers in empire and in civilization. But Roosevelt was at bottom ambivalent about civilization, or "the world movement," as he called it. He took a more measured view of its potency, questioned the degree to which it had taken hold, and was openly skeptical about some of its alleged benefits. Whereas Taft tended to see civilization as an accomplished fact, for TR it was an uneven and contradictory process whose end was not yet in sight. Although Roosevelt was a phenomenal embodiment of the cosmopolitan type, extraordinarily gifted in languages, history, science, and whatnot, his cosmopolitanism was of the elitist variety that paid scant attention to the humdrum commercial and cultural contacts that were doing the work of global unification. Issues of character and morality, individual and national, excited Roosevelt far more than technology and commerce while the classical republican in him always distrusted marketplace morality for its cupidity and its cowardice. In judging the effect of his time upon national character, the overall relaxation of life brought about by a more peaceful civilization grated on his militant temperament, which assumed that individuals and nations still needed to fight to achieve the right.

Taft, on the other hand, was more impressed by the novelty and importance of modernity. He had clearly thought about this issue more deeply than Roosevelt, who was bored by economics. For Taft, globalization was beginning to overshadow traditional power politics. This difference in emphasis was summarized by Taft's declaration that "modern diplomacy is commercial," an assertion that lay at the heart of his "dollar diplomacy." That statement needs to be understood both as an expression of narrow commercial and financial interests and as an affirmation of the importance of the underlying reality of globalization, or what Taft referred to as "modern times" or the "enlightened tendencies of modern times." Taft insisted that "the successful conduct of our foreign relations demand[ed] a broad and a modern view." Dollar diplomacy proceeded from the assumption that the world had changed so dramatically that there was little choice except for the United States, now a great power in a new global era, but still a nation that continued in many ways to behave like a small eighteenth-century polity, to catch up with it. If left unmodified, the "great guiding principles" associated with isolation threatened to become "outworn dogmas." "We must not wait for events to overtake us unawares," he warned. In asserting that the nation had been too "self-centered," Taft signaled that a broadening of horizons was in order.[27]

This preoccupation with the new had major implications for foreign policy. Political geography continued to be of primary importance to Roosevelt, but for Taft, who early in his term described the world as being "very small," distance was losing its centrality. Apart from the kind of narrowly functional and sometimes grudging cooperation that lies at the heart of a division of labor, Taft believed that international society also required active collaboration among the major powers on larger questions of international order. Formerly preoccupied with "domestic questions," America's foreign relations had been based on "temporary expedients natural to a people to whom domestic affairs are the sole concern." But now the nation was caught up in "a larger relation with . . . obligations to others than ourselves." The United States had a greater and more active role to play in global affairs for the purpose of advancing a historical process that was leading to global interdependence and consolidation. As his secretary of state, Philander Knox, pointed out, "The tendency of modern times is manifestly toward international unity."[28]

Dollar diplomacy has been much maligned and poorly understood as a Republican policy that catered to rentier capitalists. It did not help that members of the administration insisted on using words like "hypothecate," Wall Street banker–speak that pretty much assured that the policy would be misunderstood. Though often associated with an expansive commercial and financial capitalism, the only diplomatic biographer of Knox has rightly argued that the "economic motivations for dollar diplomacy were secondary." That is not to say that dollar diplomacy was softhearted in its promotion of American economic expansion, but it also had larger objectives in view—motivated by that combination of greed and belief in the common good that cohabit uncomfortably at the core of capitalism. In the words of Francis M. Huntington Wilson, an assistant secretary of state, dollar diplomacy meant "the creation of a prosperity which will be preferred to predatory strife. It means availing of capitalism's self-interest in peace. It means taking advantage of the interest in peace of those who benefit by the investment of capital. It recognizes that financial soundness is a potent factor in political stability; that prosperity means contentment and contentment means repose." Among other things, capitalism required a rule of law, openness to foreign investment, fiscal discipline, secure property rights, and a host of other culturally embedded norms that the fiscal proconsuls of dollar diplomacy would attempt to disseminate to peoples who lacked them.[29]

It is difficult to find a clearer statement of the belief that capitalism and peace went hand in hand. Taft well understood that economic interests sometimes clashed, but he was convinced that such conflicts of interest did not lead automatically to political or military conflict. Quite to the contrary, for when Taft talked about replacing bullets with dollars, it was not about using trade as an economic substitute for war, an approach that William James had mocked as "a better avenue to plunder." At worst, in Taft's view, economic disagreements created mere "passing points of friction." Despite all the change and turmoil introduced by capitalism, in the long run economic processes were not socially destabilizing. As Knox explained in 1912, "True stability [was] best established not by military, but by economic and social forces." For Taftians, the expansion of trade was "the foundation in practical life of most advances in civilization." By explicitly relating the primacy of international society to the nation's only strong suit, its outstanding record of economic development, dollar diplomacy aimed to restore the sense of the United States as a nation at the forefront of history.[30]

Like Roosevelt, Taft treated the Caribbean as a vital interest, but his globalizing outlook produced a willingness to step outside the boundaries of the Western hemisphere to advance his vision of great power cooperation. In self-consciously seeking to align the nation with powerful globalizing forces, Taft sought by various routes to put political and legal clothing on the rapidly maturing body of international society. He was far more audacious than Roosevelt in drawing the political corollaries that flowed from interdependence. In his presidential message of December 3, 1912, Taft asserted that "only the failure of small nations to maintain internal stability could affect the peace of the world." That declaration suggested that relations among the great powers were on the whole less problematic than those with less developed nations. While one side of dollar diplomacy focused on the provision of capital, financial expertise, and oversight to underdeveloped peoples, Taft was far more optimistic about exploring the untapped possibilities for promoting cooperation among the great powers themselves. Whereas dollar diplomacy was a two-sided approach, Roosevelt had clearly been more interested in maintaining law and order on the wrong side of the tracks.[31]

The tensions between TR and Taft were most clearly defined in their spat over attempts to apply dollar diplomacy in China. The controversy broke out in connection with Knox's scheme to form an international financial consortium in which loans for railway construction in China would be jointly administered by the treaty powers. If approved, this new institution would represent a rejection of the old pattern of railway diplomacy in which the powers had competitively extended their imperial domination over large portions of China in a "battle of concessions." From the standpoint of immediate self-interest, this plan if adopted would have given American capital a seat at the table and a share of the profits, but the benefits were projected to be more far-reaching for all concerned. In theory, this multilateral lending consortium (it is not too much of a stretch to see it as a forerunner of the International Monetary Fund [IMF]) would moderate competition among the powers, safeguard American investments, strengthen the sovereignty of the shaky Chinese government, and increase the likelihood that a modern rail network would speed China's economic growth. The more rapidly that China developed, the sooner the dream of a vast China market could become a reality and the faster imperial authority over China could be lifted. It would fully satisfy the two basic principles of the Open Door policy, which sought to assure equal commercial access and to promote a strong, prosperous, and democratic China.

Conceptually, the scheme was both ingenious and extraordinarily ambitious, but it was also politically naive. Sniffing the potential for danger here, Roosevelt worried that the gambit might backfire and irritate the Japanese to the point of endangering the Open Door policy in China and perhaps even igniting a war. But as Taft was at pains to point out in his final address to Congress, his China policy was simply a continuation of "the principle of international cooperation in matters of common interest" that had been the basis of American policy as one of the China treaty powers for at least a half century. Membership in the proposed consortium was entirely voluntary, prompted by enlightened self-interest rather than coercion. TR, however, believed that Taft was playing with fire, because China was a vital interest for a regional power like Japan, whose leaders suspected that Taft's scheme of cooperation would result in a loss of imperial influence. To this accusation, Taft responded that the possibility of war with Japan was preposterous. In any event, the proposal came to naught, its chief achievement being to arouse Japanese and Russian suspicions.

Arbitration was another issue on which Taft and Roosevelt parted company. The "great jewel" of Taft's policies was his promotion of arbitration treaties that actually provided for the settlement of important issues on the basis, wherever possible, of legal rulings—"justiciable disputes," he called them. International arbitration as a feature of US foreign policy had been around since the eighteenth century. As early as 1794, the controversial Jay Treaty had included provisions for arbitration of debt and boundary issues, but the major milestone was the Treaty of Washington of 1871, which allowed an arbitral panel to settle claims arising from the British practice of outfitting Confederate commerce raiders during the Civil War. At the time, this treaty was hailed as "a victory for modern civilization, . . . of good sense over bad blood, and of the pen over the sword." Many pundits expected that the treaty would start the ball rolling in a gathering momentum for arbitration. As one writer put it, "every successful instance of arbitration like that at Geneva, will tend to elucidate the process, and suggest new provisions for its future success." The *Nation*, a journal not normally given to panegyrics, acclaimed the treaty as "the greatest gain for civilization which our age has witnessed, the most solid victory which the great cause of Peace has ever won."[32]

Enthusiasm for arbitration declined after 1871, only to be revived in a big way after 1898 as the administrations of McKinley, Roosevelt, and Taft committed themselves in varying degrees to the principle. In his first inaugural, McKinley described arbitration as "the noblest forum for the settlement of international disputes" and stated his intention of pushing the idea forward in future. He described the arbitration treaty with Great Britain that led to the settlement of the Venezuela crisis as presenting to the world "the glorious example of reason and peace, not passion and war, controlling the relations between two of the greatest nations in the world, an example certain to be followed by others."[33]

Roosevelt also promoted arbitration treaties and negotiated quite a few, all the while insisting ad nauseam that certain kinds of disputes — the irreducibly important questions of national honor or vital interest, for which nations would continue to fight — could not be settled in this fashion. There was no need for TR's expostulations on this score, because the bloodletters in the Senate so weakened the treaties that they could leave the chamber only when effectively drained of vitality. But Taft believed that Roosevelt was missing the point, for if arbitration was to be more than the trivial expression of a pious sentiment, it needed to recognize the force of new social realities that visionaries like Lieber had anticipated. The social roots of arbitration were best described a few years earlier by Elihu Root, who suggested that diplomacy "now consists chiefly in making national conduct conform or appear to conform to the rules which codify, embody, and apply certain moral standards evolved and accepted in the slow development of civilization." In other words, arbitration was not some vain hope; it was a practical a way for diplomacy to catch up with the unexpectedly rapid maturation of international society.[34]

Following this line of thinking, Taft pushed the idea as far as he could by signing controversial treaties with Great Britain and France that provided that even matters of "national honor" be submitted to arbitral panels and decided if possible on the basis of legal principles. In this conception, national honor was emptied of its primal meaning as a value that could not be compromised. One had to start somewhere, and Taft hoped that treaties with Great Britain and France would create a powerful gravitational core to which other nations, especially Germany, Russia, and Japan, would soon be attracted. The idea was not as preposterous as it looked to many. The Anglo-American relationship was the leading example of a recently fraught relationship that had evolved to the point that war was unthinkable. True, this "special relationship" was much indebted to peculiarly bilateral factors such as a common language, culture, and parallel national interests, but instead of being seen in this restrictive way this newfound amity was thought to be a groundbreaking expression of the kind of intimacy that more and more nations, expanding from the continental core, would share. As the leading progressive intellectual Herbert Croly argued, "The emancipated and nationalized European states of today, so far from being essentially antagonistic to the American democratic nation, are constantly tending towards a condition which invites closer and more fruitful association with the United States." Under Taft, the State Department also pushed a judicial arbitral scheme for Latin America that had been hatched under Root in the previous administration. More than his other initiatives, Taft's emphasis on international law was a vote of confidence in the existence of a "thick" international society that was capable of supporting such law.

The enthusiasm for arbitration would last a few more decades—it was promoted most avidly in the League of Nations in the 1920s—after which it declined and became a historical curiosity. Its adherents would come to be widely viewed as Pollyannas who overlooked the continuing human attachment to organized killing as the principal way of settling major international differences. Realists had never liked it, nor for that matter did advocates of international law, who thought that arbitration encouraged unprincipled compromise based on cynical calculations of power. But in the context of the time, this enthusiasm for arbitration was not as foolishly idealistic as it later came to look. Taft's willingness to enter into such treaties was an accurate reflection of the absence of serious threats to the nation; the occasional notes of fear and danger in the foreign policy discourse of the day seem even more far-fetched in retrospect.

But at a deeper level the vogue for arbitration was an expression of the belief in the power of an unrelenting process of globalization to change international relations for the better. The currents of international society were so swift and powerful, it was assumed, that other nations would be swept along in the same direction as the United States. This was typical of the nineteenth-century view that liberal industrialization was creating peaceful but powerful societies that were leaving behind the economically debilitating institutions and practices of militarism, a view that continued to resonate throughout the twentieth century and beyond. This underlying view received different expressions over the span of these three presidencies, as imperialism, great power relations, and dollar diplomacy were linked to a globalizing civilization and a shared concern for international cooperation.

This internationalist reasoning (Roosevelt's as well as Taft's) failed miserably in Europe, the undisputed center of civilization, where the system was based on heavily armed alliances and a balance of power, coupled with an obstinate attachment to authoritarianism, luxuriant militarism, and deep ambivalence about liberal democracy. Looking from afar upon this scene, informed American observers since the end of the Franco-Prussian conflict had foreseen a major war looming on the horizon, the only unpredictable element being when it would break out. A very few prescient policy analysts even anticipated the United States being drawn into such a war as a consequence of its traditional attachment to neutral rights. Though they could not have known the impact that submarine warfare would have, the inescapable pull of European conflict upon American neutrality had been clear since the 1790s. With their thinking still dominated by a hemispheric definition of national security, neither Roosevelt nor Taft appreciated the degree to which a major war in Europe could disrupt global society.

This failure to accurately size up the state of international relations was due less to blindness than to overoptimism about the positive forces at work in international society. Even with allowances for the more sanguine temper of those times, objective causes for pessimism among American policy makers were few. Global society was not a figment of the imagination, no more so than the common belief in the family of nations. The assumption that globalization was producing a growing likeness among societies as well as global integration was well founded. The emergence of American internationalism was supported by the fact of diminishing differences between the United States and Europe, and between the peoples of the West and those of the rest. America was becoming like Europe; Europe, like America. The experience of Great Britain, France, and the United States afforded good reason to suppose that advanced democracies did not fight each other. One can acknowledge that the American view of the world during these years was much too simple, but Taft's proposals were no more ridiculous than many economic measures that would be adopted as important foreign policy tools a half century later (IMF, modernization, foreign aid), nor were the assumptions of convergence and the growth of common values so wildly removed from reality. And, lest we forget, American policy makers were no more badly mistaken than the many presumably more realistic European leaders and cognoscenti who expected a bloody but brief conflict. No one had access to a crystal ball.

Even so, it remains a fair question why dollar diplomacy should merit discussion in any detail. The parched desert of research on the Taft administration suggests that historians have seen little point in investigating a foreign policy with so little significance apart from its expression of an outmoded and discredited zeitgeist—a worldview immortalized by Norman Angell's "the great illusion," which is remembered (inaccurately) for its naïveté. Yet, in the aftermath of the failure of his proposals, Taft continued to maintain that his ideas had a future. In a letter to Knox reflecting on the experience, he remarked that "you and I seemed to be a little in advance." And he was right to think so, for in the 1920s, dollar diplomacy was revived to much greater practical effect until the Great Depression and diplomatic crises of the 1930s brought a turn to a more political approach. Even then, dollar diplomacy refused to go away. Its underlying assumptions about international society persisted and became even more prominent in American foreign policy throughout the century and beyond. Despite its failures, dollar diplomacy at least introduced important themes having to do with the organization of international society to the agenda of diplomacy. Other ideologies have done far worse.[35]

But the path ahead would be far more perilous and full of surprises than anyone had imagined. In 1911, a journalist wrote that "America without great foreign affairs cannot remain in the forefront of nations." The self-perception of the United States as a great power was clearly present in this statement, as was the assumption that the nation had engaged in traditional great power behavior. But had it? The turn to empire gave such an impression, but it had been more thrust upon the United States than seized aggressively. It was accepted more as an international responsibility than a national opportunity and only on the condition that it was a way of fitting new global realities to the American tradition of isolation. Following the annexations, the chief concern of Roosevelt and Taft became how best to promote the cooperative world order that the nation had supposedly entered. But neither Roosevelt nor Taft had required the United States to behave politically in a radically different manner, or to redefine the nation's core interests in a groundbreaking way. As long as the United States continued to play only a supporting political role on the world stage, its ability to shape the course of international relations would be quite modest. Only when it felt the need to impose its preferences and had earned the ability to do so would others take seriously its ideas.[36]

If Americans had trouble understanding this, foreign observers did not. Judging from the memoirs of European diplomatists of the time, the United States was dismissed as a negligible factor in European and imperial affairs. Given its continued lack of interest in adhering to old world principles of realpolitik, it is not surprising that the powers took little notice of America in matters affecting their vital interests. There was no cause for offense in this, for the European lack of regard comported with the self-image held by many Americans of a nation that existed outside the political mainstream of the world. In the election campaign of 1912 scarcely a word was said about foreign policy: no warnings of looming danger, no discussion of alternatives. In retrospect, that a nation could conceive of itself as a world power without some meaningful discussion of its foreign policy staggers the imagination. A telling exception was the 1912 Progressive Party platform, which deplored "the survival in our civilization of the barbaric system of warfare among nations with its enormous waste of resources even in time of peace." Thus when a cataclysmic war broke out in Europe in August 1914, no one thought to consult the United States out of concern that it had a vital stake in the matter; no one asked for assistance; nor did anyone fear American disapproval. Nor for that matter did the United States demand to be consulted. In 1908, Roosevelt expressed the wish that "every American felt that American policy is a world policy and that we are and shall be identified in the future with all great questions." By that standard, the nation had yet to make the grade.[37]

Foreign policy in the years between the Spanish-American War and the Great War did not signal the rise of the United States as a great power traditionally understood, but rather the coming out of a nation that was tentatively beginning to redefine what it meant to be a great power. While the greater engagement in world affairs was unmistakable, there was no expectation of American geopolitical primacy. Such modest leadership initiatives as it put forward were carried out, rather poorly, in the new key of a growing commitment to the advance of international society. At the time, despite the growing recognition that globalization was having an impact on international relations, this fresh approach had few political ramifications. But that would change with the coming of World War I, which came to be known as the Great War for Civilization.

4 The Wilsonian Anomaly; or, The Three Faces of Wilsonianism

Most Americans in the early twentieth century who thought about global trends believed that international relations were changing profoundly for the better. As an example, in his first State of the Union address to Congress, Taft's successor as president, Woodrow Wilson, reaffirmed the prevailing expectation that smooth sailing lay ahead. "Many happy manifestations multiply about us of a growing cordiality and sense of community of interest among the nations," he ventured to say, "foreshadowing an age of settled peace and good will." That sunny view would be severely tested by the outbreak of the Great War in Europe in 1914 and even more so three years later, when the United States became a key participant in one of history's most destructive wars. Nevertheless, this grim turn of events became an occasion for extravagant optimism, thanks largely to Wilson's rhetorical ability to reshape the meaning of a conflict that originated in murky reasons of state into an ideological crusade. Wilson's dream of turning the struggle into a "war to end war," as it was often called, ended in epic failure, but his ambitious quest would continue to have an impact long after his time.

Among a host of other important consequences the war also launched the career of Wilsonianism as the ideological embodiment of America's ingrained belief that it was the world's redeemer nation. Despite its postwar fall from grace, for both its die-hard supporters and its critics Wilsonianism would remain the supreme expression of the nation's exceptionalist spirit. In the eyes of one major historian, Wilsonianism was "a potent definer of contemporary history." "In the history of America's encounter with the world," says another scholar, "Woodrow Wilson is the central figure." And for a legion of hardheaded detractors, this president became the foremost example of an abiding exceptionalist delusion. Thus for Henry Kissinger, a high priest of realism, "Wilson's principles have remained the bedrock of American foreign policy thinking." Whatever the persuasion, historical perspectives have portrayed Wilson's presidency as a critical point in exceptionalism's historical journey. Even if the evidence for exceptionalism had not been particularly compelling up this point, Wilsonianism appeared to unleash a long pent-up impulse, a deep trait in the national character that would continue to find expression in American foreign policy. For those who took inspiration from his ideas, his personal tragedy was but a prelude to the long-term survival of an indomitable idealist impulse. For those who did not, the saga of Wilsonianism was proof of the tenacious durability of cultural illusions.[1]

But there are other ways to view Wilsonianism. Perhaps a multifaceted perspective, in which Wilsonianism presents three rather different faces, may be more revealing. When seen from the customary frontal viewpoint, the distinguishing feature of its countenance is its close association with collective security; but when looked at from one profile, its outstanding feature is its role as a guardian of long-established liberal doctrines; and from another angle, one sees what was then a groundbreaking view of national security. The composite of these three images makes for a rather different portrait of the man and the era in which, far from setting the standard for future binges of exceptionalism, Wilsonianism comes across instead as an eccentric and ephemeral creed, an aberrant episode in the history of US foreign relations whose trademark feature failed to survive it.

The basic story is so well known as to require only the barest retelling. After quickly declaring neutrality and vowing to remain on the sidelines of the conflict, Wilson got caught up in disputes with the belligerents over their violations of international law as it governed neutrality—with Britain, over its illegal blockades practices; with Germany, for engaging in submarine tactics that violated the rights of American merchant vessels and passengers to free passage on the high seas. In retrospect, it was virtually impossible for Wilson to steer clear of the war while continuing to insist on neutral rights, given the irresolvable contradiction between neutrality and isolationism, as Robert Tucker and others have pointed out. Despite Wilson's sincere desire to remain neutral, the US insistence on the right to trade and to profit from the war made involvement pretty much inevitable given that it was at loggerheads with the belligerents' pressing need to assure that neutral commerce would not work against them.[2]

The particulars of the disputes with the warring powers differed in some fateful ways, however. The quarrel with Great Britain, though testy at times, never threatened to spin out of control, whereas the German declaration of unlimited submarine warfare in January 1917 forced Wilson's hand and shattered his chimerical hopes of playing the peacemaker. During the years of neutrality, Wilson had become increasingly invested in the idea of mediating the dispute with an eye to finding a solution to the more general problem of great power war. But with the failure of both neutrality and mediation, he took the nation into war, pledging that "the world must be made safe for democracy." During the nineteen months of American belligerency, Wilson delivered a number of addresses, the best known being his Fourteen Points speech, in which he outlined his plans for a peaceful world order. At the heart of his program was American membership in a radically new kind of international organization whose chief aim would be to prevent the outbreak of yet another great power war—an idea that would later come to be called "collective security." Following the defeat of the Central Powers, the final chapter in Wilson's personal drama featured a sickly, stubborn president striving unsuccessfully to convince the US Senate to ratify a peace treaty that would have committed the United States to joining the League of Nations.

The story is quite dramatic, poignantly tragic even, but unfortunately its meaning within a broader narrative arc remains unclear. Wilson believed that history, past and future, was on his side, even if the present was not. "I would rather lose in a cause that will some day win, than win in a cause that will some day lose," he said in a notable chiasmus. But if

Wilsonianism is judged by the president's own long-term standard, in the light of what had come before and what was yet was to happen, its signature foreign policy proposal had little grounding in American history and an unpromising future. Wilson, who was elected to the presidency of the American Historical Association before his death in 1924, strove mightily to anchor his exceptionalist foreign policy views in American history, a stratagem subsequently embraced by many historians of US foreign relations. "We have always fought for humanity," Wilson (quite misleadingly) insisted. In his war message to Congress, he declared that the United States was fighting "for the things which we have always carried nearest our hearts—for democracy . . . for a universal dominion of right by such a concert of free people as shall bring peace and safety to all nations and make the world at last free." Such assertions were in turn linked to his view of America as an idealistic nation. His statements about the uniqueness and universal importance of America are too numerous to itemize, but he was quite unembarrassed about his predilection for dressing up issues in visionary terms. "Sometimes people call me an idealist," he said. "Well, that is the way I know I am an American. America is the only idealistic nation in the world."[3]

But how American were his ideas, actually? In the case of the League of Nations, the pivotal institution of Wilsonianism, the ideas were genetically far more British and European than American. The utopian belief in an association of nations was already well formed in 1837, when Alfred Lord Tennyson wrote his first Locksley Hall poem looking forward to the end of war "in the parliament of man, the Federation of the world." In this work, Tennyson gave poetic luster to an idea that was already well established in European thought, thanks to the work of sages like Immanuel Kant. In contrast to the idea of a world parliament, America's homegrown tradition of internationalism gravitated toward less glamorous advances in international law, arbitration, and advocacy of disarmament. Prior to Wilson, this vision of a parliamentary internationalism had never been seriously considered as a policy option—its public career was limited to a lonely conjecture by a postpresidential Roosevelt. At the lower echelons of public opinion, the idea first came to life in 1915 with the creation of a pressure group, the League to Enforce Peace.[4] Once it took hold, Wilson made no attempt to stake a claim of intellectual property to the project, choosing instead to be its chief sales-man. In short, for Americans the League was a fresh enthusiasm, a great leap forward born of optimism about the advanced state of international society, while for Europeans it was the coming to fruition of a much longer and more complicated story.

When one takes into account its foreign genealogy, the narrative of the League idea is better understood as a chapter in international history than as a plot element in an exclusively American drama. As one histo-rian has pointed out, "the [League] Covenant built upon the nineteenth-century Concert system rather than replacing it."[5] The same holds true for the history of the League as a functioning institution, which for Euro-peans and many others had a more protracted ending than its American wraith. After its creation, the League, which enjoyed more secure politi-cal footing in France and Great Britain than it ever did in the United States, stayed in business for more than two decades. If one considers the League to be an idealistic organization, one reasonable conclusion is that its member nations were even more starry-eyed than the United States, yet somehow we have failed to brand the hard-nosed Europeans as dupes of idealism. Nevertheless, despite all these non-American at-tributes, the president's eloquent advocacy on behalf of the organization has forever after stamped the League with a Wilsonian trademark and an American identity.

Wilson's League was a European-born child that enjoyed only a brief political life in the United States before being abandoned by its Ameri-can foster parents. In 1918, the League had the look of an idea whose time had come. It had popular support and also enjoyed backing from influentials in both political parties. But in retrospect, 1919 and 1920 marked the first and last time in the history of US foreign relations that membership in such an organization had any realistic chance of politi-cal acceptance. Though a small band of Wilson's disciples would con-tinue to argue that America's rejection of the League was attributable to contingent circumstances (that was a polite way of eliding the martyred president's stubbornness), its flaws ran much deeper than that. Insoluble problems condemned the organization to failure—not personal hatreds, not Wilson's unwillingness to compromise, not the parliamentary ma-neuvering of Henry Cabot Lodge, and not the die-hard opposition of senatorial "irreconcilables." Though it would take longer for them to realize it, this would be no less true for the nations that did join the League, for they were participants in the institutional elaboration of a bad idea that could not have worked in any circumstances, with or without American participation.[6]

If one stops to consider how extraordinarily ambitious the organization was, the reasons for its historical failure become painfully clear. With its goal of attaining world peace, it was arguably the most radical experiment in international organization ever. By comparison, for reasons that are perfectly understandable in retrospect, its institutional successor, the United Nations was straitjacketed from the start by the more modest scope of its objectives. The League's raison d'être, however, was to eliminate what for millennia had been the central feature of international relations, war as an institution, by creating organizational machinery that would make conflicts like the Great War impossible. And it is by this standard that, quite rightly, though perhaps too harshly, it has been judged, for virtually all dissections of the League's policies in the 1930s spotlight its failure to stop great power aggression. As a rule, such postmortems suggest that the League, by its very constitution, had been impotent or incompetent to deal with its overambitious mission.[7]

But in its design the League was hardly a toothless organization. Its approach to the veto power provides a good example of the lengths to which it was willing to go to constrain bad behavior by the great powers. First of all, there was no absolute veto; indeed, there could be no veto if the organization was expected to check one of the great powers. According to Article 5 of the covenant, council decisions required unanimity, "except where otherwise expressly provided" in the covenant. That express provision was located in Article 15, which said that council resolutions were authoritative if "unanimously agreed to by the members thereof other than the Representatives of one or more of the parties to the dispute." That is, the votes of parties to the dispute were not counted. There was also a veiled threat of war in such a council recommendation, which was implied in the promise of members not to make war against a nation that abided by its recommendations. In certain cases, again according to Article 15, a simple majority vote in the assembly, which had to include the unanimous council members, was sufficient to express the League's will in a dispute. And, as later became evident, even where the veto was supposed to apply it could at times be bypassed.[8]

The problem with the League was not that it was congenitally crippled by constitutional or procedural birth defects. Though conceivably it might have been given even more authority (which Wilson resisted), the real difficulty was that its more powerful members refused to exercise the formidable powers and responsibilities that they had already been granted under the covenant. The most prominent nations, most notably Great Britain, had no stomach for imposing sanctions and risking war, choosing instead to practice within the League the appeasement that later became characteristic of their foreign policy outside the organization. In other words, it lacked precisely the kind of commitment to collective security that Wilson, in his 1919 speeches, had identified as the quality indispensable to making it a going concern. Only a fully committed United States, Wilson believed, could provide the necessary backbone. In the absence of such an underlying commitment, Wilson predicted that the League would be "only a debating society." That is to say, the League suffered from a debility of the spirit, not the body.[9]

The enduring historical what-if? is whether the United States, had it joined, would have made the League a success. One popular answer is that the US would have functioned, in the words of Wilson's close adviser Colonel Edward M. House, as "the gyroscope of world order." This was in line with Wilson's vision of the League as a collegial body that could not function effectively without American leadership. My guess — and it is only that — is that it would not have made enough of a difference. There is no reason to suppose that American membership would have been able to arrest the League's slide into irrelevance in the 1930s, or that the nation's willingness to intervene in faraway places would not have evaporated. Even if the treaty had been ratified, both Democrats and Republicans would have gravitated naturally toward more limited nonpolitical forms of international cooperation (a topic that will be dealt with in the next chapter). The commitment to collective security that lay at the heart of the Wilsonian project reminds one of the brilliant arcing of a lamp filament just prior to its failure, or a supernova explosion whose dazzling luminosity fades quickly into stellar obscurity. For Americans, the League controversy was a short-lived flirtation that somehow came to be viewed as crucial to the subsequent history of US foreign relations.[10]

Wilson's proposal for an international guarantee of freedom of the seas, articulated as point two of his Fourteen Points, offers another instance in which Wilsonianism marked the end of an era. The doctrine of neutral rights, which was more firmly anchored in the American past than the League idea, posed a difficult problem for Wilson. While British and German practices on the high seas managed to arouse US public opinion to the point of war, Wilson's complaints about the belligerents' violations of US rights, though well clothed in the language of international law, remained nationalist arguments that lacked the ideological pizzazz needed to mobilize public sentiment on behalf of his peace program. Wilson's idealistic rhetoric managed to galvanize not only the American public but also convinced people around the world of the righteousness of the allied cause.

However, the mixture of nationalist and internationalist motives used to fight the war formed an unstable political compound. Nineteenth-century US liberals had long recognized that the doctrine of neutral rights was a formula for entangling the United States in European wars, and they also realized that it was inconsistent with any strict doctrine of isolationism. They were aware, too, as subsequent events would prove, that the doctrine of neutral rights was at odds with commonsensical notions of neutrality because the United States was likely to be forced into choosing sides in any future war—unless it was willing to fight all the belligerents or cede its rights. This was the same problem James Madison had faced in the run-up to the War of 1812. Admittedly, the principle of neutral rights was internationalist in two respects: it presumed economic interdependence, and it was an established feature of international law. Ultimately, though, it was a nationalist dogma dedicated first and foremost to the selfish pursuit of profit that presupposed the ability to maintain internationalism by purely national means. And that made it a historical dinosaur.

Behind the doctrine of neutral rights and freedom of the seas lay the idea that international society could and should continue to function normally, or at least with minimal disturbance, in the event of war. Once

Wilson was pushed into asking for war in response to Germany's submarine tactics, there was no way in which he could make the defense of this principle the centerpiece of his war aims because it was an appendage of the old diplomacy. If, as he later argued, modern wars tended to be global, simply vindicating the principle would imply that the United States would be pulled once again into the next European war. Where was the progress in that? The only way of getting around the problem was to transform the system that gave life to the principle. Wilson's solution was to internationalize neutral rights by tying them closely to the League. In the past, the idea that the ocean was a commons could only be enforced by going to war against great powers who sought to exploit wartime commerce to their advantage. In response to criticisms that the treaty made no provision for assuring neutral rights (which the British negotiators in Paris were not about to concede), Wilson pointed out that there was no need for such legal protection under a League regime because in future conflicts there would be no neutrals; or, better still, if the League could prevent wars from breaking out in the first place, there would be no need for neutral rights.

Wilson proved to be correct in his prediction of the obsolescence of neutral rights in a global context, but for the wrong reasons. Even without the League, in retrospect 1919 was the last gasp for this traditional idea. That would not become evident until the mid-1930s when Congress, in a series of neutrality acts passed between 1935 and 1937, fled from the traditional idea of neutral rights as if from the plague. Subsequently, the issue has faded into historical oblivion. If anything, in the Cold War years the United States found itself on the opposite side of the issue as it attempted to coerce neutrals into going along with trade restrictions against communist countries. In his role as prophet, Wilson got some predictions right, but on this one he was quite wrong: future crises would have neutral nations, but the United States would not be among them.

A notable recent work carries the title *The Wilsonian Moment*. And that is precisely what 1919 was: a moment. Wilsonian idealism, in one of its faces, was the last stop of a historical journey in which liberalism placed its faith in international organization as the principal means of regulating political relations among states. Given the rapidity with which the League of Nations was abandoned by Americans, along with its failure in practice in the 1930s, it is clear that this institution, the centerpiece of Wilsonianism thinking, was a nineteenth-century solution to twentieth-century problems. So this face of the Wilsonian moment, expressed in the enthusiasm for the League, was the culmination of one prominent theme of nineteenth-century liberal internationalism rather than the beginning of a twentieth-century ideology. Similarly, the Great War marked a historical end for the principle of neutral rights as the principle for regulating relations between the United States and Europe. In both these important respects, Wilsonianism was a conclusive ending rather than a beginning.[11]

But if Wilsonianism was a historical terminus, in a variety of other ways it was simply an entrepôt, a temporary place of storage for a body of liberal ideas that could later be profitably shipped to market. Part of the problem in making sense of Wilsonianism originates in the tendency to conflate Wilsonianism and liberalism, when many supposedly Wilsonian doctrines were, strictly speaking, not Wilsonian at all. As long ago as 1938, the British historian E. H. Carr had pointed out that "the 'new gospel' which Wilson brought to Europe at the end of the War was in the main a faithful reflexion of mid-Victorian liberalism in its palmiest days." Wilson's thinking, according to another historian, was "like a throwback to the assumptions of a previous century." In his articulation of the basic tenets of liberal internationalism, Wilson was less original than people like Mazzini, Richard Cobden, or Francis Lieber. Free trade, democratization, disarmament, international law, international cooperation, and ending war among the great powers were all staple ingredients of Victorian liberal orthodoxy. Some of the more somber reflections that we identify with Wilson—the pessimism about armaments, the horrible consequences of modern war, the inevitability of the United States being drawn into European conflicts—also haunted late nineteenth-century liberals. And as we have already seen, the belief in a global civilization was a key ideological element of that earlier liberal era. These pre-Wilsonian themes and ideas were kept cryogenically alive by Wilson, and would spring back to full life only with the revival of globalization in the 1980s. Thus it makes little sense to confer a proprietary Wilsonian trademark upon a body of liberal ideas that had been in circulation internationally for the better part of a century.[12]

Free trade, democratization, and anti-imperialism offer good examples of how Wilsonianism served as the historical analog of an electronic step-up transformer for the long-range transmission of ideas. Next to the campaign for honest and efficient government, free trade had been the reform most avidly pursued by nineteenth-century American liberals. Unfortunately for them, the stunning record of economic growth under a high tariff regime nurtured after the Civil War by the newly dominant Republican Party made it politically impossible to put free trade principles into practice on the British model. Besides the impossibility of overcoming powerful vested interests, liberal economic theory in the United States had to deal with a powerful protectionist theory—ably articulated by Henry C. Carey—in which suspicion of free trade as a British Trojan horse loomed large. Moreover, in the late nineteenth century free trade was still a contested doctrine in economic science. A substantial body of thought was headed in the opposite direction, most worryingly in Germany. Beginning around 1880, political economy there began to be studied nationally rather than as a body of universal truth, a turn of events that made it even more difficult for liberals to make a convincing scientific case against protectionism.

Although tariff policy never stopped being debated theoretically, the continuation of protectionism was determined less by ideology than by interest-group politics that made it impossible to dislodge even if economic science had been entirely on the side of free traders. Given the political and ideological gridlock, the Democrats, who remained the minority party between 1861 and 1933, were in a position to make only marginal reductions to American tariffs when they briefly assumed power in the administrations of Grover Cleveland and Woodrow Wilson. The two Democratic tariffs enacted during this period, the Wilson-Gorman tariff of 1894 and the Underwood tariff of 1914, despite percentage cuts in overall rates, still left the United States as the leading protectionist among the developed nations. The larger problem, apart from protectionism being the default position in the United States, was the dwindling of free trade sentiment throughout the developed world. Significant opposition to free trade had already been raised in Great Britain by Joseph Chamberlain, while import barriers, albeit less imposing than America's, had become the norm on the continent. Thus, had

Wilson somehow been able to drastically cut tariffs, the failure of other nations to follow suit would have resulted, in one historian's opinion, in a program of "unilateral tariff liberalization" that "could not achieve reciprocal access to foreign markets."[13]

With a global regime of free trade becoming less likely, Wilson responded to real-world pressures by steering foreign economic policy in an unfree direction. During the war, growing concern about foreign competition and the political carving up of markets fed fears about the ability of American manufactures and banks to compete. The passage of the Webb-Pomerene Act and the Edge Act in 1919 exempted export combines from antitrust regulation and allowed banks to join forces in foreign banking activities. This patently antiliberal push to form large export associations led one writer to wonder whether "there is danger lest the pursuit of large trade groups will tend to upset once more the peace of the world." According to historian Burton Kaufman, Wilson's progressivism envisaged "economic coordination and cooperation" at the expense of the market. Given these forbidding domestic and foreign obstacles, the achievement of free trade was a more utopian political objective in 1919 than the creation of the League of Nations. The most that Wilson could do for the time being was to offer the idea for discussion, but with no realistic prospect of adoption. Predictably, then, little or nothing was done at the Paris Peace Conference to advance the cause of free trade. It was one of the many Fourteen Points that fell by the wayside, with scarcely any attention paid to it by indifferent passers-by.[14]

Wilson's proposals, then, need to be looked at in the broader context of a stalled liberal international agenda, whose lack of momentum would grow even more pronounced in the mania for higher tariffs in the 1920s. Free trade had been part of the international environment for which Great Britain had largely been responsible, and whose continuation and expansion under US leadership was, though perhaps logically conceivable, a political impossibility. Only the domestic economic crisis and the collapse of international order in the 1930s, coupled with the political realignment that took place in the election of 1932, abetted by the now-widespread embrace of free trade axioms in economic theory, and topped off with a world war made it feasible at long last to rebuild the international economy on a free trade foundation. But once again:

there was nothing distinctively Wilsonian about economic international-ism, which was, properly speaking, a liberal nostrum peddled before and after Wilson's time by many people who could scarcely be described as Wilsonians.

Democratization also fits into this pattern of the cultural transmission of ideas that had no immediate political prospects of success. The num-ber of democracies in the world in 1918 was quite small, constituting, depending on how one counts, fourteen to twenty-one countries that made up 24 to 38 percent of the international community. In Wilson's time, there was little likelihood that this number could be increased dra-matically, especially not by interventionist means that forced peoples to be free. Apart from the paradoxical nature of such an enterprise, the forc-ible spread of democracy violated the liberal — and conservative — princi-ple that freedom in the last analysis came from within as an outgrowth of the organic political maturation of a people. As a self-professed admirer of Edmund Burke, who insisted that peoples could not hope to enact ideas that departed radically from what their traditions had organically prepared them to implement, Wilson was not disposed to impose demo-cratic norms upon peoples who lacked the requisite cultural capital. In this respect, he was no different than his hero, Thomas Jefferson.[15]

For Wilson, making the world safe for democracy did not mean de-mocratizing the world. As John Milton Cooper Jr. has noted, the phrase was crafted in the passive voice that did not envision an American ji-had against nondemocratic infidels. Rather, this phrase presupposed the existence of a core group of democratic developed nations whose combined weight would assure the preservation of a global political en-vironment favorable to the continuation and future expansion of liberal-ism. Apart from his insistence on the downfall of the *Kaiserreich* at the armistice negotiations, Wilson, with seven interventions to his credit, showed little enthusiasm for promoting democracy elsewhere. This re-luctance to intervene for the purpose of installing democracy abroad would continue to be the norm for succeeding American policy makers throughout the twentieth century until the administration of George W. Bush in 2003.[16]

Wilson's administration did attempt a few experiments in imposed democracy in Latin America, but except for the far-fetched possibility that the Dominican Republic and Haiti be considered synecdochically as universally applicable models this is hardly indicative of global aspirations. In this region, his Republican predecessors and successors alike showed just as much and perhaps more zeal for the idea than Wilson. If anything, the failure of attempts to implant democracy in places like Cuba, the Dominican Republic, Haiti, Nicaragua, and Panama produced a growing skepticism among policy makers and legislators about the wisdom of introducing democracy at the point of US bayonets. Following American withdrawal in the 1920s and 1930s, these countries lapsed into authoritarianism, with American acquiescence if not outright assistance. In the long run, the examples of this allegedly Wilsonian impulse at work paled by comparison with the far more numerous instances in which the United States either tolerated authoritarian regimes or connived at their creation. By the 1980s, what had always been an inescapable vice would even be transformed into a virtuous principle by the Reagan administration. In the event, the number of democratic states in the world did not begin to expand significantly until the 1970s and 1980s, an outcome that elicited much wonderment when it occurred.[17]

The history of anti-imperialism is yet another complicated and drawn-out story in which the Wilsonian moment was only a way station. Most American liberals of the nineteenth century anticipated an end to colonialism once the civilizing mission had been completed, though they showed no sense of urgency about setting a date. From the developmental point of view, many societies were thought to be seriously lacking in the skills needed to administer a complex national community, which meant that acculturation would necessarily be a drawn-out affair. Like democracy, nationhood was a historical outcome that could be sustained only by the patient acquisition of political and cultural capital. For the foreseeable future, democratization and national self-determination for most peoples was a pipe dream.

The acceptability of imperialism suffered a huge blow when growing numbers of liberals, and left-wing liberals especially, came to see it as a contributing factor to the outbreak of the Great War. Nevertheless, there was zero chance that the colonial powers in 1919 would take seriously the idea of imminent decolonization. Faced with this political intransigence, Wilson had little choice at the peace conference but to cave in to the unregenerate colonial aspirations of his partners, most controversially (but not exclusively) in his decision to hand over German rights in China's Shantung province to the Japanese. The mandate system was a small but significant step in the anti-imperialist direction, at least in the abstract, but in many instances the de facto operation of mandates worked contrary to its stated purpose of preparing subject peoples for independence. In this political context, anti-imperialism was little more than a devout wish, for it stood little chance of widespread adoption in the near future. Here, as with free trade, Wilson was simply keeping ideas alive, although when looked at from a long-term perspective a strong case can be made for 1919 as the year in which the imperialist tide finally began to recede.

Finally, and not least, Wilson as a custodian of liberal ideas kept alive the belief in the power of international society. This was evident during the period of attempted neutral mediation, when the core of Wilson's message was that the belligerents had underlying interests in common, namely, their mutual stake in international society. His subsequent appeals to public opinion abroad were intended to rouse forces that ran deeper than parochial politics. Time and again he emphasized that the key to the success of the League of Nations was "world opinion." "Force will not accomplish anything that is permanent. . . . The only thing that will hold the world steady," Wilson insisted, was "[the] silent, all-powerful opinion of mankind." The League could not succeed without it; and without something like it, the idea of the League made no sense at all.[18]

But world opinion was not fully global nor could it be until modernization and democratization had spread significantly beyond its Euro-American core. As it was, much of non-Western opinion was not in sync with what Wilson wanted to hear. Thus when confronted with the maelstrom of enthusiasm for self-determination that his speeches had helped to touch off in Europe's colonies, Wilson was not a particularly receptive listener. By default, then, world opinion amounted to the informed opinion of the leading democracies, who happened also to dominate the international system. Even though world opinion was not yet universal, Wilson, like Taft, believed that among the nations that counted there existed a critical cultural mass sufficient to make the League a success.

For Wilson, the support of the American public was an indispensable part of this core. If the core was stable, peripheral nations would follow the great powers out of self-interest if not out of conviction. In keeping with the belief in the power of international society, the inference to be drawn was that the problems of the world originated at the top, not at the bottom.

In these three areas—free trade, democratization, and anti-imperialism—the liberal ideas sustained and transmitted by Wilsonianism were part of a broader international outlook, a liberalism that was already a global ideology and not uniquely American. Unlike Carr, who was able only to see backward from Wilson, we also have the advantage of being able to see a good distance forward in time from 1919. From this roomier perspective, it is now clear that many of the nineteenth-century liberal themes echoed by Wilson went on to have extraordinary success. But these were, strictly speaking, not Wilsonian ideas, for they both antedated Wilson and outlived him in ways that would have astounded him.

Wilson's presidency was transitional in one other important respect: In addition to passing the torch of liberal ideas to the next generation, it was also a stage on the road to world power. American internationalism was not created in a single day, and certainly not by a Wilsonian deity. The United States did not instantaneously globalize when Wilson arrived on the scene. It would take a half century for the United States to become a full-fledged global actor in a process that had many notable contributors: McKinley, Theodore Roosevelt, Taft, Wilson, Republican leaders of the 1920s, Franklin D. Roosevelt, and the policy makers of the Truman administration. Moreover, as part of this process, many of the developments since 1919 that have all too often been painted in a Wilsonian light—the United Nations, multilateral international cooperation, pell-mell decolonization, to name a few—have actually been regressions from Wilsonian conceptions.

But if Wilsonianism was the end of the road for overly optimistic nineteenth-century liberal ideas and an important link in the chain of liberalism's evolution, it was also a beginning. It is bitingly ironic that the idealistic Wilson painted a world picture bleaker than anything liberalism thus far had entertained, or, for that matter, far more pessimistic even than the views held by many of Wilson's critics. This apocalyptic side of

Wilsonianism would have a far greater practical impact on foreign policy than the League fiasco or the other Wilsonian themes discussed above because it uncannily anticipated the way in which Americans would conceive of threats in the twentieth century. In going far beyond the traditional liberal critique of war as wasteful, Wilson was the first American policy maker to define the new kinds of dangers facing the United States as a result of conditions that were historically unique. Starting with his wartime speeches and extending into the postwar period, Wilson began to articulate a new conception of what was at stake in the Great War, a question that had puzzled many people who could not understand why nations had become insanely caught up in such a monstrous orgy of violence.[19]

Wilson claimed to see a new kind of international reality in process of formation in which the old rules and standards had little applicability. The immediate problem was the prospect of a German victory, which Wilson argued would threaten liberal civilization. Whether Wilhelmine Germany really presented such a danger, or whether this was the rhetorical exaggeration of a wartime leader, is open to question. More consequentially, Wilson foresaw the likelihood of even greater world wars that would threaten to consume the nations that engaged in them and also endanger all liberal societies in a world civilization. A successful aggressor might unhinge the system; but, equally worrisome, a protracted all-out war against that aggressor might do the same. Either way, the continued existence of international society itself was at stake. Industrial technology, coupled with global interdependence, had made great power war an institution that a liberalizing world could no longer afford, an intuition that the stalemate on the Western front brought home with devastating clarity to many who did not enjoy Wilson's rarefied vantage point.[20]

Besides being enormously wasteful of lives, money, and materiel, the war threatened to destroy the very environment in which it thrived. Beginning in obscure crises like the assassination at Sarajevo, failure to stop a conflict in its opening phases could easily mushroom into a global conflagration that had the potential to overwhelm international society. It was not that war was no longer affordable, as prewar liberals had predicted, for governments had found all sorts of ways to pay for it. Rather, the problem was that war, the traditional institutional method of resolving international problems through victory, now threatened to make victory meaningless. Even a "good war" fought for the right reasons, could now result in a Pyrrhic victory, a "typhoon" in which the devastation and disorder at war's end could create revolutionary unrest that itself might explode the system.[21]

Viewed in this light, the war had exposed appalling weaknesses, instabilities, and contradictions in a globalizing process that had automatically and almost effortlessly swept all before it in the nineteenth century. What was the proposal for the League of Nations, after all, but an institutional effort to rein in some of the destructive forces of modernity? Wilson was not alone in harboring such dark thoughts, for even relentless opponents of the treaty like Senator Henry Cabot Lodge were aware of the dangers posed by another European war and of the desirability of doing something to avert it. The difference was that the treaty guaranteeing French security (which Lodge favored) was framed in terms of specific dangers and obligations, not in terms of the global system maintenance that Wilson envisaged.[22]

While many of Wilson's ideas later became objects of vulgar caricature and propagandistic excess, this new sense of threat became central to the way the United States defined its national security between 1939 and 1991. In this respect, Wilson was a prophet of doom, not the redeemer who had failed to found a new religion. Wilson's consciousness of the new kinds of perils faced by the world in the twentieth century, particularly the dangers flowing from great power war, marked the beginning of another story in which Wilsonian problems would find non-Wilsonian solutions. Put another way, Wilson's historical success in pointing to new strategic predicaments was complemented by the absence of a viable liberal political alternative to the problems that he so eloquently pointed out. His answer—the League—proved to be no answer. But while this aspect of Wilsonianism survived to become a foundational aspect of American foreign policy in the future, it too faded away with the end of the Cold War. The problems that Americans encountered after 1991 and the solutions that they brought to bear upon them would be post-Wilsonian.[23]

Another irony: the failure of the public to take seriously Wilson's

113

prophecies of doom was largely due to the fact that his outlook remained at bottom thoroughly optimistic. Though he predicted more devastating wars in the absence of effective international organization, the belief that the League of Nations was a workable solution to the world's problems made sense only if one presupposed the existence of a resilient international society with a highly developed capacity for political cooperation. Wilson's brand of liberal internationalism assumed that the chief problems of international society could be solved through market processes, which would produce international cooperation, through the evolution of international law, which was the institutional vehicle of such cooperation, and ultimately through collective security, which as a last resort could mobilize a threat so overwhelming that individual members of the League would not need to agonize over making the sacrifices normally demanded when going to war. For the League to successfully impose economic sanctions required a degree of interdependence so thoroughgoing that economic boycotts alone could bring aggressor nations to heel. Wilson's willingness to rely upon world opinion as the underpinning of the League of Nations assumed that international society, though it had just passed through a near-death experience, was fundamentally healthy and capable of effectively mustering such power.

In his positive view of the expansion and progressive future of world society, Wilson differed little from his predecessors. Unfortunately, his optimism about the basic health of international society was the undoing of his program for, as a rule, a fear-based foreign policy always sells more readily. In the absence of an obvious threat, more traditional-minded and skeptical Americans wondered why a league was necessary in the first place. Assuming that, for the sake of argument—and many Americans did not—that Wilson's strategic hypotheses were solidly grounded, the underlying belief in the solidity of international society worked against the argument for accepting a league. The Republican Party was home to many internationalists who had their own ideas about what was appropriate. If autocracy and militarism were problems, the defeat of Germany and Austria-Hungary had gone a long way toward stamping them out. Wilson's League envisioned the possibility of checking another rogue great power in the future, but opponents of the League believed that this "black swan" would not be seen again. For them, the solution was simple: with militarism dethroned, one needed only to await the benefits of workaday international cooperation made possible by the existence of a vibrant international society.

When disaggregated in this way, Wilsonianism looks far more complicated than a beginning in which the United States became a world power at the very instant that its primordial idealism ran amok. It was, as one scholar suggests, "a many splendored thing." Like Chicago's Picasso, a monumental sculpture that takes on a radically different appearance (bird? woman? insect?) when viewed from different angles, Wilsonianism was an amalgam of liberalism past, present, and future, with collective security, its best-known element, being the least enduring part of the mixture. Some elements were better suited to the nineteenth century, some to the middle of the twentieth, and some to the late twentieth and twenty-first centuries. In the family of Wilsonian ideas, his intellectual children had very different life spans. The legacy of nineteenth-century liberalism, with its emphasis on free trade and liberal democracy, survived into the twenty-first century. The new sense of strategic threat that he intuited came to maturity around 1940 and thereafter enjoyed an eventful life span of a half century. But Wilsonianism's favorite child, which inherited the defective gene of an unworkable brand of international organization, was stillborn, a progeny that had no future.[24]

Be that as it may, it is Wilson the bereaved parent that Americans have chosen to single out as the leading example of something essential and enduring about the United States. For his admirers, the Wilsonian tragedy, in which a sickly president, "in a supreme act of infanticide . . . slew his own brainchild," was a missed opportunity to create a peaceful world order based on a "higher realism." But it was hardly the last chance for future advocates of multilateral cooperation who would continue to find inspiration in Wilson's noble failure. Others have found less to admire. Myriad critical accounts have fed the mistaken belief that Wilsonianism was the quintessential expression of a deeply ingrained idealist impulse, which, like sexuality for Freud, needs to be repressed for the sake of civilization's survival. For this strain of argument, the assumption of Wilsonianism's built-in character was a necessary foil, a structural requirement of a realism that, in its capacity as a critical outlook, would otherwise be left with little to criticize. Without a feminine Wilsonianism to serve as an indispensable counterbalance to a radically cantilevered argument, realism as a prescriptive disposition would lose its masculinity. Thus Wilson himself becomes merely a figurehead. This is quite strange, if one stops to think about it, for it entails elevating a failed program, one that was summarily rejected by succeeding generations of American policy makers, into a status approaching cultural centrality.[25]

....

So what was Wilsonianism, then? A historical embodiment of the disappearing Cheshire cat? If the analysis sketched above has anything to it, many of the features of US foreign relations commonly attributed to Wilsonianism vanish under the light of a historical analysis in which Wilsonianism comes across as not particularly American to begin with. How significant was it? In David Fromkin's harsh judgment, "Wilsonianism is not any political program of which Woodrow Wilson was the author; nor was it any program of which he was the original political sponsor; nor was it any coherent body of doctrine or principle guiding the president in making his decisions." Given its lack of substance, Wilsonianism was no more than "a certain way of talking about international relations in terms of concepts that are inspiring and high-minded but in practical application provide no guidance."[26]

While there is some truth to this formulation, it is much too extreme. The liberal dimension of Wilsonianism was quite substantive, while its geostrategic side, the way in which Wilson defined modern threats, would have an enormous, though largely unacknowledged, impact. But if Wilsonianism was not original, Wilson most definitely was. Ideas and programs aside, it is the personal aspect that stands out—Wilson the orator, the salesman, the tragic figure, the prophet. It is difficult to imagine an episode of this kind without Wilson. One can envision many policies that could have been implemented by all sorts of people, but in this case, we can picture only one person—Wilson—who was capable of promising redemption while ending as a tragic failure. Superficially, at least, the way in which Wilsonianism has tended to center on the man resembles how Christianity became a faith that focused more on Christ than on Christ's message. Judging by the large number of biographies and character studies that have appeared since his time, it is difficult to disagree with the finding that a large part of Wilsonianism is simply about Wilson.

In some ways, Wilson resembled another great statesman, Otto von Bismarck. A nineteenth-century journal once observed of Bismarck that the tragedy was that there was no Bismarckism to survive him. "The secret of his power will be buried with him in the grave," lamented one writer. There could not be a succession, in the *Nation*'s view, because Bismarcks were "among the rarest products of this world." Much the same could be said about Wilson, who was a fascinating, charismatic man. But there was no institutionalization of his charisma, no replication of his genius, no enduring establishment of his pet project of collective security. In some ways, the comparison is unfair, for Bismarck had at least compiled a substantial record of institutional achievement in foreign relations (squandered by his successors) and realpolitik continues to pass for practical wisdom in some quarters. Wilson, by contrast, was a world-historical figure without a world-historical idea—at least in the Hegelian sense of an idea that was fated for historical success. In this sense, Wilson became a redeemer without a religion; and Wilsonianism became a short-lived cult, not an enduring church.[27]

An empathetic understanding of the Wilsonian imagination from the perspective of the twenty-first century requires an anthropological knack for entering into a world of thought that is quite familiar in some respects yet utterly alien in others. Trying to understand it requires breaking through the kinds of cultural barriers one encounters when trying to understand Roman slavery, the religious medieval worldview, the Greek attitude toward homosexuality, or the beliefs of any markedly different culture. Most difficult of all to grasp is the conviction that a League of Nations could exercise significant power, a highly questionable belief shared even by Wilson's senatorial foes, who feared that joining this new body would spell the end of American independence. The admission ticket to such an understanding, I would submit, is to be found in Wilsonian views of the promise and perils of international society. While the connection between global society and the politics of globalization would continue to be a central theme of international relations throughout the century and beyond, the terms of the relationship between the two would change so greatly as to make strangeness inevitable.

117

The story of the League fight suggests that Wilsonianism was not the paradigmatic example of American idealism at work, but an anomaly in the history of US foreign relations—an exceptionalist exception whose guiding ideas were short-lived in practice. Wilsonianism was not the purest illustration of a deep and enduring impulse of American culture because its core conviction, that international organization was indispensable to the eradication of great power war, had shallow roots in American political thought and was quickly abandoned as a political goal, never to be reclaimed. But that is not to say that all elements of the Wilsonian worldview were aberrations. Clearly, Wilsonianism was too complicated an outlook to make that kind of simple generalization. Among its enduring elements, the mainstay of the Wilsonian view—the belief in global society—was something that Americans would continue to share throughout the century and beyond.

5 Restarting Global Society in the 1920s

By war's end, the United States was unquestionably the world's leader, politically and economically. Europe's turn at the helm had been cut short by death and destruction, mountains of debt, and wholesale demoralization, but even a healthier continent would have left a comparatively unscathed America at the wheel. Militarily, Wilson's crash program of naval construction made the US Navy the equal of Britain's. Economically, having made the passage from debtor to creditor nation during the war, the United States became "the world's banker," the principal source of badly needed financing for postwar reconstruction, stabilization, and investment. Following some early postwar stumbles, America extended its economic lead over the rest of the world, prompting foreign admirers to introduce "Fordism," *Fordismus*, and *Fordizatzia* into their vocabularies.

Complementing its prowess in mass production, during the 1920s the United States emerged as the world's first large-scale middle-class consumer society as it pioneered the transition, in Herbert Hoover's words, "from the full dinner pail to the full garage." The United States even closed the gap in high culture with Europe and drew ahead in some fields. The American university system had become a world leader, American letters, music, and the arts had risen to global stature, while

American science and social science began a spectacular ascent. American popular culture also made a dramatic impression, most conspicuously in Hollywood's domination of the global motion picture industry. Incongruous images of America as "a sort of wild west with skyscrapers and enormous wealth somehow thrown in . . . a fabulous land of crime and graft" still abounded, but these anachronistic impressions reflected a cultural lag in world opinion, not the American reality.[1]

Unlike the late nineteenth century, when its power potential lay dormant, in the 1920s the United States took over the reins of world leadership. Only recently a junior member of the firm, it was now recognized as the senior partner to whom everyone looked for direction and support, a position that not even Theodore Roosevelt had coveted. Even die-hard opponents of American participation in the League of Nations accepted a central feature of Wilson's thinking: that the United States needed to play a leading role in the world, albeit not the part that Wilson had in mind. More congenial to the Republican administrations of the 1920s was the example of dollar diplomacy, whose scope was quickly expanded beyond anything contemplated in Taft's prewar baby steps. In its original version, dollar diplomacy had little to do with Europe's economic problems, but in the 1920s it became crucial to the continent's economic recovery and to political stabilization. In Asia, too, where the Anglo-Japanese Alliance had far outweighed the Open Door policy in importance, the developmental premises of the Open Door were expanded and systematized in some important regional agreements brokered by Washington. And quite consistently, all this was done while retreating from the bipartisan tradition of gunboat imperialism in the Caribbean.

Despite the painful awareness that American leadership was required to deal with postwar headaches, US policy stopped considerably short of challenging the fundamentals of the prewar approach toward the world. By comparison with its bare-bones prototype, this full-featured version of dollar diplomacy was far more vigorous, geographically comprehensive, and consequential. Nevertheless, Republican internationalism in the 1920s continued to be based on the assumption, shared by Wilson, his critics, and preceding presidential administrations that international society was fundamentally healthy. Whatever problems existed could be resolved at the societal level. To this way of thinking, the postwar rough patch could be smoothed out by having the United States take a larger measure of responsibility for global recovery, after which the inherently robust constitution of international society would allow for a resumption of its normal functioning.

This was a self-consciously apolitical mentality. The prevailing view at the time held that America could meet its global obligations by relying on the economic wherewithal of the private sector, with only minimal government support from the sidelines. In retrospect, when viewed from the more muscular mindset that came into vogue a few decades later, it has come to seem curious—feckless and irresponsible, in some quarters—that policy makers were blind to the crucial part played by politics in the world's problems and in failing to recognize the continuing role of power, including the resort to force and violence, in getting things done. But such disdainful judgments ignore the fact that the United States did try to steer affairs on a global scale, which was something that not even the European powers at the height of their influence had attempted. Moreover, they overlook the absence of serious political threats at the time. Those threats only materialized as a consequence of the Great Depression, a nearly complete and wholly unanticipated breakdown of international society that even critics of Republican foreign policy acknowledge touched off the crisis of the 1930s. At the time, the Republican approach was perfectly rational because it was in keeping with the slow but successful decades-long drift of American policy toward international cooperation.

....

Although in office for only two and a half years, President Warren G. Harding lived long enough to define the boundaries of the new era's internationalism. From the very beginning, it became clear that his campaign promise of "normalcy" did not envision turning back the policy clock to its prewar settings. In his inaugural address, Harding was quick to use the language of dollar diplomacy in recognizing "the new order in the world, with the closer contacts which progress has wrought." He also reminded his listeners of America's new status. "We aspire to a high place in the moral leadership of civilization," he said, sounding as if he were attempting to nip in the bud what would later be called "the myth of isolationism." "Those who assume that we played our part in the World War and later took ourselves aloof and apart, unmindful of world obligations," said Harding, "give scant credit to the helpful part we assume in international relationships." After outlining some familiar avenues of cooperation such as progress toward disarmament and international law, he reminded his listeners that, notwithstanding a commitment to high tariffs and "an unwillingness to assume the correction of all the ills of the world," the United States was prepared "to cooperate with other peoples or to assume every just obligation to promote human advancement anywhere in the world."[2]

On other occasions, Harding let it be known that the United States was prepared to wield an unprecedented degree of global influence, albeit with the voice "of good counsel, not of dictation." This was his way of saying that American leadership of a mature international society would settle problems by cooperation, consultation, and inclusion, unlike the coercive political methods that ostensibly had been laid to rest as a result of the Great War. In suggesting the manner in which the United States would exercise its influence, Harding was affirming in a nontheoretical way Francis Lieber's point that the United States existed primarily as a civil society, not as a political or governmental entity. This outlook, sometimes called business internationalism, envisioned a night watchman state in a night watchman world in which the harmonizing effects of the global market would drastically reduce the need for defense. When seen from this perspective, the politically fraught reparations question could honestly be described by Harding's successor, Calvin Coolidge, as "not a political but a business problem." American investment bankers and the money market could successfully handle the matter because this was the kind of thing businessmen were good at and governments had yet to tackle.[3]

There was a startling exception, however, one that did not require clearing away the typically dense cobweb of Harding's rhetoric to understand, in which he conceded that the rescue of civilization itself might be worth a military effort. After reminding his listeners that "when World War threatened civilization we pledged our resources and our lives to its preservation," he went on to suggest that the United States would intervene again, if necessary. "There was no American failure to resist the attempted reversion of civilization," he declared. "There will be no failure today or tomorrow." At this time, only the uncalled-for Wilsonian aftermath of the war, but not American participation, was viewed as a mistake. Fifteen years later, a large body of isolationists would see things very differently.[4]

But in the 1920s, the likelihood of another such crisis was a far-fetched prospect. Like an attack of appendicitis from a vestigial organ, the near-death experience of civilization was thought to have been the product of militarist institutions that the war had surgically removed. The affliction, though near fatal, was neither congenital nor chronic, and the prognosis for future good health was favorable. "There never again will be precisely the old order," Harding said. "For out of the old order came the war itself and the new order, established and made secure, never will permit its re-currence." In this new "established" and "secure" order, Wilsonian fears of civilization's collapse were sequestered. American leaders, like their counterparts in Europe, operated on the assumption that war was not on the horizon as the benefits of interdependence crowded out contem-plation of its possible downsides. This optimism comes across as naive in retrospect, but at the time it was difficult if not impossible to see the decade as a prelude to the catastrophic failure of the global economy or as the beginning of an intermission between two world wars. In the eyes of American statesmen, the worst was behind them.

Indicative of the confidence in the overall good health of interna-tional society was the broad-minded approach taken by the United States toward the three nations that later turned out to be its most dan-gerous adversaries: Germany, imperial Japan, and the Soviet Union. By underwriting a contentious reparations settlement that was threatening to choke off postwar recovery, American policy toward Europe demon-strated an unprecedented willingness to become involved in continental affairs of the greatest moment. According to Secretary of State Charles Evans Hughes, it was "manifest that there can be no improvement in world conditions in the absence of European recuperation." Economic growth, coupled with imaginative debt rescheduling, it was hoped, would shrink the reparations problem to insignificance over time.[5]

At first, the success of the government-encouraged flow of private capital to Germany exceeded expectations. As a result, the connection between Germany and the United States became so close as to make the United States Weimar Germany's best friend, a relationship that would have been inconceivable only a decade earlier. All this was achieved by what Herbert Hoover, then secretary of commerce, described as "pure economic diplomacy." Well, maybe not so pure, as it was subsequently revealed that strings were being pulled behind the scenes by the State Department. Nevertheless, this approach did pay a huge political dividend. The Rapallo treaty of 1922, a Soviet-German entente in which the two pariahs sought to derive mutual advantage from their outcast status, portended for a time a struggle between the ins and the outs, but the most important prodigal son, Germany, was welcomed back into the family fold in 1926, when it was allowed to join the League of Nations. True, the punitive terms of the Treaty of Versailles remained in force and added a poisonous element to German politics, but the hope was that lasting prosperity would eventually turn a still-open wound into a harmless memory.[6]

Less receptive but surprisingly inclusive was the tolerant posture adopted by the United States toward the new Bolshevik regime in Russia. Domestically, the red scare of 1919 made clear the degree to which Americans feared radical left ideologies, but on the international plane, the mindset was more confident. True, the Soviet state was a political pariah because the US policy of nonrecognition stayed in effect until 1933, when diplomatic relations were restored following the regime's agreement to discuss repayment of czarist debts. Nevertheless, despite this official antagonism, Americans continued to cultivate informal relations with the newly named USSR (1922), where American capitalists, engineers, and travelers were made to feel welcome in the 1920s. Many of the sojourners were dissidents who rejected Western market societies, but many others were not.[7]

Thanks to the belief in the basic soundness of international society, even the worrisome creation of a communist state would soon be pooh-poohed with the argument that it was the product of an unnatural childbirth whose congenital deformities condemned it to a short life. As many leaders of the 1920s saw it, the Bolshevik determination to create a developed society with an autarchic command economy was akin to paddling a canoe up the waterfall of history. A political quarantine of the Soviet state, in combination with commercial and cultural inclusion, would, in Herbert Hoover's words, allow the regime's ideology to "burn itself out in the hearts of the people." Hence the willingness of many nations and entrepreneurs to deal with the USSR in the belief that exposure to the outside world would have a corrosive effect on Soviet institutions. Influential politicians like Senator William Borah campaigned for recognition on the pragmatic basis that trade was mutually beneficial and because it was a potent way of integrating an otherwise dangerous outcast into international society. This kind of integrationist thinking would be even more prominent in the 1930s in attempts to appease Nazi Germany.[8]

Sooner rather than later, as was true of all other nations in the world, the Soviet Union could not avoid being swept up in the globalizing process. Lenin famously insisted that capitalists would hang themselves if given enough rope, but the capitalists, for their part, were convinced that exposure to the West was likely to be the regime's undoing. Bolshevik rule, so repulsive to many, was widely considered to be unnatural and hence vulnerable to Thermidorean collapse at any moment. But if engagement worked to the disadvantage of the Soviets, so too, as later became evident, did the self-imposed isolation that followed the New Economic Policy. Though reliant on the West as a market for the grain exports needed to finance a crash program of state-directed industrialization, Stalin's program of Socialism in One Country mandated, in theory, economic separation from market economies. Leon Trotsky later described this turn as one in which "the historical process of the struggle of hostile forces is replaced by the evolution of Bolshevism in a vacuum." But this could not last. Not unlike Tokugawa Japan, the Soviet Union would at some point have to lower the drawbridge of self-imposed sequestration.[9]

Japan was not a pariah nation, but Americans had long worried that it might become such in the event of a failure to integrate sufficiently into a global fraternity. The threatened breakaway over the Shantung issue at Versailles, postwar clashes over cable rights, tensions over Japanese ambitions in China, and an ambitious program of Japanese naval expansion made for a daunting set of challenges in the relationship. The American solution was to completely restructure the way of doing business in eastern Asia. At the Washington conference of 1922, Secretary of State

Charles Evans Hughes coordinated a striking series of agreements whose hallmark was a naval disarmament treaty that set fixed ratios for the major powers, thus effectively halting a three-way postwar arms race in the construction of capital ships and even reducing British and American naval strength. It also provided for four-way political consultation, dissolved the Anglo-Japanese alliance, and settled a variety of other knotty problems relating to the Pacific region.

This complex set of accords is typically seen as a bargain based on a realistic calculation of interests that would fall victim to changing circumstances a decade later. As best as the technical experts could make out, the naval numbers did provide for a military balance that was acceptable to all. But it is easy to get lost in the numbers, for there were also novel elements at work that a hard-nosed accounting calculus fails to explain. The agreements, which were premised on self-restraint, were in many respects self-denying. As a distinguished member of the US delegation, Elihu Root, pointed out, "Cynics are always near-sighted, and often and usually the decisive facts lie beyond the range of their vision." Secretary of State Charles Evans Hughes, the presiding genius of the conference, made the same point to his negotiating counterparts. "There was much cynicism in the world, and many people were trying to criticize the treaty," he said. "Even more important than the scrapping of ships," to his mind, "was the development of a right sentiment in the world."[10]

Looking at the naval treaty from a historical perspective, the report of the American delegation ventured that "probably no more significant treaty was ever made." But while the arms deal attracted the greatest amount of attention, it was a secondary factor, for it depended in the first instance on a prior political agreement. Typically, disarmament negotiations have been stumped by the "you go first" problem in which a lack of trust, or the suspicion that the other side was seeking to take special advantage, prevent either party from making the first move to disarm. It was no different in this case, where the bookkeeping cost-benefit aspects could only be toted up amid a changed atmosphere of trust among the powers. The American delegation's retrospective summary put it this way: "To stop competition it is necessary to deal with the state of mind from which it results. A belief in the pacific intentions of other powers must be substituted for suspicion and apprehension. The negotiations which led to the Four Power Treaty were the process of attaining that new state of mind."[11]

But . . . the removal of distrust required that the underlying causes of competition be eliminated, which in this case meant China. The solution was for everyone to accept America's long-standing prescription for dealing with China, the Open Door policy. Though the details of the China accord were mind-numbingly detailed, and the Chinese themselves were hardly delighted, they were less about minutiae than about general principles of dealing with imperial rivalries in China that threatened to get out of hand if not moderated. The general approach was "the substitution of international co-operation for international rivalry in China," which resulted in what was optimistically described as "a Magna Charta for China." But, to pursue the chain of questioning still further, one needs to ask what induced others to accept the cooperative principles of the Open Door. Why should the powers have abandoned the political and military pursuit of special preferences that might lead to war in the event that imperial interests should collide? Disputes had gotten out of hand not long before, after all, most explosively in the Russo-Japanese War of 1904–5. Somehow, the Open Door and its promise of international cooperation with a view to overseeing the rise of a modern unified China was preferable, but why?[12]

The Open Door needs to be understood, not in a narrow sense as an expression of America's interests in China, but as a metaphor for a larger worldview in which economic competition did not entail political antagonism, as mercantilist and realist assumptions would have it. From the liberal viewpoint, economic competition was not a zero-sum game of winners and losers; rather, trade and foreign investment would generate economic growth that was advantageous to all. The result would be China's growing prosperity, its increasing value as a market and a trading partner, its incorporation as a welcome addition to the number of democracies into the world, and an end to the diplomacy of imperialism. Whatever might be said about the quest for balance that lay behind the arms accord, the nine-power treaty on China was *not* about preserving the status quo in the Pacific. In essence, adopting the Open Door meant going along with the larger American view of a globalizing world in which the solution to political problems would lie in the salutary extension of international society. True, in the larger scheme of things it was still only a regional agreement. An analogous bargain was not possible in Europe on the question of land armaments, as a decade of futile negotiations under the auspices of the League would prove. Success was also achievable because it required only a moderation of the diplomacy of imperialism, which was easier to tackle than showdowns in which the great powers confronted each other directly over more fundamental problems of national security. Nevertheless, it came down in the end to everyone agreeing on the workability of the American view of the world.[13]

The emphasis on international cooperation and trust also meant that enforcement of the treaties was left to the good intentions of the contracting parties. The treaties had no political teeth in part because the legacy of George Washington's dictum against entangling alliances in peacetime continued to make such deals politically taboo in the United States. But it would have made no difference had the Farewell Address never been delivered, for such alliances were thought to be unnecessary in an era when the commercial and cultural winds of international society were blowing in a favorable direction. The treaties were intended to be reflections of a new international state of mind among diplomats that finally harmonized with social realities. At one difficult point in the negotiations, Hughes said that "rather than disappoint world opinion it would be better that the attempt had never been made to reach this agreement. "A few months later, he maintained that "there is no artificial method by which adjustments can be reached in the absence of a sincere desire for accord." And that desire for accord was thought to be essential for a conference that, in his words, "had a great moral objective in view." The treaties were an attempt at the practical codification of this underlying reality of world opinion. Cooperation, he had indicated a few years earlier, depended "upon the fostering of firm friendship springing from an appreciation of community of ideals, interests, and purposes."[14]

As a result of these negotiations, the kind of great power club that Taft had so ignominiously failed to establish in his railway diplomacy was now accepted as a basic principle of the Washington treaties of 1921–22. Harding described it as "a conference of friends," whereas in negotiations it was described as a "quadruple entente" in the Pacific. By roughly accepting the existing global distribution of power and allowing Japan to maintain regional naval superiority, the ratios were reminiscent of the kind of global-cum-regional thinking that had informed TR's policies. The conferees, Hughes pointed out, "were all dealing fairly *and confidently* with one another." Disarmament, great power cooperation, and group unity in handling a transition to complete sovereignty for China were accepted in a deal that constituted a remarkable reversal, at least in theory, from prewar ways of doing business.[15]

This kind of comprehensive agreement would have been inconceivable only ten years earlier. For example, Theodore Roosevelt in 1908, when requesting appropriations for four new battleships admitted that naval disarmament was preferable, only to conclude that "there was no likelihood whatever of obtaining it in the future within any reasonable time." In the interim, Roosevelt's expectations were proved wrong. For Western nations, the devastating consequences of the war confirmed the belief that militarism had sought to overturn the normal functioning of international society. The war's dreadful aftereffects made it much easier to remove the kinds of nationalist obstacles that had stymied Taft's prewar initiatives. The position of the United States had changed, too, which was made plain by the conference being held in Washington on American initiative. This deal was, for relations in the Pacific region at least, the purest expression of the liberal ideal of a world without politics, purer even than the Wilsonian vision, which assumed that political dangers would never go away entirely. It was the twentieth century's liberal moment.[16]

Behind the US approach to all three powers, unpoisoned by bitter nationalist memories of catastrophic relations in the past, was the idea that they were integral members of a liberal world community of nations united by a compelling harmony of interests. In their belief that politics was an epiphenomenon, a by-product of more fundamental societal forces, American policy makers exemplified in practice the theoretical Marxist distinction between economic base and political superstructure. "The dominating fact of this last century," said Herbert Hoover, then secretary of commerce, "has been economic development. And it continues today as the force which dominates the whole spiritual, social and

129

political life of our country and the world." This integrationist approach was an indicator of the perceived power of attraction of international society, undergirded by the expectation that economic advance was a solvent that, over time, would cleanse the world of its rivalries. One could attempt to explain this outlook by reference to the liberal belief in a harmony of interests, but to do so would imply that an abstract, logically articulated theory was at work when policy makers actually operated from a latent understanding of powerful historical trends that in its totality could not be spelled out with precision.[17]

This commercial and cultural approach sought to capitalize on the interdependence produced by the burgeoning of cross-national societal contacts of every sort. Herbert Hoover, the most influential policy maker of this period, approached international relations as if it were an overseas version of his domestic ideology of "voluntaryism," in which corporations and industry groups were supposed to come together and hammer out cooperative solutions to industry-wide problems. Informal cooperation, or at least the semblance of it, was the rule, as in the relationship between Benjamin Strong, head of the New York Federal Reserve Bank, and Montagu Norman of the Bank of England. In this scheme, the proper role of the US government was to serve as a facilitator and a helpmate, not as a decider. One sees the fingerprints of this perspective at work also in the Rogers Act of 1924, which created a professional Foreign Service within the State Department, but whose was passage was due chiefly to the desire for greater governmental expertise in the promotion of trade. The creation of the Foreign Service was less an indication of a growing realism than of the growing sway of an outlook that took international society as a given. Hoover's creation of a foreign trade bureaucracy within the Commerce Department was another indication of this belief that life was to be lived on the economic plane of foreign affairs.

The expectation that commercial and cultural forces would resolve problems was also dramatically evident in the Caribbean, where the Republican administrations sought to break the pattern of armed interventions established in the aftermath of the Spanish-American War. After an unhappy eight-year occupation, American forces left the Dominican Republic in 1924. At the same time, policy makers were searching for an exit strategy in neighboring Haiti and a solution to the continuing quasi-imperial oversight of Nicaragua. There were a number of reasons for this retreat from empire. With exhausted Europe unlikely to flex its muscles in the immediate future, the United States no longer needed to be concerned about the possibility of foreign intervention in the Western hemisphere. But the spirit of the age had changed, too. As the State Department's 1928 Clark memorandum pointed out, the Monroe Doctrine had been articulated at a time "when the political morality of Europe sanctioned, nay encouraged, the acquisition of territory by force; and when many of the great powers of Europe looked with eager, covetous eyes to the rich, undeveloped areas of the American hemisphere." Since TR's day, what had recently been one of the principal fields of international politics, the diplomacy of imperialism, had been largely abandoned, the turning point being the Washington agreements of 1922.

The era of high imperialism had passed in Europe and also in the United States, where the civilizing mission, whether through direct military occupation or indirect economic influence, was in disarray. In Haiti and the Dominican Republic, the American occupations, notwithstanding professions of good intentions and many good works, proved to be intensely unpopular with local populations. This would have counted for little only a few decades earlier, but the coming together of an anti-imperialist coalition in Congress during the 1920s was a marker of a growing modern sensibility in which imperialism was stripped of its once-fashionable cachet. This made it possible for the United States to change gears toward an internationalism that relied more on market mechanisms of economic integration and newer techniques of cultural relations in which the marketplace of ideas would substitute for political supervision. Anti-imperialists of the 1920s preferred to rely on international society to get what the United States wanted from these countries. Consistent with this political disengagement, many of the most avid anti-imperialists of the 1920s became staunch isolationists of the 1930s.[18]

In a context where the diplomacy of imperialism was clearly backpedalling, the policeman could afford to become the good neighbor, though not without some ironic results. American policy makers were more than willing to allow the republics to adopt authoritarian polities following American withdrawal so long as regional stability was not endangered. The United States was often indirectly responsible for this authoritarian trend because it created the constabularies that were later used by local strongmen to cement their rule. In more instances than not, acceptance of these noxious regimes was excused by the belief that the nations under dictatorial rule were not ready for democracy, that an autocrat often served as a bridge to democracy as had been the case with the ancient Greek tyrants, and that despotic governments were not necessarily injurious to international society. But the noninterventionist approach applied also to a toleration of more radical states like Mexico, where testy disputes over rights to oil and other sensitive issues were dealt with in a pragmatic fashion.

It is true that Americans believed, as an article of faith, in global democratization as the ultimate guarantee of peace (though not in a global republic). As Harding put it, "When the Governments of the earth shall have established a freedom like our own . . . the last sorrow and the final sacrifice of international warfare will have been written." Until that day arrived, however, there was no compelling need to democratize the entire world. Although the number of autocracies in the world was growing in the 1920s, in the absence of any danger there were no compelling reasons to pursue regime change. And in some conservative quarters, there was outright admiration for the ability of these regimes to suppress radical leftist movements. It was quite possible to get along with dictators, many of whom, particularly in Latin America—Duvalier in Haiti, Trujillo in the Dominican Republic, Somoza in Nicaragua—owed their positions in one way or another to American policy.[19]

There was nothing new about this behavior; throughout its history the United States had supported authoritarian regimes, if only via diplomatic recognition, far more often than it had promoted the creation of democracies. In the few instances in which democratization by force had been tried—in Cuba, the Dominican Republic, and Haiti—the results were dismal. The United States had been able to impose order and to mandate the holding of elections, but it could not transplant democratic habits of the heart. Bitter experience showed that one could expect only growing resistance, from foreign insurgencies and domestic critics, to long-term occupations. Anyway, democratic regime change had never been pursued for its own sake. Only when the alluring promise of the civilizing mission beckoned, or the peril of a growing German presence in the Caribbean loomed in the 1910s, did the United States take force-ful action toward democratization, but more as an afterthought than as part of an original scheme.

This functional thread of 1920s internationalism was intertwined with a legal strand. Harding's two most important cabinet appointees, Hoover and Hughes, were also the foremost representatives of economic and legal internationalism. Whereas the former emphasized economic processes and the latter looked to world opinion—structure versus cul-ture, as it were—both relied on the same underlying sociocultural real-ity. Both disarmament and legal attempts to abolish war as an instrument of national policy presupposed the existence of a mature international public opinion that was primed to accept a new legal-rational order in foreign affairs. The traditional critique of this outlook contends that Americans were quite naively projecting their particular cultural under-standing of legal order onto a world that operated by different principles entirely. But a more complicated view, one that comports more readily with the historical facts, suggests that the belief in an effective interna-tional legal order sprang from a rather different underlying assumption: that the globalizing process had laid a cross-cultural foundation for the creation of new international legal structures.[20]

Although legal internationalism enjoyed bipartisan support, it was unable to muster the votes necessary to get the United States to join the Permanent Court of International Justice at The Hague, no doubt because nationalists, no matter how many reservations were attached to the resolutions, always suspected that enforcement would in the end come down to the use of military force. Nevertheless, international law registered an impressive triumph in 1928 with the signature of the Kellogg-Briand Pact, which was perhaps the highest expression of legal internationalism ever. Ultimately, sixty-two nations agreed to renounce war as an instrument of national policy, excepting always the right of self-defense. The multilateral form of the treaty was as important as the content because it allowed for universality. Among its enthusiasts, the treaty, like law generally, was supposed to reflect an underlying moral sentiment in the international community. According to the interna-tionalist scholar James Shotwell, "the will to peace is paramount in the civilized world; and it is in this fact that the Pact of Paris resides." Or, as

Hoover put it, "Peace is not made at the council table or by treaties, but in the hearts of men." By outlawing war, which had never been illegal, a major barrier to the continued expansion of international society would be removed. In the opinion of the influential philosopher John Dewey, unless war was outlawed there was "no opportunity for existing moral sentiments to function effectively in international relations, and next to no hope for the speedy development of a coherent and widely accepted body of moral ideas which will be effective in determining international relations."[21]

As these comments suggest, the pact relied on the power of a maturing world opinion to shape international politics, much as the attentiveness to public opinion had become an inescapable part of domestic politics. It was doubtful whether the signature of the document by such a large body of nations was expressive of such a commitment, for in many cases adherence to the treaty was prompted by ulterior motives for purposes of public relations. In one sense, it did not matter. If the tendency to global pacification that was inherent in the civilization process performed as expected, questions of political enforcement were superfluous. But what if world opinion proved to be a chimera and nations continued to resort to war as an instrument of foreign policy? In that case, too, the result need not be disastrous as long as conflicts were not allowed to become global. As the nineteenth century had demonstrated, competitive world politics would continue to coexist with the continued growth of civilization and the pacification process would continue to move forward, though more fitfully than legal internationalists desired.

But then the big question: What if international society itself was threatened with collapse, as Wilson had predicted? Was international society worth saving? In that case, how would the United States respond? There was no arguing with the fact that the United States belonged to international society or that American participation in a leadership role was indispensable to the health of the world community. But the reverse questions—Was international society essential to America's well-being? If the lights went out elsewhere, would they go out also in the United States?—were left unasked by nearly everyone, because there was no need to ask them at the time. In keeping with the rule that politicians make decisions on big issues only when they have to, this was not a judgment that leaders in the 1920s felt called upon to make. In the 1920s, that kind of question was not worth asking much less answering.

Reminiscent of Wilson's optimism in 1913, to the policy makers of 1929 the world was wakening to the dawn of a new age of peace and prosperity. The prospects of peace, now-president Hoover stated in his first message to Congress, "were never brighter than to-day." This was not simply public posturing, for he privately told his secretary of state the same thing. "It seems to me," he said to Henry Stimson, "that there is the most profound outlook for peace today that we have had at any time in the last half century." Predictably, Hoover continued to peddle the now well-established nostrums of dollar diplomacy: a renewal of the commitment to arbitration, international law, membership in the Permanent Court of International Justice, along with continuing negotiations on the limitation of armaments. Fidelity to the sacredness of contracts was another principle, although on this matter Hoover was willing to propose a brief moratorium on debts. The effects of the great global Depression of the 1930s would make Hoover's statements look terribly naive. But, at the time, there was no compelling reason to anticipate disaster around the corner.[22]

Contrary to the portrait of a reactionary conservative that would later linger in the minds of many Americans, Hoover was as innovative a president as one could expect, given what the American political system was then willing to support. Hoover, who had as deep a practical grasp as any man alive of the workings of international trade and finance, would have been the first to admit that the world economy was important to the United States. In his inaugural address, he accepted "the profound truth that our own progress, prosperity, and peace are interlocked with the progress, prosperity, and peace of all humanity." Consistent with this global view, he argued that the burgeoning political problems of the decade had their origins in international social forces, as when he blamed the prolonged Depression on "the continued dislocations, shocks, and setbacks from abroad." Obviously, Hoover had a political interest in blaming the Depression on external causes. It was a convenient way of deflecting blame for Republican economic mismanagement of the bubble economy of the 1920s and of sidestepping the accusations that the worldwide Depression was made in America whence it radiated outward. Wherever the responsibility lay, the cairns on the path forward pointed clearly toward peace, disarmament, and restoration of economic confidence through "organized economic recovery." As he told Congress, "the welfare of mankind and the preservation of civilization depend upon our solution of these questions."[23]

The Manchurian crisis of 1931, in which the Japanese conquered and made a de facto colony of a major Chinese province, was notable because it foreshadowed the issues that arose later in the decade. After experiencing a disastrous downturn in their export-oriented economy, the Japanese elites gave up on international society and set out on a career of empire building that would make Japan independent of a liberal world economy. Although the Japanese tried to finesse the Kellogg-Briand Pact by resorting to the legal fiction of calling their invasion an "incident" and, instead of outright annexation, by creating an ill-disguised puppet state called Manchukuo, their behavior raised the issue of whether and how to respond to the now-illegal use of force by a major power. The administration was split between the president, who felt that no forceful measures were called for, and Secretary of State Stimson, who saw Japan's behavior as a threat to global society. Stimson believed that Japan might be bluffed into withdrawal by the implied threat of US military action, but Hoover made sure that American policy would never get to that point by preemptively declaring that the use of force was off the table.

The disagreement between Stimson and Hoover was important because it raised many of the fundamental questions that beleaguered the country later in the decade. How seriously should one take crises in faraway places of little nominal value? Stimson, clearly, was thinking about far more than defending America's interests in China. To this point, China had not been a vital interest of the United States, and the Open Door policy, when first announced in 1898, had not been thought worth a war with other China powers. But for Stimson, the problem was much larger than China. If Japan were allowed to get away scot-free with the conquest, he feared that international society might collapse. For Stimson, the disagreement with Japan centered on "an issue between the two great theories of civilization and economic methods." Because this was not the Japan of 1922, he found it "almost impossible that there should not be an armed clash between two such civilizations." As he explained a few years later, the problem resonated far beyond Asia: "in the interconnected and industrialized world of today war has become immeasurably more destructive and likely to spread than in former ages, and . . . unless it is controlled, our civilization will be in real peril." Modern civilization, he warned, was more fragile than was commonly understood. In retrospect, the importance of Stimsonianism—which was in point of fact a restatement of the pessimistic side of Woodrow Wilson's thought—is that it showed how expansive American internationalism could be, even in the absence of a clear and present danger.[24]

As a matter of principle, Hoover's voluntarist approach to legal internationalism stopped short of enforcement measures. In the Manchurian crisis he refused to go beyond imposing the toothless legal sanction of nonrecognition, after which he went on to compete with Stimson in taking credit for the policy. Though nonrecognition was a victory for Hoover's point of view, Stimson later sought to put the best face on his defeat by arguing that world opinion was not inconsiderable and that the Japanese, in particular, had always been sensitive to it. That only thirteen states recognized the puppet state of Manchukuo suggested that world opinion frowned on such behavior. Nevertheless, assuming that something like world opinion did exist, this crisis was throwing its continued solidarity and efficacy into question. The idea of world opinion had never depended on impressive governmental head counts or majority sentiment among the world's peoples; rather, it was premised on the growing like-mindedness of the small number of civilized core states, two of whose leading members, Nazi Germany and imperial Japan, were now on the verge of abandoning the commitment to international society.

The falling out between Hoover and Stimson showed how radically two eminent internationalists could disagree about the importance of the international order. Stimson would later declare openly that the preservation of international society was worth fighting for, whereas Hoover, who had ample firsthand experience in coping with the postwar chaos in Europe, had come to believe that the cure of war was worse than the disease. Though highly knowledgeable about foreign lands and cultures, and possessing an incomparable firsthand understanding of the world economy based on decades of travel and business experience, Hoover never set the same store in international society as other internationalists. He did not conceive of civilization—the then-existing civilization, anyway—as the key to America's future.

While international society was nonessential to Hoover, that did not mean that it ought to be ignored. During the crisis, Hoover energetically worked both the economic and the legal sides of the internationalist street. He invoked a one-year moratorium on intergovernmental debts. He tried actively to create movement in the disarmament talks at Geneva, which, being principally a Franco-German issue, revolved around the snarled issue of reducing land armaments. And he pushed for an international economic conference that would foster stability and confidence, encourage trade, and stabilize currency values. Cooperation at the economic level may not have been necessary, but it was still highly desirable. As he put it, "any effort to bring about our own recuperation has dictated the necessity of cooperation by us with other nations in reasonable effort to restore world confidence and economic stability." Beyond these limited forms of international cooperation, however, he was unwilling to go. As the fallout from the Great War suggested to growing numbers of people, that conflict had multiplied the problems of international society instead of resolving them.[25]

In the end, his thinking was governed by his appreciation of America's continuing difference and uniqueness, by an old-fashioned sense of exceptionalism that distrusted European values and traditions. Geographical distance still mattered, but even more important was cultural distance. He agreed with the idea that there should be a growing harmonization of cultures and societies, but European politics continued to be a snake pit that the United States should take great care to avoid. Ideally, cooperation could make the system work better, but in the absence of teamwork it was better to leave international society to its own devices and hope for improvement in the long run. In his view, Europe and the world needed America more than America needed them. In the worst case, civilization could be preserved in the Western hemisphere. While other nations could only dream of autarchy, he believed that America's economy was largely "self-contained." Quite consistently, then, he insisted that "we can make a very large recovery independent and irrespective of any foreign influences."[26]

The limits of American devotion to international cooperation were most evident in the assumption that protectionism was consistent with the smooth functioning of the world economy. US trade policy, which had been based on Careyite premises for nearly three-quarters of a century, had been reaffirmed by Harding in 1921: "it is not to be argued that we need destroy ourselves to be helpful to others." Following a modest downward adjustment, the Fordney-McCumber (1922) and the Hawley-Smoot (1930) tariffs surpassed the already high rates levied in nineteenth-century tariffs. It is not certain that Republican tariffs caused the Great Depression, as has often been claimed. Democrats had long argued that protectionism had the effect of weakening international society, and academic economists by now solidly endorsed free trade, but these arguments were rejected by Republicans who noted that protection, American prosperity, and the progress of civilization had long marched together and in step. Because the United States and the world had thrived side by side, there was little reason to fear the potentially disastrous global implications of American economic nationalism.

This was not simply a case of ideological pig-headedness. Economically, the US economy was more self-contained than previously, as the proportion of GNP attributable to foreign trade had dropped since the end of the Great War. And culturally, the dependence on Europe declined as Americans continued the process of building up a high culture of their own. Even when cosmopolitan borrowing from Europe did take place, it often took the form of importing extreme ideas that worked against forging a closer American relationship with international society. In other matters having to do with culture, Americans were becoming less internationally minded in the 1920s. The end of open immigration was indicative of a fear that the country could no longer afford to take in peoples from eastern Europe who were thought to be racially inferior. The explosive growth of the Klan as a powerful pressure group reflected the renewed vitality of a racialized and hence hierarchical view of the world even as science was on the verge of concluding that the idea of race had no scientific usefulness whatsoever. And the vogue for things Latin American in the 1920s presaged a shift away from the previous obsession with European culture.

In the end, the internationalism of the 1920s was a form of cohabita-

139

tion without marriage—an intimate relationship, hopefully for the long term, but subject at all times to sudden termination. The fundamental mantra, as Calvin Coolidge rephrased it in 1925, remained unchanged: "Especially are we determined not to become implicated in the political controversies of the Old World." The belief in international society operated in a world system where the League of Nations was, to all intents and purposes, effectively sequestered in a political world of its own. This reluctance to accept politico-military responsibilities outside the hemisphere was glaringly obvious in the behind-the-scenes stage management of the reparations problem and in the wording of the Four Power treaty, which required the signatories only to confer with one another in the event of serious controversy or aggression. So despite its newfound status and its substantial commitments to managing the world economy, the United States refused to behave like a traditional power.

More importantly, policy makers of the 1920s remained convinced of the continuing strength, vigor, and resilience of international society. The prospects for success of policies pioneered in the 1920s were premised on the likelihood of "gradual, long-term stabilization." Looking back on this period with the benefit of hindsight, later observers would assail such an assumption for its lack of political sense. Subsequent generations, wondering how American leaders could have been so blind, have tended to blame an unrealistic view of the world anchored in American idealism. Was this naive? Did American policy makers live in an "Alice in Wonderland universe" of diplomacy, as many historians like to remind us with ill-disguised contempt? Less charitably put: Were they really that stupid?[27]

But such criticisms ignore a basic point of doing history: to judge the American faith in international society on the basis of a standard that was quite alien to the times is unfair and distorts our understanding of the past. What has been judged foolish in retrospect becomes understandable and perhaps even defensible when the cultural background is spotlighted. American policies at the time were made largely on the basis of past experience, which had been quite successful on the whole. What later would be called deluded idealism, capitalist utopianism, or informal imperialism was an incremental extension of a decades-long policy of international cooperation that would not have survived had it not been working. One can continue to blame American policy makers for a botched economic policy, but this failure was evident only in retrospect and its fatal flaws remain unclear given that the causes of the Depression continue to be the subject of vigorous debate among economic historians. To expect that Americans could somehow have anticipated the perfect storm of the 1930s is unrealistic; it also reflects a fanciful view of what is historically possible at any given time. These criticisms also ignore the crucial fact—about which I will have more to say below—that this limited internationalism would remain the indispensable foundation for a more robust policy in the very near future. For even in retrospect, the assumption that continued economic growth would set the stage for political cooperation was quite sensible. To imagine a world in which crises among the major powers are resolved without resorting to force was not preposterous.

Perhaps, then, Americans can be excused for not fearing what had never before happened: the collapse of the world society whose durability they did not think to question. Judged by the political and economic practices of the day, to take seriously this possibility would have made little sense. Having recently excised what many believed was a militaristic threat to its survival, civilization could continue its ascent. The default political position of this commitment to international society was isolationism. In addition to being influenced by geography, isolationism was to some extent a by-product of the belief in the powerful backstage workings of international society. For if international society was really an unstoppable force, it would, with occasional help of the nonpolitical variety, be capable of surviving even the most intense political storms. As the careers of many Republican internationalists—Senator William Borah and Herbert Hoover—showed in the 1930s, this kind of internationalism did not automatically point to political interventionism.

How thoroughgoing was the internationalism of the 1920s? American policy during this period has been summed up by Joan Hoff in an authoritative work as an "independent internationalism." But it was not all that strange or different. Internationalism was always a matter of degree for all nations; by definition, the United States was never less than independent in a world of sovereign nations. It was less nationalistic than some, and more internationalist than many others. And there was plenty of guilt to go around, as other nations ostensibly more realistic ignored warning signs and continued to place their faith in international cooperation. For most parties, taken-for-granted beliefs about the autonomous functioning of international society continued to condition responses until a sequence of eye-opening events shattered those convictions.[28]

To gauge the importance of the still unforeseen events of the 1930s, it might be useful to ask what American policy would have looked like if there had been no global Depression, hence no Hitler, no Japanese militarism, and no rush to the exits of nations seeking to withdraw from international society. Most likely the United States would have continued down the path of international cooperation that it had been treading since the 1890s on its journey to global influence, but not as a world power wedded to military force as a way of attaining international social goals. In this undisturbed environment, the United States would have continued to rely on the instruments of culture, commerce, and international law. It would have continued to be unexceptional—or exceptional only in its relative modesty as a great power. There would have been no immanent impulse at work seeking expression in the nation's global ascendancy. Without a world crisis, American exceptionalism would have remained politically isolationist at heart and the exercise of American influence would have been felt primarily at the subpolitical level. If history had ended in 1930, Wilsonianism would have looked like an embarrassing interruption of dollar diplomacy, a dramatic interlude that briefly separated the acts of a longer and less complicated story than the one that ultimately played out.

The true departure would come with the discovery that a foreign policy limited to commercial and cultural relations was inadequate. But it is a mistake to assume that the shift to politics meant an abandonment of the long-standing emphasis on international society. If anything, international society became even more important in the decades to come. The prospect of its collapse would push policy makers to radically transform America's military and political stance toward the world, but it would also lead them to go beyond dollar diplomacy's reliance on the private sector by making it the explicit responsibility of the state to promote and assure the health of international society. Before that could happen, however, the nation needed to decide that international society was in peril and worth defending by war. That would mean abandoning the tradition of free security; it would also require a redefinition of America's vital interests. That redefinition would take place in the 1930s, a decade in which deeply sedimented beliefs were dredged up and closely interrogated.

6 The War for International Society: The Coming of World War II

Prior to the 1930s, international society had been left to operate behind the scenes of foreign relations. It finally took center stage in the Depression decade, when it seemed increasingly likely that it would fall victim to a plague of power politics, economic nationalism, and neomercantilist imperialism. The result was an all-encompassing international crisis that led to the great conflict now known as the Second World War. It was this war that marked the extraordinary turn in US foreign policy in which the defense of international society became its primary interest. Before going down that road, however, Americans were forced to reexamine their deepest assumptions in the only foreign policy debate in the nation's history that seriously explored fundamental questions of national security.

If one looks comparatively at the domestic politics of the decade, the United States and Europe continued in many ways to become more similar, though not necessarily more integrated. The initial impulse of the New Deal was definitely toward European-style dirigisme: unconcealed state intervention in the economy, planning, regulation, the adoption of social welfare measures, and solicitude for organized labor. In foreign relations, however, for the greater part of the decade the Roosevelt administration drifted away from the intimate participation in communal governance that was the norm in the 1920s. Hoover's reluctance to commit political and military resources to maintaining the postwar order has been criticized as insufficient, but for more than a half decade the policies of his successor, Franklin D. Roosevelt, were even more wary of intimate engagement.[1]

This standoffishness came out most clearly in FDR's decision to quit the London Economic Conference in 1933. FDR's justification—his claim that "the sound internal economic system of a nation is a greater factor in its well-being than the price of its currency in changing terms of the currencies of other nations"—suggested that economic recovery could be achieved by national means. Specifically, his decision to abandon the conference was prompted by the hope that the Depression might be ended by means of inflationist monetary tinkering, which would have been more difficult under a rigid gold standard. The willingness to engage in such autarchic experiments suggested that the nation was not yet irretrievably enmeshed in the global economy. His references to the "fetishes of international bankers" marked a stinging populist rejection of the idea that the needs of international society should take preference over sovereign designs. Coming as it did from a confirmed internationalist, this bombshell was indicative of how little classical liberal economics had been internalized by the policy community. It also showed how difficult it was to break away from self-centered economic habits of three-quarters of a century. A massive devaluation of the dollar that followed contributed to the contagion of competitive devaluations that depressed world trade during the decade.[2]

This slap in the face to the idea of world economic cooperation was partly reversed a few years later when a currency stabilization agreement was reached with France and Great Britain and the United States began to promote reciprocal trade agreements. Not so in political matters, however, where leadership had been ceded to the Europeans, who since the 1920s had been left to run their own affairs in a rump League of Nations. For much of the postwar decade they looked to be doing so admirably, by moving forward with a program of disarmament and peaceful settlement of disputes. After disarmament negotiations stalled in the early 1930s, Roosevelt handed over the reins of leadership to the League, most notably by proposing legislation that would have allowed the United States to take economic measures that harmonized with League sanctions against aggressors. But Congress was in no mood to follow the president's wishes. Instead, it mandated a more unilateral approach that ran contrary to the president's cooperative intentions.

The neutrality acts of 1935–37, which imposed arms embargoes on belligerents, forbade loans, and prohibited American passengers from traveling on belligerent passenger ships were a historical milestone because they repudiated the doctrine of neutral rights that had pulled the United States into war in 1812 and 1917. Less obviously, they also rejected the novel definition of threat that Wilson had begun to articulate following America's entry into the Great War. This new isolationism was of a different order entirely from the stance that animated opposition to Woodrow Wilson's internationalist policies. For opponents like Lodge, Knox, Theodore Roosevelt, and even Harding, a stable Europe had been worth fighting for. But the new consensus on the meaning of the Great War saw it not as a "great war for civilization," but as a sordid affair in which the United States had been bamboozled by some shady self-seeking characters: arms dealers who came to be known as merchants of death, British imperialists and their minions, and moneylenders. Isolationists of the late 1930s were convinced that the looming war would bring more of the same. Even FDR, in his famous "I Hate War" speech at Chautauqua in August 1936, agreed. His declaration that "we are not isolationists except in so far as we seek to isolate ourselves completely from war" appeared to rule out the possibility of military intervention abroad.

By mid-decade, there was no shortage of premonitions of disaster ahead, but neither was there any lack of optimistic pronouncements about the fundamental health of international society and the continuing possibility that international cooperation might yet save the day. For example, in his 1937 "Quarantine" speech, despite the spread of dictatorial regimes as the norm in "civilized" Europe, FDR attributed difficulties to a small, if troublesome, minority. "The peace, the freedom and the security of ninety percent of the population of the world is being jeopardized by the remaining ten percent who are threatening a breakdown of all international order and law," he said. "Surely the ninety percent who want to live in peace under law and in accordance with moral standards that have received almost universal acceptance through the centuries, can and must find some way to make their will prevail."

In this striking but factually shaky account of world public opinion, FDR was not describing a Hobbesian or Machiavellian world, but a more amicable Lockean state of nature that was being disturbed by only a few troublemakers. In his most famous analogy, FDR likened the international crisis to a community experiencing an epidemic, a disease of civilization in which the chain of infection was made possible by human proximity and a threshold density of population. His proposed quarantine presumed that the contagion could still be isolated. "When an epidemic of physical disease starts to spread," FDR continued, "the community approves and joins in a quarantine of the patients in order to protect the health of the community against the spread of the disease." He ended with the now-standard appeal to world opinion to make itself felt: "the will for peace on the part of peace-loving nations must express itself to the end that nations that may be tempted to violate their agreements and the rights of others will desist from such a course." This belief in the thickness and resilience of international society survived late into the decade.

In retrospect, it has been difficult to understand why Roosevelt (like many European leaders) should have persisted for so long in seeing the international system as fundamentally healthy. Subsequently, historians have tended to argue that the writing was on the wall as early as 1931, at which time preventative measures ought to have been taken. But the inability to recognize a threat was partly due to the spell that the idea of a cooperative international society continued to cast on the minds of statesmen. Even though the last European attempt at cooperation came with the appeasement of Germany in September 1938, FDR continued to dangle the lure of trade concessions well into 1939 in the hope that the promise of access to markets and raw materials would induce the renegade nations to rejoin international society. Appeasement itself was predicated on the idea that the world contained enough social space to comfortably accommodate even the dictatorships. International society was still thought capable of absorbing and accommodating members with vastly different political and cultural complexions.[3]

That faith received powerful confirmation in spheres other than politics. Even the dictatorial states in the 1930s occasionally trimmed their policies in deference to this assumption. The way in which Hitler dialed back Nazi ideology in the 1936 Berlin Olympic Games provides one interesting example of the ongoing potency of international norms and structures. As one American said of international sport, "nations can no longer be isolated, self-determining, or governed by policies independent of the standards, practices and desires of the rest of the world." The ongoing campaign by the Soviet Union to organize nations into an antifascist coalition in the League of Nations was another example of the belief in the inherent resources of international society. It was, obviously, not the communist ideal of what international society should be, but it still had its uses. The concern expressed by Republican editor Frank Knox in a 1937 letter to FDR for "American self-respect and respect for America abroad in a world that has apparently gone drunk and mad" suggested that sobriety was the default condition.[4]

Unfortunately, though this was not well understood at the time, the Atlantic powers were offering the benefits of membership in a world to which German and Japanese rulers had no desire to belong. "We no longer are dependent on the good graces or disgraces of other States or their statesmen," jibed Hitler in 1939. Whereas FDR's guarantee of access to raw materials and markets implied that the so-called have-nots could be accommodated, Germany was rejecting the entire conception of international society as it had evolved over the preceding century. Once it became evident that appeasement had failed, its inadequacy was not viewed pragmatically in the sense of "oh, well, it didn't work this time, but it was still worth a try." Appeasement, only recently viewed as a practical and quite respectable way of doing business, suddenly became the cardinal sin of policy making, an abandonment of moral standards that led only to continual extortion and ultimately to catastrophe.

Only when international society itself was considered to be at risk did these optimistic attempts to salvage the situation come to an end. Thereupon, FDR begin to change direction with a stepped-up tempo of initiatives—financial aid to China and embargoes against Japan in the Pacific, the destroyers-for-bases deal with Britain in 1940, lend-lease aid in 1941, and aggressive convoying in the Atlantic. By December 1941, he had tilted American policy dramatically toward Great Britain and

China, while stopping just short of active participation and intervention. These policy shifts, particularly FDR's pugnacious approach to the war in Europe, provoked enormous domestic controversy. The historian Arthur Schlesinger Jr. recalled "the isolationist-interventionist debate of 1940–41 [as] the bitterest time of all."[5]

Following those tumultuous days, in the eyes of both the public and most historians (a combination that ought to raise warning flags) World War II became the "good war," both necessary and just. Partly as a result of this consensus, as one historian has pointed out, this war took on "a historical peculiarity that tends to make it analytically invisible." Not entirely so, however, for historians and novelists have long written negatively about the war from a worm's eye point of view, tactical and strategic blunders aplenty have been exposed, and some have criticized the morality of certain policies like strategic bombing, but only a few have argued that it was a problematic war of choice. Most notable among the critics was the great historian Charles Beard, who in an act of self-immolation destroyed his eminent public standing by arguing that FDR was taking the nation high-handedly into a war not worth fighting. After 1945, retrospective critiques of American participation, most notably by his contemporary Charles Callan Tansill, were also hooted down, a lesson that would not be lost on succeeding generations of historians. Thus while postwar revisionists felt free to treat virtually the entire history of US foreign relations as an intellectual free-fire zone, World War II remained the glaring exception. Even those historians who earned their reputations by arguing that imperialism was the default condition of US foreign relations chose either to avoid contact with the sacred cow of war against Nazi Germany or to focus on the softer target of Japan.[6]

So accustomed have we become to the idea of world wars that we tend to see them as natural events produced by deep historical forces. By 1940 and 1941, before the United States became a belligerent, Roosevelt was already describing the conflicts in China and in Europe as a "world war," and referring to the Great War as "the first world war." For those who approached the topic from a geopolitical framework, the world wars amounted to no more than geographically expanded instances of age-old political behaviors; apart from their global scale, which could readily be explained by modernization and globalization, understanding these wars required no major conceptual retooling. Thus one favored way of understanding the interventionist decisions of these years is to see them in realist terms as rational responses to the threat posed by Germany's mastery of the continent and its alliance with Japan. According to this way of looking at things, the United States belatedly recognized this danger for what it was and, very late in the day, took action to meet it. Viewed in social scientific terms, American belligerency was predictable, for this was the sort of thing that a great power did when faced by stark realities. The Pearl Harbor attack, later reinforced by the revelation of the genocidal practices of Nazi Germany, subsequently clothed American justifications for American entry into World War II in the impregnable armor of necessity and the spiritual shield of moral rectitude.[7]

At the time, this danger was expressed in the scientific-sounding language of geopolitics, a field of growing popularity in American universities during the 1930s, in which global "correlations of power" were the chief objects of analytical concern. Take, for example, how one geopolitically attuned interventionist described the danger in June 1941: "When Europe is taken, most of Africa goes with it. Leadership of the Eurasian land mass by the totalitarians (Nazi and Soviet) is assured in such an event, leaving the American continents as the next natural stepping stones of conflict." Occasionally, FDR would slip into this kind of talk. Doing the global math of world domination at a press conference, he concluded, "From Hitler's point of view, it is rational. And, if any of us were in his place, with his methods, we would do it." Weasel words notwithstanding, one would like to think that FDR would not have behaved like the führer were he in his place, but here he was insisting that "it is a perfectly open and shut thing and, if you have the complete, physical power to do it, you win."[8]

This geopolitical argument has long exhaled the air of gospel truth. But, as one scholar cautions, "the so-called dictates of necessity are not self-evident." Certainly for many noninterventionists of the time, the situation was not at all clear-cut. Rather than being governed by imperative circumstance, for the United States and for the other major powers as well the onset of the war was accompanied by a large number of imposing what-ifs? As Ian Kershaw has argued, "What seems to posterity an inevitable course of events did not look like that at the time." An impressive number of intelligent public figures, though disgusted and horrified by the path of events in Asia and Europe, refused to believe that a compelling threat to the nation existed. For these isolationists, realism and globalism were at odds, and such dangers as existed came primarily from home rather than from abroad. "We lack only a leadership that places America first," said Charles Lindbergh on May 23, 1941 in a speech at Madison Square Garden sponsored by the nation's leading isolationist group. Its name, America First, deserves a moment's reflection because it suggested that the Roosevelt administration was placing something else ahead of the national interest. That something else, as I will argue below, was international society[9].

However depressing, for Lindbergh the troubles were "Europe's and not ours"; or, as Rick the saloon keeper would say in the 1942 classic film *Casablanca*, "The politics of the world are not my problem." By this time, Hoover had come a long way in articulating the ideas that were rattling around in his subconscious in 1931. He saw the war as an ideological conflict, a war of ideas, but he felt that ideas could not be defeated through war. He argued that "evil ideas contain the germs of their own defeat . . . we do not need to despair that these evil ideologies will continue forever on this earth." Repulsive ideologies were at any rate nothing new. "The democratic nations," he pointed out, "have always had to live with such bedfellows." Hoover believed that peace was far more efficacious in puncturing the appeal of dictatorships than the damage done by fighting them. "If we enter such a war we only increase the moral and economic wastage of the world," he argued. "If we stay out, we preserve much for the reconstruction of the world. . . . Here in America today is the only remaining sanctuary of freedom, the last oasis of civilization and the last reserve of moral and economic strength." Such an eventuality might be seen as a catastrophe akin to the fall of Rome, but nevertheless tolerable when seen from the Byzantine point of view. Hoover preferred to place his bets on the far more profound truths of geography, relative American independence, and American uniqueness.[10]

Internationalists could not begin to make sense of this point of view. In 1937, the anthropologist Ralph Linton wrote an essay, "One Hundred Percent American," which lampooned the idea of commercial and cultural isolation by showing how the many taken-for-granted appurtenances of daily life had originated elsewhere. But though people like Linton believed that civilization had always been international, isolationists begged to differ. Should the Dark Ages return to Europe, Lindbergh insisted that the essentials of civilization "must not go down here as well as on the other side." The challenge was "to carry on Western civilization," which he and like-minded followers believed could be preserved in a non-European local setting, if it came to that. Unlike isolationists of the past, they were prepared to abandon international society the way one would evacuate a dangerous ramshackle structure. Subsequent lampooning by cartoonists of this outlook as ostrichlike neglected to mention that that real-life ostriches do not bury their heads in the sand and, when cornered, are capable of delivering a powerful defensive kick.[11]

Only a few years earlier, at a time when it was still difficult to discern a threat to the United States, Roosevelt had given the impression of agreeing with the isolationists. From time to time, advisers would point out, as William Bullitt did in 1937, that "the future is obscure. . . . There is no basis of policy more unreal or disastrous than the apprehension of remote future dangers." And at first FDR was not insensible to such arguments. On one occasion, he was forced to concede that he was basing policy on "possibility only," on "conceivable consequences," and even on a "pipe dream," or perhaps on "a crazy picture," but in the end he gave in to his worst-case expectations because it was his responsibility as a statesman to think about "ultimate consequences." Looking at things this way, the potentially disastrous results of inaction outweighed the cost of direct involvement. As one political scientist put it, the prewar debate demonstrated "why decision makers err on the side of safety in their power calculations."[12]

Whatever FDR's initial doubts and political zigzags, by late 1940 his mind was made up. Giving the back of his hand to "wishful thinkers and sentimentalists," he asserted in a radio address that "the first and fundamental fact is that what started as a European war has developed, as the Nazis always intended it should develop, into a world war for world domination." In a December 1940 fireside chat, he claimed that "the Nazi masters of Germany have made it clear that they intend not only to dominate all life and thought in their own country, but also to enslave the whole of Europe, and then to use the resources of Europe to dominate the rest of the world." By this time, appeasement having proved futile, FDR insisted that the United States had "no right or reason to encourage talk of peace," despite only recently having been the nagger-in-chief on behalf of world peace. He also ventured a grim forecast of what would likely follow a British surrender: "the Axis powers will control the continents of Europe, Asia, Africa, Australasia, and the high seas—and they will be in a position to bring enormous military and naval resources against this hemisphere. It is no exaggeration to say that all of us, in all the Americas, would be living at the point of a gun—a gun loaded with explosive bullets." The following year, one week after a provocative encounter between the destroyer USS *Greer* and a German U-boat, he stated that "the Nazi danger to our Western world has long ceased to be a mere possibility. The danger is here now." Put this way, the threat was existential in nature. The issue was no less than "the preservation of American independence."[13]

The Great Debate of 1940–41 was a dual crisis of foundational beliefs, as much a crisis within each worldview as it was a contest between contending outlooks. World War II raised a fundamental question: what is foreign policy about? The usual answer, security and welfare, is tautologous. But FDR offered two more specific answers: there was a military threat and a danger to the continued existence of international society. One answer was more effective, while the other was more illuminating, but the isolationists rejected both. There was no military danger, they believed, that could not be handled short of war. To the second argument, they responded that the essentials of civilization could be preserved even if global society should collapse. For the isolationists, the world crisis had destroyed the belief in the fundamentally beneficial character of international society, making pointless the traditional willingness to fight for the affirmation of commercial rights. As for the cultural advantages of civilization, those could be preserved without the societal involvements. If the debate settled nothing in intellectual terms, and if the events that followed shed no light on the rightness or wrongness of the contentions of each side, it did have this virtue: it illuminated the huge gulf between those who believed that international society was a vital interest and those who believed that the nation could do without it. The argument was not simply about military matters, but about what societal factors mattered militarily.

With the Japanese attack on Pearl Harbor on December 7, 1941, the strategic case of the interventionists was resoundingly confirmed in the public mind. A few days later, FDR described the tumble of events that landed the United States in war as proof that "powerful and resourceful gangsters have banded together to make war upon the whole human race." "It is an unholy alliance of power and pelf to dominate and enslave the human race," he insisted. "We know also," he added, "that Germany and Japan are conducting their military and naval operations in accordance with a joint plan." Many of the justifications that he advanced have since become strategic truisms, soon to be revived in only slightly altered form as the strategic rationale of the Cold War. The basic argument was that the pace of warfare and the rapid introduction of enormously destructive weaponry had made geographic barriers obsolete; and with the Axis powers on the verge of commanding the bulk of the world's resources, they would soon be in the position to amass military power on a scale that would lead inevitably to an attempt at world conquest. FDR attempted to portray all this as a hardheaded understanding of new global realities in which "the Nation [was] fighting for its existence and its future life." In Dean Acheson's subsequent picturesque explanation of his interventionist position, one could hear "the roaring of the cataract" as the United States drifted perilously near to the waterfall.[14]

If realism were truly in touch with the real, we would long ago have had a scientific politics. In this case, the threats that Roosevelt described with great self-assurance simply did not exist. While he was right to acknowledge the novelty of the situation, it was misleading to suggest that he knew the terrain, for neither past experience nor current knowledge could be relied upon to explain with authority what was going on. To take one example, while American policy makers assumed that the Axis powers were engaged in a global conspiracy, we have since learned that the relationship between Germany and Japan was not intimate. The racial philosophy of the Nazis and the differing geographic interests of the two nations worked against any sort of ideological coherence or deep collaboration. We know, too, that the Japanese were suspicious of the

Germans and, just as the Germans refused to share or coordinate their plans, they preferred to keep their own counsel.

As for their hatching a global plot, the strategic ambitions of each power were regional. The territorially bounded Japanese sensibility was expressed in the subsequently notorious idea of a Greater East Asia Co-Prosperity Sphere. This regional outlook, as opposed to a global framework, persisted long into the postwar period, as generations of Japanese insisted on calling the conflict "the Pacific War" instead of World War II. The same applies to Germany. Conceptually, the land-based expansion envisioned by the Nazi policy of *Lebensraum* was actually less ambitious geographically than the *Weltpolitik* of Wilhelmine Germany. It strains credulity, moreover, to imagine a statesman with credentials as parochial as Hitler's plotting a global takeover. As for the Italians, they had shown the realistic limits of their imperial expansion with the Ethiopian adventure of 1935–36. Mussolini's ambitions did not extend beyond Africa and southeastern Europe, and even those relatively modest desires exceeded his even more modest capabilities. Illustratively, the attack on Albania in 1940 had all the makings of a disaster until the Italians were bailed out by Germany's intervention.

We also know that there were no plans to invade and conquer the United States. It has been argued that the absence of any such plans was irrelevant; the Germans would inevitably have trained their sights on the United States because it was in the regime's ideological DNA to seek a military showdown as part of an intrinsic ambition for world conquest. But the traditional response to that kind of danger, workaday stuff as far as foreign policy goes, is deterrence, not preemption. In this case, however, it was the Axis partners who were seeking to do the deterring. Hoping to intimidate the Americans, they signed the Tripartite Pact in September 1940. This ersatz global alliance among powers who preferred to act independently and locally was formed in the misconceived expectation that the United States would not dare to act globally. But even if the Germans and Japanese had fulfilled the worst fears of American policy makers by creating a worldwide condominium of gangster nations, there were all sorts of eventualities, possible and probable, that would have worked against the achievement of world conquest: the survival of England (the Battle of Britain had failed by the end of 1940),

155

the building of the atomic bomb by the United States, the likelihood of a truce between Hitler and a USSR that refused to stay down for the count, or a continued unwillingness of Japan to march in lockstep with Germany. In retrospect, the United States probably could have survived a worst-case situation of hostility, long enough at least to outlast the flimsy Axis coalition.[15]

Egregious misreadings of the international situation were common to all the major policy makers. In the Munich negotiations, in which the British (along with many others, including the United States) assumed that giving the Sudetenland to Germany would satisfy Hitler's appetite for additional territory, Americans and others continued to misjudge Hitler by assuming that he could be handled by diplomacy. The British also misread Mussolini, hoping for far too long that he could be turned against Hitler. The alarmist American view of Nazi intentions and capabilities in Latin America was far off base. For their part, Axis leaders also consistently came up with policy judgments that were incredibly wide of the mark. Hitler expected that the British and French would do nothing following his invasion of Poland. Despite numerous warnings to the contrary, Stalin believed that the nonaggression pact with Germany would hold; so too did the Japanese, who based their policy of Southern Advance in large part in the belief of continued German-Soviet friendship, only to be shocked to learn of Operation Barbarossa, the German invasion of the USSR in June 1941. And that is not to mention all the military miscalculations that followed.[16]

There was much more of this short-sightedness. It was assumed that the Tripartite Pact of September 14, 1940, would intimidate the Americans, when it wound up doing precisely the reverse; and the American economic embargoes against Japan, inspired by the expectation that the Japanese would in the end cave in, prompted them instead to attack the United States, a response that surprised the Germans as much as it did the Americans. This misunderstanding of Japanese thinking extended also to the failure to realize the degree to which policy between Tokyo and Berlin, commonly thought to be the result of a close-knit global conspiracy of gangster nations, was instead uncoordinated and fraught with tension and mutual suspicion. All of these overturned expectations underscore what Maurice Matloff once referred to as "the 'fog' surrounding the intentions and capabilities of potential enemies and friends." Whereas the source of the Great War in great power competition was easy to see—the big question being responsibility for war guilt—the global origins of the Second World War, where war guilt has long been a settled matter, were far murkier. Mountaintops sometimes afford amazingly clear views, but for policy makers the view at the top is typically quite cloudy.[17]

How does one explain all these misperceptions? To start, uncertainty is a feature found in all foreign policy making. While there is always ample room for rational individuals to differ radically on ways of meeting a threat, knowing with assurance whether a threat exists at all is more problematic still. In the absence of reliable knowledge of imminent danger, one cannot hope to respond realistically because realism requires a clear understanding of objective realities for statesmen to make their calculations. But the only certainty in this situation was uncertainty. The threat was not objectively real in the way that an animal instinctively senses and reacts to danger or in the way that nations like France and Germany responded to each other's military buildups prior to the Great War. In this case, threats existed at a level of abstraction far removed from clear and present dangers. Whatever the structural realities of world politics, the mental worlds of policy makers were shot through with confusion and indeterminacy. The predictive aspirations of political science notwithstanding, experience thus far suggests that neither policy makers nor intellectuals command much insight into the future—accurate predictions on crucial issues are merely luck, or at best, educated guesses masquerading as knowledge.[18]

Leaving to one side a focus on the objective side of things, with its emphasis on a rational calculation of expected utilities, perhaps a more productive approach, one that has the virtue of being cognitively realistic, would be to look at the influence of uncertainty in decision making. The phenomenological facts of life, which were quite different from the cocksure public declarations, were in the end quite telling about America's unique world role. Only in mid-1941 did FDR, after realizing that there was an enormous information deficit with regard to the Axis powers, authorize the creation of what would become the nation's civilian intelligence agencies (on one notorious occasion the accuracy of the evidence on which Roosevelt was acting was challenged by Senator William Borah, who claimed to have more reliable sources). Whether or not isolationists had a superior claim to the title of realists is arguable, but the existence of such a completely contrary understanding of the situation among so many intelligent people underscores the fact that no one really *knew* what the state of affairs was or where the global order was headed. Given the lack of conclusive evidence from both sides about the nature of reality, it is difficult to avoid the conclusion that the disagreement was the product of the differing conceptual apparatuses that each brought to the situation. For each side, seeing was not a passive empirical process but an active product of the human mind. In foreign affairs, more so than in many other areas that require informed decisions, ex cathedra declarations of truth deserve to be received with skepticism.[19]

Thus far history has chosen to treat the disagreement by concluding that the isolationists were wrong while the interventionists got it right. But on the facts of the matter as they were available at the time, either side might have been right, wrong, or a mixture of both. Even in retrospect, it is difficult to make an open-and-shut case for an existential threat to the United States. To take but one possibility, Great Britain and the Soviet Union might well have survived, creating a new balance of power on the continent, though there was no guarantee of that. For that matter, what would a military defeat have brought? Given the profoundly regional outlooks of the Axis powers, even a vanquished United States would likely not have been reduced to the abject status of Vichy France. Twenty-twenty hindsight offers little help here. We cannot even say with confidence that FDR guessed correctly, for America's participation in the war destroyed the ability to test the genuineness of the danger that it had been intended to remove. One of the characteristics of human activity is that subjective intentionality creates new social facts, observer relative, whose establishment makes pointless any debate over the appropriateness of their creation in the first place.[20]

But the bewilderment ran deeper than that, for the uncertainty went beyond this particular situation; it was a general phenomenon that lay close to the very heart of modernity. The most explicit statement of the issue was supplied by the German thinker Arnold Gehlen, who argued

that the built-in rapidity of change in modern society produced deinstitutionalization, the disappearance of the social machinery that provided
order and predictability, whereas traditional societies had durable institutions that, by contrast, were reliable and seemingly permanent social
facts. Gehlen spoke of modernity as "objectively blurred, objectively indeterminate," as a process that created a reality "which shares . . . the
property of allowing for conflicting judgments." Gehlen was a Nazi. But
if taking seriously the views of a politically tainted German thinker is too
off-putting, it might help to point out that pretty much the same idea lies
at the heart of the true-blue American concept of "cultural lag." Or, if
one sees modern life in Joseph Schumpeter's terms as a process of "creative destruction," one could say that the institutional flux of modernity
was outpacing the ability of humans to create stable new cognitive forms.
But however stated, deinstitutionalization had the effect of decreasing
confidence in the taken-for-granted character of social structures. In this
way, modernity could not help but generate baffling and contradictory
images of the world.[21]

The tumultuous condition of international politics in the late 1930s
bears a striking resemblance to the kind of world described by Gehlen.
Everything that had been well established in the previous century was
up in the air: the European balance of power, the nature and scope of
military power, the ideological structure of the world, the role of imperialism, the relationship between Europe and Asia, and, not least, the
very nature and utility of diplomacy, which was thrown into question
by the disastrous failure of appeasement. Hitler's cynical repudiation of
appeasement's underlying principle of reliable statesmanlike behavior,
which even in a competitive world had been beyond question, underscored this rapid collapse of the formerly accepted order of things. In
situations where the objective foreground is blurred and indeterminate,
subjective judgments are called upon to fill in the blanks and to supply the information, or what passes for information, needed to arrive at
decisions. This shift of emphasis from the external situation to the way
it which it was construed shifts an enormous amount of the explanatory burden from the objective to the psychological side of the ledger. If
this is right, despite the very real fear that the international crisis evoked

among American internationalists, then the choice for internationalism was just that—a choice—one that was neither culturally nor externally determined.[22]

The argument from uncertainty makes a case against social scientific realism, but it does not offer a positive counterargument. Fortunately, there is plenty of evidence that something solid other than survival was clearly at stake. Despite all the bewilderment among policy makers about whether or not an existential threat existed, there was a more objective danger on which a decision could be based: the threat to an international society that had arisen in the nineteenth century and that was a product of centuries of evolution. That kind of peril had little to do with the physical survival of the United States and everything to do with America's identity, especially so in the eyes of internationalists who believed that globalization had provided a hospitable matrix for the fulfillment of republican aspirations. Despite loose leftist critiques of rootless cosmopolitanism, it did have a secure anchorage in international society, without which the United States would have been cast adrift ideologically. As Secretary of State Hull asserted in his Toronto address of 1937 in which he emphasized the need for international order, "the activities of individuals and of communities are so intricately interdependent that the fullness of the individual's life is powerfully determined by the character of the social organization of which he is part."[23]

In his "Arsenal of Democracy" speech of December 29, 1940, in which he announced his program of lend-lease support to anti-German nations, Roosevelt envisioned "a new and terrible era in which the whole world, our hemisphere included, would be run by threats of brute force." Survival might not be in question in this era, but only at the unthinkable cost of becoming a garrison state. "To survive in such a world," FDR continued, "we would have to convert ourselves permanently into a militaristic power on the basis of war economy." Recast in this form, the interventionist argument was about the survival of the American way of life rather than the survival of the American state; it was a question of essence, not existence, in which America's identity was presumed to depend on international society. FDR had already taken this line of argument for a test drive in a 1938 letter to Ambassador William Phillips in Rome: "if we get the idea that the future of our form of government is threatened by a coalition of European dictators, we might wade in with everything we have to give."[24]

The cause-and-effect relationship between international society and democracy was sometimes inverted so as to credit the United States with principal responsibility for inaugurating the era of democracy in human affairs. In his 1940 Armistice Day address, Roosevelt offered a historical interpretation of the "new order of the ages," the motto found in Latin on the great seal on the back of each dollar bill. In his questionable telling, this new order had radiated outward from the Americas: "truly and fundamentally, it was a new order. Nothing like it had ever been seen before. We must accept it because the new order spread into almost every part of the civilized world. It spread in many forms, and over the next century almost all peoples had acquired some form of popular expression of opinion, some form of election, some form of franchise, some form of the right to be heard." What this speech lacked in historical accuracy—the historical tide was clearly running against democracy in the 1920s and 1930s—it made up for in conviction. But the emphasis on international society was more to the point. Now that this "new order of the ages" was endangered, FDR sought to focus attention on "the maintenance of the new order to which we have been accustomed and in which we intend to continue." From an internationalist's point of view, the point of no return had been reached from which there was no turning back.[25]

This covered far more territory conceptually than national security or physical survival. "Our type of civilization," FDR said on another occasion, "though saved for a generation by the first World War, is once again a world issue." In a speech to the governing board of the Pan American union, FDR emphasized the necessity of avoiding "an organization of world affairs which permits us no choice but to turn our countries into barracks, unless we are to be the vassals of some conquering empire." Again, in 1940, he asked, "What shall we be defending?" The answer: "a way of life which has given more freedom to the soul and body of man than has ever been realized in the world before." Such statements indicate clearly the importance of the survival of an international society that was congenial to a liberal civilization. In the president's mind, at least, the continued existence of a liberal globalizing world had become essential to maintaining the national character.[26]

Instead of relying upon suspect rhetorical declarations, there is another, perhaps more persuasive, way of making the case that the United States was acting to preserve international society. Compared to states that were faced beyond question with existential threats and forced to act from concrete understandings of their national interests, America's behavior differed radically. The degree to which the American decision for war was sui generis becomes evident when one compares American strategic thinking with the kinds of decisions made by other powers who would become partners and enemies in what came to be called the Second World War. "Modern politics is world politics," Evan Luard has written, but that was not true of international politics through most of 1941, in which most state actors assumed the priority of the local over the global. I have already pointed to the regional ambitions of the Axis powers, but the foreign policies of their immediate enemies were equally local when it came to vitally important questions of war and peace. Great Britain, France, and the Soviet Union were no less regional in how they approached the wars in Europe and in Asia. Each of these powers had imperial interests in Asia that it was willing to sacrifice to more pressing European concerns.[27]

Great Britain's sprawling empire, which had been instrumental in the creation of a global society, encompassed a geographic assortment of interests that dwarfed those of the United States. But by 1940, the threat to the British Isles had narrowed the focus of British foreign policy to surviving a Nazi invasion from the continent. Were it not for the United States, the British would have been willing to allow Japan to have its way in the Far East. Provided that India, Australia, and New Zealand were left untouched, some kind of deal was imaginable. Because the primary goal of Prime Minister Winston Churchill was to induce America to join the war against Germany, showing solidarity with the Americans against Japan was necessary, but this was not a war that the British, on their own, were eager to instigate. It followed, once the British found themselves at war with Japan, that they played only a supporting role in the Far East—a separate "theater" of war (as if the war were a multiplex cinema)—in comparison to their marshaling of men and material in preparation for the D-day landings. The heavy lifting in the Pacific war was left to the United States.[28]

Stalin's USSR also took a narrowly defined geographic approach to its difficulties by giving priority to Europe over interests in the Far East. After protecting himself against Germany with the infamous Ribbentrop-Molotov Pact of August 1939 (God's gift to realists who believe that ideology is a secondary concern in international relations), the following spring Stalin hedged his bets by signing a nonaggression pact with Japan. This was a brilliant wager, as it turned out, for it allowed him to transfer forces from Siberia to Europe to stem the German invasion that began in June 1941. The USSR continued to honor this agreement until August 1945, when, with Germany out of the way, it entered the war against Japan in its closing days. That the Soviets were strongly encouraged to do so by their American allies does not mean that they did not have reasons of their own, but the timing underscored Moscow's regional priorities.

The role of defeated Vichy France is less important—quite understandable for a state that has been described as impotent—but still instructive. Marshal Philippe Pétain's puppet state could not hope to have an independent foreign policy. Its first task was incorporation into the Euro-German new order. But it did enjoy some flexibility in the administration of France's empire, which Americans hoped to keep out of German and Japanese hands. Harking back to the imperialist tack taken in the decades following defeat in the Franco-Prussian War, some Vichy officials hoped to retrieve at least a vestige of great power status via the empire to compensate for lost status on the continent. Unfortunately for this aim, France was only nominally in command of all its colonies and in no position to defend them. Thus when the Japanese insisted on the military occupation of northern Indochina in 1941, the Vichy regime had no choice but to acquiesce. By the end of 1942, Vichy's attention shifted closer to home as a result of the Anglo-American invasion of its African possessions and the now-total German occupation of France.[29]

The central point is simple enough: whereas other major nations made their decisions on the basis of regional priorities, the United States chose to act on the basis of global thinking. The United States was the only major power to risk, perhaps even to invite, war on both sides of the world even as other powers went to great lengths to avoid placing themselves in that kind of situation. Why they chose to focus on local security concerns is not mysterious. With immediate dangers staring them in the face, decisions on ends, means, and priorities could be made almost intuitively. In the case of the United States, no such patently compelling dangers existed. The necessity for the other powers to adopt regional approaches to their security problems highlights, by way of contrast, the interpretative latitude that existed in the American case. This interpretive elbow room was further highlighted by the panoramic range of issues taken up in the Great Debate.

Though American officials assumed that the crisis was global and required a global strategy, this did not mean that a war of unbounded geographic scope was desirable. Prudent military strategy dictated a more moderate course of action. However, strategic military planning that called for a one-war-at-a-time approach was never converted into a diplomatic strategy of delay with Japan that would have allowed the United States to focus exclusively on first defeating Germany, which was thought to be the greater danger. Instead, American policy did the exact contrary by plunging the country into war with both enemies at once. Though it had abandoned any pretense of neutrality in its naval policies in the Atlantic, the United States was actually more cautious in dealing with Germany than with Japan. By stiffening its stance in the Pacific, many historians have argued that Japan, backed into a corner by an American-led oil embargo, had little choice but to strike back at the United States, hence the attack on Pearl Harbor. Still, there were no apparent regrets at this colossal foul-up in the execution of strategic planning, for having to fight a two-front war substantiated, in a self-fulfilling way, the administration's case that the threat was at bottom global.

All this raises an interesting question: In view of the local priorities of the other major powers, if the United States had not become a belligerent in 1941 would there have been a Second World War? Given the regional predilections of the other participants, it is plausible to conjecture that the Sino-Japanese War that began in 1937 and the European war that erupted in 1939, in the absence of any compelling incentive to link them together, would have remained separate and distinct conflicts. Only the United States had a weighty rationale for merging the two wars, the threat to global civilization, which saw the two conflicts as being inseparably connected. The conjecture is unprovable, but this much is clear: With its unique geopolitical sensibility, the United States helped turn what were two concurrent regional wars in Europe and in Asia into a genuinely global conflict of a kind that rendered the so-called Great War positively provincial and anemic by comparison. Instead of responding to a conflict that was already global, American participation globalized two regional struggles.

If America's entry as a belligerent resulted in a Second World War, it is not altogether mischievous to say that America "caused" World War II—in a proximate sense, anyway. The argument that World War II was an American creation may be excessively provocative, but it has a productive side that questions the widespread assumption that objective strategic conditions led inevitably to a global contest. If one rules out superior knowledge and acknowledges that the American position was not based on a panoptic understanding of the world crisis—and the profusion of uncertainties and outright errors makes clear that it could not have been—any serious account of the origins of the Second World War needs to take into account the way in which American policy makers, in their minds' eyes, connected the wars in Europe and Asia into a unified geostrategic picture of the world. This leaves open the possibility that Americans may have assigned too much importance to global linkages—but then again, maybe they were correct to believe that local political habits lagged behind the social and economic unification of the globe.

It was not inevitable that they should make such connections. Apart from the study of foreign relations, American historical scholarship since the middle of the twentieth century has tended to privilege the social and economic at the expense of the individual and the political, but in this instance individuals mattered enormously. We accept the importance of leadership decisions readily enough when contemplating the impact of someone like Hitler. But if, let us say, someone with a less expansive definition of the national interest than FDR like Herbert Hoover had been in charge, he might have ruled out a tough approach to Japan, as he had already done in 1931, and he might also have displayed a more detached attitude toward the drift of events in Europe. Without Roosevelt at the helm, policy might well have gone in the opposite direction. But the internationalist Roosevelt believed that the United States had become a part of international society, a nation that was embedded in the narrative of globalization. As he stated in his final inaugural address, "We have learned to be citizens of the world, members of the human community." For FDR, civilization had become the indispensable context for the flourishing of American society. International society made up the landscape of Roosevelt's world picture. If one can infer reasons for intervention from the far-reaching economic and social war aims that were in process of being formulated even prior to the United States becoming a belligerent, clearly the poor health of international society comes across as the primary reason for getting involved in the war.[30]

Only the Japanese attack on Pearl Harbor transformed what would have been a war of choice—what was the Great Debate about, if not about making a choice?—into a war of necessity. The metamorphosis was so rapid that a stunned minority, unable to believe that they had misread the situation so completely, insisted that the attack had been a trick conjured by FDR in order to plunge the nation into war, never mind that this would have been an absurd approach to attaining the desired interventionist end. Even though such a conspiracy has never come close to being proved, the belief that it existed continued to smolder in the popular consciousness for many decades, like an underground coal fire, before the dying embers of isolationism finally burned themselves out. For internationalists, Pearl Harbor "proved" their case, but it did so only by skating over the fact that American involvement had not been the product of a realistic reading of the world political situation. It concealed something equally important: that what had only recently been a deeply controversial assumption about the fundamental importance of the international society had become firmly embedded as the foundation for a revolutionary postwar foreign policy.

There were, then, two intertwined strands that together formed a strong line of argument on behalf of American action in the international crisis: one centered on a military threat, the other focused on societal dangers. The strategic justification has long been the more eye-catching thread in explaining what was at stake in the world crisis. But with the passage of time, the case for an existential threat to America's independence and survival, which was enormously controversial at the time, has gotten weaker while the argument about the threat to the American way of life stemming from the collapse of international society has grown more plausible. It was also more persuasive at the time. All the talk of a threat to the American way of life should not be interpreted as so much ideological smoke and mirrors aimed at converting idealistic sorts who were unable or unwilling to address more pressing real-world problems. On the contrary, FDR's argument for removing the danger to international society was a more solidly grounded policy rationale than the wobbly case made for a geopolitical peril.

It was already a truism that the First World War had been more a conflict between societies than armies, but it was still very much a traditional political conflict, basically a fratricidal European spectacle with sideshows in Asia and Africa, whose origins could be explained in old-fashioned political terms. The threat to international society became apparent to some only toward its close. But if the second war was from its very beginning about the future of international society, it deserves to be understood, for both geographic and structural reasons, as the first authentically global war and the only great war for civilization. Once one acknowledges the war's societal character, it should come as no surprise that traditional political explanations should come across as somewhat shaky. While geopolitical warnings were intended to arouse fear, and thus were subject to exaggeration and scaremongering, an appreciation of the menace to international society was supported by hard social facts. Unlike the arguable outcomes of the various military scenarios, it was clear that without an American rescue of a global civilization that was gasping for air, the political and moral economy of the world would likely have gone under even without an Axis victory in Europe.

Such views of the future were less marketable to the public or attractive to the pundits, but they were far more compelling in their predictive power. In a geopolitical setting that would uncannily resemble the world described in George Orwell's dystopian novel *1984*, all of the normal functions that people had unthinkingly assumed to be the environment of everyday life—financial and commercial practices, the availability of goods, travel, professional associations, the functioning of education and science, the collection and transmission of news, and much more—

would have been transformed. Patterns of trade, finance, technology flow, and migration would have been disrupted. Intellectual and cultural exchange would have been straitened and diverted into narrower and less productive channels. At the same time, the antidemocratic floodwaters of recent history would have continued their worrisome surge. Viewed in this way, the references to a threat to the American way of life are the crux of the interventionist argument, not just an ideological accessory.

A globalist foreign policy makes sense, but only if there is a global society worth fighting for, which leaves open a big question: How dependent upon global society *was* the American way of life? Unfortunately, no conclusive answers are available. Historians do not command the equivalent of climate change models in which the past can be rerun by inputting different variables. All that can be said with assurance is that American internationalists, having witnessed the United States develop in a globalizing setting, were convinced that international society was essential to the nation's way of being. There is no way of proving that inaction would have led to a garrison state in which traditional liberties would have been increasingly eroded. Strong arguments were made about such an eventuality, but they were countered by isolationists who, for their part, were convinced that FDR's internationalism led down a slippery slope to dictatorship. These contrasting perspectives would survive into the postwar period in long-running but inconclusive debates about the national security state and the imperial presidency.

Once again, the historian is left with a humbling list of unprovable what-ifs. But, weighed against the Cold War that followed, the global economic and political disruption resulting from a continent divided between Germany and the USSR and an Asia dominated by Japan might well have proved far worse in the end. And one should not discount the moral dimension, even though it was not the dominant rationale for intervention. The case for WWII as a good war became stronger over time as awareness of the Nazi death camps sank in; the war ended domestic divisiveness; and, by most accounts, it restored prosperity. All these blessings depended on victory, of course, and victory of a particular kind, at that. For this triumph avoided a countervailing danger, a possibility that had been recognized by Wilson and played up by the isolationists, that even a war fought for all the right reasons, could result in a Pyrrhic victory. Making World War II a war of choice does not mean that it was any less the "good war" that Americans continue to celebrate in their historical memory; it merely highlights its extraordinary character.

....

This is a good spot from which to stand back and reflect on the singularity of this historical turning point. There was, in the first place, the unusualness of a situation whose central aspect was inconclusiveness about the very nature of the threat and about what would constitute an appropriate response. No one then or later could be sure of the gravity of the danger or whether a life-or-death threat existed at all. Adding to the perplexity were radically opposed appraisals of the value to the United States of what not long ago was thought to be an irresistible globalizing process. Wilson was among the first to argue that threats to global society required radical action, but his views had failed to gain traction in public opinion. In view of the uncertain anchorage in American political culture of this internationalist interpretation of the crisis, it would have been rash to predict, on December 6, 1941, the swiftness with which the importance attached to international society would sweep aside definitions of national security that not long ago had enjoyed the status of holy writ.

The suddenness and the scope of the shift in American policy were striking. After denying for more than a century and a half the national security importance of politics and warfare outside the Western hemisphere, the United States was suddenly defining dangers and interests in an expansive global way that was out of the question for every other power. American policy makers had by this point abandoned the assumption that underlying social forces, if left to themselves, would push history in a favorable direction. In the new view, the world's social environment had displaced political geography as the bottom line of national security. For interventionists, American identity and security had become so closely linked to the well-being of international society that the need to safeguard the social and cultural environment of the world had deposed the long-reigning obsession with political calculation.

For the remainder of the twentieth century, the United States would continue to base its foreign policy on the assumed primacy of the world social and economic environment. But it was also during these postwar years that the raison d'être of this singular approach—the restoration of international society in a way that would allow national flourishing—was severely tested. A few geopolitical savants predicted that the central story line of the postwar period would revolve around a falling-out among the wartime allies and their subsequent struggle for power. They were correct, but their nearsighted focus on politics failed to appreciate the degree to which US foreign policy and the broad arc of postwar history were tied up with the events of the previous century. These soothsayers failed dismally to foresee that the Cold War years would not be a traditional political conflict but a struggle to revive and reinvent international society, a challenge abounding in radically new problems that only the United States was in a position to address.

7 Economics versus Politics in the Reinvention of International Society

Not long after the war ended, it became the norm among students of foreign relations to draw a sharp line between the postwar era and everything prior, as if the real story of American foreign policy began after 1945, everything else being prehistory. This sense of sharp discontinuity was attributable mainly to the huge gap that opened up between optimistic wartime expectations and a disillusioning postwar reality, for it took but two years for the prevailing assumption of international cooperation among sworn allies to be replaced by an increasingly ominous and at times terrifying period of mutual hostility known as the Cold War. With only occasional embarrassed glances at its isolationist past, the United States plunged energetically into a new career of worldwide political and military activism. The past, to the degree that it mattered, was no longer seen as a storehouse of wisdom and precedent, but as a cautionary prologue, a repository of "lessons" drawn from callow behaviors that were to be avoided in future.[1]

That picture of postwar America starting over with a clean slate skips over an inconvenient fact: American policy in the postwar period continued to be governed in powerful ways by ideas inherited from the Victorian era. A friendly world economy had been a given in the nineteenth century, thanks in large measure to Great Britain's commitment to free trade after 1846, which flourished despite the protectionist restrictions that European nations began to impose in the 1870s. This was the world elegized with deep feeling by John Maynard Keynes in his *Economic Consequences of the Peace* when he exclaimed, "What an extraordinary episode in the economic progress of man that age was which came to an end in August 1914!" But by the 1930s, that system was no more. In the minds of American policy makers, its breakdown was the underlying cause of the Second World War, while Axis militarism was only the most conspicuous symptom. Given the importance of a flourishing international society, the United States began to formulate economic plans looking toward its revival even before it plunged into the conflict. Ideally, economic and political planning would be "pursued simultaneously," but in practice the particulars of the New Deal's economic program ran far ahead of preparations for postwar security.[2]

Far from being a relic of failed policies, the idea of international society would have a long and productive foreign policy life ahead of it. But for those sobered by its near-death experience, the more pressing need was for reinvention as opposed to mere reconstruction. Simply eliminating the immediate danger through military victory, as after the Great War, would no longer do. While globalization in peak condition was extraordinarily powerful, it had also shown that it did not have the ability to repair itself when confronted with serious reverses. On this understanding of the problem, American policy makers pushed for the creation of global economic institutions that went far beyond anything that Woodrow Wilson had contemplated. Inspiring this new style of international economic architecture was the recognition that the market economy was not a self-regulating entity that could be relied upon to operate securely and automatically at a remove, out of sight and out of mind.

The central task was to shore up the structural weaknesses that led to the political secession of Germany and Japan and set in motion the global civil war. Unlike domestic market economies, international society had grown up without the necessary backstops provided within liberal states: police power, contracts, and rule of law. For that matter, these basic elements were still lacking in many sovereign states, and, as the 1930s demonstrated, even developed nations felt free to secede and to contest, in Hobbesian fashion, the norms by which international society functioned. In view of these shortcomings, a politically shaped order would need to replace the self-directed system of the nineteenth century. And such a regulated structure was indeed created during the war. Despite the self-seclusion of the state-directed economies in the USSR and the Soviet bloc countries, their numbers augmented by a small number of economies that experimented with permutations of the command economy, the United States succeeded in reviving, expanding, and transforming the global system that first came into view in the nineteenth century.

Ordinary Americans may not have grasped the geopolitical intricacies of the war, but it is certain that they understood its social significance as a conflict whose goal was to assure "the good life." At American insistence, the Atlantic Charter—a prewar document—addressed the betterment of social conditions—improved labor standards, economic advancement, and social security, later supplemented by FDR's Four Freedoms. This emphasis on social security went far beyond Wilson's Fourteen Points, whose economic proposals pretty much began and ended with the promotion of free trade. As an indicator of this reawakened appreciation of international society's importance, the proposed United Nations organization was charged with a host of social and cultural tasks to be performed by specialized agencies whose numbers and responsibilities would increase over time. These nonpolitical functions of the UN marked a significant amplification of the mission of the League of Nations, allowing many of the League's technical staff to restart their careers in the new organization.[3]

This was internationalism with a huge difference. The system as constituted was an amalgam of traditional nineteenth-century liberalism, supranational institutions, and a mild American suzerainty that would later come to be called "liberal hegemony," or, less charitably, the American empire. Another way of looking at this pattern of American dominance would be to call it the nationalization of internationalism, in which the United States played a de facto role that, had international society been shaped by abstract logic instead of history, would have been undertaken by autonomous supranational bodies. The newly created institutions would have been powerless—indeed, they could not have come into existence in the first place—without the United States. This internationalism was emphatically Americocentric because the world needed the United States even more than United States may have needed the world.

The new way of doing business came to be called multilateralism, which, superficially, was a procedural updating of the legacy of international cooperation. But multilateralism was extraordinary in its concern to avoid the appearance of top-down rule by fiat. The system was a flexible, collaborative structure in which the views of smaller members were taken seriously, to the point of allowing serious disagreement to be voiced and sometimes heeded. Though the United States was clearly the first among equals, it was commonly understood that these institutions were to be run on a consensual basis rather than by imperial command. As President Harry S Truman acknowledged at the San Francisco conference that organized the UN: "We all have to recognize, no matter how great our strength, that we must deny ourselves the license to do always as we please." This determination to combine leadership and uncoerced like-mindedness provided a best-case illustration of how the international system *might* have functioned if the United States had joined the League.[4]

With the establishment of the so-called Bretton Woods System in 1944, US foreign economic policy entered a new era in which nationalism and protectionism were replaced by a free trade internationalism the nation had long spurned. Its elements, whose provisions and principles were boring if not impenetrable to many, were based on the simple idea, in Secretary of State Cordell Hull's formulation, that "the political line-up follows the economic line-up." As Harry Dexter White, the American architect of the Bretton Woods agreements, put it, "unrestrained economic warfare . . . will undermine one of the foundation stones for a secure peace." Translation: an economically stable international society was the underpinning of global political order. The chief institutions were two international bodies, the IMF and the World Bank, which would perform some of the functions of national banks but at a supranational elevation. Given the disproportionate sums contributed by the United States to their capitalization, these financial instruments were American dominated. The supervision of international currency values in a systematic way was also new, as was the definition of what constituted currency in the first place. Lessons of the past were dominant here, though the various actors had internalized different lessons. The British, still haunted by the disastrous decision to overvalue the pound in 1925 and leery of being boxed into maintaining a parity that their enfeebled economy could not sustain, sought flexibility in setting exchange rates. The United States, recalling the crippling cascade of currency devaluations in the 1930s, preferred stable currency ratios. Such differences were settled by compromises that allowed the British, among others, to delay full currency convertibility for more than a decade.[5]

The creation of the Bretton Woods system provided international cooperation with a supranational organizational structure that previously had received little consideration. Conferences aplenty had been held before, and informal cooperation between national banks had long taken place. But, as one historian has argued, "This openness to large-scale institutional solutions was, arguably, the key difference between World War I and World War II–era plans for a more stable and prosperous world order." Another historian went so far as to describe American policy makers as "revolutionary internationalists." Before long, the operation of these game-changing institutions was routinized to the point of being quite humdrum. Though many people, then and later, could not explain what they did, there was no need to understand them. They were intended to operate unobtrusively as part of the international wallpaper, save for crises in which they momentarily stepped out of the background. But it was their power, especially that of the IMF, to head off globally contagious economic crises that undergirded the smooth functioning of the market.[6]

It spoke volumes about the American conception of international relations at this point in time that the United States was quite determined to assert its primacy in the economic dimension, in contrast to the political sphere where establishing the principle of great power equality, at least with the USSR, was the prime concern. Perhaps the most remarkable example of outsize American influence in this new order was the dollarization of the gold standard whereby the US dollar became the international benchmark currency, effectively as good as gold. Although in theory the gold standard still governed in the last instance, this new currency regime was not nearly as internationalist as it looked on the surface; instead, it was an early example of how the traditional relationship between the United States and world society was being inverted. The enormous privilege of currency creation conceded to the United States was not far removed from the nationalist ideas of Henry C. Carey and the inflationists of the nineteenth century. Instead of the US money supply being tied to gold stocks, the system was now effectively dependent for liquidity on the economic health and power of the United States. Before long, this nationalization of internationalism in which the United States was granted such enormous authority, so apparent in economic matters, became apparent in other fields of foreign policy as well.

Initially, the United States continued to post healthy trade surpluses, and manufacturing industries remained strong. By the 1970s, however, the country was running ever-larger deficits in its current accounts, which it sought to remedy by going off gold and allowing devaluation of the dollar in a new system of floating currencies whose values were determined by market forces. Devaluation diminished the role of the dollar, but America's centrality remained, as foreign nations continued to buy vast sums of US Treasury bonds, thereby providing Americans the financial wherewithal to indulge their growing appetite for foreign goods. As the world economy's principal consumer, America's trade deficit served as a major buttress of foreign production, much as the spendthrift nobility of bygone days had justified their profligacy as a way of supporting the lower orders. Though the flood of cheap foreign goods hastened the ruin of many noncompetitive American industries, the felt need of policy makers to maintain international society outweighed the economic dislocation caused at home. Federal borrowing allowed other states to adopt export-oriented strategies that helped them to develop consumer societies of their own. As long as the American economy continued to grow, the United States was willing to allow other nations to become "free riders" in the same way that it had taken advantage of the open international system in the late nineteenth century.[7]

The reliance on the United States was also evident in the new free trade regime, something that the nation had fiercely resisted not all that long ago. The lowering of tariffs occurred gradually over the decades in successive bargaining "rounds" known as GATT, short for the General Agreement on Trade and Tariffs, whose complex negotiations were only spottily reported in the press. The low-hanging fruit was easily picked at the start, but by the mid-1990s the process of liberalization slowed down as the discussions grew in complexity, an ever-increasing number of participants made negotiations unwieldy, and less tractable issues such as agricultural subsidies, services, and intellectual property rights made a consensus more difficult to reach. To enforce the rules of the road put in place by earlier agreements and to handle trade disputes, a new supranational institution was formed in 1995, the World Trade Organization. For opponents of globalization, the WTO soon became the symbol of all that was wrong with the world, but, possessing no enforcement authority other than the willingness of members to abide by its rulings, it was hardly the Leviathan that some critics imagined it to be.

At first glance this leap into international oversight looked to be a natural counterpart to the New Deal's penchant for intervention in the national economy, a global New Deal. Unsurprisingly, the World Bank and the International Monetary Fund have been described as "a macrocosm of the New Deal regulatory state," or, more mildly, as a global expression of Keynesian distrust of unregulated markets. But the correspondence is illusory, because the World Bank and the IMF were not regulatory institutions in the way that central banks were. They acted more like regular banks who provided loans to individuals than as entities concerned with the liquidity of the economy as a whole. Instead of seeking to replicate abroad the kind of interventionism that characterized economic policy at home, in practice the international face of the New Deal placed far more trust in the functioning of the international market. If one likens these institutions to systems of water management, these institutions did not create elaborate networks of water diversion, canals, dams, dredging, sluices, and flow control. Instead, they were more like levees that encouraged the international current of the market economy to flow freely and more swiftly with minimal danger that the embankments would be breached.[8]

Over time, the freeing up of international trade in this cooperatively managed global economy made international society the stronghold of market liberalism. Because there were fewer restraints in the international arena than within nations, where governments still wielded considerable regulatory power, national economies were exposed to global market forces that they were increasingly unable to resist. As the system took hold, it was able to roll back market-restricting unions and neo-mercantilist schemes of protection. Ironically, under the aegis of these politically sustained institutions, after the passage of four decades classical liberalism was able to launch a counterattack against lingering predilections for state economic direction. If there was a contradiction here between the domestic and the international sides of the New Deal—and there was—it was not acknowledged at the time. But as globalization advanced, the increasing dominance of the market meant that more managerial solutions, such as concerted Keynesian attempts at providing economic stimulus, became more difficult to pull off. In the verdict of one international financial guru, "The markets win in the end."[9]

By the 1970s, the predominance of international markets became dramatically apparent in a number of crucial sectors. America's dependence on foreign sources for more than 50 percent of its petroleum needs became evident in the oil embargo of 1973 and in another brief oil drought touched off by the Iranian crisis of 1979. The 1970s were also notable for the enormous inroads made by foreign producers into core segments of the American economy, most visibly in automobiles and consumer electronics. The "self-contained" America described by Hoover, still much in evidence in the immediate postwar years, was gone. In the span of a generation, the United States had become so deeply enmeshed in the international economy that the semi-autarchic or nationalist options of the 1920s and 1930s were no longer available.

But the international payoff was stunning. "The result," Paul Johnson has written of the first twenty-five postwar years, "was the most rapid and prolonged economic expansion in world history." In western Europe, this period formed "the golden years," a time when mass consumption came to societies whose workers and peasants had never before had the opportunity to chase after consumer goods. In promoting economic recovery and expansion, the United States was relying in the first instance on societies that already possessed the cultural and institutional skills needed for industrial success. American aid programs like the Marshall Plan were successful largely to the degree that they built upon well-laid societal foundations. But the economic renaissance in western Europe was soon succeeded by something altogether new when Europe's successes were trumped by an Asian miracle. By the 1960s, the Japanese economy was in the midst of a spectacular ascent that in the mid-1980s threatened to eclipse all its competitors. By that time, upstart modernizers were emerging in the form of the Asian "tigers" and, looming ever larger on the horizon, a new global economic giant: China. Beginning in the 1980s, the Asian tigers, in particular—Hong Kong, Taiwan, South Korea, Singapore, and to a lesser degree Malaysia and Thailand—made dramatic economic progress with extremely high annual growth of GDP, doubling at a rate of every seven years.[10]

Elsewhere, the progress of economic modernization was less heartening. The idea of universal development had been a conspicuous element of American thinking about international relations ever since the late nineteenth century, particularly among missionary groups and organizations engaged in philanthropic activities abroad. Planning the rapid modernization of peripheral regions became a notable aspect of foreign policy only as a result of the Cold War competition, in which the superpowers tried to outdo one another in demonstrating their anticolonial bona fides. To blunt the appeal of so-called sacred wars that combined anti-imperialist nationalism with socialist ideology, geopolitical reasoning dictated that decolonization be accompanied by accelerated modernization programs. More often than not, however, attempts at modernizing undeveloped societies and newly independent nations by means of foreign aid programs proved disappointing. Even with highly optimistic assumptions about constant rates of growth, simple calculations based on compounded rates of increase suggested that it would take late modernizers the better part of a century, if not longer, to catch up with already-developed societies. In most cases, the sanguine assumptions were wildly off base.

Heading a long list of problems was a lack of knowledge about how to turn foreign aid into an instrument of modernization. There were limitations on funding, which was unpopular with a skeptical Congress. Too much effort was expended on showcase projects that were unrelated to more fundamental needs. Moreover, much of the aid was given for ill-concealed political reasons without due regard to efficacy, as a form of gift giving in the expectation of securing political fidelity. Thus a disproportionate amount of money went toward ill-conceived vanity projects or the purchase of military baubles, which often reinforced the rule of feckless autocrats. Geopolitical priorities also led donor nations to look the other way when confronted with the corruption and inefficiency of client states. On the whole, modernization programs did little to create the cultural and human capital required for good democratic governance and economic take-off. And in many cases, they retarded rather than advanced modernization. In the judgment of the economist Paul Krugman, "globalization, driven not by human goodness but by the profit motive, has done far more good for far more people than all the foreign aid and soft loans ever provided by well-intentioned governments and international agencies."[11]

And yet, despite false starts, the "lost decade" of the 1980s, and the enormous gap between early developers and late arrivals, by the end of the century economic development did spread to other nations and regions, including some promising growth in Africa. Economists debated whether the gap between rich and poor was narrowing or becoming wider, but by the end of the twentieth-century globalization had made significant inroads into nearly every society. Nations like Brazil, India, and Russia were only the leading edge of a larger group of rapidly developing nations that gave new life to globalization. While the human development statistics were arguable, international society was clearly more powerful than ever. Reflecting this influence, the so-called Washington consensus of the 1980s issued a catechism of neoliberal precepts elaborated by the IMF and World Bank types—fiscal discipline, rule of law, deregulation, property rights, privatization, anticorruption, good governance, and much more—that offered a template for market-based modernization in place of the import substitution schemes and social scientific planning of an earlier generation. There were still many failures, and, even more basically, some "failed states," but increasingly the blame was laid at the feet not of the system or on flawed aid schemes but on the home-brewed shortcomings of would-be modernizers.

Not limiting itself to economic successes, international society struck even deeper roots in 1948 with the adoption of the UN Declaration of Human Rights. Hitherto international law had been preoccupied with the behavior of states toward one another. The decision to prosecute Axis bigwigs as war criminals had already introduced crimes against humanity as a legal principle, but the declaration took matters one step further by declaring that the sovereignty of the state was, at least in principle, newly subject to an international standard of behavior. The principles contained in the declaration did not have deep cultural footing in many societies, and enforcement was problematic. Many of the member states who affixed their signatures to this document did not take it all that seriously or signed for questionable reasons, as rights and wrongs continued to be defined in local and particularistic ways that sometimes clashed with the declaration. Yet despite all the loopholes and backsliding, the idea of universally shared ethical standards and societal rules, which reform types had been proclaiming for at least a century, had been inscribed in international law. Just as importantly, the ability of nongovernmental human rights organizations to "name and shame" offending states testified to the maturation of a world opinion that could not be taken lightly. Following a postwar latency period, human rights became a major theme of international relations from the 1970s onward.[12]

Inevitably, foreign policy desiderata often conflicted with the desire for universal moral standards. The Grand Alliance with Stalin was only the most prominent example. In this case, the expectation of postwar cooperation and ideological change made it easier to stomach what was considered by New Dealers to be a nonthreatening dictatorship. In response to the question of whether communism and capitalism could coexist in the same world, the widely shared belief of the editor of the *Economist* was "of course they can. The world had never been a philosophic unit." Beyond mere coexistence, there existed the expectation of a productive partnership on the political plane. This went beyond the kind of toleration that existed in the 1920s, when the Soviet system was thought to be running on borrowed time. Instead, New Dealers preferred to believe that socialism was evolving in a direction compatible with liberal democracy. The fashionable wartime view was that the two kinds of society would meet at a social democratic midpoint (more like 60–40, in FDR's view). In the opinion of Harvard sociologist Pitirim Sorokin, the world was witnessing "a progressive mutual convergence of the economic forms of the two countries." This was not good news to all. A source of great concern to old-fashioned liberals was the likelihood that all societies were becoming administrative aristocracies. As it turned out, this expectation of a Great Bureaucratization was a bogeyman for, if anything, the growing integration of international society actually widened the gap between market societies and administrative states.[13]

Nonconforming right-wing autocracies posed less of a conceptual problem. Making the world safe for democracy could also mean making it safe for autocracy. To the profound dissatisfaction of Americans stationed in China, the United States supported Jiang Jieshi (Chiang Kai-shek) in the civil war against the communists; it consorted with Franco in Spain and Salazar in Portugal; and it tolerated a motley crew of caudillos and dictators in the Western hemisphere, the Middle East, and Africa. These were the kinds of regimes the United States had long been willing to live with. Unlike Nazi Germany and militarist Japan, these dictatorships were not perceived as international outlaws. (It may be useful to recall that political democracy was not one of FDR's Four Freedoms—speech, religion, want, fear—many of which had been tolerably provided by authoritarian governments.) By the 1970s, it came to be argued that such regimes were acceptable because they could serve as bridges to democracy. Besides, there were worse alternatives, and for the moment such states could be politically useful. Beyond mere toleration, dictatorships could serve as outright allies or as bulwarks against the establishment of governments that might be more threatening to the international system. In the case of the Middle East, the United States was willing to ally itself to culturally hostile regimes like Saudi Arabia, the bedrock of the ultraconservative Wahhabi sect of Islam, for example, and with Islamic mujahedin who contested the Soviet occupation of Afghanistan in the 1980s.[14]

But the postwar years also departed significantly from the latitudinarian past. Beyond merely tolerating unsavory governments as it had in the past, in the postwar period the United States engaged repeatedly in a number of pro-authoritarian interventions in which the justification previously used in Latin America in the heyday of American imperialism shifted from a need to maintain law and order to a geopolitical rationale. During the Cold War, the United States intervened on numerous occasions to replace regimes suspected of planning to desert the Western camp and side with the socialist world. In Iran (1953), Guatemala (1954), the Dominican Republic (1965), the Congo (1961), Chile (1973), Grenada (19835), and Nicaragua (1985), the United States acted, in most instances covertly, to avert hostile takeovers. And yet, rather unexpectedly in view of all this, a democratic explosion did take place in the 1970s and 1980s in which the ranks of democratic nations were significantly expanded.

Cold War enemies posed less of a problem for international society than authoritarian or recreant states. The existence of large self-segregated areas like Russia, eastern Europe, or China was tolerable because they had never been vital organs in the body of globalization to begin with. Far more important than their immediate exclusion was the task of sustaining a global environment that would have the capability of incorporating them in the future. Less respectable regimes could always join in as full partners at a later date when a cultural coming of age would make it possible for them to shed their authoritarian skins. So long as the overall system was stable, it could afford to be pluralistic, thereby allowing policy makers to focus on making the world safe for democracy rather than on imposing it. The foremost consideration was ensuring the survival of an open world order that was dominated by its leading liberal nations. Despite the ideological hostility that divided the globe, it was still possible, as John F. Kennedy said in a crafty play on Wilsonian rhetoric, to "make the world safe for diversity." This statement would have made no sense if international society had not been reestablished on a firm footing. Despite occasional bouts of gloom and doom, by the end of the twentieth-century global society was wider and deeper than ever.[15]

The Cold War Impasse

The Cold War was a stalemated geopolitical contest in the course of which a revitalized globalization developed to the point that it was able to exercise a critical impact on the outcome of the competition. With the onset of the struggle between the superpowers, news of the reconstruction of international society was relocated to the business sections to make room on the front pages for international politics. This came as an unwelcome surprise to American policy makers who, in planning for the postwar world, were at first clueless about the degree to which the United States would need to exert enormous amounts of political and military power—which may help to explain why political planning for the postwar had lacked a sense of urgency. Even after the Cold War had clearly begun, the reliance on economic initiatives in its early years owed much to the expectation that economic questions would dominate the postwar era, as they had in the 1920s. There had been next to no anticipation of the need for the United States to provide "core public goods" in the form of a secure environment for saving, investment, and trade, all of which, it had been expected, would resume their normal functioning following a messy but brief transition period of demobilization and reconversion.[16]

The prewar assumption that international society could take care of itself had been a whopping error; no less grievous a misconception was the optimistic expectation that economic poultices alone would suffice to cure postwar economic ailments. But an awareness of the need for forceful political measures came only gradually to the minds of policy makers. After relying initially on remedial economic initiatives like aid for Greece and Turkey and money for Europe in the Marshall Plan, American policy makers concluded by 1948 that even financial guarantees and economic expedients could not succeed in the absence of political commitment. Thereafter, in rapid succession, came charter membership in the North Atlantic Treaty (NATO); intervention in Korea in 1950; crises in the Taiwan straits, Berlin, Cuba, and Vietnam; and a nuclear arms race—and this was only the short list. By 1950, following a decision for peacetime rearmament, American policy was headed well down the road of militarization. Slowly but surely, politics came to dominate perceptions of the postwar years, thereby creating the perception of extreme discontinuity between the war and postwar periods.

Compared to the well thought out architecture of the international economy, the political planning for the postwar period looks fanciful in the extreme. In Woodrow Wilson's day, political reform had seemed eminently doable, while the possibility of economic change in favor of free trade lay dead in the water. In the 1940s, the reverse was true, as epochal economic changes were made with relative ease while politics proved to be the stumbling block. The leading illustration of this lack of political foresight was the fate of the United Nations organization, which was initially advertised as a more practical successor to the League of Nations. The UN was intended to fulfill the marquee political goal of the United States during the war by providing postwar security for the world. In retrospect, its prospects for success in this mission were nil. Nevertheless, the organization survived, thanks in no small measure to the ability of the superpowers to avoid another world war outside its auspices and because the organization served a large number of indispensable functions having to do with social and economic progress and the (now déclassé) expansion of international law. Thus it was later argued that the UN, after more than a half century of political futility, was "more indispensible than ever."[17]

Hope for the UN's success as a security organization was possible in the first place only because it sidestepped the problem that was the League's raison d'être: how to restrain a rogue great power. Whereas the League of Nations assumed that the threat of a breakaway power would not go away, the veto power within the Security Council made it impossible to take any punitive action against its permanent members. By design, then, the organization could deal only with minor troublemakers. As Evan Luard has pointed out, the UN was "founded on the premise of agreement among the powerful to subdue the weak." This neutering of collective security followed logically from the disastrous League experience, which suggested that any organization designed to prevent great power aggression was doomed in advance to failure because collective security could never be collective enough.

But that did not mean that the founders of the UN believed in an anarchic state of affairs. There was a more powerful, antirealist explanation for how so many intelligent people could be so astonishingly wrong: the stubborn persistence of the belief in great power cooperation. The UN's design harked back to pre-Wilsonian expectations that uncivilized smaller powers were the remaining obstacles to peace. Unlike the Great War, when the United States had kept its distance from the allies and refused to see the League as a postwar successor to the alliance, the very name "The United Nations" presupposed the continuation of the working relationship established among the coalition partners. Hence it was unnecessary to arrive at detailed political understandings while the war continued to rage.[18]

The assumption that problems would ultimately work themselves out to everyone's satisfaction also applied to the treatment of the enemies. Apart from a desire not to repeat the disastrous experience of the 1919 peace conference, there was no urgency to conclude a formal peace following the end of hostilities because the roots of a solution had already been planted during the war. Thus peace treaties would be signed on an ad hoc basis. No rogue powers would remain after victory had been achieved because it was clear that the principal troublemakers, Germany and Japan, would remain under the supervision of the victors, making it highly unlikely that the era of world wars would extend into round three. Thus the absence of a general peace treaty after the war, besides reflecting the inability of the superpowers to agree, also suggested a mutual understanding that the defeated nations would not be reintegrated as political equals. That assumption, at least, proved to be correct.

The composition and the operating rules of the Security Council caused some idealists to scorn it as a forum of traditional power politics, whereas more realistic types believed that great power domination would make the UN more effective than the League, but both views were far wide of the mark. The UN as it was conceived was not a political organization at all, because the idea of cooperation that lay behind it presumed the absence of traditional competitive international politics. The expectation that the wartime "principle of unanimity" would carry over into peacetime collaboration assumed that the predisposition to get along would see the powers through the inevitable rough patches—a rose-colored vision that for a time beguiled all the members of the Grand Alliance. By institutionalizing the optimism about international cooperation that characterized the years before World War I, the UN turned out to be far more idealistic in its expectations than the League, which had been created precisely because it was thought likely that a Godzilla state would arise in the future. Helpless by design in its ability to deal with such possibilities, it is small wonder that it was impotent to resolve the major disputes of the age. As soon as the unanticipated postwar falling-out among former allies took place, then, the United Nations was quickly abandoned as the primary site of world politics.[19]

The Cold War that ensued is a familiar tale in which the United States finally took on the "adult" responsibilities of a world power. Once policy makers became convinced that friendly cooperation with the Soviets was impossible, the United States changed from unarmed to armed prophet, to use Machiavelli's terms, by demonstrating a willingness and ability to dirty its hands in the muck of politics. Given this dramatic turnabout, the Cold War continues to be understood for the most part as yet another episode in an age-old story of great powers contending for mastery through grand strategy, alliances, armaments, and war, whose maxims and motives conformed to key ideas advanced long ago by seminal thinkers like Thucydides, Machiavelli, and Thomas Hobbes. This dramatic U-turn in American policy was reflected in the way that American scholarship on international relations quickly shifted its focus from the study of a polite world of international law to a preoccupation with conflict-based theories of power politics and with technocratic means of achieving its foreign policy objectives. If America's narrow preoccupation with the progress of international society had been the problem, politics was now the solution.[20]

The propensity to define the Cold War in political terms becomes clear when one looks at the long-range strategy of "containment," first articulated by the diplomat George Kennan in 1946 and 1947, and later codified in cruder form by National Security Council Memorandum 68 of April 1950. Kennan's major achievement was his ability to get Washington policy makers to redefine the relationship with Moscow in adversarial terms in place of the long-standing American assumption that great power cooperation was the default state of affairs in the world. This regime, he made clear, was not the cooperating kind. It was, instead, unremittingly hostile to international society. In its eyes, "Everything must be done to advance relative strength of USSR as factor in international society. Conversely, no opportunity must be missed to reduce strength and influence, collectively as well as individually, of capitalist powers."

Kennan's solution to the Soviet problem was also political. Procedurally, he argued, "the main element of any United States policy toward the Soviet Union must be that of long-term, patient but firm and vigilant containment of Russian expansive tendencies." In his classic long telegram, he advised that "if the adversary has sufficient force and makes clear his readiness to use it, he rarely has to do so," which was yet another way of stating the ancient maxim, "If you desire peace, prepare for war." Kennan later complained that the subsequent militarization of containment distorted the nonbellicose diplomatic approach that he had in mind. This smells a little of special pleading after the fact, for at the time he believed that there was nothing to negotiate. Until the Soviets came to their senses, attempts at traditional diplomacy were pretty much doomed to failure. In the meantime, their acute understanding of power realities was as much reason as one could expect them to see. In his concern to hammer home, with little regard to subtlety, the need for a tough-minded stance, he was, as he later ruefully admitted, perhaps too successful. Thus the Hobbesian notes of his analysis were easily read as a call for a policy based on the sustained display of American military might, even though, over the long term, Kennan preferred the restoration of stable balances of power in Europe and Asia that relied mostly on the operation of local political forces.[21]

But in whatever manner the power was to be mobilized, the purpose was to hold the line until the USSR became more tractable. In his "long telegram" and the "X" article published the following year in *Foreign Affairs*, Kennan envisioned the Cold War epoch as a period of tension that would avoid major war until it culminated, perhaps in ten or fifteen years, in the "mellowing" of Soviet power. Convinced that "Soviet power bears within it the seeds of its own decay," Kennan expected that Western resoluteness, by patiently allowing the USSR's congenital malignancies to metastasize, would eventually lead to significant political changes in the Soviet system. Uneven economic development and the limits beyond which a "tired and dispirited population" could not be driven would put a damper on Soviet capabilities. Thermidor, when it came, was likely to originate at the top from an increasingly disillusioned and frightened elite. He especially emphasized the possibility of a succession crisis in which "Soviet Russia might be changed overnight from one of the strongest to one of the weakest and most pitiable of national societies." While the particular form of the crisis was unforeseeable, the inherent infirmities of the Bolshevik state would force it to abandon its stance of hostility to the outside world. Then, once it rejoined international society, one could do business with it.

In his grand vision of how the Cold War would play out Kennan had little to say about the possibility that external economic and cultural forces could spark the dissolution of the USSR and its empire. Apart from containing the Soviet Union, the United States needed only to keep its powder dry while the Leninist state undid itself. Kennan, a social and cultural conservative by temperament who was deeply put off by many features of the modernizing world that surrounded and besieged him, showed no inclination to put his trust in the global success of liberal commercial and cultural forces. Thus beyond calling for "a much more positive and constructive picture of the sort of world we would like to see," in which Americans should seek to suppress the ethnocentric temptation to urge other peoples "to develop political processes similar to our own," he had little to offer beyond the straitjacketing of a system that would self-destruct or "mellow" as a result of defects in its political DNA. In Kennan's view, time was on America's side—no thanks, however, to the industrial civilization that he disdained.[22]

The Cold War did not follow Kennan's script; in different circumstances it might well have done so, but in this case it did not. In broad terms it was undeniably a power struggle, but to leave the matter at that is like resting content with a description of Leonardo da Vinci as an Italian—it barely scratches the surface. Containment contained, but the reliance on power turned out to have serious limitations and introduced some daunting new problems. Besides failing to bring about victory, rearmament and the willingness to use counterforce whenever necessary also made victory impossible. The Cold War turned into a cold peace because the destructive power of nuclear weaponry and delivery systems had evolved to a point that all-out war was rendered meaningless. Going to war to meet the threat from Nazi Germany and Japan made sense from the standpoint of a means-ends calculation. But by the mid-1950s, Wilson's intuition about the futility of modern warfare was given revelatory force when prudent policy makers on both sides began to realize that war could now destroy both international society and all societies. These hitherto hypothetical possibilities for destruction forced political leaders and military strategists to adopt, often with great reluctance and in the face of criticism from an uncomprehending public, a novel self-limiting approach to war. Like many cars whose capabilities far exceed any real-world applications, the novel Cold War system had a built-in speed limiter that restricted politicians from effectively stepping on the gas pedal past a certain point.

The key to avoiding all-out war was a new politics in which the ability to maintain American credibility became an ersatz substitute for victory, while its loss became a token of defeat. Credibility, not to be confused with the self-centered fixation with prestige, was the old concept of national interest transposed to a new global key. Because credibility was the soft underbelly of world opinion, its chief point of vulnerability, the object of the politics of credibility was to shore up confidence in the sustainability of international society. The worst-case fear of a credibility-based policy was not a Waterloo imposed by force of arms, but the concern that credibility would collapse, and the institutions of the West along with it, in a domino-like tumble. As Dean Acheson once mused, "we could lose without ever firing a shot." Though there was violence aplenty, the novel aim of limited wars was to frustrate the enemy, not to defeat him, all the while remaining careful not to escalate to a level that might unloose all-out war. This singular approach evolved out of necessity as a series of improvisations because the world had not yet evolved institutional procedures for resolving major disputes on any other basis than wars waged without stint until military victory was achieved.[23]

Although containment sought to check enemy designs, the politics of credibility also produced unintended exasperation closer to home—the MacArthur near-mutiny of 1951, mass protests over Vietnam, a nuclear scare over Cuba in 1962, and widespread concern over the long-term wisdom of nuclear deterrence in the 1980s. Credibility-based policy was doubly unfortunate in its effect on public opinion: it enraged Cold War critics who thought the United States was being too interventionist while at the same time it exasperated cold warriors who believed the United States was not doing enough. For those who preferred a bolder approach, containment was a way of playing defense with one hand deliberately tied behind one's back. "Why Not Victory?" asked the 1964 Republican presidential candidate Barry Goldwater. In addition to trying the patience of the American people, containment also worried America's allies in Europe, whose confidence was supposed to be shored up by US displays of worldwide commitment.

Thanks in large measure to the lessons learned from early confrontations, over time the Cold War settled into a deadlock that clearly could not be decided by force. The so-called crystal ball effect in which both sides clearly previsioned a future of mutually assured destruction meant that they could only play not to lose. As a series of inconclusive credibility crises played themselves out, their frequency and intensity abated, though it took twenty-five years for the two parties to acknowledge that taking the military road led off a cliff. By the 1970s, the rise of détente, institutionalized in the SALT (Strategic Arms Limitations Talks) nuclear arms limitation treaties, signaled the attenuation of such confrontations. Alliances like NATO and the Warsaw Pact remained, but, minus the smell of danger in the air that had sparked their creation, they functioned more as instruments of alliance cohesion than as deterrents to external threats. And the crises that did erupt no longer operated as interventionist triggers. As an example, American outrage over the Soviet invasion of Afghanistan in 1979 produced only some symbolic retaliatory measures that inflicted little noticeable pain on the Soviets. Alas, among the chief victims were American farmers whose profitable grain exports were gutted by US sanctions.[24]

Though it may seem counterintuitive at first, in addition to the mutual restraint imposed by nuclear stalemate the internationalist ideologies of the two contenders also helped to prevent the outbreak of a third world war. More often than not, ideology has been viewed as a secular equivalent of religious extremism in which zealotry is given license to run amok. That is how many Americans perceived the Soviet leadership; in much the same way, that is how realist critics of America's Cold War ideological excesses tended to view the American public and its leaders. But realism, normally seen as a prudential outlook, may actually have been more dangerous. With traditional instrumentalities declared off limits due to a fear of nuclear war, and with its emphasis on conflict and military power as the last word in solving disputes, realism prompted disgruntled cold warriors to strain against those limits by looking for ways to win nuclear wars, by means of a preemptive first strike, fighting a limited nuclear war, pressing for escalation of limited wars, and so on. The penchant for mirror-image thinking also led realists to overestimate the willingness of the enemy to risk all-out war, thereby destabilizing the nuclear standoff. A thoroughgoing commitment to realist theory would have further militarized the Cold War than was already the case.[25]

By contrast, ideology was a fire retardant, not an accelerant. The governing assumption of containment was that the Soviet Union, fueled by ideological ambition, would use military power and geography to its advantage unless checked by the "preponderant power" of the West. But this depiction of an innately power-hungry USSR was a caricature of Soviet motives that completely ignored a fundamental assumption of Marxist ideology, namely, that the world's problems, which arose in the first place from the play of social forces, would be resolved as a result of the natural evolution of those forces. Admittedly, the Leninist reworking of Marxism had magnified the importance of human willpower in seizing opportunities for astute political and military action to speed up history. But even in this radically revised version of the ideology, whereby revolutionary takeovers could be achieved through political cunning, in the long run these kinds of successes could only be tactical. Russian communists were acutely aware that the revolution in Russia was an anomaly that could not be generalized. Final victory could come only by the ripening of secular historical trends in the wider world, without which the entire belief system stood to be exposed as an ideological fraud, a cover for a politico-military worldview. Nationalism, by contrast, saw military conquest as the preferred route to victory. Had Hitler intended to conquer the world, he would not have acted from internationalist motives, which is what made him all the more dangerous.

Often seen as opposites, ideological internationalism and realism turned out to be well matched in the Cold War context. Whereas traditional realism alone led to a conceptual cul-de-sac, internationalist ideology pointed to a way out of the dilemmas and aporias of containment. Ideology may have been the enemy, but it was also a necessary friend and helpmate in keeping the Cold War within manageable bounds. Crucial to the compatibility of this odd couple was a common commitment, from the inception of the confrontation in 1947, to the reordering of international society. As militarized as the struggle was, this civilian emphasis worked in favor of tamping down the shared will to power. In the absence of a belief in the evolution of international society on the part of both the United States and the USSR, which in each case amounted to a belief that time was on one's side, the Cold War would have been much more difficult to hold in check. True, Khrushchev boasted that "we will bury you." But that was a metaphorical description of what would come to pass in the long term, and it was certainly better than everyone lying dead on the nuclear battlefield in the here and now.

At the time that he put forth his idea of containment, Kennan believed that ultimate success depended on immanent causes of decay within the Soviet Union, as a result of which the Soviet system would mellow or possibly self-destruct. The militarization of containment, contrary to many of Kennan's later arguments, made possible a diplomatic resolution of many of the Cold War issues of war and peace in the period of détente and after, during which the resulting US-Soviet relationship could be better described as one of cooperation and conflict. But while the Cold War mellowed, it lived on as an armed truce because the underlying problems of ideological hostility and great power competition remained. Though it was not part of Kennan's scheme, the idea of containment harbored within itself the possibility of an alternative route in which the evolution of international society would settle the outcome of the Cold War. How exactly this could take place remained up in the air, but it was at least crystal clear that this contest could not and would not be decided through superior force or other forms of power.[26]

As it happened, an alternative metric by which success and failure could be appraised received a prominent airing in the simultaneously silly and sagacious 1959 "kitchen debate" in Moscow between Vice President Richard Nixon and Soviet leader Nikita Khrushchev. Noting the capacity for mutual destruction, Nixon asked, "Would it not be better to compete in the relative merit of washing machines than in the strength of rockets?" Once launched down that road, the colloquy was reminiscent, though with far less wit, of that masterpiece of one-upmanship from *Annie Get Your Gun*, "Anything You Can Do (I Can Do Better)." Whatever the final tally of propaganda points registered by the vice president and the premier, the two men apparently shared an understanding that the Cold War victory could be achieved by the superior performance of one system or another—relative superiority, because in other circumstances each could have provided the basis for effectively functioning social systems. After all, the Cold War was in part an ideological struggle between adversaries who shared a commitment to thoroughgoing modernization. Both powers adhered to a fundamental ideology that disparaged the inherent importance of politics in favor of the primacy of the social processes that produced an industrial way of life. They also agreed on the way in which success should be measured—by production and, increasingly, by making possible the good life for their peoples—although as we shall later see, on this point there were some crucial differences that would have an enormous impact on the Cold War's outcome.[27]

On occasion, policy makers were able to advance, albeit in an impossibly hazy way, a nonpolitical method for resolving intractable problems. A notable example of this approach was the "magnet theory" proposed by Eisenhower's Secretary of State John Foster Dulles for ending the division of Germany. The idea was that communist East Germany would in the long run be irresistibly attracted by the West's superior way of life. At the time that it was put forward, this was less a plan than a way of maintaining hope in the absence of a plan, a stab at assuaging a restive West German public opinion at a time when diplomacy was impotent to bring about reunification. As a political program, it was a nonstarter, but it did eventually catch on in the 1970s when the West German state adopted a modified version of this idea in the form of an *Ostpolitik* that abandoned a political resolution of the German question in favor of a reliance on the favorable long-term outcome of economic and cultural processes. At the very least, the reasoning went, mutual contacts would keep alive the idea of a united Germany. From a wider perspective, a good case can be made that Dulles was not being entirely cynical in playing to German public opinion, because in retrospect America's overall approach to the Cold War resembled a global version of the magnet theory.

The Soviet Union's call for "peaceful coexistence," which sought to redefine the superpower competition in social terms of class struggle, was cut from the same cloth. Nevertheless, the foreign policies of the two antagonists were never up to the task of operationally defining the relationship of international society to Cold War victory because ideas like the magnet theory and peaceful coexistence could not be codified as policy. The idea of a peaceful fight to the death had its superficial attractions, but a commitment to adjudication of the Cold War by social and economic forces was utterly impractical, for without an agreed way of keeping score and officially determining a victor, there was no obvious way of winning an economic competition. In this competition, everyone knew that only the gold medal counted, whereas the prize for winning silver was to be lowered into the grave of history.

The Achilles' heel of an economic competition was that it could not reliably establish beforehand how and in what circumstances a death certificate would be issued. Were economic inferiority the trigger for losing power, most regimes in the world would have to accept their inadequacy and surrender their rule. It was especially unlikely that the economically plodding Soviet regime would agree to commit *seppuku*, given that the dictatorship of the proletariat had at its disposal extraordinary instruments of discipline that allowed the regime to hang on for a very long time. Also, system changes tended not to be peaceful affairs. With a Soviet regime at death's door, it still remained possible for a panicked communist leadership to resort to desperate measures and touch off a spiraling crisis that ended the Cold War with a big bang. In short, apart from the extreme unlikelihood of being accepted in the first place, an economically centered strategy lacked a peaceful "endgame" for managing the decline and fall of communism. Or, to describe the plot in literary terms, there was no sense of an ending. As far as policy was concerned, there was nothing specific to work toward other than a vague sense that time was on one's side.

Compounding the political uncertainties of an economic strategy were other serious problems that had to do with the unpredictable functioning of the free enterprise system. The prognosis was dicey even in the event that things went America's way, but the possibility of bad economic news made for even less cheery scenarios. What about the chance, which became a worrisome possibility for a brief spell in the late 1950s, that the Soviet economy might prove to be the more dynamic, and hence more attractive? Or what if the world economy produced another crash, a prolonged period of stagnation, or massive inequalities? The economy was capable of all kinds of surprises, both good and bad, whose consequences could not be rationally calculated, least of all by the arcane theories of professional economists. The market economy, which was notorious for the ups and downs of the business cycle, was, by definition, not fully controllable by political command. Even the successful creation of consumer societies had the potential to erode the constant readiness to sacrifice that might be needed in a long-term struggle. True, foreign policy was not all that reliable to begin with, but economic decision making could not provide even the minimally dependable cause-and-effect calculations that need to be weighed in purposive decision making. Thus, relying on the economy to win the Cold War would have been like allowing ocean currents and breezes to do the entire job of navigation.

In any event, some compelling strategic imperatives dictated that economics take a back seat to politics. The fatal shortcoming of an economically based policy was that it could not function without the shelter provided by a political and military umbrella—the "public goods' provided by the United States. The allegiance of important partners in western Europe and in Asia depended in large part on the expectation of economic prosperity, which relied in the first instance on the security and predictability afforded by the American military shield. Thus politico-military concerns clearly remained uppermost for fear that demoralization or intimidation could lead to both economic and political collapse. Economic policy smacked too much of the "capitalism is peace" isolationist mentality that had been discredited by the war. What nation had prevailed in a conflict solely by a reliance on economic means? By such reckoning, economic growth created the enormous advantage of being able to more easily support advanced military establishments. Hence the buck stopped with more and better bangs.

Despite its obvious importance, then, economic policy operated in the shadow of high policy. If prewar policy privileged the social over the political, postwar policy reversed the equation. To confirm this prioritization one needed only a brief glance at the proportion of government spending allotted to military outlays or to the status pecking order among Foreign Service personnel within the Department of State. Politics was a glamorous and heroic affair, whereas the business world produced uncharismatic figures in gray-flannel suits. Moreover, once established, economic policy was a matter of "set it and forget it," a question of administration rather than policy, in which economic activity was left to its own devices to run backstage, attended to by technocrats who were committed to rule-governed behavior. This is unfair, for good economic policy making involves many complex and important high-level decisions on an ongoing basis. Nevertheless, this de facto functional stratification carried over into historical interpretations and international relations theories whose explanatory conventions reinforced the functioning of the new caste system.

The difference between the economic and political spheres went beyond mere hierarchical separation. Because many of the economic policies adopted by the United States were designed to address problems that arose prior to the Cold War, the postwar preoccupation with problems of global power had the political and the economic worlds of American policy operating as if they existed in parallel universes. While economic policy focused on international society, politics dealt with the Soviet Union, its allies, and threats to the Western alliance system. The two sets of policies overlapped in time and intertwined in some important respects, yet they remained distinctly separate in other ways, with different logics, different audiences and objectives, and different timetables. The political turn was a revolutionary break, while economic policies were evolutionary. US diplomacy in the postwar period entered onto new and unfamiliar terrain, but for economic policy there was no paradigm shift in the sense put forth famously by Thomas Kuhn, in which, following a conceptual revolution, scientists found themselves "living in a different world."[28]

Because of this overlap, the postwar reshaping of America policy was not the kind of all-or-nothing break that is commonly suggested by the clear-cut contrast between isolationism and internationalism. The Cold War was not a new story written on a recently erased blank slate; it was more like a political overlay on a preexisting map of international society. If pre–Cold War policy approaches had been genuinely outdated, the privileging of politico-military affairs would have been justified; instead, making politics the center of attention had the effect of obscuring how policies formulated to deal with the problems of one era turned out to be crucial to the success of political arrangements designed in another. The foreign policy journey to the end of the Cold War was traveled on two separate paths—one political, the other economic; one prewar, the other postwar—which together contributed to solving a problem that by itself neither was able to address. The institutions put in place by Bretton Woods and GATT influenced the texture of the Cold War, turning it from just another power struggle, however epic, into a very different kind of affair in which power was used in novel ways to achieve a victory without force. The privileging of politics, at the time and in subsequent scholarship, has made it easy to overlook the impact of nonpolitical innovations in international society that led ultimately to the Cold War's resolution.

Over time, as both sides came to understand the limits of power politics in a novel military environment, containment turned quite conservative as Americans and Soviets grew more comfortable with the status quo. The détente policy of Nixon and Kissinger attempted to codify this mutual understanding. One could make the case that Kennan's vision of a more reasonable USSR became a reality in the late 1960s, but if so it was a turn of events that departed considerably from his original script. For while containment did succeed in preventing Soviet expansion, Kennan's prediction that the Soviet Union would soon fall prey to its internal contradictions was quietly abandoned as the Soviet regime grew even more powerful militarily at the same time that it delivered what, by Russian standards, was an historically unprecedented level of prosperity and security to its citizens. Because some militant strategists doubted that the Soviets could be trusted to keep their word, the only realistic response was to further increase America's military might, which, by itself, offered no promise of ending the impasse. By the 1980s, the Cold War seemed on track to last forever, with scholars and statesmen increasingly reconciled to the indefinite prospect of an unwinnable competition.

The political standoff offered only one rational way out: some form of peaceful change. The frozen status quo of the Cold War contributed to this end, for while it could not achieve victory, it did make way for a nonpolitical solution to emerge from the more fluid environment of international society. As a result of the revolution in weapons technology that made war an unrealistic way of settling issues, an interesting inversion took place in which the pressures created by the Cold War logjam found their outlet in new channels that confirmed the nineteenth-century intuition about the revolutionary impact of globalization upon politics. This was a deliciously ironic outcome in which the postwar turn to power politics, which had dismissively superseded a prewar foreign policy keyed to international society, once again wound up relying on international society as a force for reshaping international politics. Incredibly, an international social order whose failure so recently had been the source of the world's problems would once again become the key to success.

However, the solution would not come, strictly speaking, from the economic sphere. An explanation of how the Cold War ended requires going beyond the consideration of political and economic policies. In the long run, though the wartime economic plans turned out to be infinitely more consequential than the short-lived political plans for the postwar world, neither politics nor market forces proved ultimately decisive. As a conjectural way of shifting our focus away from conventional modes of explanation that fail to explain what was going on, one could do worse than to think about the role of politics in the Cold War in a neo-Aristotelian sense—what Aristotle might have argued had he lived in the twentieth century—as a project of global civic formation in which the function of statecraft was soulcraft. For Aristotle, politics was not simply about power. Political knowledge was the highest form of social knowledge as well as an autonomous sphere of activity that shaped everything else in society—a point of view that believers in the primacy of social forces have been at pains to deny. In this classical conception, politics was an activity at the highest level of practice and the polis was a shaping community built on friendship, indispensable to human fulfillment and flourishing, the object of which was to facilitate the Good Life.

Clearly, that is not what politics at the international level had been about; in the family of nations, in the absence of a something resembling a general will, agreement was a product of power differentials. But if we transpose the Aristotelian view of politics to American foreign policy, the Cold War can be seen as a project that went beyond the insular promotion of the national self-interest or mindless enhancement of state power by creating a favorable context for the flourishing of an international community. Just as individuals could not fulfill their natural purposes without a state, global society could not perform its functions in the absence of a political order that only the United States was in a position provisionally to supply.

Indispensable to the effective functioning of that order was the existence of human beings imbued with a certain kind of character. Notwithstanding its ideological obsession with individual autonomy, liberalism has always been concerned with character formation with a view to creating a liberal culture of individualism. This was not always apparent, but on occasion a few American policy makers were able to step back and reflect on the larger meaning of what they were doing. President Truman's secretary of state Dean Acheson, for one, frequently depicted as the embodiment of a brutish mind-set that focused on amassing preponderant American power, came very close to articulating such a conception in March 1950 when he sought to define the objective of foreign policy. Its positive goal, he said, must be "to create those economic, political, social and psychological conditions that strengthen and create confidence in the democratic way of life." When approached in this fashion, any aspiring explanation of the Cold War needs to look beyond politics and economics by taking into account the emerging ideological and cultural outlooks that strengthened America's influence in international society and set the stage for the eventual collapse of the Soviet world.[29]

Overly schematized, the process worked something like this: politics created a congenial environment for economic development; in turn, economic advancement opened up a cultural route to the resolution of the Cold War thanks to the unexpected emergence of Americanization and consumerism on a global scale. But, because it was cultural in nature, this denouement was not determined by power, whether political or economic. Individual decision makers mattered, but American foreign policy, vitally important as it was, did not have the ability to end the Cold War. The end, when it came, was a complete surprise because it was the result of changes that took place outside the jurisdiction of policy making. Why and in what ways these cultural processes came to be so important will be the subject of my next chapter.

8 Ideology and Culture as Ingredients of the Cold War

To forestall any misunderstanding: political economy mattered. The extension of an American politico-military umbrella over the so-called first world, in combination with the superior productivity of free enterprise economies, was indispensable to ultimate success in the Cold War. But, however necessary, political and economic policies were helpless to end the Cold War, thanks to a military impasse that made it impossible to force the socialist world into acknowledging its inferiority or dismantling its top-down way of doing things. While the recovery and expansion of international society worked wonders for the West and a growing number of flourishing societies in other regions, no exit from the superpower deadlock was in sight. Because change in the socialist world could not be imposed from the outside, it would have to come voluntarily from within—an end result that lay beyond the purview of foreign policy.

American popular culture and liberal ideology turned out to be indispensable contributors to this unlikely outcome. From the earliest days of the republic, the expectation had been that the world would emulate America's republican political system. A century later, as the first wave of globalization rolled in, it was assumed, more modestly, that the nation would do its share in carrying out a collective civilizing mission and, more ambitiously, in promoting cooperation among the civilized powers. Within this shifting picture of the nation's international role, American culture, whether high or low, was never considered to be a significant export; nor was ideology, for that matter, as republicanism was not sophisticated enough to compete with the new ideologies that originated in Europe. Quite unexpectedly, then, in the context of a Cold War in which power politics led down a blind alley, cultural relations, with American culture featured prominently, helped reanimate an international civil society that had escaped a near-death experience in the 1930s. As a bonus, they also provided a way out of the Cold War impasse.

Culture and ideology do not spring readily to mind when one thinks about the fundamentals of international relations. This is understandable, for these are hazy concepts that have been fought over by scholars for more than a century, yet it has never been made clear how they function or in what ways exactly they matter. Culture, especially, has encountered tough going because of its association with amorphous mental processes that presumably account for the differences among peoples but whose causal importance in fact remains murky. Its shortcomings are compounded by the methodological handicap of being studied by literary and humanistic methods. In a knowledge industry where science reigns supreme, culture's humanistic status demotes it to a lower rank than the study of objective economic and political phenomena. When matched against the confusion about what culture is and does, the operation of the economy and of military power can be shown to have a demonstrable impact and, in principle, their efficacy can more readily be explained by quantifiable measures of causation. In brief, we have here another instance of the long-running war between the sciences and humanities, a war that, in the study of international relations, has been won in a rout by science. It is no surprise, then, that most of the scholarly world has succumbed to the temptation to subordinate ideology and culture to the study of social and physical power.

And yet, contemporaries persisted in talking about the Cold War in a prosaic way that assigned more importance to these mental processes than scholarly opinion would have approved. To take the most obvious example, the Cold War was continually portrayed in public discourse as a war of ideas between capitalism and communism. It was commonly described, even in official declarations, in a portentous nationalist idiom as a struggle to preserve "the American way of life." The cultural stakes were not entirely national, however, but were also understood to refer to a conflict, in some deep sense, of incompatible ideas or belief systems that were universal. Actually, the very idea that culture and ideology were vital ingredients of a worldwide competition implied that a global society was already in existence, for an ideology cannot exist apart from a host culture, while a culture, for its part, cannot exist without being embedded in a society. No one could say with scientific authority how exactly cultural and ideological struggle fit into the overall scheme of things, not least the academic clerisy whose attempts to plumb the intricacies of ideology and culture plunged them down a conceptual rabbit hole. Yet everyone somehow understood that something of great importance was at issue, that the fabric of everyday life, in the United States and elsewhere, was at stake.[1]

But culture and ideology were not equally downtrodden. If one were to hold a referendum asking Americans to choose between ideology and culture to characterize the ideational side of the Cold War, ideology would win in a landslide because Americans habitually rely on the political rhetoric of freedom to extol their way of life. From an academic standpoint, moreover, ideology receives a token measure of respect thanks to its close family relation to power, the common assumption being that the gravitational pull of power can attract fidelity to its belief systems. I want to suggest, however, that popular culture proved far more important in the end because governmental programs in public diplomacy, even those that professed to focus on culture, were in fact ideological and therefore political in nature, which made them subject to the same kinds of limitations that constrained America's military and economic policies. Mass culture, by contrast, had a different and more far-reaching impact because it could not be contained within political channels. Operating outside the political embankments made it possible for global cultural changes to create an opening for political change.[2]

Ideology and culture mattered enormously in the Cold War—not simply as geopolitical window-dressing—but, in the end, culture mattered more than ideology. Specifically, the unexpected arrival of what came to be called a "global culture," by providing body to a world opinion that hitherto had been skin deep, reinforced enormously the operational linkages and networks of global society that had been reconstituted after 1945. In yet another example of cultural lag at work, in the postwar years a nascent global culture began, however tentatively, to come into view as an emergent property that pushed global society toward becoming something more cohesive: a global community. For millennia, culture had been a source of discord among states and within empires, especially in the era of high nationalism, so this was something new for a world in which socioeconomic institutions and military power, and, to a much lesser extent ideology, had long been the chief centripetal forces that operated across political boundaries. The novel presence of a global culture would have enormous political cash value, because even though liberal ideology by the 1980s exerted a more powerful grip on the minds of policy makers and intellectuals than ever before, the ideological consensus in the West was incapable of resolving the Cold War.[3]

The argument is at least worth listening to given the fact that the military and diplomatic sides of the Cold War have been chronicled ad nauseam without coming close to providing a convincing explanation of what it was about or how it ended. No attempt will be made here to repeat or to summarize this enormous literature or to address long-asked and still-unanswered questions such as who started the Cold War and whether it was avoidable. Instead, I want to suggest how and why culture and ideology were indispensable to ending the Cold War and in allowing a more inclusive resumption of the process of globalization that had first captivated Americans in the nineteenth century. In turn, that should underscore how the Cold War was not simply a geopolitical episode, but part of a larger and ongoing story in international history.[4]

Rebuilding the Core

The impact of American mass culture first showed itself in the military occupations of Germany and Japan. Maintaining some form of oversight over these former enemy states was enormously important, given their strategic locations and power potential, but equally vital was the need to reincorporate them into a global society whose core had shrunk to a perilously small number of advanced states. Anglo-Saxon societies alone, which had long prided themselves as being at the cutting edge of globalization, could not sustain international society without outside support. This while Germany and Japan had been problem members, failed modernizers from a liberal point of view, their rehabilitation was critical to rebuilding global society. Given their indispensability, advocates of a Carthaginian peace like Treasury Secretary Henry Morgenthau, who would have preferred to turn Germany into an impoverished untouchable nation, were from the outset destined to fail. Granted, the decision to reintegrate Germany and Japan into the world community was prompted in part by the Cold War need for allies, or at least to prevent them from siding with the Soviet enemy, but it is likely that a welcoming of the prodigal sons would have taken place had there been no Cold War, given the long-standing American emphasis on global integration. Besides, integration, done well, was the most effective form of control.

Unlike most occupations, which were machines for producing bad memories and festering resentments, the American occupations successfully shepherded Germany and Japan into becoming functional democracies with close ties to the United States and to world society. A crude construal of what happened is that they were "forced to be free" by having liberal ideology and institutions imposed upon them. But the use of Rousseau's paradox, with its insinuation of hypocrisy, is questionable in this case because in a deeper sense the outcome was not forced, certainly not in the way that communism was inflicted on eastern Europe. A more convincing argument would hold that the democratization of Germany and Japan mirrored a consensual general will that genuinely reflected the wishes of the people. All the force in the world cannot impose freedom in the absence of the cultural preconditions for an open society. In any case, there is no such thing as an absolutely free choice, for all choices are to some extent conditioned by a people's historical endowment. Though they prefer to think otherwise, Americans, for example, owe their freedom not to choice, but to historical circumstance.

As it happened, in these countries the preconditions for democracy were already present. Though the two occupations differed in many important details, each country was able to draw on a cultural heritage that included significant experience with democracy, industrial growth, and exposure to international society, which helps to account for the favorable reception given to the occupiers in each land. Undeniably, defeat for each country was so overwhelming that there was no choice but to embrace it, however grudgingly, which was what FDR had in mind when he insisted upon "unconditional surrender" instead of a negotiated peace. But the willingness to accept American political guidance was conditioned by cultural affinities that became increasingly evident. Democracy, in particular, was not some alien transplant. It had organic roots in each nation, which the Americans self-consciously relied upon. Contrary to a widespread wartime sense that the German and Japanese peoples were akin to aliens from outer space, intercultural contacts demonstrated a surprising capacity for like-mindedness. As Secretary of War Henry Stimson reminded President Truman, "Japan is not a nation composed wholly of mad fanatics of an entirely different mentality from ours. On the contrary, she has within the past century shown herself to possess extremely intelligent people, capable in an extraordinarily short time of adopting not only the complicated technique of Occidental civilization but to a substantial extent their culture and their political and social ideas." Along with their bayonets and chocolates, the conquerors also brought with them values that had native appeal.[5]

But there was more behind the welcoming dispositions than superior force, the relative leniency of the occupations, or preexisting cultural compatibility. As the American occupation of Germany proceeded, it became clear that it was less American art or highbrow music than the demotic aspects of American culture—the easygoing informality of GIs, their popular music, jazz, and consumption patterns that captivated the Germans and other Europeans. There was some resentment of the occupiers, which was only to be expected, but it was more than offset by a fascination with the way of life that they brought with them. This allure might well have faded over time had it not been for the postwar economic miracle that gave West Germans the chance to savor that way of life for themselves. The same was true, in delayed fashion, of the Japanese occupation experience. To a significantly lesser extent, the Soviets achieved something similar in their occupation of the eastern zone of Germany, where they were able to draw upon the values of a powerful tradition of German socialism. The long-term result was that the social rights bequeathed by communism became deeply embedded in East

Germany's culture—a *Mauer im Kopf* that remained standing even after the fall of the Berlin Wall—something that West Germans painfully discovered after reunification finally arrived in 1990.[6]

The remarkable degree to which the occupiers were welcomed, admired, and emulated testified to a degree of compatibility in political cultures that was absent from the previous US occupations in Latin America, where baseball often caught on but democratic politics did not. In stark contrast to the disappointing attempts to modernize underdeveloped countries like Cuba, the Dominican Republic, Haiti, and the Philippines, the successful occupations of Japan and Germany exceeded expectations, though it took some time for the realization of success to sink in. For at least twenty-five years, American policy makers fretted about the degree to which democratization and Westernization were taking root. Even well into the twenty-first century, they were not taking any chances, as tacit occupations of Japan and Germany continued. As one might expect, the United States had co-opted pro-Western leaders and proscribed potential nationalist and communist competitors, while congenial intellectuals were recruited to do ideological combat against the communists. In the long run, however, it became glaringly apparent that worries about the viability of the democratic cuttings grafted by the conquerors onto the political stems of these two societies had been exaggerated.

The postwar reformations of Japan and Germany rebuilt the developed core into something resembling the World War I status quo ante. But that core, though restored in numbers, was much shakier than it had been before the Great War. In Great Britain, America's closest partner in globalization, the low public esteem for free market society was made shockingly apparent when the larger-than-life wartime leader Winston Churchill was turned out of office in July 1945 in favor of a Labor Party that promised a cradle-to-the-grave welfare state. Across the English Channel in western Europe, liberal democratic traditions were quite insecure, most alarmingly in France and Italy where powerful communist and social democratic parties threatened to gain power through legitimate popular elections. The appeal of the left was not the only problem. Large segments of these societies continued to be guided by the teachings of Roman Catholicism, which persisted in treating liberalism as an ideological abomination. Marshall Plan propaganda certainly helped, but it was questionable whether it was able to overturn deep-seated European misgivings about the merits of American-style capitalism.[7]

The roadblocks were formidable enough in the European core, but the conditions for cultural reconstruction were largely absent in many peripheral nations and regions. It had been fashionable at one time to promote development under the aegis of imperialism and the civilizing mission, but in an increasingly nationalist world imperialism was no longer defensible as a modernization strategy. The same held true for the racialist ideas that lent support to enduring colonial domination. The periphery had not been critical in the past, but the Cold War produced a dramatic change in its geopolitical market value. As the Soviet example generated a growing appeal in newly independent nations, a revitalized Marxist thought envisioned anti-imperialist revolutions in a global "countryside" that would engulf the developed "city." Areas that not long ago were looked upon as backwaters now had to be taken seriously by American policy makers, if only out of concern for a collapse in the credibility of US foreign policy. How to attract or at least not lose third world nations who lacked democratic traditions and showed little fear of the Soviet Union was a problem that took a worrisome political turn with the arrival on the scene of the nonaligned movement in the mid-1950s.

Given the inability of government policies to break up the political logjam of the Cold War, the unforeseen global cultural phenomenon that soon came to be called Americanization took on immense significance. At first the thrust of American cultural policy was to convince skeptical foreigners that American culture was worthy of its own niche in the pantheon of civilization, an ambition that went back to the nineteenth century. That worked well enough, as far as it went, but that kind of policy approach appealed chiefly to elites. Much to the surprise of nearly everyone, it was American popular culture, heretofore much derided by Europeans and American cosmopolitans alike as lowbrow, that caught fire globally. Ironically, it was not the export of American democracy, but the worldwide spread of the American way of life that became central to the novel period in the history of international relations known as the Cold War. Confounding long-standing expectations about the nature of America's appeal, the nation's most effective attraction turned out to be not its political system or its peculiar brand of capitalism but the relative affluence of the new American consumer society, its informality, the breadth of life choices available to its citizens, and the vitality of its mass culture. The relative affluence of the American everyman had long served as a magnet to immigrants, but Americanization expanded the cultural horizon of mass consumption beyond the core nations to the rest of the world.

The Limits of Cultural and Ideological Warfare

Leaving little to chance, by 1950 the US government had added cultural diplomacy and ideological warfare to its arsenal of policy weapons as part of an all-out effort that Dean Acheson called "total diplomacy." Although this expansion of the government's reach into all aspects of foreign relations can be seen as an inevitable part of the modernization process, to highlight the unrelenting administrative aggrandizement of the state suggests a greater measure of command over outcomes than governments can effectively exert. Cultural relations did have a transformative impact, but not as a result of soft power programs or as part of what one writer has called "a multi-dimensional strategy of challenge to the Soviet system." Although cultural and ideological changes would play their part in ending the Cold War, government-directed cultural programs deserve only minor credit for the outcome.[8]

Any serious consideration of the possibility that culture and ideology were indispensable to ending the Cold War begins—and often ends—with the damning fact that soft power received little attention or funding from the US government. Despite the commonsense view that values of universal importance were at stake, policy makers showed only passing interest in the potential of ideas to become America's greatest asset in its foreign affairs. On the contrary, programs designed to address culture and ideology tended to be treated with great suspicion and sometimes outright hostility by Congress. Which raises the question: How could it have been such a game-changing resource if it was generally scorned

209

and dismissed as insubstantial, ineffectual, and programmatically sus-pect? The answer: "soft power" was not a difference-maker because it was a menial form of power.[9]

If one considers the very basic measure of funding, for example, the information and cultural programs were treated as poor relations of their well-to-do military and diplomatic kin. Among diplomats and warriors for whom power competition was the main attraction of international relations, cultural relations were considered something of a midway diversion from the strategic spectacle taking place in the big tent. In the status hierarchy of Foreign Service officers, cultural specialists were viewed as deacons whose ministrations were only marginally relevant to the priestly functions of high policy. Out of fear of contaminating the purity of the process, cultural specialists themselves contributed to their marginalization by insisting that intellectual communication be hon-estly open and not politicized. Not least, the programs at times operated at cross-purposes, with cultural and information policy makers devoting as much time in bureaucratic combat as in fighting the Cold War—or so it looked at times to outsiders.[10]

Partly for such reasons, cultural relations never did become a basic ingredient in the recipe for making Cold War foreign policy. But these barriers to their acceptance were minor compared to other obstacles that proved to be insurmountable. Foreign policy—any policy, for that matter—typically requires a convincing connection between means and ends in which it can plausibly be claimed that the proposed measures will produce a desired outcome. But the cultural programs met with unrelenting skepticism from Congress because their effectiveness could not be justified in such instrumental terms. And the congressional critics of cultural policy, many of whom were parochial yahoos, were perfectly correct to doubt their effectiveness. Because the cultural relations pro-grams were more about consciousness-expanding processes than about outcomes, no one could explain in a clear-cut way what cultural rela-tions accomplished. Why have them at all, then? Missiles and aircraft carriers may have been no more effective at ridding the world of the Soviet Union, but at least their protective benefits plainly justified the jaw-dropping expenditures.[11]

By many subjective and objective measures (audience size, number of exchanges, polling data, etc.), these programs were highly successful. Cultural relations worked best at producing "international understanding" when liberal rules applied, with friends more so than with foes, where a let-the-chips-fall-where-they-may approach was acceptable. Despite their problems in generating support at home, the cultural programs contributed to cementing elite allegiances within the first world, especially with close allies whose foreign policy interests corresponded with America's. Where opportunities for contact with the socialist world opened up, the programs enjoyed some limited success in expanding the horizons of communist elites and publics, and in so doing, contributed to change. Given the favorably one-sided results of the cultural programs, some historians have contended that they could have ended the Cold War sooner and more cheaply had they been taken more seriously. A few have gone so far as to argue that the cultural effort was the principal reason for eventual victory in the Cold War, by virtue of its effect upon elite targets within the USSR.[12]

This type of approach would have made sense in the days of the ancien régime when politics was still aristocratic, but since then the site of ideological legitimacy has been relocated to mass culture. Moreover, the cultivation of elites sometimes miscarried. The limitations of public diplomacy were glaringly exposed in a number of high-profile fiascos in which even successful elite-centered programs of cultural relations ran up against popular indifference to or even alienation from American values. In the collapse of Nationalist China and in the creation of an anti-American regime in Iran, to take but two instances, thin strata of Western-educated intellectuals were unable to resist the rise of radical groups with sure-footed stances in mass culture. Unlike ideology, mass culture did not require fine articulation; if anything, as a lowbrow resource potentially available to all, its effectiveness depended on beliefs that did not have to be spelled out. At a time when the cosmopolitan vision of internationalism was being overwhelmed by a new populist variety, the cultural programs were self-limiting by virtue of their targeting of elites. Their potential effectiveness was also compromised by tightly regulated schemes of bilateral relations, like the cultural agreements with the USSR, where the participants were carefully chosen and strictly monitored, leaving little room for any meaningful penetration of the upper echelons of Soviet society.[13]

For the advocacy-driven information programs, numbers were less of a problem. Despite the jamming of radio frequencies by communist regimes and other attempts at restricting the amount of information that reached their populations from the West, these programs were able to create a small tear in the iron curtain that allowed curious mass audiences a peek at life outside the Soviet bloc. In the case of the 1956 Hungarian rebellion, they even helped set a spark to dry tinder among restive eastern Europeans who nursed long-standing resentments toward the Russians. But because a sudden buckling of the Soviet empire in eastern Europe threatened to spiral out of control, US broadcasters were enjoined from encouraging insurrection. "Liberation was American political rhetoric, never U.S. foreign policy," says one historian. Originally conceived as a cheap way of finessing politics, in this case the information programs instead ran up against the limits imposed by politics. If the cultural programs were successful with the wrong people (allies), the information programs were unsuccessful with the right people (enemies). Though the programs did hearten some dissidents in iron curtain countries, until the 1980s political disaffection was easily subdued by the resort to softer post-Stalinist techniques of repression.[14]

The bigger problem of the information programs was their openly ideological character, which undercut their ambition of transforming mass opinion. One of the characteristics of ideology is that it calls for a sophisticated understanding of its various branches and their relationship to one another. For example, a command of Marxism and liberalism requires in each case that one be conversant with economics, theories of society, the role of politics, the place of the individual, and a theory of history. Given the steep intellectual cost of entry, the club of fully paid up ideologues is populated by an elite few. Moreover, because ideologies define themselves in part by opposition to other ideologies, they have to deal with a built-in resistance to infection from opposing worldviews. Reinforcing this natural immunity was the material self-interest of the neo-aristocratic communist "new class" or *nomenklatura*, for whose members allegiance to Marxism was the precondition of their privileged status. In the end, no degree of investment in propaganda, however great, could defeat Soviet ideology by arguing it to death. The best that could be said of such programs is that they somehow "weakened" the adversary.

Ideology was also a limiting factor for the cultural programs, which many liberals saw as apolitical and ideology free. True, many supporters of the programs had little interest in using them to fight the Cold War and bridled whenever it was suggested that they make greater efforts to sell the foreign policy line du jour. They took pride in professing to be free of political taint and in claiming to be interested only in promoting pure dialogue with a view to achieving "mutual understanding." But one needs no paternity test to be certain that the close family resemblance between the support for free flow of ideas and free trade identifies cultural internationalism as a scion of classical liberalism, which was surely an ideology. A belief system based on elements such as a contractarian theory of society that privileged the individual and his desires, an economic theory in which markets were driven by consumer preferences, a cultural theory in which the rational choice of individuals superseded the demands of tradition, and a supracultural theory of humankind that pointed ultimately to the recognition of human equality across various domains could hardly be called politically neutral. Belying the widely held image of cultural relations as a genteel, tolerant, and innocuous process, promoting the unimpeded exchange of ideas, coupled with free economic exchange, was in fact a potent recipe for the destruction of traditional polities and societies.

President Truman once described the Cold War as a struggle for the minds of men, a turn of phrase that cultural cold warriors embraced as a political imprimatur for their tradecraft. But that did not mean the Cold War could be won as a struggle of ideas. As a branch of politics, government cultural programs were, in practical and conceptual terms, from the very beginning an unworkable approach to Cold War victory. As their most thorough (and normally quite generous) chronicler argues, "In the final analysis one is struck by the limits of public diplomacy." Effective cultural policy, in this view, depended first and foremost on a good foreign policy, which implied that public diplomacy was inherently incapable of playing in the major leagues of statecraft. Assuming,

213

for the sake of argument, that the cultural and informational programs had been the equals of military strategizing and political deal making, with greatly augmented funding, they still could not have succeeded.[15]

If soft power, like other forms of power, was powerless to make the command economy systems collapse, the ambition of "winning" hearts and minds or capturing "the soul of mankind" was an aspiration even further removed from the reach of the Cold War's political arts. Rather than focusing on official programs, therefore, one needs to look at more penetrating cultural processes where the power of attraction and voluntary emulation operated on a global scale.[16]

The Cultural Background

The shortcomings of public diplomacy can be traced back to a larger problem: the inability of foreign policy to reliably manipulate transnational intellectual and cultural flows. Obviously, governments are not powerless to shape cultural relations, whose various currents can be slowed down or speeded up, promoted or discouraged, and whose amplitude can be regulated. But states cannot effectively direct many aspects of life within their own boundaries much less outside of them. Over the long run, top-down policies cannot completely stifle or steer bottom-up impulses; no matter how expansive its ambitions and extensive its reach, in the end all government is limited government when dealing with deep historical currents. A case in point is the crucial role in resolving the Cold War played by the widespread appeal of the Western way of life — popular culture as opposed to high culture—which took place principally outside the carefully policed boundaries of the Cold War. This rise to prominence of mass culture, whose global attractiveness came out of the blue without benefit of policy planning or official oversight, created a setting that was increasingly inhospitable to Soviet ideology.[17]

An embryonic global culture became possible only because postwar international society had much greater sweep than its nineteenth-century forerunner. Despite its pretensions to universality, nineteenth-century "civilization" had been restricted to an inner circle that consisted of Anglo-American societies and France, occasionally Germany and perhaps Italy, supplemented by thin strata of liberal elites in other countries

214

who were engaged in an uphill contest for power with traditional and radical competitors. Given its limited sweep, this civilized core by itself did not possess enough cultural drawing power to attract peoples under the sway of Soviet influence. The potential impact of the globalization process, however, was far greater. If liberal ideas were institutionalized and normalized on a global scale, a geographically much-expanded version of civilization might have sufficient gravitational pull to draw in those outside its Euro-American sphere. Before this could happen, however, unprecedented cultural changes needed to take place. Because an ideology, if it is to exist at all, has to be implanted within a culture, the worldwide spread of liberalism needed a favorable global cultural environment in which liberal ideas could take root and grow. International society would provide the basis for a global culture, which in turn would have an impact on ideologies with global pretensions.[18]

Before the second half of the twentieth century, international society suffered from a cultural deficit. Not counting a thin cosmopolitan membrane of high culture, international society was pretty much a cultureless entity before World War II. Although a thickening web of commercial practices made reliably available a diverse array of goods from distant places, there was hardly any cultural glue to hold this network together. The kind of contractarian behavior that is fundamental to liberal societies was neither widely institutionalized nor culturally absorbed, not even in some European societies that were familiar with liberal ideas. In general, the *Homo economicus* held up by free market theorists as the model of natural man had yet to be culturally shaped. Those market-friendly norms had matured over time in the United States and other early modernizers, but the contractual culture described by Durkheim or the bureaucratic legal-rational norms described by Weber had not yet been firmly embedded in international society. If the events of the 1930s had taught any lesson, one that was further underscored in the Cold War, it was that the future of a liberal international society was still uncertain. The entire structure had been built on an unstable foundation.[19]

In a sociological parallel to philosophy's mind-body problem, all societies have a cultural counterpart, common ideas that reinforce coherent behaviors. While a functional division of labor produces social interdependence, a reliance on specialization and differentiation alone cannot hold a social system together. Considered as ideal types, societies can be situated on a scale that ranges from the completely individualistic to those forcefully controlled from the top down. At one extreme lies an ultra-Hobbesian society of individuals operating purely from self-interest with no cultural bonds of community to hold them together. But, as Clifford Geertz once remarked, "a cultureless human being would probably turn out to be not an intrinsically talented though unfulfilled ape, but a wholly mindless and consequently unworkable monstrosity," that is, he would not be human. A society composed of such atomistic individuals, Emile Durkheim recognized long ago, would be "a veritable sociological monstrosity." At the other extreme, even totalitarian societies cannot be held together solely by force, because effective power always requires some degree of cultural legitimation. If a culture of individualism is necessary for an individualistic society, and if some degree of cultural legitimation is necessary to the maintenance of a society based on power, the same would apparently hold true for international society, which cannot be wholly anarchic or be held together exclusively by power. So, one might reasonably conclude that there must be something like an international culture.[20]

And yet, despite the dovetailed fit between society and culture in a single society, the idea of a global culture seems strange, even unnatural, when viewed in an international setting. The very idea of a global culture is oxymoronic, for how can one have a global culture and particular cultures at the same time? Since one is based on the principle of identity and the other on the assumption of difference, the two would look to be mutually exclusive. After all, one's humanity runs through one's culture, which is to say that one's own culture is the unavoidable medium for whatever cosmopolitan or humanitarian sentiments grow out of individual experience. Because of its localist bent, over the centuries, culture, with its resistance to change from the outside, has been a force for particularism and separation. Small wonder, then, that it became a mainstay of nationalism. Unlike cosmopolitanism, which revels in creating a coherent mosaic out of unique cultures, culture in the everyday sense has the effect of making other cultures look strange, leading at the extreme to clashes of cultures and civilizations. On the scale of forces that promote human convergence across social boundaries, then, culture deserves to be ranked quite low in comparison to changes induced by, say, technological innovation or the forceful imposition of international norms.

Moreover, if culture and society do fit together, hand in glove, and if the idea of a global culture is inherently problematic, then the very idea of a global society that has been featured in this narrative is thrown into question. Just as the fallacy of composition warns against assuming the identity of the part and the whole, what holds true for individual societies is not necessarily true of international society, which might more accurately be described as a society of societies. That is one reason why most theorists consider international relations to be anarchic in nature. In this view, such functional order as exists can be explained by power exercised through military force, diplomatic negotiation of mutually acceptable behaviors, or ideological consensus promoted and enforced by hegemonic powers. International relations are thus preeminently a political, not a social, domain. To the extent that something like international society exists, it is a mere effect of politics, something that has no independent existence. This weak version of international society is but a one-sided coin without a cultural obverse. Thus the intellectual problem of how to provide a cultural dimension to international society, to construct something that might intelligibly be called a global culture that is more concrete and compelling than the abstract unity of mankind, has no straightforward solution.

But that kind of either-or logic is often at odds with the messiness of history, for not all international traffic is routed through the marshaling yard of the state. Societies in particular, with their openness to exchange and external connections of all kinds, have been more porous than cultures and polities. And all social organisms do not necessarily entail culture, for society precedes culture. The existence of social animals tells us as much, and the existence of cultural lag would tend to confirm it at the human level. Institutions, created by human beings, tend to take on a life of their own, precipitating unforeseen social changes that precede cultural acceptance. As a result, despite the absence of a common source of political authority in international relations, substantial institutional networks have grown up that to a large extent operate autonomously of political relations, with roots in the societies of sovereign states and lateral offshoots that connect with other societies. These social processes have produced functional interdependence in a complex division of labor as well as norms that permeate international dealings.

Then too, in the case of regions, cultural commonalities have been shared by many civilizations whose members, thanks to numerous connections and familiar features, did not view each other as complete aliens. Instead of a global culture, then, it may be more appropriate to speak of global civilization in the postwar years as one in which a cluster of mutually shared cultural attributes had spread throughout the world. Nineteenth-century types had it right when they commonly employed the term "civilization" to describe the transformation of societies and cultures on a global scale. But, inasmuch as the word has fallen out of favor, for the sake of convenience I shall continue to use the prevailing term of art, "global culture," by which I mean a common element among cultures throughout the world that in other respects continue to retain their distinctiveness. In the twentieth century, the coming into prominence of this cultural dimension was called by various names — Americanization, consumer culture, or simply consumerism. But, whatever the nomenclature, as culture it actually did important international work by shaping behavior in ways that provided greater depth and coherence to transnational relations than merely functional connections could offer.[21]

This global culture was at the same time deeper and shallower than commonly conceived. Global consumer culture was more profound than a vulgar materialist way of life that was driven by cupidity, a lust for possessions, the desire to affirm one's identity (e.g., "I shop therefore I am"), or to rid oneself of status envy. Consumerism was only the tip of an iceberg whose submerged features were much more substantial than its hedonistic surface might suggest. At first sight, the longing for a particular commodity might appear to be an uncomplicated impulse that is devoid of broader cultural consequences. This was not so, however, in the case of consumer desire, which carried with it — though not necessarily at the level of articulate self-consciousness — a de facto approval of the complex social and cultural system that produced and distributed the goods, much as the European sweet tooth had presupposed the acceptance of the slave plantations that made it possible to satisfy the craving for sugar.

Though individual appetites were the motor force of acquisition, consumerism was a profoundly social phenomenon. The desire to consume was politically charged because it signaled an approval of the kinds of rules and practices that were taken for granted in capitalist economies: running an airline system, shipping, supply chains, international monetary transfer routines, quality control, and expert systems all backed by a complex international law of property and contract. The effective functioning of that background required a mastery of productive skills that could be brought into play only within complex market structures that were capable of satisfying consumer desires. An open society, observed one Soviet visitor to the United States, was "a system of very small, tiny details that you cannot see in reading magazines or academic books." Those details could not be supplied by command economies. So the desire to consume was an indicator that a growing number of countries had assimilated a host of unspoken assumptions into their cultures about how an advanced society ought to work.[22]

In addition, the eager consumption of one commodity had a multiplier effect that linked it to the consumption of others and to a bundle of related behaviors. In the words of Peter Berger, the enjoyment of rock music symbolized "a whole cluster of cultural values—concerning self-expression, spontaneity, released sexuality, and, perhaps most importantly, defiance of the alleged stodginess of tradition." In a world where nothing existed in isolation, the desire for material goods and the enjoyment of stuff had potentially vast ramifications: the promise of gender and racial equality, careers open to the talents, democracy, social and spatial mobility, freedom to think and create, as well as the liberty to succeed and fail. In other words, the desire for a commodity carried with it a lot of social and, potentially, political freight.[23]

In this way, the desire for certain commodities amounted to an endorsement of the kind of social system that was able to produce them. The global preference for mass consumption had cultural and social implications that made it easier for people to think well of the liberal political ideology with which the goods were identified. Here the Soviets were at a disadvantage, for the appeal of Marxist ideology to the global Everyman was minimal while the cultural appeal of Soviet life was virtually nil. The mutual aversion of the two ideologies was more than offset by the allure of Western consumer culture. This was not the kind of problem that could be solved by importing one million pairs of Levi's, as the East German regime did in the 1970s, or by the USSR's large-scale purchases of Western grain as feedstock for increased meat production.

But while this novel prospect of an ecumenical consumer culture was quite impressive, its penetration of second world societies was limited. Owing to the political segregation of the two worlds, international society was unable to exert the kind of coercive force upon the socialist enclave that it had exercised in the wide-open world of the nineteenth century. Though an emerging global culture enjoyed the advantage of operating through desire rather than through compulsion, insurmountable obstacles existed to its spread in communist lands. For those who lived in the Western core, consumer culture became deeply embedded in the fabric of daily life. But for inhabitants of the second world, aspiring to this kind of lifestyle was the stuff of pipe dreams because the absence of an institutional structure geared toward the satisfaction of consumer desires offered little or no hope of creating something similar. There was no stampede of shoppers trampling one another to gain admission to the emporium of the West. In the USSR, there was no deep revolutionary undertow of consumerism that threatened to drown the regime.

If the attractiveness of the democratization of luxury in Western societies was unable to effect regime change, the desire for political freedoms, human rights, and a thick civil society was even less potent. Most residents of iron curtain countries had little understanding of democracy, market mechanisms, or the habits of the heart embedded in liberal civil society. Any further penetration of Western culture was inhibited by the absence of democracy in Russian tradition and by the large measure of legitimate authority enjoyed by the regime. The citizenry as well as the *nomenklatura* were vested in the system. The top-down political structures of communist countries allowed elites to rule in part because they enjoyed considerable popular support. Just as the appeal of liberal capitalism in the West sprang not from abstract virtues but from a vibrant culture that gave it an attractiveness that it might not otherwise have possessed, socialist societies had many admirable features of their own that would be culturally internalized and become the objects of widespread nostalgia following their disappearance. For all their flaws and inefficiencies, the command economies of eastern Europe's socialist states had done a decent job of supplying life's necessities and smoothing out many of its uncertainties. For goldbricks, persons not driven by ambition, and those satisfied with the basic necessities provided by an industrial system—a sizeable percentage of people in any society—life was tolerably good under socialism.[24]

The absorption of Western culture was quite limited in some other ways as well. With a few notable exceptions like Aleksandr Solzhenitsyn, not even political dissidents stopped to consider the less attractive underside of the Western way of life (some of which their official propagandists had long been at pains to point out). Concealed from view behind the glittering surface of commodities were the messy and dysfunctional side of liberal democracy, the hidden injuries of class, the uncertainness of life, the perils of unemployment, the indignities of old age, and the cruel vagaries of the market—which, upon firsthand acquaintance after the Cold War, would generate much nostalgia and regret among many former citizens of socialist regimes.

Then too, the standard propaganda contrasts between freedom and slavery or the struggle between the sovereign individual and the overweening state overlooked the degree to which both socialist and market systems had become administered societies. Some sociologists have gone so far as to suggest that liberal societies have insidious ways of manipulating their citizens, a point most notoriously argued by Herbert Marcuse in his countercultural classic *One Dimensional Man*. But this was only a radical expression of a view held widely even among liberals that all states, increasingly challenged by the unruly complexity of modern life, have expanded their administrative arms into nooks and crannies of society once thought to lie beyond the reach of government. While totalitarian regimes have been the most notorious offenders, various liberal writers have argued that the bureaucratic state was fast becoming the norm in democratic polities as well. This point of view has been associated most prominently with the sociology of Max Weber, who forecast the expansion of bureaucratic authority as the inevitable outcome of the process of rationalization that lay at the heart of modernization. Weber's was, ultimately, a depressing vision of society as an "iron cage" whose residents freely consented to being governed as things.[25]

Such pessimistic opinions, buried in the fine print of the Western social contract, received scarcely any notice from the discontented in socialist societies. But the rocky post–Cold War histories of many eastern bloc states suggest that they had not internalized the meaning of even its main clauses. The limited penetration of Western values was evident from the persistence of authoritarian proclivities in Russia in the 1990s and after, which had the effect of deflating optimism about the country's democratic future. Under Vladimir Putin's leadership, the absorption of globally established commercial, financial, and political practices proceeded with painful slowness, if at all. The difficulty of transplanting Western norms was also evident in the poor performance of democracy in many post-Soviet states in eastern Europe and central Asia. But even in places where economic progress was more rapid and consumption was becoming glaringly conspicuous, as in China, the advent of the new market society did little to loosen the tight grip of one-party rule. Measured ideologically or culturally, the direct political results of consumerism were quite meager. In short, while it is obvious that a consumer culture became established in large portions of market societies in the second half of the twentieth century, it is questionable whether this caused a crisis in the socialist world.

Yet consumerism did have a major impact. Briefly, my argument is that the global success of this new way of life produced a sense, among those who participated in it and those who did not, that it was normal and that the socialist style was a deviation. Perhaps a little bit of philosophy, which is often a stranger to history, might be helpful here in understanding the global scalability of culture. Though admittedly the point is made in an oversimplified manner, it enables one to see that a surprising number of diverse thinkers in the twentieth century have sought to make sense of a phenomenon that they have called by different names. John Searle has pointed to the influence of what he has called the "background," Charles Taylor has discussed the "social imaginary," Maurice Merleau-Ponty has spoken of "sedimentation," Pierre Bourdieu of *habitus*, and Michel Foucault of the power of discourse and regimes of truth. Earlier, Emile Durkheim took a similar tack in his description of a highly individualistic society that was nevertheless backstopped by a form of deep solidarity. Other thinkers like Cornelius Castoriadis, Martin Heidegger, his student Hans Georg Gadamer, and no doubt many more could also be connected to this story. For that matter, with a bit of stretching one can find early anticipations of such ideas in Aristotle's conception of *logos* as the source of human community, or in Rousseau's notion of the General Will.[26]

Despite their many differences, most notably over whether culture is a repressive form of power or a condition of emancipation (or both), these thinkers were all struggling to define something that runs at a level deeper than politics, economics, and ideology, something so deeply embedded as to be a naturalized way of looking at the world. All of them were referring, I think, to the unspoken understandings and proclivities that we carry around in the backs of our heads and provide a foundation for our humanity. For my purposes, Taylor's characterization is as good as any. An imaginary, as he defines it, is "that largely unstructured and inarticulate understanding of our whole situation, within which particular features of our world show up for us in the sense they have." Though it may be conceptually daunting, as a matter of experience there is nothing inherently mysterious about the background, which inhabits all of us in one form or another and exercises a profound influence on how we see the world. In this case, the ideas of these diverse thinkers can be applied to the formation of a global imaginary or background in which, to one degree or another, people of very different cultures come to take for granted and to consider as normal certain elements of a way of life whose most striking facet is consumerism.[27]

Cultural borrowing and appropriation have always taken place, but in this case something distinctly different was happening. The recognition that one's inherited folkways were not a self-evident standard by which to judge the value of others was an indispensable first step on the way to breaking away from the constraints of one's traditional culture and substituting a more open approach to the world. It replaced what had been a hallmark of culture, its ethnocentric predisposition to closure and rejection of foreign values, with a degree of acceptance of the practices of other cultures, ranging from a grudging live-and-let-live tolera-

223

tion to an open respect for and even a welcoming of alien ways. And inasmuch as this acceptance was cultural, it was itself normalized in due course through a process that amounted to the opposite of consciousness raising. Other forms of cultural adaptation such as multiculturalism, acculturation, and hybridism allowed for the possibility of leaving the cultural core basically untouched or, when taken to extremes, of destroying it entirely. But the normalization of consumer culture meant that a critical mass of people in quite distinct cultures acquired the sense that other peoples were leading a normal existence, not some queer or repulsive lifestyle threatening to homegrown mores. But again, this appreciation of Western societies as normal did not mean that citizens of communist societies were being subverted by democratic values or that they were aching to undergo the kinds of profound transitions through which Western societies had passed.

So it was not culture as a package, which does not travel well, nor ideology, which does possess the capability for universality among elites, but rather it was this small yet critical segment of cultural code that migrated throughout the world's peoples and became the basis of important cultural commonalities.[28] If this were the nineteenth century, these changes would have been attributed to a zeitgeist. In the twentieth century, however, the spirit of the age resided not in the heavens above, but collectively in the cultural imaginary of a growing number of societies. This might be dismissed with a "so what?" shrug until one stops to consider the many profound changes in innermost sentiments that have taken place over the past few centuries on a global scale. Among them, one can point to turnabouts in attitudes—many still in progress—toward slavery, the inequality of women, racism, ethnocentrism, imperialism, genocide, cruelty toward animals, homosexuality, the use of torture, and, however problematic, doctrines of human rights. Often such changes in the background proceed at a snail's pace, though occasionally with surprising speed thanks to the quickening pace of generational change, but even with frequent setbacks in the face of tenacious resistance their influence eventually spreads to the point where those who think otherwise are looked upon as weird and out of touch. The establishment of an international consumer culture should be added to the list of issues in which changes in sentiment have had an enormous effect upon traditional behaviors.

One way of looking at the expansion of global society and its normalization is to view it as an unscheduled referendum on human nature. There have been many definitions of human nature: Aristotle's political animals, Freud's and Nietzsche's seekers of power, Confucian goodness and Augustinian sinfulness, Marx's *Homo faber*, Hobbes's creatures of appetites and aversions, utilitarian pleasure seekers, the free choosers of existentialism, the game players of Huizinga's *Homo ludens*, the rational choice utility maximizers of liberal economic theory, and the communitarian creatures of socialism, among others. All of the foregoing viewpoints emphasize a certain side of what it means to be human. All have serious problems. But even though it has problems of its own, perhaps the international cultural background associated with globalization deserves to be put on the short list of such components of human nature. This was culture in a "shallow" sense, as many elitist critics of mass society have delighted in pointing out, but it was wider, deeper, and more consequential than cosmopolitanism in its expression of an admirable longing: a human desire for liberation from pinched and narrow lives that had been cribbed, cabined, and confined in almost every conceivable way. It was, in its own way, an expression of a desire for universality before which the appeal of socialism as a way of fulfilling humanity's "species-essence" ran a very poor second.

Why and how this global cultural background helped to end the Cold War will be the subject of the next chapter.

9 Americanization, Globalization, and the End of the Cold War

Telling the Part from the Whole: Americanization versus Globalization

With a few exceptions, until the middle of the twentieth century American culture was of little interest to the rest of the world. But then, complementing the global reach of America's power in the Cold War, American popular culture spread like wildfire as mass media, tourists, businessmen, soldiers, scholars, and other agents of dissemination fostered a widespread acquaintance with American ways. Hollywood became even more dominant, solidifying and expanding a global primacy that had already been established in the interwar period; American TV programming was similarly ubiquitous; American popular music, particularly rock and its successors, could be heard everywhere sung in English, further cementing the status of English as the global lingua franca. As one historian has argued, "U.S. artists, from Louis Armstrong to Frank Zappa, from Ray Charles to Marilyn Monroe (not to mention their animated compatriots, Mickey Mouse and Donald Duck) did more to win sympathies for 'the American way of life' than any U.S. politician or military leader."[1]

This unexpected appeal of things American went far beyond music and mass media. Foreign students poured into American universities;

and, increasingly, publics abroad embraced American consumerism as their preferred way of life. As the 1940s stretched into the 1950s and 1960s, this new form of Americanization gained even more momentum. American clothing—sweatshirts, sneakers, denim pants, baseball caps—surfaced everywhere. It was aided by the arrival of an era of popular consumption in which people demanded refrigerators, televisions, telephones, and automobiles, even as some governments viewed these consumer goods as annoying frivolities. Eventually, the elite-oriented cultural programs of the US government got the message and began to ride this wave by incorporating popular culture into their programmatic mix. In colloquial parlance, the "Coca-colonization" of the world was taking place.

Once under way, the process was often greeted with considerable resistance. European elites had long prided themselves on Europe's superiority as the center of high culture, but this cultural tsunami from abroad and below also provoked the wrath of ethnic particularists and nationalists, conservatives, radicals, and some liberals, too. ("I don't need one, my wife is my washing machine," opined one Brit.) From a left perspective, it was easy to hurl accusations of cultural imperialism. But these were lame allegations that confused the imposition of something unwanted with desire and choice; for this was less the forcible exportation of a way of life than the igniting of a latent desire that was already present among people who were "consumer ready." Thus, despite efforts by European elites and nationalists to erect seawalls against the waves of mass culture, there was no holding back the tide. One could imitate, or maybe on occasion even beat the Americans at their own game, like the Beatles or the Rolling Stones, but no globally attractive alternative could be devised.[2]

However, to focus on Americanization is to distort what was going on at the level of the global whole, of which Americanization was only a part. Americanization did not turn others into copies of Americans. To a significant extent, as converging trend lines over the past centuries showed, the Europeans were already like Americans, and to the degree that Americans remained different, they had long expended considerable energy in trying to become like Europeans. But the growing techno-material similarity of societies—skyscrapers, automobiles, telephones,

227

department stores, and all the rest—did not erase the differences in mentality that continued to shape men's minds. The consumption of rock music and Levi's no more signified the Americanization of a European consumer than an American's purchase of a Toyota suggested her Japanization or the purchase of Dannon yogurt signified Frenchification. Though American culture was certainly a catalyst for globalization, Americanization was a lazy metonym for what was taking place.[3]

Americanization often failed to promote the objectives of US foreign policy. It was possible for the French to lead the charge against American cultural imperialism and yet remain an important if prickly ally of the United States. The same was true of the amiable Canadians, who became increasingly alert to the need to delineate and preserve—perhaps, even, to create—a distinctive cultural identity vis-à-vis the giant society to the south that was in many ways so similar. America's other next-door neighbor, Mexico, similarly sought to stay clear of the magnetic field of American culture despite extraordinarily close ties between the two countries' elites and the massive traffic, legal and illegal, across their common border. In other cases, receptiveness to American culture did not translate into slavish pro-Americanism, as the Federal Republic of Germany demonstrated in the 1990s and 2000s.

Nor did this homogenization of experience amount to the creation of a uniform "global culture." In the nineteenth century, the idea of a global culture would have struck liberals—for whom cosmopolitanism connoted a pluralistic world of nations, each blessed with uniquely valuable characteristics that were to be cherished—as both unlikely and undesirable. By the 1980s, many observers believed that something resembling a global culture was coming to be, but globalization no more produced a global culture than did the spread of hunter-gather societies across the world during the Paleolithic period or the triumph of agricultural civilizations during the Neolithic period. Each of those earlier global transitions had disseminated ways of life that were structurally similar in broad respects, but the cultures that adapted to the process remained sui generis, distinguished by environmental differences, language, unique religious practices, mythologies, and much more. In the case of globalization, preindustrial agrarian civilization was being destroyed, not cultural distinctiveness. The so-called Americanization of the world left ample room for the continued existence of other industrial and postindustrial societies with unique features of their own while reducing the number of societies that lived outside the preindustrial world to a vanishing few.

Thus for all the talk of the Americanization of Germany and Japan, these countries remained no less German or Japanese after their tutelage. To the extent that the occupations succeeded, it was not because Americans had been able to refashion the Germans in their own image, but because in large measure they were already like Americans as a result of their historical experience with modernization and globalization. In Japan, which since the late nineteenth century was second to none in its willingness to adopt foreign products and ways, it is ridiculous to argue that the nation was any the less distinctively Japanese as a result. It was "like" other societies by virtue of having globalized—and one could plausibly argue that on the whole the cultural distance between Japan and the rest of the world had narrowed—but it nevertheless retained its peculiar Japaneseness. The difference with Japan of the past had to do with the new context in which Japan operated. As a result of having rejoined international society, it increasingly depended on a host of background changes that made Japan a modern society, not an Americanized one.[4]

What this suggests is that attributing deep cultural influence to Mickey Mouse is, well, cartoonish. So too with the impact of Big Macs, for it is not as if McDonald's took possession of people's souls as well as their stomachs. Alert to the possibility that McDonald's was in danger of being perceived as a foreign invader, its executives were quick to realize the danger and to take corrective action. Sensitivity to accusations of cultural imperialism led the fast food colossus to preemptively tone down its foreignness by conforming to the architectural and gastronomic peculiarities of the societies in which it did business. Besides promising "a regional touch in your hamburger," overseas franchises were designed to harmonize with existing architectural forms. This was not simply a chameleonlike deception, for global product identities, manufacturing facilities, and sprawling multinational corporate structures were making the national identities of corporations increasingly problematic.

To the extent that the consumption of its products was a matter of consumer preference, the allure of McDonald's lay in its association with a new lifestyle that was based on the consumption of iconic non-essentials as desirable goods. Sometimes, as Peter Berger has suggested, "a hamburger is just a hamburger," but when consumed beneath the Golden Arches, it was "a visible sign of the real or imagined participation in global modernity." By itself, the desire for consumption cannot produce thoroughgoing cultural metamorphoses. Yes, consumerism was important, vital even, but at the same time one should be aware of the limits of its influence. When compared with the weighty symbolic loads carried by exchanges in premodern societies, exchange and consumption in the postwar world were not as heavily freighted with cultural implications. Nevertheless, they mattered.[5]

Americanization was always a matter of degree. In the case of western Europe, the spread of the English language merely added another tongue to societies that were already multilingual. Americanization thus took the form of cultural assimilation, refashioning, and accretion, more so in certain spheres of culture and society than in others, which left the cultures of European societies basically intact. There were, moreover, many important areas in which Americanization was rebuffed. While Hollywood, American popular music, and TV programming were triumphant, other industries suffered rejection. The social response to the US manner of food production and consumption was a case in point. Other nations did not adopt the American automobile-dependent, suburbanized way of life, with its strip malls. Nor were they comfortable with its go-go capitalism, its niggardly social welfare system, or its religious peculiarities. Just as East German socialism differed from the Hungarian or the Soviet varieties, so too did the capitalism of these nations differ from the American form, thanks to the influence of culture and history. American football and baseball remained exotic New World species of sport. American social science was a bloom that prospered only within narrow planting zones. Americanization did little to further the acceptance of American-style constitutionalism or republicanism, the two-party system, or the narrow ideological spectrum of American politics. European cities retained a different look and feel. Attitudes toward religion, sexuality, gender relations, race, and much more remained unaffected. For their part, Americans continued to flock to Europe because it was genuinely different, not merely because it was old in the mind's eye.

Tradition continued to play a large role in Asia's modernization, too, as China and neighboring societies were able to draw on large reserves of cultural capital that had long prompted numerous predictions of their imminent modernization. In the booming societies of Asia, Americanization clearly took a back seat to globalization. Propagandists for the Asian miracle delighted in trumpeting the role played by Asian values such as family, hierarchy, education, and social order, while pointing to the leading role of the state in planning and directing top-down modernization initiatives. In some cases, like Singapore, the nation's leaders made a point of drawing contrasts between their disciplined society and the flabby Americans. In Japan, periodic gaffes in which Japanese politicians voiced disapproval of the racial pluralism of the United States pointed to the continuing power of racial exclusivity as a cultural barrier in Japan. Fear of permanent cultural damage inflicted by Americanization should have been allayed by evidence that the tide of Americanization had crested and begun to recede, as rapidly modernizing nations developed cultural resources of their own that were available for global export: music and musicians, cartoons, films, (e.g., South Korea, Hong Kong and China, Romania), cuisines, and so on.

Overall, however, tradition remained more hindrance than help in societies whose people craved the benefits of modernity but could not put in place the institutions that made it possible. The use of tradition as a resource for modernization usually required a supportive political elite, a rarity in authoritarian states where the conditioned reflex was to use custom to maintain the status quo. Lack of political will was often combined with reactionary resistance to creating the cultural capital needed to modernize. Political change was not necessarily a solution to the problem. In North Africa and the Middle East, the chief threat to the rule of despots increasingly came from zealous conservative strains of Islam that were deeply hostile to the core institutions of liberal modernity. Not coincidentally, especially during the early Cold War, many of these were for a time drawn to the Soviet top-down model, which promised an easy form of modernization by fiat that did not require the cultural preparation that was crucial to success stories elsewhere. One could easily draw up an inventory of reasons for failure, but even an exhaustive checklist of the prerequisites for modernization would not provide a sure-fire formula for success. There always remains the unwelcome possibility that some societies simply do not have what it takes to transform themselves. And in such cases Americanization was a nonfactor.

The mystique of Americanization also tends to overlook the very heavy cultural traffic in the other direction on what was a very broad two-way street. The globalizing impact was plainly evident on the higher levels of cultural life in the United States as well as on the consumer culture. Symphony orchestras, whose American origins went back to the late nineteenth century, multiplied at an amazing rate while playing European classical music as their core repertory. The American university system developed scholars with specialized expertise in foreign lands that the nation being studied often could not match. The spread of foreign language training made the United States one of the most cosmopolitan societies even as it remained linguistically provincial on the mass level. And if one looks at a program like the Peace Corps, a strong argument can be made that it had a deeper impact on its volunteers than it did upon the people of the lands in which they served. The point was more readily apparent in consumer goods. The United States depended on the rest of the world for more than half of its energy needs: China for capital to pay for an enormous smorgasbord of imports; Japan, Europe, and Korea for cars; Asian societies for shoes, clothing, and electronics. Perhaps the most dramatic (and welcome) changes came in American eating habits as the cuisines of many other nations were combined into a complex gastronomic system. Such examples of cultural feedback underscore the point made by historian Richard Pells that the United States was "as much a consumer of foreign intellectual and artistic influences as it has been a shaper of the world's entertainment and tastes." All this back and forth suggests that globalization, like tennis, is a not a one-sided game.[6]

Like other countries, the United States demonstrated its own dogged cultural resistance to some globalizing pressures. Despite its reputation as the liberal society par excellence, the idea of free trade was never internalized by the American public, and the same might be said for internationalism. The continuing influence of religion made the United States the foremost example of resistance to the secularizing effects of modernization. The fierce popular opposition to Darwinian evolution, the theoretical bedrock of biological science, was testimony to the inability of the American public to digest the signature intellectual dish of the modern scientific worldview. Though racism was delegitimized at the elite level, a hierarchical view of humankind based on cultural differences was still all too apparent at the level of mass culture, even as mass ignorance of the world became something of a running joke among pollsters and late-night comedians. During this period, soccer, the only true world sport, was unable to gain a strong foothold in the United States as Americans continued to invest their enthusiasm in the far more parochial pastimes of baseball and football.[7]

On balance, societies were caught up in an intricate global process of convergence of social forms and cultures that the one-way notion of "Americanization" fails abysmally to convey. If one insists on using the term, should we say that America was being Americanized? Of greater import than Americanization was the amazing interpenetration of cultures across the globe of the kind that nineteenth-century liberal thinkers had predicted. The spread of English as a second language, the steady assault of ever more intrusive global media, and the standardization of technology made it possible for human beings from different cultures to talk about shared experiences as never before. People, ideas, images, money, and goods crossed borders with a scale and speed previously unknown. In the light of these intensifying exchanges among societies, Francis Lieber's intuition about how internationalism would take root was prescient. By the 1980s, it became increasingly apparent to observers that many of the quickening currents of change that first became apparent in the late nineteenth century had swelled into an overwhelming torrent. Awareness of this epochal change prompted the coining of a new word, "globalization," that quickly became a scholarly cliché in the 1980s and a political buzzword in the 1990s.[8]

It was within this context that a "third wave" of democratization inundated the world in the 1970s and 1980s. Since the middle of the nineteenth century, the number of democracies in the world had remained disappointingly small. But now most nations denominated themselves officially as democratic, though in many cases this was little more than greasepaint smeared over the otherwise unappealing faces of authoritarian regimes. But this change, however qualified, could not have taken place without an international society that provided a welcoming setting for democratic regimes and the diffusion of ideas that made an international way of life seem normal and desirable. This was an astonishing turn of events. In view of the political rigidity imposed by the Cold War, few observers were expecting a wave of genuine self-government. Nevertheless, a surge of democratization took place, and it was powerful enough to wash over the barriers thrown up by a faltering world economy in the 1970s: the run-up in oil prices, economic sluggishness, third world debt, the difficulties of the dollar and the collapse of the Bretton Woods pegged exchange-rate system. Unfortunately for the socialist world, its problems were far more serious.[9]

Culture Change, Leadership, and the End of the Cold War

A detailed explanation of how the normalization of global society was connected to political change in the Cold War is beyond the scope of this book. Obviously, the political walls of the socialist bloc would not have been breached without the existence of Western consumer societies that exposed how little socialist economies had to offer by contrast. But given the enforced separation of systems, the collapse of the Soviet world was not the product of the coercive force of international society; nor was it the result of an irrepressible desire to emulate Western societies, for the Westernization of peoples under communist rule mostly amounted to a disquieting understanding that they were not like the West. Conspicuously lacking, apart from those states in eastern Europe that saw themselves as victims of Russian imperialism, was the political motivation needed to overturn a well-entrenched order that commanded formidable repressive resources. Consequently, instead of looking to mass culture, any explanation of how the Soviet system collapsed must turn to the thinking of socialist political elites who set in motion the system's dissolution. For it was only the elites who were able to convert background changes in international society and in their own jurisdictions into a political about-face that left behind Cold War mindsets. Traditionally, elites have been notoriously averse to dislodging themselves. And yet, remarkably, in this instance a political cave-in of this kind did take place.

A major part of the explanation for this epochal change lies in the shortcomings of Marxist ideology in the face of new global realities. The burgeoning global fascination with mass consumption presented a fundamental challenge to a regime whose system was best suited to running a steady-state economy. Marxism, like liberal economics, had long focused on production and supply rather than consumption and demand. The stunning appearance of consumer societies, something that even the early bourgeoisie had rejected, was an unwelcome surprise to a socialism that through much of its history had practiced a "left asceticism" that sneered at a bourgeois style of consumption that was looked upon as historically atypical and unsustainable. In the limited consideration that he gave to the contours of life after capitalism, Marx envisioned a system that would satisfy basic needs, thus leaving ample time for leisure and cultural activities. This lifestyle would blossom courtesy of the marvelous productive machine bequeathed by the bourgeoisie to their socialist heirs.[10]

But while the machine would remain, the fuel of innovation would vanish. In a postrevolutionary world where there were no longer any competitive pressures to maximize return on capital, the impulse to continuously introduce new products and improve efficiency would not—in point of fact, could not—survive the collapse of a capitalist society. With no more revolutions in productivity and no more new stuff mandated by cutthroat competition, production would be routinized—administered by a bureaucratic "dictatorship of officials" because factories could not run themselves without hierarchical direction. This form of managed society, as Max Weber understood, would effectively stifle any lingering impulses toward innovation. This was a far cry from the image of dynamism that the Soviet model had once projected, whose attractiveness rested on its apparent ability—quite appealing to authoritarian nationalists—to create industrialized societies that could provide the basic necessities but not much else. Marx had been quite vague on the subject of life under communism, but the torpid socialist systems of the second world offered a convincing sneak preview of what one could expect in the worker's utopia.[11]

Powerless to unleash or to stamp out what had once been disdained as commodity fetishism, socialist societies in the late Cold War years imperceptibly internalized an appreciation of consumerism that their leaders thought prudent to appease as best they could. As early as the 1930s, the Soviet regime had sought to introduce a greater element of choice in consumer purchases, and even made available—at a steep price—limited quantities of luxury goods that in future were restricted to the *nomenklatura*. Consumerism also made notable strides during the Brezhnev years, albeit in a very modest way by Western standards. Nevertheless, even during these good times people understood that life was better elsewhere. The widespread popularity of *samizdat* and *tamizdat* underground literature literally spoke volumes about popular interest in Western culture and, by comparison, about the barren soil of Soviet cultural creativity. The treatment of travel as a privilege and reward implied that the grass was much greener on the outside (as those who visited the West quickly found out for themselves), while the large audiences that tuned in to Western radio broadcasts showed curiosity about life in the West and a corresponding cynicism about glowing official descriptions of domestic life under socialism. How many people in the West tuned in to Radio Moscow?

The most telling aspect of this latent consumerism was the public's awareness of being excluded from international society. Take, for example, the growing number of citizens of the USSR who during the closing years of the Cold War expressed the desire to live in "a normal country" as *normalniye lyudi*, that is, normal people. What was it like to live in a normal country? It was to be international, to participate in something that once would have been considered impossible: a cosmopolitan mass culture. There was a long list of standard features of life, to which the rest of the world had grown accustomed, that the Soviet public was aware of not enjoying: pop music, travel and tourism, vibrant literature, entertaining movies and TV programs, and stylish clothing, among other aspects of vigorous mass cultures. Teenagers desired the right to be rebellious and alienated. There was an egalitarian aspect, too, to this dilation of desire and its satisfaction, a democratization of luxury in which the gap between the wealthy and the average man was closed considerably—the practical gap between chic Rolex and lowly Timex was virtually zero.

Overall, the quality of life for middle-class individuals in the West had become demonstrably superior to that enjoyed by the upper classes a generation earlier. The Marxist slogan "from each according to his abilities, to each according to his needs" was trumped by a capitalism that promised to fulfill each person's desires.[12]

Whereas the socialist standard of sufficiency had been realized in the USSR in the form of a spartan barracks socialism, the benchmark of consumer civilization turned out to be superabundance, or as Mark Twain once put it, the "limitless multiplication of unnecessary necessities." Consumerism, as Hegel had been among the first to recognize, was "something inexhaustible and illimitable." But, as sociologists have been at pains to reiterate, the kinds of goods promised by a global consumer society were nonessentials: access to art and entertainment, a wardrobe that allowed some enjoyment of fashion, the opportunity to travel, the sampling of varied foods and cuisines beyond the monotonous fare of the local diet and, perhaps most of all, getting a car, which was the most sought-after diploma certifying that one had gained entrée to the good life. Unfortunately for the communist aristocracy, the rise of this new standard in which mere adequacy had become inadequate required an ability to meet expectations of abundance that the regime was abysmally suited, in principle and in practice, to fulfill. By resting their economic appeal on the promise of sufficiency, the Soviets contributed to the alienation of their populace and forfeited any possibility of creating a global background of their own.[13]

Hitherto the long-standing historical tendency in the creation of desire had followed a top-down pattern of cultural transmission. In the diffusion of etiquette, clothing styles, or new standards of beauty like foot binding in China, the arbiters of taste had been aristocrats. Adam Smith, for example, believed, with a touch of Calvinistic disapproval, that much consumption was driven by the desire of commoners to emulate one's aristocratic betters, an assumption that lives on as the rationale behind product endorsements. However, the drivers of consumption were very different in the Cold War world. In mass society, the wellsprings of taste flowed increasingly from the ranks of society itself, from designers, inventors, fashion dictators, jazz musicians, rock performers, and celebrities whose status depended on the ability of markets to materialize their ideas into widely saleable commodities. There was no way that top-down socialist societies could dream of releasing such energies or of commanding them. Whereas the Soviet system excelled at suppressing creative impulses, the bureaucratic architects of the new Soviet man could not command muses for the kind of innovation needed to match the consumer cornucopia of the capitalist West. In a global society in which Calvinist frugality was no longer the norm, recognition was now a matter of keeping up with one's consumerist equals. In this sense, too, international society was egalitarian, though not in the restricted socialist sense of imposed equality. This was a far cry from the socialist prediction that the unification of mankind would come about in the wake of capitalism's globalization of misery. Instead, unification was going forward as a by-product of capitalist abundance.[14]

In addition to the disheartening example of the West, the economic success of a growing number of formerly preindustrial nations also gave life under socialism a lackluster appearance by comparison. For more than a century and a half, spectacular economic growth had been restricted to a small number of early developers in the West. That began to change in the 1970s and 1980s, as Japan, the so-called Asian tigers, and then China joined the globalization caravan. Those societies provided eye-popping contrasts to the arthritic Soviet economic scheme. Their successes also cast doubt on the appeal of anti-imperialism as a global strategy, for their advances were made possible only by participation in a capitalist world economy that, if one were to believe the axioms of the anti-imperialism creed, was bent on squeezing surplus value from dependant peoples.

From a Marxist perspective, there were crucial ideological reasons for taking seriously the global consumer revolution. Though the love affair with consumerism did not stir a primal yearning for democracy, communist leaders as well as traditional elites in countries like France were quick to sense the global political implications. Obviously, the widespread democratization of prosperity made a mockery of the axiomatic Marxist prediction of the inexorable impoverishment of the working class; but in more practical terms, it also challenged the revolutionary strategy of the Soviet Union. The Bolshevik revolution in its beginning phase had been understood by Lenin as a historical anomaly that was explained away by the expectation that revolutions were sure to follow in more developed countries, specifically in Germany. The revolution would be rescued and brought to completion from abroad. When external deliverance failed to materialize, the Stalinist strategy of "Socialism in One Country" resorted to a scheme of self-strengthening in order to guard against the ideologically given likelihood that the capitalist powers would plunge into a fratricidal war that would endanger the USSR.

While World War II validated that analysis, the Cold War did not. Instead of going to war, the first world came closer together; under permissive American hegemony, there were disagreements aplenty, but no fundamental rifts emerged among the capitalist powers. Briefly, salvation from the outside once again seemed possible as hopes were invested in the theory of third world revolution. This idea, whose origins lay in the early Soviet period but which moved to the forefront in the late 1950s, was a conspicuous abandonment of the traditional Marxist idea that revolution would spread outward from the industrialized center. For a time, the vogue of radical third world nationalism confirmed this revision, but it was gainsaid by the proliferation of consumer societies and, as socialist states stumbled economically, by the absence of any effective countermovement against globalization. This posed a theoretical problem: If the revolution would come from neither center nor periphery, where would it come from—Mars? Up to a point, it was easy for Soviet leaders to rewrite history, or to tactically shift ideological course, but the postwar trajectory of events suggested that a complete rethinking of their ideology was in order, which risked forfeiting their identity and reason for being.

The biggest blow to Soviet pride was the defection of China, whose newfound economic dynamism contrasted with Soviet stagnation. The arrival of the People's Republic of China in 1949 had given an enormous boost to the idea that communism was the global wave of the future; but, by the same token, its rancorous departure from the Soviet-led camp in the 1970s consigned the command economy to the bin of old-fashioned ideas. Like the USSR, an initial reliance on bureaucratic administration had transformed the PRC into a formidable power, albeit an impoverished one. Dissatisfaction with Soviet tutelage had already taken a geopolitical turn in Mao Zedong's shift toward a rapprochement with

239

the United States in 1971. That was followed by an even more radical move following Mao's death in 1976, when China switched to a mixed economy that depended on global export markets and massive imports of technology and raw materials.

In pursuit of the so-called Four Modernizations, the nation plugged itself into a world economy whose chief guarantor was the United States. Underscoring the value attached to its participation, China lobbied hard, and successfully, for admission to the newly founded World Trade Organization. The holding of the summer Olympics in Beijing in 2008—a quadrennial pageant seized upon by other former outcast nations as a way of gaining recognition as a respected member of global society—highlighted China's dramatic century-long journey from a geographic expression to a world power and gave the regime a degree of the international respect that it craved. But it also highlighted its membership in the global guild of post-Stalinist modernizers. Ideologically, with some intellectual contortions this turn could be interpreted as a kind of hyper-Menshevism, though whether it had much to do with Marxist theory at all is open to question.[15]

As the most recent of "free riders," China provided the most spectacular example of the gap between globalization and Americanization. The Americanization of China had long been the fond hope of missionary types and China hands from the middle of the nineteenth century through the heyday of the Open Door policies, but Americanization was not on the agenda of the economically supercharged China of Deng Xiaoping. In particular, the brutal suppression of the Tiananmen Square protests in 1989 showed that the Communist Party had no intention of relaxing its political grip. Afterward, the Chinese government took action to prevent the importation of unwelcome American products such as pornography and open access to news from the outside world. By the 1990s, political anti-Americanism began to grow side by side with a cultural nationalism, which showed its face in periodic flare-ups over the future of Taiwan and territorial disputes about unimportant unpopulated islands. Also, China's leaders began to talk about the "cultural security" of their nation, which suggested both a well-founded fear of the cultural by-products of globalization and a shaky understanding of the way that culture and globalization were connected. On the political side, China was often loath to cooperate in the United Nations Security Council and in international climate negotiations.[16]

Nevertheless, despite post-Maoist China's failure to satisfy America's longing to see it democratize, relations were tolerable because it was ruled by the kind of authoritarian regime that the United States had long been able to stomach. Stripped to its bare essentials, China policy was also the premier example of the enduring faith that Americans demonstrated in the beneficent workings of international society over the long term. The way in which the endgame would play out was more readily visible than it had been in the days of containment, when economic integration was an unlikely possibility for socialist societies. US policy makers envisioned the continued blending of China into the world economy and looked forward to the eventual growth of a powerful middle class with liberal leanings to rein in the authoritarian behavior of the regime. Besides, the Chinese economy had become so closely linked to that of the United States that a wholly adversarial relationship was out of the question. This was too much to swallow for some critics who saw international relations in a more threatening light. China's willingness to accept American debt obligations to finance American imports led to the two nations being bound together in what one pundit disparaged as "Chimerica . . . an economic monster."[17]

The Soviet Union, meanwhile, was experiencing a "crisis of industrial statism" in which an increasingly sluggish economic engine showed signs of stalling. The objective measures of decline were coupled with a worsening crisis of faith. Marxist ideology had long since left behind the days when it could spur the kind of enthusiasm that had energized the Bolsheviks and the crash programs of industrialization. The mature system was enfeebled by black markets, alienated workers, and an anomie that found expression in rampant alcoholism. Even basic statistical measures on which the regime had long prided itself began to turn down, especially an alarming drop in life expectancy and a stunning decline in the birth rate below replacement levels. After a period of postwar privation, Soviet citizens had become accustomed to a growing standard of living, but by the 1980s, when a demographic crisis showed its face, the formerly tried-and-true expedient of adding more labor inputs was no longer available.[18]

The consumer expectation of more meat in the diet, made possible by grain imports, could no longer be covered by the petro-dollar proceeds from oil exports once prices on the international petroleum market collapsed in the late 1980s. But while it is easy to blame economic ups and downs, the truth is that nothing was working well. In the Soviet imperial borderlands, long-smoldering anti-Russian nationalism showed that the idea of Soviet citizenship was a chimera and that the West, if only for reasons of the grass being greener, was far more attractive. At the same time that the command system was incapable of satisfying the growing material expectations of the population, the official ideology was being hollowed out, setting the stage for a legitimation crisis down the road. For many, Soviet communism was becoming an established religion in which neither the church leaders nor the faithful placed much store. This ideological rot was accompanied by physical decay.

Despite all these gloomy signs, the mixed brew of inchoate dissatisfactions and objective indices of decline found in the Soviet Union of the 1980s did not contain the highly combustible elements needed to set off a revolutionary explosion. The cultural unease in the Soviet Union was less the product of an intense desire to create their own version of the Western good life as it was the product of the understanding that the attributes of the outside world, the normal world, underscored the abnormal character of their own society. This sense of being second-rate was hardly the sensibility expected of the vaunted new "soviet man." Though the intention was to be a model for the rest of the world, Soviet citizens increasingly developed noxious personality traits that traduced the values of the superior human being that the regime was supposed to be creating. But behavior that was openly at odds with the system posed little threat to the regime. The desire for entrepreneurial freedom found expression mostly among black marketers, while the right to dissent was the rallying cry of rebellious, creative, and artistic types, the kinds of people that comprise a small minority in any society. Such popular dissatisfactions as existed were not the stuff of mass revolutionary sentiment. A change of direction, if it was to come at all, would necessarily have to come from above. Thus when the system did finally collapse, it was as if, in the words of one writer, the Russian people had "sleepwalked away from Communism."[19]

For many outside observers then and afterward, social discontents were less a spur to drastic change than the worsening power position of the Soviet Union. In the absence of some kind of far-reaching transformation, Hu Yaobang, the secretary general of the Chinese Communist Party, predicted in 1985 that "the Soviet Union will disappear as a great power in the twenty-first century." Hu's comment to the visiting Richard Nixon reflected a common view that an obsession with national power was the principal consideration in forcing decisions for reform in states like China and the Soviet Union. The ambitious military buildup of the Reagan administration, coupled with heavy investments in new military technologies, threatened to upset the hard-earned power equilibrium by placing enormous pressure on the Soviet command economy to continue supplying both guns and butter. Given that a ruinous proportion of Soviet GDP was already being allocated to military investment, without a dramatic increase in economic growth something would have to give.[20]

If maintaining the power of the USSR had been the principal concern, a logical response to growing American strength would have been to take the wherewithal for military expansion out of the hides of the people, a practice resorted to by despotic regimes throughout history when forced to make a choice. The Soviet version of this kind of politically motivated mobilization would have meant reverting to Stalinist methods of repression and belt-tightening that would have ensured the indefinite continuation of the superpower standoff. Another possibility was for the leadership to kick the can down the road in the hope of muddling through, as many politicos are tempted to do when confronted with chronic problems. The Soviets actually tried this by selecting a few premummified successors to Brezhnev, but they lacked the vitality merely to stay alive, much less to put in motion dramatic change.

Finally, in 1985 the party elite gambled on a dynamic and youthful leader, Mikhail Gorbachev, who was painfully aware that the existing system could not hope to match the West economically and militarily or maintain the pretense of doing so. Gorbachev immediately set about trying to revitalize a sclerotic system by moving toward a mixed market economy under the banner of glasnost and perestroika. Taking advantage of the USSR's top-down system, Gorbachev hoped to stimulate transformational change through a loosening of the state's grip, exactly the reverse of what would have been prescribed by Russian tradition or a Stalinist approach. The extraordinary consequences of his policies—the breakup of the Soviet Union and the end of the Cold War—were wholly unexpected. With someone less venturesome and visionary at the helm, the USSR would have survived indefinitely, as most experts were predicting, and the Cold War might not have ended so peacefully.[21]

Given Gorbachev's historical significance, one needs to ask why he felt compelled to take a series of steps that set in motion the dissolution of the Soviet system, a question that is more pressing as he was by all accounts a socialist true believer. Most likely it was precisely his beliefs that hold the key to understanding his moves. Here was a man who was motivated not by apparatchik careerism but by the pained recognition that the operative ideology of the USSR had drifted far away from its mooring in fundamental beliefs, much as the pre-Reformation church had lost touch with its core convictions. Gorbachev easily passed one test of the genuineness of an ideology: the willingness of its true believers to take action when current practices no longer express basic principles, which is why disillusioned ideologues often make the best realists. More Loyola than Luther, he had no intention of precipitating the collapse of the USSR, but he understood that continuing, like some conditioned trail horse, to plod along the same path as his predecessors would only make a bad situation intolerable. Given the long-term prospects for a Soviet slide into irrelevance, Gorbachev felt compelled to initiate drastic reforms before the point of no return had been reached. Opening wide the political floodgates might wreak some havoc downstream, but at least it would relieve the buildup of pressures that would prove disastrous if nothing were done. Continuing to temporize would also be to say good-bye to the receding prospect of rescuing the humanistic promise of socialism. On one occasion he put the urgency of the need for radical change in terms reminiscent of Rabbi Hillel: "If not us, then who? If not now when?"[22]

In an information-poor society, Gorbachev's panoramic vantage point enabled him to better grasp the big picture of troubles that ordinary citizens experienced as a vague cultural unease. Much of his dissatisfaction came from the recognition that the USSR was out of step with the march of events and the spirit of the age. More than any other political leader of his day, he was able to look with fresh eyes past the day-to-day predicaments of politics to the deeper long-term implications of the recasting of the global setting wrought by globalization. Conventional political thinking, he knew, was badly out of step with the *longue durée*. Though he continued to cling to the hope of socialism as an ultimate solution, he understood that the supposed vanguard nation had dropped out of history's line of march. In contrast to American policy, where the connection to a brighter future was implicit, the ideology of the USSR was explicitly yoked to the expectation that globalization would bring universal misery to the workers of the world. As a fallback, neo-Marxists had resorted to theories of mass society, ideological hegemony—domination of culture by the ruling classes—and condemnation of the "culture industry" to explain the delay in the creation of a global proletariat that was conscious of itself as the universal class. But given the emergence of a firmly established cultural background of consumerism throughout the world, Gorbachev foresaw no prospect of an "Aha!" moment when the ideological scales would fall from the eyes of deceived workers. His retrospective description of the Soviet experiment minced no words: "from the historical point of view it was a dead end in social development." World history, he realized, had taken a different direction.[23]

Like his fellow citizens, Gorbachev understood that this was a world in which the Soviet system was not normal and had no prospect of becoming so. Despite mixed feelings about the "major changes that had occurred in the most fundamental aspects of daily life during the years after World War II," there was no longer any place for the Soviet Union's brand of socialism. Consequently, there was no choice but to come to terms with "the internationalization of economic and then of all social life" by internalizing the reality of global society. This meant rejoining the world pretty much on the world's terms. In his words, the USSR needed "to live in harmony with mankind's universal values, abide by the norms of international law, follow the 'rules of the game' in our economic relations with the outside world," including membership in the flagship institutions of globalization, the World Bank and the IMF. In his Nobel lecture, Gorbachev underscored the point: "we have to carry out measures that would enable us really to open up to the world economy and become its organic part." The contrast with FDR was instructive. Roosevelt had acted when international society was in deep disarray; Gorbachev acted because he understood that international society was historically triumphant.[24]

This appreciation of the new global setting took him to a place beyond the customary preoccupation of national leaders with power and wealth. One common reading of his stratagems was to see them as a botched attempt at enjoying the best of both worlds: revitalizing the economy to provide for both military and civilian needs and thereby resetting the competition with the United States at a higher level. This was the wary view initially adopted by higher-ups in the administration of George H. W. Bush who found it difficult to accept the possibility that Gorbachev would abandon the Russian tradition of power seeking unless forced to do so. And it continued to be the conviction of many Americans who, after the fact, were convinced that he had been strong-armed into capitulating because the United States held "the winning hand." For example, in explaining the collapse of the USSR, Bush's secretary of state James A. Baker III believed that "the Soviet leadership had concluded that they could no longer compete with the West, not economically and not militarily." But this was a superficial analysis, for Gorbachev was not compelled to act as he did by the pressures generated by American policies. On the contrary, his thinking went far beyond conventional power calculations.[25]

While tough-minded US cold warriors saw his reforms as a way of buying time for a resurgence of Soviet military might, Gorbachev understood that the trajectory of international society conflicted with a continuation of old-style geopolitics. As he put it, alongside the usual geopolitical jostling for position, "another trend, with equally objective causes, was gaining momentum—the process of the emergence of a mutually interrelated and integral world." This was a dangerous contradiction with serious consequences, for the old Soviet-style habit of thinking in term of east versus West had "placed the peoples of the Soviet Union in hostile opposition to most of the peoples of the world." Logically, but nevertheless astonishingly, he decided that accommodation to the new realities of globalization took priority over the pursuit of power. Hence his new foreign policy initiatives, or what he liked to call the "new thinking," sought to put the brakes on the arms race and to move beyond a system based on power politics, even to the point of taking some previously unthinkable measures of unilateral disarmament. Whereas the old thinking had pursued a foreign policy based on hostility, Gorbachev believed that peace demanded "movement towards globality and universality of civilization." The new thinking, commonly seen as making a virtue of necessity, was a well-reasoned derivation of Gorbachev's globalist understanding.[26]

The old way of dividing the globe into first, second, and third worlds, with the prospect of an eventual unification along socialist lines, no longer made sense because one world had already come into being. "The world economy is a single organism," Gorbachev told the United Nations General Assembly in 1988, "and no state, whatever its social system or economic status, can normally develop outside it." The only hope of success for socialism thus required working with globalization, not by operating against it. As if it were stealing a page from William Howard Taft's playbook, the party's Central Committee in 1985 spoke of "bringing international relations back into the channel of normal cooperation," that is, rejoining international society. Suggesting that policy makers had hitherto been ideologically oblivious to this epochal change in international society, his foreign policy adviser said of Gorbachev's approach: "this is a reunification of mankind on the basis of common sense." One way of defining culture is to see it as common sense, in this case a common sense that was presumably global.[27]

If sustaining a military rivalry was not at the heart of Gorbachev's new thinking, neither was the idea of economic competition. Even supposing that Gorbachev had wanted to match the affluence of the West, he acknowledged that achieving a comparable level of wealth lay well beyond the reach of his nation's system. True, he was aware of how miserably, relative to the West, the Soviet economy, archaic even by socialist standards, was performing, having witnessed firsthand the cornucopia of capitalist production. But he was no fan of consumerism, for the socialist ideal of sufficiency had nothing to do with the creation of a consumer society. Writing a decade after the collapse of the Soviet Union, he complained that "consumerism and the desire for things . . . have pushed into the background any desire for spiritual enrichment or cultural progress," though he failed to spell out how exactly socialism was better equipped to supply such a boon.[28]

All in all, the Soviet imperial-cum-ideological tradition was woefully ill adapted to deal with the globalized international environment. In this new world, to persist in power maneuvers would serve only to defend an out-of-date system that had no hope of displacing the global reality. Without drastic change, the Soviet Union was fated to be left behind, an increasingly irrelevant Cyclops of a nation in a world that had passed it by. But it was not simply Soviet behavior that was behind the times, for there was also a systemic problem. The geopolitics of the Cold War were obstructing powerful trends of a world that was "objectively united by the bonds of interdependence," which was giving rise to a new form of "international relations under which, one can no longer live under the ancient traditions of 'the law of the fist.'" By restructuring the old power-oriented politics of the world, a system that was based on coercion, the Soviet Union could make its own significant contribution to globalization by "launch[ing] the beginning of a world *perestroika*." Vladimir Putin, one of Gorbachev's reversionist successors, would later complain that "the demise of the Soviet Union was the greatest geopolitical catastrophe of the century," but for Gorbachev the old thinking that undergirded geopolitics was no longer a relevant frame of reference. The decisive consideration was, instead, global community. True, Gorbachev would continue to point out the shortcomings of the pure market model and insist on the universal appeal of socialist values, but these could only bear fruit historically, "on the other side of ideology," in a future to which the USSR would have little to contribute.[29]

As the USSR's influence contracted to the boundaries of a pan-Slavic empire, the Soviet-led "world" came apart at the seams. The collapse, when it came, was extraordinarily rapid. Within the space of a little more than two years following the surprise opening of the Berlin Wall in November 9, 1989, the communist regimes of the eastern bloc collapsed, mostly without violence (Romania being the exception). The aftermath was messy but not explosive, as many expected, for there was little danger of a global conflict. By the end of 1991, following some Byzantine internal politics, the Soviet Union had been dissolved, replaced by fifteen successor states around the perimeter of a new Russian federation. Had the Soviets deployed their tanks as ruthlessly as they had in 1953 in East Berlin, 1956 in Hungary, and 1968 in Czechoslovakia, the Cold War might well have continued, though in what form is impossible to say. But that does not obviate the fact that the erosion of the principal selling point of the Soviet system—its superiority as a system of production and distribution that catered to the deepest needs of human beings—had become an effete ideological product that could not be rejuvenated.

Culture Change as Conflict and as Acculturation

None of this could have happened without an American foreign policy that midwifed the revival of international society and the leap into a second wave of globalization in the 1970s. In the nineteenth century, the assumption that globalization was unstoppable had left little room for political tampering with its mechanisms. In the Cold War, by contrast, the effect of US policy was to give global community the political nurture sufficient to reestablish itself and to flourish. The long stretch of time during which this commitment to globalization endured underscored the degree to which policy was addressed to long-range international trends as opposed to the ephemeral issues that dominate the headlines in democratic electoral cycles. The duration of that commitment was even longer when one factors in dollar diplomacy. From a longer perspective still, international politics had traveled a remarkable distance since the dawn of international relations.

That the Cold War had ended with a political victory for the United States could not have been clearer—after all, the nation's archenemy had suddenly passed away—but the causes of this success were extraordinarily muddled. As soon as it was over, a messy and inconclusive debate took place about who or what should take credit for the result. Depending on one's predilections, one could select from a baffling menu of options. I have chosen to emphasize Gorbachev's appreciation of changes in international society, but others have opted for Reagan's tough line and willingness to splurge on military modernization. Other possibilities include the contagious spread of the courage displayed by dissidents in eastern Europe, particularly in Poland and Czechoslovakia; heretical political leadership in the eastern bloc countries; the influence of the charismatic Polish pope, John Paul II; the relative failure of communism to provide a way of life as satisfying to most people as that generally available in the West; the computer revolution; American steadfastness over the entire forty-five-year life of the Cold War; *Ostpolitik*; the amazing spread of American popular culture; the role of nongovernmental organizations; the exposure of Soviet elites to life in the West; the example of China. One could expand the list still further. With history a picture puzzle that can be put together in many different ways, it is no wonder that historians have yet to provide a convincing causal explanation of this dramatic outcome.[30]

Assembled in this way, it is obvious that all these pieces of the puzzle have some merit and that no single explanation will do, for no one factor could have been effective in the absence of others—this mighty river was the product of many tributaries. Frustrating as it may be, this inability to explain precisely how and why things happened is typical of the way that historians wrestle with explanations of large-scale events. The more the historian focuses on broad phenomena like globalization, the more he is likely to lose touch with the small but certain cause and effect relationships that lend authority to historical studies that concentrate on more modest happenings. Historians inevitably lose sight of the complex connection between the parts and the whole as they climb up the rungs of generalization and abstraction by writing histories of histories—the higher the ladder, the more unsteady the explanation. Unlike natural science, history has no plausible procedure for uniting the macro and the micro in the way that physicists hope to bring together quantum mechanics and cosmology in a grand unified theory that comes close to explaining ultimate reality. Historians are perforce more modest. For those who appreciate its complexity, history is too vast and too tangled to explain in its totality. Historians cannot hope to gather enough evidence to accurately reconstruct it, and even then they would not be able to process it systematically. While parsimony is the holy grail of social scientific theory, simple historical explanations are for the simpleminded.[31]

If we want to understand how the Cold War ended, there is no way of extricating ourselves from a dense web of argumentation in which no single strand turns out to be the Ariadne's thread that leads the way out of the labyrinth. If we seek to account for the postwar world's distinctive political characteristics, the answers must be sought at least in part in ideology and culture, but changes in the ideational sphere cannot be explained without reference to the international economy, whose performance helped to generate, transmit, and sustain certain kinds of ideas. In turn, the international economy owed much to the political buttressing that had been retrofitted after the war. And, as we have seen, an explanation of victory and defeat in the Cold War is wholly inadequate without an understanding of how global culture has functioned. In short, globalized international relations cannot be convincingly construed in reductionist terms.

Despite this inherent complexity, one-size-fits-all political explanations have tended to command the limelight. The administration of George H. W. Bush received much well-deserved credit for bringing the Cold War to a "soft landing," thus breaking a historical pattern in which periods of dramatic change in the international system were marked by horrible crashes. But skillful pilots, though indispensable, explain only so much. Self-assured "nuclear abolitionists" like Ronald Reagan and Mikhail Gorbachev were important to ending the Cold War, but to attribute the outcome entirely to their military and foreign policies, their economic programs, their preoccupation with missile defense and the danger of nuclear war, and so on, is badly to misunderstand the historical process by which this outcome was reached. The Cold War could not have been ended without the diffuse transcultural understandings that operated outside of political reach. To continue with the aviation metaphor: even more necessary was a smooth and well-prepared runway, constructed over the course of a half century of generally successful globalization, which made possible a controlled touchdown. Had the landing taken place in mountainous or rocky terrain, the outcome would have been disastrous.

Training the spotlight on international society and on culture also puts the simplistic idea of Cold War victory in a new light. Though the Cold War ended in the triumph of one way of life over another, it was not a political conquest that liberal ideas "won." As one way of gauging the importance of international society, one might try to imagine the best case outcome (the worst case being a nuclear World War III) had international society been a nonfactor. In that case, as many historians of both left and right persuasions have suggested, there needn't have been a cold war at all because disagreements could have been put to rest by realistic deals of the "this is yours and that's ours" variety. A few American statesmen, Nixon and Kissinger, even agreed. Obviously, globalization has only a bit part to play in this kind of schema, which is what one might expect from explanations that are based on realistic political and military calculations. But the Cold War was not settled in this way because it would have required that the American foreign policy imaginary be drastically scaled back and altered beyond recognition. In the absence of this necessary background, constant wheeling and dealing of the Nixon-Kissinger variety would have been construed as appeasement, as they soon enough discovered.[32]

The other extreme option—force—also had its limits. The Cold War was not really a war because it could not be fought in the first place with purposive strategies, tactics, and weaponry designed to achieve victory. Though the Cold War was contested on many battlefronts, even at its most intense it may be more useful to think of it as a "hot peace." Even as a political description, the term "cold war" is a loaded expression that fails to capture the complexities of the relationship between the United States and the Soviet Union, which, as eventually came to be realized, was highly cooperative in many areas, sometimes in unspoken ways. By the 1980s, aside from some rhetorical fireworks, it had settled down, as a practical matter, into a live-and-let-live relationship. But if the Cold War was not a real war that could be fought or won, and if its ultimate outcome was dependent upon the workings of intercultural processes that could not be politically dictated, then it is questionable whether it makes sense to think of it as a power struggle. It may be that it is better understood as part a larger story about the evolution of international society and the spiky progression of the globalization process.[33]

As a fallback, one could resort to the competitive idioms of social Darwinism by recasting the Cold War as a cultural conflict. But such a move also has its difficulties. To be sure, there was an ideological and cultural front to the Cold War, where battle was joined quite seriously by officials who were tasked with waging and winning a struggle of ideas. The problem is that the metaphor of conflict or contest, which suggests much suffering, sacrifice, grief, and death, along with its connotation of clear-cut defeat or victory, does not fit a process that occurred insensibly outside the ambit of official foreign relations. There were wars, certainly, but important changes also took place in a quite unwarlike and mostly invisible fashion in the background that I discussed earlier, changes that could not be imposed or prevented by official means. "Defeat," rather than being dictated, took the form of a belated recognition by Gorbachev and his supporters of a historical metamorphosis that the apparatus of Soviet power was powerless to effectively oppose. For individuals behind the iron curtain, acknowledging the normality of a Western lifestyle was hardly a defeat. Nor was it a defeat for socialist societies in the aggregate, for whom the end of the Cold War, because it offered the opportunity for a better life, might more accurately be considered a victory for the supposed losers.

Bereavement is always a by-product of significant and rapid cultural change, but the conviction of die-hard communists that the outcome of the Cold War was a political debacle was every bit as misplaced as the Western belief in Cold War victory. For a struggle that was waged politically but resolved by global social and cultural processes, the non-coercive language of acculturation and cooperative cultural borrowing may be more appropriate than Darwinian metaphors. If the crucial developments took place on cultural ground, the view of the Cold War as a power struggle fails hopelessly to convey what was at stake, how the issues were resolved, and how gains and losses should be weighed. The claim that the United States did not win the Cold War as much as it was resolved in its favor is certainly arguable, and one's position depends on the degree to which one believes that the historical process can be shaped by foreign policy or any other use of instrumental rationality. As totalitarian societies have demonstrated, the scope of political control is enormous, but it was the ungovernable growth and intensification of international society and the emergence of an incipient global culture that made possible what power could not achieve.

So while American policy did play a significant role in the outcome, there was no political blueprint for cultural transformation on a global scale of the kind that occurred during the Cold War. It was not possible to predict beforehand, to plan for, or to manage the wave of Americanization and consumerism that washed over the world; nor was it possible to forecast the accompanying globalization of American culture, the degree of dependence upon foreign resources, and the impact on the American labor force and wages that would result from the pursuit of an open global economy. If it is the case that cultural innovations are conditioned by one's cultural inheritance, the presence of an embryonic global culture suggested that a widespread predisposition to welcome such changes was already in place—something that policy makers could not know ahead of time nor take advantage of. Just as evolution is a process of creation without a Creator, history is a play without a playwright.

Perhaps the wisdom of the crowd (which can at times be quite stupid) has something to tell us about the validity of the war metaphor. Take, for example, the flat popular reception accorded to the news that the Cold War had ended. Given the enormous amount of ideological PR with which the public had been carpet bombed for more than a generation, Americans took surprisingly little satisfaction in their historic achievement. Though many intellectuals indulged in triumphalism, there was no spontaneous outpouring of mass euphoria, relief, dancing in the streets, or victory parades of the kind seen, say, at the end of the Second World War. Unlike the conclusion of that conflict, the end of the Cold War did not feel like an earthshaking success. It was not a hollow victory, but neither was it rousingly fulfilling—many sports fans derived greater joy from the triumph of their favorite teams. This is hardly conclusive evidence, but it does suggest that the end of the Cold War was a world-historical event to which applying the word "victory," a political term with zero-sum connotations, is wholly inappropriate. So in answer to the question, "who won the Cold War?" I say, "global society."

The reason why victory felt so joyless had much to do with the new form taken by international relations during the Cold War. Until the nineteenth century, politics was thought to be the most important realm of human activity and the centerpiece of social knowledge. Until the middle of the twentieth century, Americans had thrown in their lot with international society. In the Cold War, politics returned to take up residence in a newly receptive American milieu, but it could not resume its once dominant place. It could not displace international society from the foreign policy agenda, and it had to stand by as culture took on an essential role in deciding the outcome of international issues. This transit from the political to the social and then to the cultural encompassed a complicated pattern of interactions to which the old political vocabulary of war, peace, domination, and subordination cannot do justice. Looked at in this way, much of the world's history in the twentieth century was a prolonged stretch of turbulence in the continued evolution of international society.

After seventy-five years of self-sequestration under Bolshevik rule, the collapse of the Soviet Union marked Russia's return to the civilizational fold. But Russia was not alone in experiencing a homecoming. For the United States, the Cold War had been a major departure from the course charted at the turn of the twentieth century. With international society apparently secure, the United States, like Cincinnatus, was in a position to return to its earlier more modest station in international affairs. On the other hand, the extraordinary power that it had amassed between World War II and the end of the Cold War made it possible for the United States to exercise a kind of hegemony that was quite new in world history.

10   Global Aftermath

The half-century period of America's historical singularity began to wind down in 1991 with the downfall of the Soviet empire and the collapse of communism. At first glance, appearances suggested otherwise, as post–Cold War America was dominant on a scale never before seen in world history. Confounding the many predictions of a return to traditional multipolar international politics, there followed instead a "unipolar moment" in which the United States stood out as something unique, an unchallenged global power. In the neologism of the French foreign minister, it was a "hyperpower"; to its critics, it was a global empire; while for those who viewed it more appreciatively, it was a liberal hegemon. Uniting such disparate judgments was a widespread belief that US supremacy was both the culmination of a deep exceptionalist impulse and the beginning of a new phase in which it would seek to perpetuate its supremacy[1].

But far from being the crowning achievement of a historical career that led inexorably to this moment, these years did not mark the entry into the promised land of exceptionalism; they were, instead, a transitional period in which US foreign policy gravitated erratically toward the more modest default position embodied in dollar diplomacy. Extraordinary as it was, America's dominance during these years was only a transient state of affairs that owed much to some highly unusual circumstances: the residual legacy of Cold War military preparedness combined with the historically improbable disappearance of any serious military or ideological competitors. But there were other reasons for thinking that this ascendancy was only temporary. One had to do with hegemony's flimsy grounding in the history of US foreign relations and the absence of a home in a cultural tradition. Hegemony, which was quite new, went against the grain of a half century of policies that had revolved around meaningful international cooperation, and it also broke with an even longer tradition of modest leadership. More importantly, despite the widespread impression that the United States was able to do as it pleased, its power, like that of the Wizard of Oz, was less imposing than it seemed.

·········

The unprecedented political and military dominance amassed by the United States in the post–Cold War decades was the product of favorable domestic and foreign conditions. One enabling factor was a stupendous military capability inherited from the Cold War. American power was a legacy of its earlier investment in military technologies and the ability to profit from the so-called Revolution in Military Affairs. Once developed, this unique capability took up fixed residence in a welcoming institutional matrix from which it was impossible to evict. Since Eisenhower's farewell address in 1961, the dense network of institutions that formed the military-industrial-scientific complex had become even more parasitically embedded in the American economic and political structure. Though military spending relative to GDP declined during the 1990s, it nevertheless equaled that of the next fifteen powers combined. On the foreign side of the ledger, the disintegration of the USSR and its empire left a Russia that was in every respect a flaccid remnant of its former self. In what had amounted to a historical elimination tournament, America was the only competitor left standing.

With no credible military challenger in sight, and with no significant contraction of military capabilities, the United States stood alone atop the Everest of power while other nations were limited to surveying the world from the foothills. The American military establishment, in one of its habitual misreadings of history, would have liked to keep things that way. "Our first objective is to prevent the re-emergence of a new rival," declared a 1992 draft Defense Planning Guidance. One problem, however, was that the powerful national security state built up over more than four decades was now left without a mission. With the sudden disappearance of a threat that had long warranted the hypertrophied defense establishment's privileged existence, policy makers had difficulty in defining credible new dangers. The best that James Woolsey, President Bill Clinton's CIA director, could do was to suggest that, despite the removal of the most dangerous beast of prey, the jungle was still teeming with "a bewildering variety of poisonous snakes." Woolsey's inability to specify a threat suggests that part of the reason for continued security expenditures on a grand scale lay closer to home. It is close to a sociological law—sometimes called a bureaucratic pathology—that bureaucracies, once established, have a well-documented tendency to perpetuate themselves. In this case, the military bureaucracy was enmeshed within an institutional network so dense and powerful that radically downsizing it was unthinkable.[2]

Nevertheless, despite this military dominance, the earliest signposts of the 1990s pointed toward a diplomatic path whose waypoints had previously been set by dollar diplomacy. Expectations of cooperation had always been disappointed in the past, but President Bush gave voice to some long-suppressed hopes by painting the future in rosy colors. "Now we can see a new world order coming into view," he told Congress, "a world where the United Nations—freed from the Cold War stalemate—is poised to fulfill the historic vision of its founders." This line of thought was given intellectual cachet in the so-called end of history thesis advanced by Francis Fukuyama, in which the future promised an unchallenged resumption of liberal globalization. The most obvious signpost indicating entry into this new New Era was that the prospect of war among the great powers had dwindled to virtually zero, becoming, in John Mueller's words, "sub-rationally unthinkable." As a tangible expression of this sentiment, nuclear disarmament among the powers, hitherto the stuff of pipe dreams, was put on the slow and bumpy road to becoming a reality.[3]

The implausibility of great power war was accompanied by a degree of active collaboration that would have been utterly fanciful only a few years earlier. An uncommonly broad coalition that in 1991 forced Iraq to disgorge its conquest of neighboring Kuwait marked the high point of joint military action, but it was not the sole example. In southeastern Europe, following the breakup of post-Tito Yugoslavia into a bedlam of quarrelsome successor states, NATO and the United States, following some initial bumbling, were able to quell a conflict that threatened to unleash genocidal forces. Farther afield, the war in Afghanistan featured another diverse coalition, including NATO forces that for the first time were fighting "out of theater." Even the much derided "coalition of the willing" used to justify the 2003 invasion of Iraq recognized that the intervention needed to be legitimated by a cloak of multilateralism. The limited NATO engagement in Libya in 2011 that hastened the downfall of strongman Muammar al-Qaddafi temporarily regained some of the lost momentum of cooperation. True, Russia and China often frustrated Security Council action in the UN, but their disapproval centered on proposed actions against troublesome third parties and did not involve life-and-death differences between the great powers.[4]

With great power political tensions at a historical low, for a time in the 1990s economic policy threatened to become high policy. In international affairs as in the domestic policies of the Clinton administration, the refrain might well have been "It's the economy, stupid!" One analyst argued that "under Clinton, foreign policy has become almost synonymous with trade policy." Another commentator identified Clinton's approach with dollar diplomacy, whence the single-minded pursuit of expanded trade would bring security, democracy, and other good things. In truth, the 1990s did bear more than a passing resemblance to the 1920s as a period when the world, for a brief moment, appeared to be on the verge of becoming a liberal utopia. With some troubling exceptions, it was a decade of astounding economic growth as more and more countries entered the club of modernizing nations while others were taxiing for takeoff. Globalization, already a hot scholarly topic, was now on every politician's lips as well. Embracing these changes, Clinton spoke enthusiastically about "our commitment to globalization." His mention of "harnessing the forces of globalization" indicated clearly that international society was once again towing history in its wake.[5]

What happened next lends support to the adage that periods of happiness are the blank pages of history. In the aftermath of the attacks on the twin towers of the World Trade Center in New York City on September 11, 2001, the country veered toward a more pugnacious, unilateralist kind of globalism. Those attacks, it was endlessly repeated afterward, were said to have "changed everything" as the national mood shifted from complacency to crisis. Even the most dangerous moments of the Cold War, perhaps with the momentary exception of the Cuban missile crisis, had failed to incite the kind of deep public fear and anger aroused by the 9/11 attacks. In response to the new national obsession with terrorism, the George W. Bush administration announced a war on terror of indefinite duration. It envisioned using the nation's military superiority to remove the threat and, in the process, to resolve the unfinished business of globalization by installing democratic regimes in a Middle East region overpopulated with authoritarian regimes—"draining the swamp," in the policy speak of the day. In his 2005 inaugural, Bush declared, "The survival of liberty in our land increasingly depends on the success of liberty in other lands. The best hope for peace in our world is the expansion of freedom in all the world."[6]

The United States took the offensive first by invading Afghanistan, which the al-Qaeda network had been using as its base of operations, and more controversially, by invading Iraq in March 2003. The war in Iraq, while hotly debated at home, was wildly unpopular abroad, stirring up accusations of US imperialism and fostering anti-Americanism among people who only two years earlier had expressed deep sympathy for America. But the new American unilateralism ran deeper than Iraq. The Bush administration made no attempt to disguise its disdain for the United Nations, which it considered to be little more than a talking shop. The Senate's refusal to ratify a number of landmark treaties—the Kyoto protocol on climate change, the Rome statute establishing an international criminal court for trial of war crimes, a global ban on land mines, and others—further promoted the image of the nation as a bad citizen of the international community. Ironically, the attempt to make a case against rogue nations and terrorism was instead convincing many that the United States had become a rogue internationalist.[7]

Much of the criticism of the United States assumed, too readily, that the Bush administration had unleashed a deep trait in the American national character. On its face, the unilateralist turn of its global war on terror was the perfect embodiment of an aggressive exceptionalism. For much of the world, the Bush policies reinforced the long-standing stereotype of the United States as a "gunfighter nation," an image that American historians had done much to promote and one that the Texas-bred president sometimes played to, particularly in his "wanted: dead or alive" description of the manhunt for al-Qaeda leader Osama bin Laden. This assertive and trigger-happy America, many were convinced, was not the quirky product of a single administration; rather, it was an outgrowth of deep historical roots that would be around for a long time to come.[8]

Seeking to unearth its sources in the past, some observers sensed a revival of Wilsonianism in this efflorescence of exceptionalist rhetoric. Even before the invasion of Iraq, a writer in the *Wall Street Journal* said of George W. Bush: "The 'W' Stands for Woodrow." While the press and political pundits gnawed away at the Wilsonian theme, scholars preferred to discuss America's new global position in terms of empire. In dozens of works, academic writers sought to compare America's extraordinary position after the end of the Cold War with that of former imperial powers, with classical Rome usually the first analogy to come to mind. Rome's territorial sweep, its overpowering military, its ability to impose a Pax Romana accompanied by Roman citizenship, and its republican heritage all provided fodder for comparison. Another variation on the theme of empire saw the United States as inheritor of the imperial crown worn by Great Britain in the preceding century. This idea had enjoyed brief favor in the late 1940s when Britain's decline first became manifest, but the imperial family resemblance stood out more vividly in the new global circumstances. For some, the British analogy justified American behavior; while for others, the connection with Pax Britannica was an embarrassment in a new era in which imperialism was a dirty word.[9]

These dramatic interpretations made for good stories, but were they good history? Did it make sense to see the United States, formerly the mainstay of a liberal international order, transformed virtually overnight into an overweening power intoxicated with its own might? Was post-9/11 foreign policy the point at which the United States finally fulfilled the destiny that had been foreseen since the founding of the republic?

Legions of policy analysts and historians liked to think so. But if there is anything to my narrative, it makes more sense to see the post–Cold War decades as a residual period in which contingent events led to a temporary outburst of interventionism. Then, too, if one brackets the Iraq war and the war on terror, a look at the broader outlines of American policy shows that in most vital respects the United States continued to adhere to the basic vision of internationalism that had sustained it through the century.

The arguments about a revival of Wilsonianism, empire, and abandonment of multilateralism all suffered from fatal flaws. For one thing, these debates lacked policy relevance. Few people except the intellectuals who consulted each other's books took notice of them, and deservedly so, for the comparisons with Rome were far-fetched. One might as well have sought meaningful connections between gladiatorial contests and American football—once one gets past the fact that both wore helmets, the comparison breaks down very quickly. The image of the torch being passed from an exhausted Britain had an initial plausibility to it, but here too the superficial similarities were far outweighed by substantive differences. The displacement of Great Britain as the world's leading power was not a simple casting change in which an ambitious American understudy replaced a fading leading man. It was, rather, a new production entirely in which the United States played a radically different kind of starring role. Whether measured in geopolitical, economic, or cultural terms, the stature and influence of Great Britain at the height of its power differed enormously from that of late twentieth-century America.[10]

Analogies to Wilsonianism were equally misplaced. If there was a connection, President Bush went out of his way not to acknowledge Woodrow Wilson's influence, despite some tailor-made opportunities to do so. Bush's reluctance was traceable to a host of fundamental differences with Wilsonianism that went beyond partisan politics. Most importantly, Wilson had sought the more limited practical goal of making the world safe for democracy rather than unrealistically attempting to spread democracy by force in critical regions. In addition, Wilson's crusade, if that is what it was, placed its faith in collective security and international organization, whereas the Bush administration preferred to hold the UN at arm's length. Most of all, Wilsonianism was largely irrelevant to the world of the twenty-first century. As I pointed out in an earlier chapter, Wilsonianism offered a set of solutions to problems that, by the end of the twentieth century, no longer existed. The most striking resemblance between the two was that both approaches were historical outliers. If one looks beyond the spurious comparisons to Wilsonianism, it is not clear that the Bush administration's democratizing ambitions fit *anywhere* within the ideological boundaries of the history of American foreign relations. Wilson's brand of collective security had defined one extreme that was never again pursued; the Bush administration's justifications bookended another.[11]

In its essential long-term features, American policy in the aftermath of the 9/11 attacks changed hardly at all. Present-minded commentators liked to paint succeeding presidential administrations as polar opposites, but a look at the Clinton-Bush years demonstrated a high degree of continuity. During this period, the United States never deviated from the fundamentals of good citizenship in international society. It continued its membership in NATO, whose members even agreed to participate with the United States in the war in Afghanistan, which for a time was viewed as a good war. The United States also continued to bear its responsibilities for security in Asia and for governance of the international economy, all the while maintaining its membership in a host of functional international organizations. Even its unilateralism was little different from unpopular interventions during the Cold War, particularly the wars in Korea and Vietnam, which also had been fought as shaky "coalitions of the willing." Then, too, Clinton had advocated preemptive war in certain situations (as had Eisenhower) as well as regime change in Iraq. All of which suggests that the swerves of one presidency were being mistaken for a fundamental change in America's approach to the world.

There were other indications that the crisis was less than it was made out to be. Realist logic predicts that overbearing behavior will be countered by coalitions, thus creating a new balance of power. But the underlying continuity of American policy gave no cause for the formation of an anti-American bloc despite the uproar in world public opinion. The absence of any moves toward such a countermobilization indicated that American hegemony was more an annoyance than a genuine threat to the vital interests of the core states. More positively, it confirmed the widespread understanding, though not screamed from the housetops, that only a dominant America could be counted on to provide the public goods needed by a global society. If this was genuinely the case, then a hegemonic United States remained indispensable to world society's continued well-being. In contradiction to the self-defeating logic of the "security dilemma" of international relations theory and metaphorical accusations of imperialism, the security of the United States continued to rely on the use of preponderant American power to make other nations feel secure.[12]

America's remarkable global influence depended to a significant extent on the legitimate exercise of power as the bulwark of international society. In many cases, American domination had been invited by the dominated, who would have been terrified to see it renounced. But that hard-earned legitimacy, which had enabled the United States to establish its primacy and was equally vital to maintaining it, had the by-product of circumscribing America's military strength. The expectation of cooperation, which the United States had been instrumental in creating, severely hamstrung its ability to exercise its power. To maintain its position, the United States needed to continue to act in the spirit of multilateralism, whereas behaving like a classic hegemon was the surest way to erode or even destroy that hegemony.[13]

But there were solid reasons to think that continuing down the path of unilateralism was unsustainable over the long term. First, the precariousness of the Bush administration's policies was underscored by its highly contingent character. It would have been very easy to lead a consensual international effort against terrorism, especially in light of the extraordinary outpouring of sympathy from abroad—"Nous sommes tous Américains," said a memorable headline from *Le Monde*. But a public opinion that craved action, the availability of a superlative military machine, and the potent presence within the government of a small group of hawkish neoconservatives eager to exploit America's military superiority bent the policy needle in the direction of unilateral military action. Ordinarily, a fringe group of this kind would not have been able to exercise such influence, but in the post-9/11 environment its members were presented with a golden opportunity to leverage their unconventional views. And they did, only to encounter rapidly diminishing returns.

Economic difficulties posed even more serious obstacles to a continuation of unilateralism. By the 2010s, a multitude of domestic problems cast a shadow over the ability of the United States to sustain its extraordinary position. For a time after 9/11, the desirability of having an almighty military was virtually unchallenged. One decade and a trillion dollars later, however, questions of affordability began to set limits on how much military might the United States could effectively wield. Victory could be easily achieved against conventional military opponents, but the costs of fighting open-ended and inconclusive wars in which the United States was hard-pressed to hold its own against substate actors were enormous. In the 1950s, Eisenhower believed that permanent military mobilization would sap the strength of the economy. In the 1980s, Paul Kennedy prematurely predicted that "imperial overstretch" would afflict the United States, as it had so many other great powers in the past. But it became increasingly clear that the prospect of huge budget deficits, coupled with chronic trade imbalances financed by the borrowing of enormous sums from China and other nations, made it impossible to sustain such high levels of military spending. Something, at some point, had to give. So while the power position of the United States was clearly unprecedented, it was approaching the point at which it could no longer sustain that power.[14]

But chronic economic troubles were only the most visible symptoms of a descent from the heights, as a growing inventory of serious domestic problems suggested that hegemony was no longer practically viable. When one looked at societal indicators, lying beneath the surface were some festering domestic ills that increasingly constrained America's options. Ironically, at the very moment that American military power reached heights previously imaginable only in the dreams of would-be world conquerors, the domestic basis of that superiority was being undermined. In the middle of the twentieth century American society and culture had been paramount in many different areas, but the advent of the millennium showed the country receding into the middle of the pack in many sectors. In some ways, American society had regressed to a status reminiscent of the late nineteenth century when the nation had failed to stand out in most head-to-head comparisons to other developed nations. At that time, it had been an economic giant and a military pygmy. Now even its unequaled economic dynamism and productivity, formerly its most compelling claim to distinctiveness, was in process of being eclipsed by a band of energetic upstarts and reinvigorated old-timers.

One writer has pointed to "the other exceptionalism," a long list of fields in which the United States lagged far behind the standards set by other developed countries. The American standard of living, once unparalleled, was matched or exceeded by a substantial number of countries that boasted higher per capita incomes (In 2011, the UN Human Development Index ranked the United States in twenty-third place.) While the American middle class had stagnated over a stretch of thirty years, other nations passed the United States by. The gap between rich and poor threatened to make America a class society, making it increasingly difficult to view it as the land of opportunity. Some comparative studies even suggested the heretical possibility that Europe offered stronger prospects for social mobility and better life chances. Although higher education remained a bright spot, it was becoming increasingly unaffordable, whereas other nations provided much greater support to their young. In primary education, the situation was execrable, as other countries routinely outperformed American students by wide margins on standardized tests. Scientific education in particular was lagging. To compensate, the United States relied increasingly on the "brain drain" in which foreign-educated scientists and engineers made up the intellectual deficit.[15]

Americans worked longer hours, took fewer vacations, and were less well paid than counterparts abroad. The country spent more per capita on health care than any other country but without corresponding returns to health and life expectancy, whereas other nations did far better with less. The American Constitution was less and less attractive as a model for other democracies. "I would not look to the U.S. Constitution if I were drafting a constitution in the year 2012," said Associate Justice Ruth Bader Ginsburg. In areas where it was in the forefront, such as its incarceration rates, there was no cause for pride. And, in the minds of European critics, the continued resort to capital punishment was semi-barbarous. Similarly, the nation's stingy and porous social welfare safety net struck some foreign observers as a denial of economic human rights. If one compares the United States at the turn of the millennium with Charles W. Eliot's list of American contributions to civilization in the 1890s, America had lost its distinctiveness. Notwithstanding its remarkable ability to successfully integrate large numbers of immigrants, the United States was no longer the trendsetter in international law, standard of living, advances in eliminating war as a method of settling disputes, mass suffrage, religious toleration, and the diffusion of well-being. On top of everything, massive gridlock in Washington suggested that the political system was incapable of addressing the lengthening list of serious national problems.[16]

Given these disturbing trends, the situation was ripe for a return to a more modest policy outlook built atop deeper historical footings. For most of its history since the late nineteenth century, the United States had been content to be among the leading nations, first as follower and later as leader, pursuing a vision of foreign relations as a cooperative enterprise. Even at the height of its Cold War influence, an extraordinary degree of diplomatic effort, perhaps the bulk of it, was expended on tending to relations with allies. The delayed return to normal internationalism began in the administration of President Barack Obama, who, in his words, "made a commitment to change the trajectory of American foreign policy." According to one widely read interpreter, Obama hoped to bring US policy into line with the nation's "core interests," which also happened to be the central concerns of dollar diplomacy, namely, "dealings with the great powers and [the] embrace of larger global issues." His version of internationalism reinstated a central conviction of the 1990s that global society was composed increasingly of like-minded states that would pull together on the major problems facing them. Not surprisingly, the ugly international image of the United States was reversed almost overnight, almost embarrassingly so. The desire to see the United States restored to its former status was transparently evident in the award of the Nobel Peace Prize to Obama, in advance of accomplishments he had yet to record.[17]

Confronted simultaneously with the sharpest economic downturn since the Great Depression, a budgetary crisis, and a rapidly diminishing public appetite for the war on terror, the president planned a with-drawal from Iraq and scheduled a drawdown from Afghanistan. But he also sought to steer American foreign policy away from the unilateralism of the Bush years by pursuing a greater degree of international collaboration. An important instance of this shift was his patient construction of an international coalition to impose effective sanctions against Iran as a way of discouraging the Islamic republic from developing nuclear weapons. Another was the intervention in support of anti-Qaddafi rebel forces in Libya. Rather than rely on American troops, NATO air power provided the bulk of the force while the United States contented itself with supplying indispensable logistical and intelligence support, an approach that some called "leading from behind." There were some failures of cooperation, too, but whatever the outcome it was unlikely that American policy would continue down the byway taken during the Bush years.[18]

In the face of such indicators of American decline, the future of exceptionalism suddenly became a charged issue. "The age of American predominance is over," declared a leading economist who went on to predict that China would take over America's economic role. Younger Americans especially were increasing likely to exhibit "a declining belief in our special virtue as a world power." Obama himself caused a stir and handed Republican politicians a campaign issue when he gave the impression of disavowing American exceptionalism by relativizing it. At a press conference in Strasbourg on April 4, 2009, he stated, "I believe in American exceptionalism, just as I suspect that the Brits believe in British exceptionalism and the Greeks believe in Greek exceptionalism." This touched off a brouhaha back home. "God did not create this country to be a nation of followers. America is not destined to be one of several equally balanced global powers," thundered Republican presidential aspirant Mitt Romney. In response to the political fallout from his statement, Obama retreated somewhat. The most quoted line in his 2012 State of the Union address was "anyone who tells you that America is in decline or that our influence has waned, doesn't know what they're talking about . . . America remains the one indispensable nation in world affairs." But then the next year, he argued for taking action against Syria "with modest effort and risk," concluding, "That's what makes America different. That's what makes us exceptional." To equate the uniqueness of American policy with only modest effort and risk was a significant comedown from US foreign relations at its most ambitious.[19]

Both the requiems and the exceptionalist swagger were intellectually dubious because they were based on a "rise and fall" model of thinking about power that no longer conformed to how the world functioned. Admittedly, if one works from that kind of perspective, then the second half of the twentieth century cannot help but look like the booster stage of America's rise to supremacy. In contrast, the story I have presented in this book portrays these years as a period of extraordinary influence that could not be sustained. It was, moreover, not a record likely to be copied or surpassed by any other power because the international system was no longer about single powers selfishly, and unrealistically, seeking dominance. The story was not about the United States or potential competitors, but about the future of the global society that the United States had been so instrumental in saving and reviving. The more interesting question was whether international cooperation had become institutionally and culturally established among nations to the extent needed to sustain a global society whose continued success was far from certain.

Just as liberal economic theory correctly predicted that America's disproportionate economic superiority in 1945 would wane as other countries recovered and prospered, it was equally foreseeable that the US star would shine less brightly in the firmament of nations. But this was hardly a tragedy. At its inception, the American empire was intended to be temporary, pending the restoration of an international society in which cooperation rather than hegemony would be the norm. In 1941, the publisher Henry Luce wrote an essay in *Life* magazine advocating what he called "the American Century." Luce, with his China missionary origins, envisioned a world that was converted to American ways. Often seen as an imperialist Urtext, it is worth pointing out that he did not envision an Americanization of the globe. "America cannot be responsible for the good behavior of the entire world," said Luce, "but America is responsible, to herself as well as to history, for the world environment in which she lives." Elsewhere, he wrote, "Emphatically our only alternative to isolationism is not to undertake to police the whole world nor to impose democratic institutions on all mankind." The point was to assure the continued operation of global society, not to dominate it.[20]

The American Century, unlike the Third Reich, was not intended to be "the American millennium." Only the twentieth century would be an American century, "our century." And so it was. To an amazing extent, Luce's vision was realized in practice, which helps to explain why it has been so compulsively revisited. Luce did not address the question of what would succeed it, but American policy makers did. From the earliest days of the Cold War, they recognized that the postwar world was not an American creation, and they left open the yet-to-be-realized possibility that the follow-up to the American Century would produce an international environment in which others did their share of the rowing. America's relative decline was consonant with a rapidly globalizing world in which the United States would possess a monopoly of neither virtue nor vice.[21]

Following the half century of American dominance in foreign affairs, then, the post–Cold War years were an anticlimax. After having reached the pinnacle of international power, there was no way for the United States to go but down. The extraordinary character of America' story lay in the journey to the top, not in the flag-planting ceremony at the summit. By itself, this was predictable. Alpinists, after all, do not linger on the peaks that they conquer, for getting to the top is less dangerous than remaining there. After pausing for a few moments to enjoy the view and breathe the rarefied air, they need to start the faster but still fraught descent downward to safety. To think otherwise, as did many chauvinist policy makers and cheerleaders who believed that American hegemony was a natural state of affairs, was to confuse the by-product of the journey with a permanent historical condition.

Concluding
Thoughts

At bottom, this book has been about America's continuing response to globalization. Following a half century of passive acceptance of the world revolution of modernity, the first American policy to explicitly address globalization was dollar diplomacy, which proceeded from a relatively modest conception of the nation's place in the world. Taft's policies were only a crude experimental model that generated little interest abroad, but when the production version rolled out in the 1920s the status of the United States had been radically upgraded to first among equals. In its new position of leadership, US policy sought to bolster the trend toward legal and commercial cooperation as a replacement for the old methods of political and military coercion. Dollar diplomacy assumed that the United States ought to be an active, indispensable, yet politically uncommitted participant in global affairs. Because this internationalist approach had the virtue of coexisting peacefully with the tradition of political isolation vis-à-vis Europe, it was, as has been argued elsewhere, a "normal internationalism" that was backward compatible with the republican tradition and the liberal internationalism of the nineteenth century.[1]

This optimistic temper was reshaped during the world crisis of the 1930s. Unwilling to risk a collapse of the globalization process and the destruction of international society, FDR set in motion a half century

271

of foreign policy innovation. US policy during this period broke with a time-honored axiom of foreign relations in which states looked to their own self-interest with little regard to the effect of their behavior on the health of the global environment. While the other powers continued out of necessity to follow regional approaches, American policy makers revolutionized international politics by defining national security in global terms and formulating policies to match. Recognizing that the international background could no longer be taken for granted, they also accorded much greater weight to the economic, cultural, and ideological dimensions of foreign relations than had been the case prior to the war. This was not a belated recognition of realism, but a giant step beyond.

The most remarkable aspect of this foreign policy was its global scale of conception and execution. The relative decline of major powers like Germany, Japan, Great Britain, and France provided an opening for this turn to globalism, but before it could fill the new power vacuums that emerged around the world the United States first needed to adopt a global outlook in which the constraints of geography, long a basic consideration of realism, no longer applied. One lesson taken away from WWII by American policy makers was that modern war was global and hence peace was indivisible. So while in principle Europe was more important than Asia, in practice America's global orientation led policy makers to treat problems in other regions as connected and as de facto equal. This felt need to touch all the global bases meant that another traditional realistic restraint, the tailoring of foreign policy ends to fit limited national means, was also suspended for a time. Contrary to the gloomy forecasts of realist oracles, this geopolitical globalism turned out to be sustainable over the span of more than four decades thanks to an unprecedented spell of domestic economic prosperity, a peacetime military mobilization that was capable of supporting multiple wars in different areas of the world, favorable tailwinds from globalization, and, indispensably, a worldview that made it possible for the country to steer a steady course despite a constant tacking back and forth by successive presidential administrations.

The unique mix of global policies was not built up of entirely new parts. The cultural undercarriage of globalism had been under construction since the late nineteenth century and many policies, particularly the support for international economic institutions during and after WWII, were intended to deal with problems of globalization that had become apparent long before the run-up to the war. Other notable departures, such as new doctrines of human rights that were prompted by the horrors inflicted upon civilians during the war, were evolutionary extensions to individuals of the legal internationalism that first arrived on the scene in the late nineteenth century. If there had been no Cold War, it is likely that innovation would have been restricted to elaborations on these themes, but the pressures of the ideological competition with the Soviet Union prompted still more creative initiatives, many of which were prompted by the invention of new weapons of mass destruction that rendered impossible the military resolution of international disputes. Some of the geopolitical techniques used by the United States were traditional (alliances, balance of power, arms competition), but others were quite novel (limited war, credibility crises, and the building of an international civil society).[2]

While a robust American economy and a nonthreatening hemispheric environment left ample room for implementing policy on a global scale, such favorable conditions alone could not foreordain the kinds of novel strategic decisions that were made. Most notable was the determination of the United States to intervene in formerly strange and out-of-the-way places that only recently had been considered strategically negligible. Military commitments to places like Korea, West Berlin, Vietnam, and other ordinarily trifling venues produced credibility crises that mocked the realist axiom that only vital interests were worth a fight—the formidable pundit Walter Lippman once called this global version of containment "a strategic monstrosity." But while such unfamiliar locales were lacking in conventional strategic cash value, the chance that their loss might have a disastrous effect on alliance cohesion, world opinion, and global society seemed to make them worth defending. Somehow, despite some close calls, the United States managed to intervene with enough self-restraint to prevent these crises from escalating into full-blown great power wars. After a quarter of a century of growing public restiveness, repeat performances of such faraway adventures became politically out of the question, but a worldwide network of alliances, commitments, and far-flung military deployments remained. The net result was that American power, in its depth and breadth, was without parallel in world history.

273

One could make a strong case for American uniqueness solely by focusing on such distinctive features of high policy, but such an approach would neglect its signature characteristic, namely, that the whole point of American geopolitical involvement from the time of the Second World War was the re-creation of international society. Inflated claims that American policies won the Cold War or fanciful notions that the postwar world was an American creation disregard the workings of a process in which foreign policy played the limited role of allowing the Cold War to be settled by nonmilitary means. This was not a negligible achievement, but the fact that the success of American policy was contingent on the flourishing of an unpredictable globalization process was conveniently overlooked amid the triumphalist crowing heard in the wake of the Soviet Union's collapse. If our understanding of the Cold War has suffered from ignoring this connection to globalization, so too has our appreciation of the complex texture of US foreign relations in the twentieth century.

The link to globalization, besides cutting down to size the intellectually overrated importance of military and political exploits, has another salutary effect: it deflates the provincial and chauvinistic view of the world that tends to accompany the belief in the nation's exceptionalism. American achievements, however extraordinary, were only a secondary plot line of a larger story whose main theme was the recasting of international relations from political struggle into a project centered on the management of international society. American policy was not about the United States leading the world toward its own preferred ends; it was about the United States aligning itself with globalizing trends whose continuation called for supportive measures that the United States was in a position to supply. Put another way, the United States traded up from a belief in itself to a belief in something greater than itself, a belief that many other nations also came to adopt. To focus only on national achievements is to train on the United States a spotlight that should be directed elsewhere.

This self-subordination to globalization should also remind us that America's relationship with the world was in many ways one of dependency. Whereas exceptionalism tends to evoke images of arrogant nationalism, a universalism tied to supranational currents has been far more representative of the American experience. Much of the appeal of American policies was traceable to their promotion and defense of a way of life that was not invented by Americans, the right to which was not exclusively American. US foreign policy contributed to the triumph of a universal ideology that was the intellectual property of no nation. Many of the most prominent values associated with the exceptionalist world-view—free trade, human rights, antislavery, anti-imperialism, to name a few—became American only through late adoption or naturalization. Likewise, the spread of consumerism and democracy was not particularly an American triumph. Contributing to this success of nonnationalist ideas was the willingness and the ability to cast policy in a cooperative framework that was congenial to the evolution of a liberal global society. Thus, only by virtue of a continuing commitment to collaborative globalization was American power able to reach its apex. The United States only became a hegemonic power by not behaving like a traditional hegemon.

Viewed from a globalizing perspective, therefore, as opposed to a position built on exceptionalist premises, the making of the post–Cold War world order was not an American project. All the triumphalist talk about America's outsize role credited the nation with an ambition and a degree of power that it did not possess. Because US foreign relations were always about adaptation to larger historical forces over which the United States exercised, at best, only a limited degree of influence, the most notable achievements of US policy depended on a willingness to take the risk that deep historical processes would play themselves out in a beneficial way. And so they did. The success of free trade policies and the spread of consumerism, whose most spectacular expression for a time was found in the American way of life, created a global cultural background, anticipated by few policy makers, that devitalized the appeal of both traditional and ideologically radical competing ways of life. But this was not an outcome that US foreign policy, by itself, was able to produce. The most that can be said is that the United States was instrumental in creating the political and economic context that allowed this background to ripen, in this instance with favorable results.

Finally, the connection to globalization throws cold water on the persisting conviction that the United States, more than any other nation, is naturally in tune with history. In another era, when nations were thought to be history's principal actors, it would have been uncontroversial to see America as the vehicle of history's ambitions, just as Hegel had imagined

275

Prussia to be the temporary resting place of the world spirit. That view of world history as a logical process is no longer taken seriously as a philosophical position. In its place, however, we have been left with an irrational sensibility, the kind that finds reflexive expression in political rhetoric that elevates the United States to the position of predestined world leader. This presumption, which has far more cultural resonance than a philosophical abstraction, has on occasion seduced sophisticated policy makers as well as patriotic yokels.

The belief in a providential historical role has no rational warrant because it entails a commitment to a process that no one fully understands. At least America's rise to global prominence is explainable by the facts, but we still cannot say conclusively why globalization happened or where it is going—nor are we likely to find out any time soon. One can draw up a periodical table of the main elements of globalization, but its complex chemical reactions—the emergence and subsequent trajectory of the globalization process—have yet to receive a definitive historical explanation. That is because a convincing causal account would need to explain the advent of the Industrial Revolution, a task at which a small army of talented economic historians has thus far failed. Untangling its global spread, the relation of politics to globalization, the effects of culture change, and a host of other factors, taken individually or together, is a job much too complicated for historians to handle except by resort to literary techniques in which authors take on godlike qualities. This gap between conceptualization and explanation is one of the shortcomings that most historians who deal with large topics learn reluctantly to accept. To realize that American policy makers have been betting the nation's future on the outcome of a process that no one fully understands should inspire humility rather than the cocksure confidence that radiates from evangelists of exceptionalism.

For some readers, my argument about the primary role of international society may come across as shakier than the views I have tried to throw into question—insubstantial, intangible, ungrounded, empyrean, and only tenuously connected at best to anything that we might consider reality and hard knowledge. The complementary claim about the importance of background beliefs may seem too philosophical, almost metaphysical, which is another way of saying that it is too detached from the kinds of concerns that motivate people in real life. Worse still, my emphasis on a cultural imaginary may strike some as itself being imaginary. It would not be surprising, therefore, if some readers should choose to reject my account as yet another variation on the theme of idealism. For those who are so inclined, the traditional way of telling the story remains attractive because the main contention of my narrative—that US foreign relations in the twentieth century revolved around a commitment to globalization—violates time-honored principles of statecraft based on self-interest, geography, and power drives.

But this ongoing connection to globalization was not conjured out of thin air, nor was policy based on idealism. No nation bases its foreign policy on idealism, and it is just plain silly to think otherwise. As I have argued throughout, few American policy makers and liberal intellectuals in the twentieth century believed that foreign policy was about refashioning a corrupt world in America's idealized self-image by a laying on of hands. Rather, it was about keeping clear the road for globalization. This prioritizing of the general process allowed for the unseemly willingness to tolerate and do business with ideologically odious regimes, provided that those governments posed no fundamental threat to international society. In this matter and many others, global problems took precedence over particular annoyances. The urge to spread American ideals far and wide, which was far more evident in private projects than in public policy, paled before the need to come to terms with a globalization process that had little regard for America's inner yearnings.

Besides, globalization was not an ideal. It was not something transcendent or impossibly abstract, but a concrete reality, the most important reality of recent world history. It was a social fact in the Durkheimian sense of something that exercised real power; so much so that for a time in the nineteenth and twentieth centuries it was taken for a historical juggernaut. What I am saying is what most social scientists and historians believe—that politics is best understood as a product of society and culture. This is not to say that politics did not matter, for obviously it did. But international society, like most societies, is shaped by politics in only partial and ill-defined ways. Though the pressures exerted by globalization did not dictate the form of America's response, globalization was nevertheless an objective, structural process to which all societies, including America, were forced to adapt in one way or an-

277

other. Some nations like Nazi Germany, imperial Japan, and the USSR recognized the power of globalization only to reject it with their own versions of a *Sonderweg*. The United States, in its own way, accepted and promoted the new global reality, while many other nations simply muddled through. The meaning and implications of globalization may have been unclear, but it could not be ignored, for globalization forced nations to change their ways of doing business.

The fact is that the truisms of political realism, which are supposed to hold throughout history, have been challenged and in some respects completely upended by conditions in which the pursuit of power has been superseded by the pursuit of wealth—in which power has become a function of wealth, in which wealth is most effectively produced by market economies, and competitive markets are undergirded by trust, predictability, law, cooperation, and a safe international environment. While wealth is no stranger to power, it is a form of power that is compatible with law, democratic rule, and an autonomous civil society. It may have been possible to bring globalization to a halt before World War II, but, in the half century that followed, what had been a badly misfiring system became a firmly constituted global society. In the nineteenth century, globalization was able to coexist side by side with the established system of power politics. A century later, the possibility of a return to the old diplomacy was at least as far-fetched as the prospect of a globalized system had been a few hundred years ago.[3]

Still, a belief in globalization comes across as impossibly abstract, a concern of intellectuals, perhaps, but not of policy makers. Surely men of affairs—well, men, until recently—could not have been so removed from real-world happenings as to place their chips on something as arcane as globalization. But the whole point of talking about imaginaries is to point out that people in point of fact do think that way; what from an intellectual perspective strikes the eye as obscure and far removed from ordinary life is embedded in each and every one of us in a naturalized worldview that underlies our stance toward everything that we encounter. Just as international society exists as a social fact that affects us whether we think about it or not, globalization is concretely embedded to some degree in the cultural imaginary that we all inhabit. In the case of the United States, the presumption of international cooperation was a vital ingredi-

278

ent baked into America's political culture that internationalist statesmen could not reason their way out of. And, in many surprising ways, that imaginary was an accurate reflection of what international society was.[4]

Idealism is one possible objection to my account; imperial misconduct is another. For those who prefer to see the malevolent guiding hand of the United States behind global events, American exceptionalism is best understood as an accessory to imperialism, to which American culture has been a willing accomplice. For some radical critics of exceptionalism who reject economic determinism, the Cold War was largely an American construction born of an imperialist fantasy, the implication being that the world would have been spared much grief had the United States curbed its ideological impulses. But there were so many more facets to US foreign relations than empire, not least among which was an even more influential anti-imperialist sensibility. The chief problem with critical approaches that attribute America's position to the operation of its power is that people gravitated voluntarily, or maybe tropistically, toward the American position. Given the relative lack of coercion and tribute in the metaphorical American "empire," some critics from the left have been leaning toward the position that international society is the root cause of the problem. Even so, from this perspective, the United States remains complicit as the principal national agent of the impoverishment of humankind's lifeworld.[5]

This critical view of American behavior harbors an assumption that is commonplace in the scholarly marketplace of ideas: that America's international rise depended on negative perceptions of others, racial or cultural others who were conveniently demonized for purposes of mobilization or those who needed to be re-created in America's image. This trait, too, is assumed to have been present from the beginning. In the abstract, the structuralist argument in which good can only have meaning in the face of a contrasting evil makes good sense, hence the appeal of the notion of a "constitutive other." But those who point to America's peculiar arrogance as the source of its exceptionalist claims tend to forget that this trait is not uniquely American. Structural oppositions are a universal property of language making. As a way of creating and maintaining their distinctive identities, all societies need others to other: the French need the Anglo-Saxons and the Belgians (among others), the Canadians need the Americans, the Koreans need Japan, the Irish need the British, the

British need Europe, the Serbs need the Croats, the Swedes need Norwegians, the Greeks need the Turks, the Iranians need the US "great satan," and the Chinese appear to need everybody else, and so on. The reverse side of this coin is that othering also is at work among critics who need the United States to play the villain against the oppressed global masses.[6]

But this approach is far too simple, for identity formation involves more than a process of binary opposition. The same holds true for nations as for individual growth and maturation—besides distinguishing oneself against unlikeable others, positive identification with others is also indispensable. In the case of the United States, those others consisted at first of "civilized" nations, a grouping that was later was expanded to encompass the bulk of the human race. Among other things, globalization helped to drive home the understanding of similarities and shared interests among peoples, conveniently summarized as a common human identity. Over the long run, it is not difference and otherness, but likeness, similarity, and human identity that beg for historical explanation, whose emergence cannot be accounted for by referring to some internal cultural trait. Not least, there also happens to be a factual problem with this argument about the need for others. For if we look at the historical record, it shows that the United States went through substantial stretches in which it lacked the enemy that some find to be congenitally indispensable.[7]

To those who remain skeptical of this narrative, I would respond that the story of US foreign policy over the wide sweep clearly includes imperialism, but it is even more clearly not about empire; it involves a rise to world power, but at bottom it is not about a quest for global ascendancy; it contains ideals, but it is not principally about idealism. It was less about Americanizing the world than reinvigorating the globalization process. Globalization, though not conceived or born in America, was adopted and raised to maturity by America. This willingness to expend much blood and treasure on behalf of goals that other nations were unable to take seriously— that was unique. The end of the Cold War would not have been possible without the United States fighting for global society in 1941, building it in the postwar years, and making it possible for it to flourish throughout the remainder of the century. Despite the geopolitical disasters of the twentieth century, the history of international relations was more—much more— than a dreary tale of endless political conflict and genocidal horrors.

From the perspective of policy makers, the Cold War was not about power politics or empire, but a rescue operation aimed at righting a vessel damaged in a violent storm. It was the product of fear, not of ambition. For the decision makers who took the nation into the Second World War, it was perceived as more a matter of necessity than of choice. So too with the Cold War, which was entered into with trepidation and uncertainty, in the hope of avoiding another world war, fully realizing that another war would likely fulfill Wilson's prediction about the destruction of modern civilization. One could grant the force of subjective feelings and at the same time insist that the world would have been a better place without American leadership. Perhaps. But even if one owns up to the often irrational and excessive features of American postwar policies, of which there were many, one doubts that international society could have been reconstituted without American global activism. Antiglobalizers would not see this as a defense at all, but they have little to offer in the way of attractive practical alternatives.[8]

·········

There is no question that a sense of exceptionalism is a deep-rooted trait of the national character. But the claim that it has been a driver of US foreign relations since the days of the nation's founding and thereby deserves a place of honor among explanations of America's outsize role in the world is historically groundless. To the extent that culture has been a significant factor, this narrative has argued that the cultural background that gave US foreign relations its distinctive shape and coherence only arose and developed from the late nineteenth century onward. What is more, the content of this new outlook bore little resemblance to the kind of swagger that one hears in chants of "We're number one!" Unlike a view that sees exceptionalism as a constant, I believe that my account is empirically more consistent with America's place in world history and more sensitive to the perceptual world of policy making, with its built-in uncertainties and its background understandings, without which the ongoing activities of foreign affairs are impossible.

Those understandings are composed, in varying measures, of faith, knowledge, and uncertainty. In the American case, faith has been reflected in optimism, which is quite distinct from idealism. In the case of the United States, the nation's hopefulness about the direction of world affairs was attributable more to the conclusions drawn from a rather successful record of past experience than to the promptings of national character or Panglossian philosophy. Apart from a supportive history, this optimism also received significant backing from social science, particularly economics, which rested on solid empirical footings. This science was not value free or value neutral, but many of its assumptions stood up rather well in practice. There was a fairly solid pragmatic basis for believing that markets, science and technology, and the unleashing of the human desire to maximize one's talents would have a potent influence for the better. Experience showed that power did flow upward and outward from society while policies that allowed global markets to operate efficiently worked better than other alternatives as a powerful force for global unification, development, and human equality. This was idealism in the sense that modern economics, no longer a dismal science, is idealistic.

Policy makers also operate with an enormous fund of data that, they like to think, gives them superior knowledge of policy problems. But, like anyone else—more so than most people, who are blind to nuances and conflicting considerations—they operate in a climate of uncertainty, fortified only by imperfect knowledge, and exercise only a limited capacity to shape events. Some problems can be successfully managed, some defy human control, while for many others muddling through is the best to be hoped for. As with extraordinary success in the stock market, outcomes attributed to expert knowledge usually owe a great deal to good fortune.

In this case, the turn to globalism was a huge historical gamble that proved to be a winning bet in the short term. But, as Wall Street types make sure to warn, past performance is no guarantee of future results. Because history, like gambling casinos, takes a dim view of steady winners, there is no assurance that globalization will continue to work to America's advantage. There was no inevitability to any of this in the past, nor will there be any in the future. Perhaps coming generations will look back at America's extraordinary position in the second half of the twentieth century as little more than a curiosity in a storm-tossed history of international relations. Or, alternatively, one can imagine it as an important step on the human journey to a better world.

Historians and Exceptionalism

Because their country is assumed to be exceptional, Americans do not believe that all nations are created equal. Unfortunately, such self-evident beliefs tend to become problematic when subjected to close scrutiny. In this case, the difficulty lies in the inconvenient fact that Americans are not alone in having an exalted sense of their national destiny. Many other peoples have also been convinced of the superiority of their ways of life, oftentimes with an intensity that makes American pretentions look modest by comparison, leading one writer to conclude that "exceptionalism has become the rule rather than the exception." In theory, this presents a problem because, strictly speaking, exceptionalism implies uniqueness, but as a matter of practice the existence of cross-cultural similarities has failed to dent the deep conviction that the American way of life is uniquely designed for export. Pesky fault finding tends to be swatted away by the thought that America's exceptional status is only a temporary condition that will wither away once other peoples begin to adopt its distinctive political and social features. Until the arrival of that millennial moment, America will continue to be unique.[1]

Scholarly opinion has diverged dramatically from popular sentiment. By the end of the twentieth century, it was plain to most historians that Americans were "not exceptional . . . in any sense of moral innocence or purity." The same held true for many of the nation's societal features. For a growing number, this assessment was prompted by the desire to overhaul American history by approaching it from a new supranational perspective. In an influential work widely regarded as the manifesto of this cutting-edge outlook, Thomas Bender argued that "on the spectrum of difference the United States is one of many, and there is no single norm from which it deviates—or that it establishes." In a later volume that heralded the adoption of an international research standard, he proposed that "instead of exceptionalism, which presumes the United States to be here and the world over there, the world becomes a diverse terrain of polities, all different, all interdependent." For Bender, "a global perspective reveals that our history is not 'exceptional,' only distinctive." According to another leading scholar, the United States was "simply a nation in a dangerous world like every other—a democratization of distinction, as it were.[2]

Thus, while conceding the trivial point that the United States was different in the way that all nations differ in their run-of-the-mill particularity, such scholars think it more important to emphasize the shared experiences between America and other societies. Most Americans, in reflecting on exceptionalism, are more likely to think about the domestic virtues of their nation than its foreign policy, but the anti-exceptionalist persuasion would seem at first glance to be just as applicable to foreign affairs as to comparisons of domestic institutions and culture. The few social scientific studies that exist tend to reaffirm the view that exceptionalism has little value in explaining the history of US foreign relations. According to one survey of American foreign policy over the centuries, "claims of exceptional U.S. external behavior have been exaggerated." As one scholar has put it, once one filters out the rhetorical noise, it seems clear that "the conduct of U.S. foreign policy has been determined primarily by its relative power and by the inherently competitive nature of international politics." In other words, the United States acted much as any other nation would have behaved in the same circumstances.[3]

Unlike their colleagues in other fields of American history, historians of US foreign relations have been reluctant to abandon exceptionalism for the study of "American variations on larger global themes." Many intelligent people of every ideological persuasion remain convinced that irrepressible exceptionalist notions have left a deep and enduring impact on the history of US foreign relations. While most, though hardly all, would agree that exceptionalist ideas come up short as descriptions of the real world, they also continue to believe that myths have causal importance. For students of foreign policy, the pervasive sense of being second to none, even though mistaken, cannot be dismissed as mere ethnocentricism because wrongheaded beliefs can be as far-reaching as well-founded convictions, especially if they are held by powerful nations like the United States. Exceptionalism is thus a pernicious form of self-delusion, a deeply ingrained cultural fantasy that blocks an understanding of the world as it really is, which in turn results in a distorted foreign policy. "It is not good," as one writer understatedly puts it, "for individuals or nations, to believe things that are not true." That is why diplomatic historians continue to write about how America's exceptionalist sense of self has profoundly influenced America's foreign relations, most notably as the vehicle for various idealistic enthusiasms and imperial excesses.[4]

Condensed from a broad body of literature, the history of this belief and its impact makes for a familiar story that goes roughly like this: American exceptionalism surfaced in early colonial times in John Winthrop's famous depiction of the Massachusetts Bay Colony as a "city upon a hill." It reemerged during the American Revolution in documents like Tom Paine's *Common Sense*. Following the adoption of the Constitution, it resurfaced in the 1790s in the expectation that the revolution would spread to Europe, and it was revived periodically in the nineteenth century by enthusiastic public support for European revolutions. It also took more tangible form in missionary expansion, in an ideology of Manifest Destiny whose ambitions extended far beyond the continent, in American imperialism, and in an Open Door policy in China that foresaw a leading role for America in the Middle Kingdom's eventual modernization and democratization.

In the twentieth century, its quintessential statement was a Wilsonian idealism that saw American constitutionalism as a model for other nations and as a template for international organization. But its most assertive expression came in the worldwide Cold War struggle against Soviet communism when the American way of life became a global export. If anything, the sense of America's unique standing in the world was even more pronounced after the end of the Cold War. It was then that the sense of obligation that came with the nation's exceptional status was bluntly expressed by Madeleine Albright, President Bill Clinton's secretary of state. "If we have to use force," she said, "it is because we are America. We are the indispensable nation. We stand tall. We see

285

further into the future." The career of exceptionalism took an even more dramatic turn a few years later in President George W. Bush's democratizing crusade against terrorism whose purpose, according to a major policy document, was "to seek and support democratic movements and institutions in every nation and culture, with the ultimate goal of ending tyranny in our world."[5]

Because the nation's exceptionalist predisposition is thought to be an ingrained belief, historians have sought to trace its cultural origins to the nation's formative period. In the process of mining the sources from those years, many claim to have struck pay dirt. As one distinguished study puts it, "the normative order to which Americans appealed in the twentieth century had very deep roots in the American past." "By 1776," according to Robert Kagan, "the ambitions driving Americans toward their future overwhelming global power were already in place." The various strands of American foreign policy thought, says another scholar, are "as old as the republic itself." One recent study asserts that "cultural analysis illuminates the remarkable continuity of U.S. foreign policy flowing from a distinctive national identity," while another promises to explain foundational "preconceptions which gave a special direction to American thinking on foreign affairs."[6]

Variations on the theme of culturally embedded exceptionalism are plentiful and ingenious. Some profess to see basic patterns or "themes" established early on, often personified in the archetypal figures of Hamilton and Jefferson. If we are to believe one author's analysis of Washington's farewell address, "every major shift and dimension of American foreign policy . . . are all here in Washington, Hamilton, and Madison's rhetorical masterpiece." Another writer notes "the strength and persistence of a strong ideological impulse that stirred dreams of dominance and animated U.S. policy." Sometimes exceptionalism is described as existing side by side and in tension with other enduring outlooks. If this cultural impulse does in fact exist, it makes sense to argue, as has Walter Russell Mead, who adds Jackson and Wilson to the list of those who embody basic traits, that "American thinking about foreign policy has been relatively stable over the centuries." These kinds of references, with many more to choose from, suggest that exceptionalism is culturally hardwired. If one accepts this idea, it is easy to see exceptionalism as the enduring cultural impulse behind America's rise to world power.[7]

In my view, this belief in the impact of a belief is a beguiling fantasy about the power of a fantasy. For when one looks at it closely, the historical narrative that supports exceptionalism turns out to have some serious defects. Most notably, scholarly assertions about the effects of exceptionalism on policy turn out to be quite vague, the usual pattern being one in which expressions of American singularity are followed by foreign policy actions that allegedly flowed from them. Such post hoc arguments do little to establish whether declarations of exceptionalism were smoke screens that concealed deeper motives, rhetorical conventions whose purpose was to increase social solidarity, or causal mechanisms for translating belief into action. By and large, the case for the influence of an exceptionalist impulse in American foreign relations is assumed rather than proved; it is left for the reader to infer what the historian has failed to demonstrate.[8]

Many of the difficulties of execution stem from underlying problems with conceptualization. To begin with, it is widely acknowledged that there is no single kind of foreign policy that grows from this fertile soil of exceptionalism—things would be much simpler if this were not the case. It has long been recognized that American exceptionalism has shown different and sometimes contradictory faces to the world. One side was republican exceptionalism, first articulated during the American Revolution, which was based on the idea that America was an example or role model for the rest of the world. This idea nicely complemented the policy of political isolation from European affairs that was followed throughout the nineteenth century. But isolationism and its presumed inwardness has attracted less interest among historians than the other face, that of an expansionist, crusading, missionary America forcefully spreading the nation's power and values in a quest to reshape the world in its own image.[9]

Unfortunately, the coexistence of these contradictory Jekyll and Hyde guises suggests that exceptionalism is causally empty or a symptom of cultural pathology, about which I will have a few things to say below. If exceptionalism was two sided or open ended in its foreign policy possibilities, it would be hardly worth talking about, just as a weather forecast that predicted either a placid summer's day or a howling blizzard would not merit serious attention. Exceptionalism might still be a side dish for certain policies, it might be the stuff of pep talks, or it might serve as a justification for policies that are adopted for altogether different reasons, but the absence of an autonomous power to move and the capability of going in opposing directions would suggest that the actual course of events is set by something else. Indeed, that "something else" has been the subject of this book.[10]

There is a more sophisticated way of putting the argument, however, in which one kind of exceptionalism is succeeded as a matter of course by the other. In this view, overland expansion ripened into overseas empire, isolationism transmuted into internationalism, and regionalism evolved into world power. Typically that is done by separating expansion into "phases." As one distinguished historian argues the case, the United States changed insensibly from an empire *of* liberty in which the nation stood as a shining example, into an empire *for* liberty in which American ways were forcefully imposed upon others. Another scholar, in describing the transition from agricultural advance to commercial and cultural expansion, conjures up images of shape-shifting in which character remained constant: "a second kind of empire, a continuation of the first but seldom involving any settlement." But if one compares the two varieties of expansion, one needs to acknowledge their differences, which are not trivial at all. It may all be H_2O in the end, but whether one is sustained by water, frozen with ice, or scalded with steam makes a huge difference to the quality of life or whether life can survive at all. Another historian uses the analogy of a prudent Old Testament isolationism being succeeded by a chiliastic New Testament exceptionalism. The closest biological counterpart to this kind of change is the process of metamorphosis in which, by their very natures, tadpoles develop into frogs or caterpillars turn into butterflies. In an analogous way, isolationism and internationalism can be seen as sequential expressions of an underlying impulse, or as phases of some foreordained pattern of development.[11]

But this version of cultural determination is also open to serious objections. One problem with assertions of a cultural predestination toward a universalistic foreign policy involves the question of whether *any* culture, qua culture, is capable of generating the conditions for a universalistic outlook. There are many reasons to think not. In its most basic functioning, a culture produces and reproduces repetitive day-to-day behaviors that feel natural and commonsensical to its members. At this level, a culture, if left to its own devices, cannot be the source of novelty, except perhaps in the way that language changes through a long process of cultural drift via a slow and haphazard accretion of minor variations. The acceptance of unthinking, naturalized assumptions and behaviors leaves little room for agonizing policy choices and dramatic departures. Nor is it possible for culture to transcend itself. To the degree that culture relies upon tradition and tends to closure it is inherently hostile to cosmopolitan universalism, to the point that it comes near to being its conceptual opposite. Culture in this anthropological sense is a redoubt of localism and particularism, a grain of sand without a corresponding universe. As Walter Bagehot once observed, fixed custom "explains the necessity of isolation in early society."[12]

Breaking out of this solipsistic cage requires conscious deliberation and articulation of ideas by means of which a world outside the culture can be imagined and sympathetically experienced. But this expansion of sensibility comes via intercultural contact that breaks the spell of culture. Once prereflective assumptions are opened up to discussion, ideas and choices that formerly would not have been entertained come into view, that is, ideas that are not cultural in a deterministic sense. One could start with the more modest assumption that culture sets boundaries and creates an environment of action—that is, that culture is not instrumentally causal except in the most trivial sense—only to have other serious problems arise. Culture in this sense can only tell people what not to do while allowing a wide range of possibilities for actions in which choices are made by noncultural means. As I have argued in chapter 1, in the case of the United States those cultural boundaries, in combination with the restraints imposed by geography, from the beginning actually worked against exceptionalism in foreign policy. The cultural possibility of political internationalism was not present at the creation; it came into being only later.[13]

More problematic still, the belief in the persistence of culturally embedded drives, whether they take the form of impulses for expansion and empire or binary traits such as isolationism/internationalism or real-ism/idealism rests on a rickety biological metaphor that likens cultural change to genetic development. Biological analogies have their uses, but this metaphor is impossibly hobbled from the outset by an apples-and-oranges problem of incommensurability. For one thing, the reliance on organic metaphors does violence to our understanding of the place of individuals in the social matrix. As Friedrich Hayek once observed, the organic character of biological analogies falsely describes the position of individuals in societies, for unlike cells in a biological organism, individuals "do not occupy fixed places . . . which they retain once and for all."[14]

There is an even more damaging, perhaps lethal, confusion at work. Whereas individual organisms develop according to a fixed genetic blue-print, cultures evolve. The biggest problem with the assumption that exceptionalism is immanent, that is, that it is internally programmed or built-in, is that the analogy is based on nonevolutionary biology. Unlike the behavioral repertoires imposed upon individual organisms by their genetic programming, cultural change can sometimes occur swiftly, un-expectedly, and sweepingly, without any readily apparent predetermi-nation. Recasting cultural change in evolutionary terms also requires the addition of another variable: an environment to which the organism needs to adapt. In this instance, that external variable was the rise of an international society that accelerated and magnified the degree of cul-ture change. References to America's faith in progress or idealism miss the degree to which this outlook was not self-determining or unfolding from within, but was instead the product of a pragmatic relationship with the world.

To be sure, the present is encumbered by our historical inheritance and there is a path dependency at work in which all developments are traceable back to primordial events, but that does not mean that a telos or immanent force was present from the beginning to guide events at every step of the way. The assumption that such a force is at work is pro-foundly antihistorical, for it fails to acknowledge that historical changes are contingent upon prior developments in time that were themselves contingent. I take this to be the meaning of Kierkegaard's aphorism that "Life can only be understood backwards; but it must be lived forwards."

I have been at pains in this book, particularly in chapter 2, to show that discontinuity introduced by radically new circumstances makes more explanatory sense. Once this is factored in, America's journey to world power can more readily be explained as a series of tentative and unprogrammed responses to the contingency of globalization in which policy was a process of adjusting to unforeseen external forces that were transforming the world and American society. From this perspective, policy was clearly not the product of cultural predestination.[15]

Moreover, earlier and later cultural forms are not commensurable. They are different in fundamental respects, which is why historians are akin to time-traveling anthropologists. As noted by Maurice Merleau-Ponty, "Certain notions cannot be attained except by a series of successive steps and by a sedimentation of meaning which makes it impossible for the new sense to appear before its time and apart from certain factual conditions"—which means that Elvis, or someone like him, could not have appeared in the eighteenth century. Among other things, the process of culture change is an opening of horizons through an ongoing process of creation in which the possibilities for further change at any point in time are bounded by what a culture has become, not on what it primordially is. To assume the causal persistence of a stable identity across time of American society misses the mutation that has taken place since the eighteenth century, a time when Americans were culturally closer to the ancients than to the moderns. That is to say, cultures are as much creations as creators, akin to worlds in which tadpoles turn into princes and moths into frogs.[16] Therefore internationalism or globalism cannot be the product of a fixed culture that dictates responses and attitudes to various situations. Cultures happen to be among humankind's longer-lasting creations, but culture is more open than that. To take but one example, if language is one of the deepest forms of culture that shapes our identities, it is also the greatest source of human creativity. Biological analogies cannot capture that kind of change.

Well, then, it might be argued, the exceptionalist urge in American culture was so powerful that it simply had to find an outlet. Without it, US foreign relations would not have ascended to the dizzying heights of world power. One cannot help but notice the similarity of this line of argument to Freud's idea of unconscious libido that will find expression and get its due one way or another. Perhaps, but like Freud's theories in general, this one does not have the advantage of being testable or provable. Historians are not scientists, but the rules of the game insist that they proceed on the basis of evidence rather than assertion. The basic problem, as this book has attempted to show, is one of historical evidence rather than logical refutation. But supposing that we were to play the neo-Freudian game, it might be worth pointing out that Freud's scheme allows for repression, which is the basis of civilization. How does impulse control (a good thing) fit into the exceptionalist argument, which assumes that the exceptionalist impulse is irrepressible?

While dubious biological analogies inform much scholarship on exceptionalism, a growing number of scholars are emphasizing the role of the international environment. Probably the most important school draws methodological inspiration from the adoption of an international perspective. While the cultural approach works from the inside out, this new approach starts from the outside in. Its adherents insist on studying the United States from the international context in which the nation has always been situated. One result of this changed perspective is a radical deflation of exceptionalism. But if this is true, that leaves international historians with the task of explaining the functional role played by exceptionalist rhetoric. It may be, as Dorothy Ross has cryptically suggested, that exceptionalist ideology has "made American experience more different from that of other countries than would have been the case had Americans a more differentiated view of themselves." I take this to mean that it added marginally to American distinctiveness. Or it may have been a smoke screen or a form of false consciousness. To the extent that it has influenced foreign policy practice by animating attempts to impose those false notions, exceptionalism has made life more difficult for all concerned.[17]

Although the emphasis on international history makes allowances for the political distortions of exceptionalism, its chief effect is to minimize the role of politics. One of the pioneering promoters of international history, Akira Iriye, has called for the study of "cross-national activities by individuals and groups of people, not always or primarily as representatives of governments but as agents for movements transcending national entities." This downplaying of the importance of political affairs is implicit in the belief that the history of the past few centuries has been driven by deep sociocultural forces associated with the Industrial Revolution. Agreed. But Iriye also argues that the broad array of transnational activities that engage the attention of the new historians "have developed with their own momentum." This view parallels a larger shift among historians over the course of the twentieth century in which increasing attention has been paid to social and cultural matters at the expense of political themes—great men, politics, dates, wars—that formerly dominated historiography. As a result, they have been able to open up new areas of research and to generate a world of fresh and exciting data. Overall, the new international history provides a welcome corrective to previous navel-gazing by making it possible to see the United States as an outlier of a European civilization that itself was situated within a broader geographic and historical context.[18]

But this approach, for all its virtues, is not without its own problems. One difficulty is professional. The fascination with the sociocultural aspects of international relations has created a fault line among historians of foreign relations between those who care little for politics and those for whom politics continues to hold pride of place. Many scholars continue to focus on politics and decision making while a growing number of younger souls prefer to devote their careers to the investigation of transnational cultural and social processes. Nevertheless, despite this conceptual and methodological schism, the two approaches continue to come down on the same side of some important issues. For the social historians, the methodological devaluation of politics means that the traditional "rise to world power" narrative was an inevitable consequence of socioeconomic realities. That is to say: Put any other people in America's place and their behavior would have been much the same. This also happens to be the view of those who continue to peer at international relations through political lenses. While they differ in the weight they assign to the political and the social, both approaches also tend to uncritically accept globalization as something that just happened.

So many references have already been made within the text to realism's failure to adequately account for the transformative impact of globalization that I will not further harp on its shortcomings. But international history, with its depiction of the United States as just another country and its emphasis on social forces, has also been blind to the connection between globalization and US foreign relations. This anopsia is particularly telling in its failure to appreciate the extent to which the continued survival of globalization was made possible by American foreign policy, a political process. For good measure, one might add that by preserving the globalization process and by putting in place the institutional conditions for its revival, US policy has contributed significantly to making it possible for historians to think on a global scale in the first place. In short, international history misses the distinctive role played by the United States in relation to an exceptional historical process.

Realists neglect globalization; international historians neglect power; and both neglect culture. Thus, while the new globalized American history argues, quite correctly, that one cannot understand American history apart from the world, my view is that the modern world cannot be understood without taking into account the outsized role played by the United States. As this book has argued, globalization began as a process largely independent of international politics, but after a certain point it probably would have collapsed without active political involvement on the part of the United States. Being part of the world does not automatically make one ordinary. There have been extraordinary nations just as there have been exceptional individuals who continue to deserve biographies. One of the shortcomings of international history, which is a form of social history, is that it takes little interest in either.

The foregoing remarks should not be considered as an outright rejection of the views of historical colleagues with whom I differ. History is complicated and polyphonic. Disagreements among historians are always a matter of degree. Historians, no matter how bad, are never entirely wrong, even those who write historical propaganda for totalitarian regimes; and, by the same token, no historian is completely right. All histories are, to a greater or lesser degree, incomplete and inadequate to the task of describing the world in its nonreplicable complexity. My modest contribution to an improved understanding of the issue of American exceptionalism has amounted to pointing out that existing approaches suffer from incompleteness. When, in addition to many other factors, one tries to take into account the effect of globalization on US foreign policy, the history looks quite different, but it is by no means complete.

NOTES

295

INTRODUCTION

1. Joyce Appleby, "Recovering America's Ethnic Diversity: Beyond Exceptionalism," *Journal of American History* 79 (1992): 429.

CHAPTER ONE

1. Thomas Paine, *Common Sense* (Charleston, SC: Forgotten Books, 2008), 61. The classic assertion that the United States was born free by virtue of being unencumbered by a feudal legacy was made by Louis Hartz in his influential book *The Liberal Tradition in America: An Interpretation of American Political Thought since the Revolution* (New York: Harcourt, Brace, 1955).

2. Carl Richard, *The Founding Fathers and the Classics: Greece, Rome, and the American Enlightenment* (Cambridge, MA: Harvard University Press, 1994).

3. Bernard Bailyn, *The Ideological Origins of the American Revolution* (Cambridge, MA: Belknap Press of Harvard University Press, 1967); J. G. A. Pocock, ed., *The Political Works of James Harrington* (New York: Cambridge University Press, 1977), 147.

4. Madison's abandonment of republican localism was hardly a clean break, however, for he was simultaneously reaffirming a classical view of democracy in which the ever-present danger of mob rule needed to be kept in check by public-spirited elites. And despite his emphasis on geographic expanse, it was understood that the local politics of the country would continue to be dominated by small self-governing communities that were thoroughly republican in spirit.

5. Paul A. Rahe, *Republics Ancient and Modern: Classical Republicanism and the American Revolution* (Chapel Hill: University of North Carolina Press, 1994), 733–44; Jefferson to Joseph Priestley, March 21, 1801. Unless otherwise noted, all quotations from Jefferson can be found in Founders Online, National Archives (http://founders.archives.gov); Gordon S. Wood, *The Radicalism of the American Revolution* (New York: Knopf, 1992), 7; Paine, *Common Sense*, 22.

6. Quoted in Rahe, *Republics Ancient and Modern*, 663. The traditional view of the anarchic and warlike character of the international order was made by Alexander Hamilton in two

classic essays in *The Federalist*, numbers 6 and 11, and by John Jay in *Federalist* number 4. "It is too true," said Jay, "however disgraceful it may be to human nature, that nations in general will make war whenever they have a prospect of getting anything by it." Many other important Founders agreed. As Andrew Bacevich has noted, "the hardheaded lawyers, merchants, farmers, and slaveholding plantation owners gathered in Philadelphia that summer did not set out to create a church. They founded a republic." *The Limits of Power: The End of American Exceptionalism* (New York: Metropolitan Books, 2008), 19.

7. Paine, *Common Sense*, 1. For the argument that Madison's solution to the problem of size was also a way of addressing the classical problem of interrepublican warfare, see David C. Hendrickson, *Union, Nation, or Empire: The American Debate over International Relations, 1789–1941* (Lawrence: University Press of Kansas, 2009), 69. Hendrickson argues that the "Philadelphia system" was itself a foreign policy construct, "a self-conscious escape from the European system." One should add that the contemporary impact of Winthrop's oft-quoted statement is questionable inasmuch as it was only unearthed at the end of the nineteenth century.

8. Jefferson to George Mason, February 4, 1791; Jefferson to Tench Coxe, June 1, 1795.

9. Jefferson to Abigail Adams, 1787; Jefferson to Madame Comtesse de Tessé, March 20, 1787; Jefferson to Carlo Bellini, September 30, 1785; Joseph Ellis, *American Sphinx: The Character of Thomas Jefferson*, 150–51, describes Jefferson's revolutionary sensibility as follows: "he believed that the random violence and careening course of the French Revolution were part of a lamentable but passing chapter in a larger story of triumphant global revolution."

10. Jefferson to John Breckinridge, January 29, 1800; Jefferson to Joseph Priestley, November 29, 1802, in *Jefferson: Political Writings*, ed. Joyce Appleby and Terence Ball (New York, Cambridge University Press, 1999), 178. Lawrence S. Kaplan, *Jefferson and France: An Essay on Politics and Political Ideas* (New Haven, CT: Yale University Press, 1967); Jefferson to Lafayette, May 14, 1817, in *The Writings of Thomas Jefferson*, ed. H. A. Washington (New York: Riker, Thorne & Co., 1854), 7:66.

11. Jefferson to John Adams, September 4,1823; also Jefferson to Lafayette, February 14, 1815, in *The Jeffersonian Cyclopedia* (New York: Funk & Wagnalls, 1900), 501.

12. S. Todd Lowry, "Ancient and Medieval Economics," in *A Companion to the History of Economic Thought*, ed. Jeff E. Biddle, Jon B. Davis, and Warren J. Samuels (Malden, MA: Blackwell, 2003), 11–12; Joel Barlow, quoted in James A. Field Jr., *America and the Mediterranean World, 1776–1882* (Princeton, NJ: Princeton University Press, 1969), 15–16; Felix Gilbert, *To the Farewell Address: Ideas of Early American Foreign Policy* (Princeton, NJ: Princeton University Press, 1961), 50.

13. Michael J. Sandel, Democracy's *Discontent: America in Search of a Public Philosophy* (Cambridge, MA: Belknap Press of Harvard University Press, 1996), 138; John E. Crowley, *The Privileges of Independence: Neomercantilism and the American Revolution* (Baltimore: Johns Hopkins, 1993), xii.

14. Jefferson to G. K. van Hogendorp, October 13, 1785.

15. A strong case could be made for Hamilton being in some ways more of an economic internationalist than Jefferson, despite being wedded to traditional views of commerce. He was realistic about the need to work within the mercantilist system, warts and all, and he was less willing than the Jeffersonians to attempt economic coercion—an inversion of positions in which the warlike Hamilton believed in commerce, whereas the pacific Jefferson did not. On the impact of trade sanctions more generally, see C. Satyapathy, "Trade Sanctions and Other Barriers to Free Trade," *Economic and Political Weekly* 34, no. 51 (December 18–24, 1999): 3583.

16. Jefferson, *Notes on the State of Virginia* (Richmond, VA: J. W. Randolph, 1853), 189; Rahe, *Republics Ancient and Modern*, 742–43; Jefferson to Governor Langdon, March 5, 1810; Jefferson to Edmund Pendleton, April 22, 1799. Machiavelli had little to say about commerce, except to note that war was a way of achieving wealth, but war came first in importance. Commerce was good insofar as it increased the capacity to make war, but bad because it tended to promote a mercantile mentality, which was harmful to a republic's virtue. Nevertheless, the new commercial property-holding elites in cities seemed preferable to the feudal nobility's ownership of landed property. Robert Kocis, *Machiavelli Redeemed* (Bethlehem, PA: Lehigh University Press, 1998), 178; Frederick G. Whelan, *Hume and Machiavelli: Political Realism and Liberal Thought* (Lanham, MD: Lexington Books, 2004), 214–15.

17. Adam Smith, *An Inquiry into the Nature and Causes of the Wealth of Nations*, vol. 1 (London: Methuen & Co., 1904), 432–33; Douglas A. Irwin, *Against the Tide: An Intellectual History of Free Trade* (Princeton, NJ: Princeton University Press, 1996), 81–82.

18. Jefferson to the Republican Citizens of Washington County, Maryland, March 31, 1809, in *The Writings of Thomas Jefferson*, ed. Albert Ellery Bergh (Washington, DC: Thomas Jefferson Memorial Association, 1907), 16:358–59; Jefferson to the Citizens of Washington March 4, 1809, in ibid., 346; Sandel, *Democracy's Discontent*, 149.

19. In his notable 1793 Report on Foreign Commerce, Jefferson wrote of commerce: "could it be relieved from all its shackles in all parts of the world, could every country be employed in producing that which nature has best fitted it to produce, and each be free to exchange with others *mutual surpluses* [my emphasis] for mutual wants, the greatest mass possible would then be produced of those things which contribute to human life and happiness; the numbers of mankind would be increased, and their condition bettered." In Paul Leicester Ford, ed., *The Works of Thomas Jefferson* (New York: G. P. Putnam's Sons, 1905), 8:111.

20. Nicholas Greenleaf Onuf, *The Republican Legacy in International Thought* (Cambridge: Cambridge University Press, 1998), 243.

21. Joyce Appleby, *Liberalism and Republicanism in the Historical Imagination* (Cambridge, MA: Harvard University Press, 1992), 335; D. A. Forward, "The Tariff Policy of the United States as a Creditor Nation," *Annals of the American Academy* 95 (May 1921): 222. Or, as Onuf puts it: "Conspicuously missing from republican thought throughout its long and complex history is any conception of economic activity, of the economy as a sphere of activity that can (if given a chance) operate according to its own logic." Onuf, *The Republican*

Legacy, 247. James A. Field Jr., in his classic *America and the Mediterranean World,* relies primarily upon poetry to make his case. Neither Field nor Felix Gilbert supply much in the way of supporting quotations about the revolutionary impact of free trade. Revolutionary localism found its most concise practical expression in Hamilton's *Federalist* number 11 in which he imagined the world as "divided into four parts, each having a distinct set of interests."

22. As Michael Sandel has made the point, "the republican tradition has always emphasized that the civic project, the formation of citizenship, and the exercise of self-government must unfold in particular places, as Aristotle wrote of the polis." Interview with Michael Sandel, *Harvard Review of Philosophy* (Spring 1996): 70.

23. "It is anachronistic to speak of international thought—ways of thinking that are specific to the world of states—before there was such a world. In republican times, there could be no international thought." Onuf, *The Republican Legacy,* 3.

24. Louis-Auguste Félix de Beaujour, *Sketch of the United States of America: At the Commencement of the Nineteenth Century, from 1800 to 1810* (London, 1814), 284. So powerful did this tide of westward expansion become that historian Frederick Jackson Turner in 1893 declared the recurrent frontier experience to be essential to American democracy, a means of national renewal through expansion that was later construed by many historians as having created an expansionist pattern for the nation's international experience.

25. Alexis De Tocqueville, *Democracy in America* (New York: Edwin Walker, 1850), 441; my interpretation is informed by Ernest May's, *The Making of the Monroe Doctrine* (Cambridge, MA: Harvard University Press, 1975), which argued that the Monroe Doctrine was the product of domestic politics and an unreal danger from abroad.

26. Richard W. Van Alstyne, *The Rising American Empire* (New York and Oxford: Blackwell, 1960), 7.

27. Anders Stephanson, *Manifest Destiny: American Expansionism and the Empire of Right* (New York: Hill and Wang, 1995), sees the belief in divine sanction as a persistent source of expansionist behavior over the long term.

28. Frederick Merk, *Manifest Destiny and Mission in American History: A Reinterpretation* (New York: Knopf, 1963). Although the notion of "interests" offers a good shorthand explanation of American overland expansion, the concept of interest is actually quite slippery. Interest-based explanations would appear at first sight to offer rock-bottom causal explanations, akin to physiological drives like sex or hunger, but they quickly become quite problematic. On some of the idea's difficulties, see Richard Swedberg, "Can There Be a Sociological Concept of Interest?," *Theory and Society* (2005): 359–90. Norman Graebner, *Empire on the Pacific: A Study in American Continental Expansion* (New York: Ronald Press, 1955), with its emphasis on commercial interests, provides the classic realist interpretation.

29. Alexis de Tocqueville, Notebook, July 20, 1831, quoted in Louis P. Masur, *1831: Year of Eclipse* (New York: Hill and Wang, 2001), 188; Sean Wilentz, *The Rise of American Democracy: Jefferson to Lincoln* (New York: W. W. Norton, 1963), 263; Charles Lyell, *Principles of Geology* (Philadelphia: James Key, Jun. & Brother, 1837), 91.

30. Message to Congress, December 7, 1830, in *The Addresses and Messages of the Presidents of the United States,* comp. Edwin Williams (New York: Edward Walker, 1846), 1:7; John E. Yellen, "The Transformation of the Kelahari !Kung," in *Limited Wants, Unlimited Means: A Reader on Hunter-Gatherer Economics and the Environment,* ed. John M. Gowdy (Washington, DC: Island Press, 1998), 22–23. The process of cultural extinction continues. See Dmitrii D. Bogoiavlenskii, "Russia's Northern Indigenous Peoples: Are They Dying Out?," in *Hunters and Gatherers in the Modern World,* ed. Peter P Schweitzer, Megan Bisele, and Robert K. Hitchcock (New York: Berghahn, 2000), 326–40; George Peter Murdock, "The Current Status of the World's Hunting and Gathering Peoples," in *Man the Hunter,* ed. Richard B. Lee and Irven DeVore (Chicago: Aldine, 1968), 13–20; Robert V. Hine and John Mack Faragher, *The American West: A New Interpretive History* (New Haven, CT: Yale University Press, 2000), 27.

31. Simon Schama, *The American Future: A History* (New York: Ecco, 2009), 326.

32. Michael H. Hunt, *The American Ascendancy: How the United States Gained and Wielded Global Dominance* (Chapel Hill: University of North Carolina Press, 2007), 12; Walter A. McDougall, *Promised Land, Crusader State: The American Encounter with the World since 1776* (Boston and New York: Houghton Mifflin Company, 1997), 78; William Pfaff, *The Irony of Manifest Destiny: The Tragedy of America's Foreign Policy* (New York: Walker & Co., 2010), 172; "Barbarism and Civilization," *Atlantic Monthly* 7, no. 39 (January 1861): 61.

33. The same was true of the United States, whose government, in Tocqueville's words, "depends entirely on legal fictions; the Union is an ideal nation which only exists in the mind, and whose limits and extent can only be discerned by the understanding." Alexis de Tocqueville, *Democracy in America,* vol. 1, trans. Henry Reeve (Cambridge: Sever and Francis, 1863), 211.

34. Matthew Pratt Gutterl, *American Mediterranean: Southern Slaveholders in the Age of Emancipation* (Cambridge, MA: Harvard University Press, 2008), esp. 1–39.

35. Jefferson to Thomas Leiper, June 12, 1815, in *Jefferson's Works* 11:477–78.

36. *Sketch of the Life of Louis Kossuth, Governor of Hungary* (New York: Stringer & Townsend, 1851), 25.

37. For the influence of American constitutionalism through the first half of the nineteenth century, see Bernard Bailyn, *To Begin the World Anew: The Genius and Ambiguities of the Founding Fathers* (New York: Alfred A. Knopf, 2003), 131–49. Actually, the American Declaration of Independence appears to have been more widely copied. See David Armitage, *The Declaration of Independence: A Global History* (Cambridge, MA: Harvard University Press, 2007). For figures on democratization—fuzzy but probably the best to be hoped for—see Tatu Vanhanen, *The Emergence of Democracy: A Comparative Study of 119 States, 1850–1979* ((New York: Routledge, 1984), 70. Percentages are found in Vanhanen, "A New Dataset for Measuring Democracy, 1810–1998," *Journal of Peace Research* 37, no. 2 (2000): 259. The most detailed study of the US response to the revolutions of 1848 winds up by concluding that their chief impact was upon America's domestic politics. See Timothy

Mason Roberts, *Distant Revolutions: 1848 and the Challenge to American Exceptionalism* (Charlottesville: University of Virginia Press, 2009).

38. William H. Marling, *How American Is Globalization?* (Baltimore: Johns Hopkins, 2008), 194–95.

CHAPTER TWO

1. Eric Hobsbawm, *The Age of Revolution: Europe, 1789–1848* (London: Weidenfeld and Nicolson, 1962), 1; John Bach McMaster, "A Century of Social Betterment," *Atlantic Monthly* 79, no. 471 (January 1897): 20; Josiah Strong, *The New Era; or, The Coming Kingdom* (New York: Baker & Taylor, 1893), 2. See also [Rev. Treadwell Walden], "Man under Sealed Orders," *Atlantic Monthly* 9, no. 55 (May 1862): 530, in which the author noted that "we live in an era when progress is so new as to be a matter of amazement."

For those readers who expect me to provide a precise definition of globalization, my instinct would be to hide behind Friedrich Nietzsche's caveat that "only something which has no history is capable of being defined." Nevertheless, I would maintain that the globalization concept is simply an updated version of civilization, the main differences being that globalization, because of its connection to the social sciences, has a greater degree of conceptual differentiation and refinement, has jettisoned the nineteenth-century sense of unilinear development and cultural hierarchy, and, with some degree of success, has made a conscious attempt at value neutrality by disassociating globalization from Westernization. Obviously, late twentieth-century globalization was far deeper, wider, and more complex, but it remains clearly recognizable as a luxuriant outgrowth of more modest nineteenth century beginnings.

Some historians believe that globalization has earlier—much earlier—origins. By taking things to an extreme, from a rigorous genealogical point of view one could easily locate the origins of globalization in the Paleolithic era. Though that approach has the virtue of pointing to important global connections in centuries preceding the nineteenth, e.g., the Silk Road between classical Rome and China, this emphasis on continuity cannot explain how a global society emerged. An obsession with path dependency can also obscure the emergence of genuine novelty in history. As my argument thus far should make clear, I am not sympathetic to originalist genealogical accounts. Nevertheless, the belief that globalization is something totally new, which emerged in the 1980s, is also a historically dubious view.

2. Bruce Mazlish, *Civilization and Its Contents* (Stanford, CA: Stanford University Press, 2004); Thomas Peyser, *Utopia and Cosmopolis: Globalization in the Era of American Literary Realism* (Durham, NC: Duke University Press, 1998), x. See also the review by Johan Goudsblom, "Civilization: The Career of a Controversial Concept," *History and Theory* 45 (May 2006): 288–97.

3. [Charles Francis Adams Jr.], "The Railroad System," *North American Review* 104 (1867): 483–84. Reprinted in Charles Francis Adams Jr. and Henry Adams, *Chapters of Erie and Other Essays* (Boston: James R. Osgood and Company, 1871), 339.

4. Extract from September 1987 interview for *Woman's Own*, Margaret Thatcher Foundation, http://www.margaretthatcher.org/document/106689; Arthur Link, et al., eds. *The Papers*

of Woodrow Wilson (Princeton, NJ: Princeton University Press, 1966–94), 14:240. See Lester Frank Ward's preface to the second edition of *Dynamic Sociology, or Applied Social Science, as Based upon Statical Sociology and the Less Complex Sciences* (New York: D. Appleton & Co., 1920).

5. Ernest Gellner, *Plough, Sword and Book* (Chicago: University of Chicago Press, 1988), 108; Roland Robertson, *Globalization: Global Theory and Global Culture* (London: Sage, 1992), 8–31. An international sociology would not emerge until the 1980s, when sociologists took the lead in writing about globalization. The International Sociological Association, and its journal, *International Sociology*, were founded in 1986. For a programmatic statement of some of the new field's commonsense assumptions, see Edward A. Tiryakian, "Sociology's Great Leap Forward: The Challenge of Internationalisation," *International Sociology* 1 (June 1986): 159. Historians of foreign relations were even slower to take up this theme as they continued for far too long to write about foreign relations as a process that centered on decision makers. Evan Luard, *International Society* (New York: New Amsterdam, 1990), is a pioneering work whose argument is that an international society exists whose basic attributes differ in degree but not in kind from territorially bounded societies.

6. Bruce Mazlish, *A New Science: The Breakdown of Connections and the Birth of Sociology* (New York: Oxford University Press, 1989).

7. Émile Durkheim, *The Rules of Sociological Method*, trans. Sarah A. Solovay and John H. Mueller (New York: Free Press 1938), 10.

8. "Table-Talk," *Appleton's* 5 (January 28, 1871): 114.

9. Thomas Risse-Kappen, ed., *Bringing Transnational Relations Back In: Non-State Actors, Domestic Structures, and International Institutions* (New York: Cambridge University Press, 1995); Robert Keohane and Joseph Nye, eds., *Transnational Relations and World Politics* (Cambridge, MA: Harvard University Press, 1971); Akira Iriye, "Cultural History and International History: How They Might Connect" (paper delivered at the University of Paris 7—Denis Diderot, June 3, 1999).

10. Akira Iriye, *Cultural Internationalism and World Order* (Baltimore: Johns Hopkins University Press, 1997), sets forth the most important historical argument on behalf of the existence of two autonomous spheres. His emphasis on "visions of international community" presupposes the emergence of international society. It bears emphasizing that even Marx had great difficulty in making the intellectual shift in the 1840s from an earlier fixation on the division of labor to his thinking in the late 1850s in which he finally emphasized forces of production.

11. "What Are We Going to Make?," *Atlantic Monthly* 2 (1858): 91; Beard quoted in Peyser, *Utopia and Cosmopolis*, 14–15.

12. J. R. McNeill and William H. McNeill, *The Web: A Bird's-Eye View of Human History* (New York: W. W. Norton, 2003).

13. "Strange Countries for to See," *Atlantic Monthly* 4 (1859): 725; Nathaniel Shaler, *Nature and Man in America* (New York, 1891), 149. Iriye, *Global Community: The Role of International Organizations in the Making of the Contemporary World* (Berkeley: University of California Press, 2002), 7–8, offers a concise discussion of the scholarly literature on international so-

ciety. For my purposes, Evan Luard, *International Society* (Basingstoke: Macmillan, 1990), and Luard, *Basic Texts in International Relations: The Evolution of Ideas about International Society* (New York: St. Martin's Press, 1992), are good starting points, though still quite rudimentary in many respects. Theoretically far more sophisticated, but coming to my attention too late for use in this book was an important work, Barry Buzan, *From International to World Society* (Cambridge: Cambridge University Press, 2004). But see also Raymond Williams, *Keywords: A Vocabulary of Culture and Society* (New York: Oxford University Press, 1976), 291–95.

14. "Physical Science and the Useful Arts in their Relation to Christian Civilization," *New Englander and Yale Review* 9 (November 1851): 494.

15. "What Are We Going to Make?," *Atlantic Monthly* 2 (1858): 101; "The Ideal Tendency," *Atlantic Monthly* 1 (1857): 778; "Civilization: American and European," *American Whig Review* 3, no. 6 (June 1846): 616. .

16. Francis Lieber, "An Ode to the Sub-Atlantic Telegraph," *Living Age* 52 (March 7, 1857): 606; [Rev. Treadwell Walden], "Man under Sealed Orders," 537; Adams, "The Railroad System," 483. The compass and gunpowder, said one writer, led to "the abridgement—I may say the extinction—of despotic human power, the equalization of human physical power, the consequent diffusion of it among the people, and the just appreciation of individual rights and duties." "Ancient and Modern Civilization," *United States Democratic Review* 24 (May 1849): 131, 453.

17. Theodore H. Von Laue, *The World Revolution of Westernization: The Twentieth Century in Global Perspective* (New York: Oxford University Press, 1987); Godfrey Hodgson, *The Myth of American Exceptionalism* (New Haven, CT: Yale University Press, 2009), 70, 156–57.

18. Akira Iriye, *The Globalizing of America, 1913–1945*, vol. 3 of *The Cambridge History of American Foreign Relations* (Cambridge: Cambridge University Press, 1993), 5; Dorothy Ross, *The Origins of American Social Science* (New York: Cambridge University Press), 1991), 58.

19. Jessica Gienow-Hecht, *Sound Diplomacy: Music and Emotions in Transatlantic Relations, 1850–1920* (Chicago: University of Chicago Press, 2009): Kristin Hoganson, *Consumers' Imperium: The Global Production of American Domesticity, 1865–1920* (Chapel Hill: University of North Carolina Press, 2007); Frank Ninkovich, *Global Dawn: The Cultural Foundation of American Internationalism* (Cambridge, MA: Harvard University Press, 2009).

20. Martti Koskenniemi, *The Gentle Civilizer of Nations: The Rise and Fall of International Law, 1870–1960* (New York: Cambridge University Press, 2002), 63, 34, 36–38; Daniel Pick, *Faces of Degeneration: A European Disorder, c. 1848–1918* (Cambridge: Cambridge University Press, 1989), 57. Koskenniemi argues, 63, that in the United States, as in Europe, "liberal cosmopolitanism was increasingly limited to the outlook of bourgeois and aristocratic classes." True enough, but given the more prominent role of the American middle class, the stature of liberal cosmopolitanism grew in the United States even as it fell back on the defensive in fin de siècle Europe.

21. Peyser, *Utopia and Cosmopolis*, 14.

22. On the emergence of new key words in the early nineteenth century, see Hobsbawm, *The Age of Revolution*, 1.

23. Ninkovich, *Global Dawn*, chap. 5.

24. Richard H. Immerman, *Empire for Liberty: A History of American Imperialism from Benjamin Franklin to Paul Wolfowitz* (Princeton, NJ: Princeton University Press, 2010), 122; Charles Morris, "War as a Factor in Civilization," *Popular Science* (October 1895): 83; Seward cited in Alfred E. Eckes Jr., *Opening America's Markets: U.S. Foreign Trade Policy since 1776* (Chapel Hill: University of North Carolina Press, 1995), 69.

25. David Steigerwald, *Wilsonian Idealism in America* (Ithaca, NY: Cornell University Press, 1994), 5.

26. Rufus W. Griswold, "Henry C. Carey and His Political Economy," *International Magazine* 2, no. 3 (February 1851): 402; Walter Nugent, "Tocqueville, Marx, and American Class Structure," *Social Science History* 12, no. 4 (Winter 1988): 332, 339.

27. Henry C. Carey, *The Plough, the Loom, and the Anvil*, vol. 3 (Philadelphia: J. S. Skinner, 1851), 34; H. G. Johnson, *Economic Policies toward Less Developed Countries* (Washington, DC: Brookings, 1967), 25; H. W. Arndt, *Economic Development: The History of an Idea*, quoted in Mark Mazower, *Governing the World: The History of an Idea, 1815 to the Present* (New York: Penguin Press, 2012), 301; Rodney Morrison, *Henry C. Carey and American Economic Development* (Philadelphia: American Philosophical Society, 1986), 71.

28. Henry C. Carey, *The Harmony of Interests: Agricultural, Manufacturing, and Commercial* (Philadelphia: J. S. Skinner, 185), 229.

29. David A. Lake, "The State and American Trade Strategy in the Pre-Hegemonic Era," *International Organization* 42, no. 1 (Winter 1988): 40.

30. John Maynard Keynes, *The Economic Consequences of the Peace* (Los Angeles: Indo-European Publishing, 2010), 5. For the neo-Careyite argument that protectionist strategies have generally been the route to development, see Ha-Joon Chang, *Kicking Away the Ladder: Development Strategy in Historical Perspective* (New York: Anthem Press, 2003).

31. Frank Freidel, *Francis Lieber, Nineteenth-Century Liberal* (Baton Rouge: Louisiana State University Press, 1947); Steven Alan Samson, "Francis Lieber on the Sources of Civil Liberty," *HUMANITAS* 9 (1996): 2; Samson, "Francis Lieber: Transatlantic Cultural Missionary," in *Francis Lieber and the Culture of the Mind*, ed. Henry H. Lesesne (Columbia, SC: University of South Carolina Press, 2005), 129–31; Lieber's remark quoted in George Wilson Pierson, *Tocqueville in America* (New York: Oxford University Press, 1938), 378. In 1835, Tocqueville famously noted that "Americans of all ages, all stations of life, and all types of disposition are forever forming associations. . . . In democratic countries knowledge of how to combine is the mother of all other forms of knowledge; on its progress depends that of all the others." Alexis de Tocqueville, *Democracy in America*, ed. J. P. Mayer and Max Lerner (New York: Harper & Row 1966), 485–88.

32. Lieber to Charles Sumner, December 29, 1864, in *The Life and Letters of Francis Lieber*, ed. Thomas Sergeant Perry (Boston: J. R. Osgood and Company, 1882), 355; C. B. Robson, "Francis Lieber's Nationalism," *Journal of Politics* 8, no. 1 (February 1946), 72–73; David Clinton, "Francis Lieber, Imperialism, and Internationalism," in *Imperialism and Internationalism in the Discipline of international Relations*, ed. David Long and Brian Schmidt (Albany: State University of New York Press, 2005), 23–42; Francis Lieber, *Frag-*

ments of Political Science on Nationalism and Internationalism (New York: Scribner, 1868),
22. See also Steve Charnovitz, "Nongovernmental Organizations and International Law,"
American Journal of International Law 100 (April 2006): 348–72. The most influential work
thus far to document this transnational associational process is Daniel Rodgers, *Atlantic
Crossings* (Cambridge, MA: Belknap, 1998).

33. Merle Curti, "Francis Lieber and Nationalism," *Huntington Library Quarterly* 4,
no. 3 (April 1941): 278; Francis Lieber, *On Civil Liberty and Self-Government* (London,
1853), 250.

34. "The New World and the New Man," *Atlantic Monthly* 1 (1857): 517.

35. Ibid., 3; Josiah Strong, *The New Era; or, The Coming Kingdom* (New York,: Baker &
Taylor, 1893), 75.

36. [W. T. Stead], "Character Sketch: The Nineteenth Century," *Review of Reviews* 22
(July–December 1900): 534.

CHAPTER THREE

1. Charles W. Eliot, "Five American Contributions to Civilization," *Atlantic Monthly* 78,
no. 468 (October 1896): 433–77; Melvin E. Page, ed., *Colonialism: An International Social,
Cultural, and Political Encyclopedia* (Santa Barbara, CA: ABC-CLIO, Inc., 2003), 1144.

2. William Justin Mann, *America in Its Relation to the Great Epochs of History* (Boston:
Little, Brown, 1902); Iriye, *Global Community*, 7.

3. Walter Nugent, *Habits of Empire: A History of American Expansion* (New York: Knopf,
2008); Walter L. Williams, "United States Indian Policy and the Debate over Philippine Annexation: Implications for the Origin of American Imperialism," *Journal of American History*
66 (March 1980): 810, 831. According to Williams: "a clear pattern of colonialism toward
native Americans . . . served as a precedent for imperialist domination over the Philippines
and other islands occupied during the Spanish American war." He concludes: "Instead of
viewing 1898 as a new departure, historians might view Philippine annexation as the last
episode of a nineteenth-century pattern of territorial acquisition and direct rule of subject
peoples." A recent survey by a distinguished historian notes a "direct line between the
handling of Native Americans in the Gilded Age and the acquisition of overseas empire in
the1890s." George Herring, *From Colony to Superpower: U.S. Foreign Relations since 1776*
New York: Oxford University Press, 2008, 270.

4. "The Constitutions of Great Britain and the United States," *North American Review* 119
(1874); "Man under Sealed Orders," *Atlantic Monthly* 9 (May 1862): 536; Adams, "The
Railroad System," 487; N. C. Meeker, "Commerce and Human Progress," *Appleton's* 2
(September 18, 1869): 149. A crucial issue that all historians need to decide for themselves
is whether and to what degree history is continuous or discontinuous. My vote for the discontinuity of the modern era has been most influenced by Anthony Giddens, *The Consequences
of Modernity* (Stanford, CA: Stanford University Press), 3.

5. As a recent example, Fabian Hilfrich, *Debating American Exceptionalism: Empire and
Democracy in the Wake of the Spanish-American War* (New York: Palgrave Macmillan,
1912), 203, argues that "American debates on foreign policy follow a pattern that is char-

acterized by a high degree of solipsism and based on American exceptionalism." Robert L. Beisner's argument in *From the Old Diplomacy to the New, 1865–1900* (New York: Crowell, 1975), in which he makes the case for a transition from "incidents" to "policy," is accurate as far as it goes. But what explains the difference in the transit from one to the other?

6. Nugent, *Habits of Empire*, 159–60.

7. Julius W. Pratt, *Expansionists of 1898: The Acquisition of Hawaii and the Spanish Islands* (Baltimore: Johns Hopkins, 1936).

8. William McKinley, inaugural address, March 4, 1900. (Unless otherwise noted, presidential addresses and press conferences can be accessed in the document archive of the American Presidency project, http://www.presidency.ucsb.edu/ws/.) Of course, the United States had recently developed a very capable modern steel navy. If luck is the meeting of chance and preparation, clearly American imperialism could not have taken place without it. Nevertheless, it is worth noting that empire building was not the purpose behind the new navy's creation. The decision to begin construction of an up-to-date modern navy had as much to do with the existence of a budget surplus as with any serious concerns with threats to national security. All this underscores the conclusion that the Spanish-American War and the decision for empire were matters of choice, not policies to which Americans were driven by necessity as they had been in continental expansion.

9. Robert Kagan, *Dangerous Nation: America's Foreign Policy from Its Earliest Days to the Dawn of the Twentieth Century* (New York: Random House, 2006), 415.

10. Two now-classic works, Ernest May, *American Imperialism: A Speculative Essay* (New York: Atheneum, 1968) and Robert Beisner, *Twelve against Empire: The Anti-imperialists, 1898–1900* (New York: McGraw-Hill, 1968) make the case for change at the level of public opinion (or what later would be called discourse).

11. Henry Cabot Lodge, "Our Blundering Foreign Policy," *Forum* 19 (March–August, 1895): 17. In fairness, despite his boasting about the American record of conquest, Lodge in this essay disavows and desire for distant empire.

12. "How Colonies Are Made — Great Britain's Wonderful Success in that Direction," *New York Times*, August 9, 1895 (hereafter abbreviated as *NYT*).

13. Herbert Croly, *The Promise of American Life* (New York: Cosimo Classics, 2005), 308. This liberal rationale followed the canonical line of argument advanced by John Stuart Mill, who insisted that colonial control was justified only when a people demonstrated an incapacity for self-government and when imperial control was exercised for the good of the natives and not for exploitative purposes. See Mill, *Representative Government* (Munich; GRIN Verlag, 2008), 257.

14. Eric T. Love, *Race over Empire: Racism and U.S. Imperialism, 1865–1900* (Chapel Hill: University of North Carolina Press, 2004). This is a good place to raise a problem that does not receive enough attention. It is widely assumed that nineteenth-century social scientists like Herbert Spencer proceeded on the basis of a priori reasoning that used Western societies, and particularly Great Britain, as a standard by which all other societies could be judged and ranked. Cultural relativism, in contrast, proceeds from the understanding that the world consists of many distinct cultures whose value cannot be judged from one's

own internal standpoint. Both were true, at least until the advent of globalization, when there emerged a global reality that encompassed all cultures. That development suggests that judgments are not only possible but necessary in which the absolute standard becomes globalization. Perhaps not from a moral perspective, but from an objective standpoint, the de-pluralizing impact of globalization has the effect of de-relativizing cultural judgments.

15. Theodore Roosevelt, "Expansion and Peace," *Independent*, December 21, 1899. For the varied uses of exceptionalism in the debate, see Hilfrich, *Debating American Exceptionalism*, 87–94 passim.

16. Eric Love's *Race over Empire* makes clear that racism was a major roadblock to empire due to of the fear of assimilating large numbers of nonwhite peoples into the American polity. The anti-imperialists were those more strongly opposed to empire on racial grounds. Once the empire was in being, the civilizing mission emerged as the central policy goal of imperial administration. Paul Kramer's *The Blood of Government: Race, Empire, the United States and the Philippines* (Chapel Hill: University of North Carolina Press, 2006) traces in detail the functioning of a "calibrated colonialism" in which the independence of the Philippines would be judged by the pace of progress toward political stability and democratic forms.

17. David Healy, *US Expansionism: The Imperialist Urge in the 1890s* (Madison: University of Wisconsin Press, 1970), 128.

18. Samuel Flagg Bemis, A *Diplomatic History of the United States*, 4th ed. (New York: Henry Holt and Company, 1955), 463–75.

19. President McKinley's Last Public Utterance to the People in Buffalo, New York, September 5, 1901; McKinley's first Inaugural Address, March 4, 1897.

20. The 7 percent share of the Boxer indemnity, which roughly reflected the US troop contribution in quelling the rebellion, can also be used as a rough measure of American influence in China vis-à-vis the other powers.

21. James Bradley, *The Imperial Cruise: A Secret History of Empire and War* (New York: Little, Brown, 2009), and Evan Thomas, The *War Lovers: Roosevelt, Lodge, Hearst, and the Rush to Empire*, 1898 (New York: Little, Brown, 2010). These accounts are entirely too lurid and one-sided in their emphasis on politics. The case for a strong connection between personality and foreign policy is put best by Sarah Watt, *Rough Rider in the White House: Theodore Roosevelt and the Politics of Desire* (Chicago: University of Chicago Press, 2003).

22. TR to Henry White, August 12, 1906, *The Letters of Theodore Roosevelt*, ed. Elting E. Morison (Cambridge, MA: Harvard University Press, 1951–54), 5:359. Roosevelt had been awarded the 1906 Nobel Peace Prize for his role in mediating an end to the Russo-Japanese War.

23. TR, paper delivered before the American Sociological Congress, December 31, 1914, in Theodore Roosevelt, *Writings*, ed. William H. Harbaugh (Indianapolis, IN: Bobbs-Merrill, 1967), 357.

24. A short list of the main events of Roosevelt's presidency reads as follows: he put an end (mostly) to the bloody Filipino insurgency that had begun in 1899; acquired the canal zone

in a high-handed fashion; discreetly forced the Germans to abandon forcible debt collection from deadbeat countries in the hemisphere; announced a "Corollary" to the Monroe
Doctrine that justified the imposition of customs receiverships in Latin American countries;
mediated an end to the Russo-Japanese War; participated in a conference in Spain that
resolved a dispute between France and Germany over their respective positions in Morocco;
and sent a naval squadron on an around-the-world cruise in 1908.

25. Theodore Roosevelt, *An Autobiography* (New York: the Macmillan Company,
1913),566.

26. John P. Campbell, "Roosevelt, Taft, and the Arbitration Treaties of 1911," *Journal of
American History* 53, no. 2 (September 1966): 279–98; Taft speech, "McKinley and Expansion," January 29, 1908, Taft papers (microfilm).

27. Taft, message to Congress, December 3, 2012.

28. Taft speech at Carnegie Hall, December 13, 1909, quoted in Paige Elliott Mulhollan,
"Philander C. Knox and Dollar Diplomacy" (PhD diss., University of Texas, 1966), 56;
Philander Knox, "International Unity; Address Delivered before the Pennsylvania Society of
New York, December 1909," *International Conciliation* 28 (March 10, 1910): 3–5.

29. Mulhollan, "Philander C. Knox and Dollar Diplomacy," 42; Francis H. M. Huntington Wilson, address to the Third National Peace Congress, quoted in ibid., 48–49. The
hardheaded case for dollar diplomacy is also made by Huntington-Wilson, "The Relation of
Government to Foreign Investment," *Annals* 68 (1916): 298–311. On the sense of responsibility for acculturation felt by dollar diplomats, see Emily Rosenberg, *Financial Missionaries
to the World: The Politics and Culture of Dollar Diplomacy, 1900–1930* (Durham, NC:
Duke University Press, 2003). Translation of hypothecate: to allocate the revenue raised by a
tax for a specified purpose.

30. US Department of State, *Papers Relating to the Foreign Relations of the United States,
1909* (Washington, DC: USGPO, 1909), xv (hereafter cited as *FRUS*); quoted in Mulhollan,
"Philander C. Knox and Dollar Diplomacy," 54; 1912 speech of Willard Straight, quoted in
Henry Pringle, *The Life and Times of William Howard Taft*, 682–83.

31. Taft, message to Congress, December 3, 1912.

32. Philip Quilibet, "England and America," *Galaxy* 12 (July 1871): 112; S. W. Boardman,
"Arbitration as a Substitute for War," *Princeton Review* 3–10 (1874): 315; "The Week," *Nation* (May 25, 1871), 349.

33. McKinley's first Inaugural Address, March 4, 1897.

34. Quoted in Benjamin Zasloff, "Law and the Shaping of American Foreign Policy: From
the Gilded Age to the New Era" (PhD diss., Harvard University, 2002), 105.

35. Taft to Knox, December 18, 1913, Knox papers, Library of Congress, Manuscript
Division.

36. Frederick McCormick, "What Does the Secretary of State Mean?," *North American
Review* 193 (February 1911): 209.

37. André Tardieu, *The Truth about the Treaty* (Indianapolis: Bobbs-Merrill, 1921), 470.

CHAPTER FOUR

1. Akira Iriye, *The Globalizing of America, 1913–1945*, vol. 3 of *The Cambridge History of American Foreign Relations* (Cambridge: Cambridge University Press, 1993), 71–72; Robert W. Tucker, "The Triumph of Wilsonianism?," *World Policy Journal* 10, no. 4 (Winter 1993): 83–99; Henry Kissinger, *Diplomacy* (New York: Simon and Schuster, 1994), 52, 30.

2. Robert W. Tucker, *Woodrow Wilson and the Great War: Reconsidering America's Neutrality, 1914–1917* (Charlottesville: University of Virginia Press, 2007).

3. For the argument that Wilsonian idealism can be explained as a derivation of religious belief, see Milan Babik, *Statecraft and Salvation: Wilsonian Liberal Internationalism as Secularized Eschatology* (Waco, TX: Baylor University Press, 2012).

4. Mazower, *Governing the World*, 45; Roosevelt's Nobel lecture of May 5, 1910. One could add disarmament to this list, whose failure, over the long term, was every bit as pronounced, but this story has too many ups, downs, twists, and turns for the kind of summary treatment offered here.

5. Paul Kennedy, *The Parliament of Man: The Past, Present, and Future of the United Nations* (New York: Vintage Books, 2006), p. 8.

6. Stephen Wertheim, "The League That Wasn't: American Designs for a Legalist-Sanctionist League of Nations and the Intellectual Origins of International Organization, 1914–1920," *Diplomatic History* 35, no. 5 (November 2011): 797–836, suggests that an organization founded on international law and vested with coercive power might have had more success. In principle, yes, but it is difficult to imagine the powers consenting to the creation of an organization with more coercive power than the League.

7. E.g., W. H. Brands, *Woodrow Wilson* (New York: Times Books, 2003), 137, argues that, apart from the veto, "the essential philosophy of the United Nations . . . was pure Wilsonianism." But this is like comparing a man whose heart has been torn from his body to a living person. In order for the heart of Wilsonianism to remain beating, denying the veto to an offending great power was essential.

8. Alexandru Grigorescu, "Mapping the UN-League of Nations Analogy: Are There Still Lessons to Be Learned from the League?," *Global Governance* 11 (2005): 36. Thus in the vote condemning Italy's attack on Abyssinia, the Italian vote against the resolution was not counted.

The veto as it was most commonly discussed in 1919 was in reference to America's responsibility to intervene on behalf of League under the terms of Article 10 in faraway lands where the United States did not have a direct interest. As Wilson put it, the League council could not make the United States intervene. "We have an absolute veto on the thing," he said, but then he added the important qualifier "unless we are parties to the dispute." Woodrow Wilson, "An Address in San Francisco," September 17, 1919, in *The Papers of Woodrow Wilson* (Princeton, NJ: Princeton University Press, various dates), 63:318. In the case of sanctions against Italy in 1936, creative lawyering in the assembly allowed the resolution to pass, though only by making the sanctions voluntary, i.e., by making room for what later would be called "a coalition of the willing."

9. John Milton Cooper Jr., *Woodrow Wilson: A Biography* (New York: Knopf, 2009), 508.

10. For what it is worth, my view is that America's membership under any conditions imposed by the Senate would have afflicted US policy with the same debility that proved fatal to Britain and France. I cannot prove that this would have happened, but neither can those who argue that American membership would have made a decisive difference prove their contention.

11. Erez Manela, *The Wilsonian Moment: Self-Determination and the International Origins of Anticolonial Nationalism* (Oxford and New York: Oxford University Press, 2007).

12. Review of *The Origins of the Foreign Policy of Woodrow Wilson*, by Harley Notter, *International Affairs* 71, no. 4 (July 1938): 595.

13. Alfred E. Eckes, review of *The Politics of Trade: American Political Development and Foreign Economic Policy*, by Cynthia A. Hody, *American Historical Review* 102, no. 2 (April 1997): 573. The Wilson-Gorman tariff of 1894 dropped rates by 10 percent, but still left them at very high levels. The Underwood tariff of 1914 that was passed into law in the first Wilson administration, which saw Wilson breaking tradition to deliver a message to a joint session of Congress, advocated a "competitive tariff" and a straightforward return to ad valorem duties as a way of plainly advertising the cost of protection. Tariff rates were reduced by an average of 26 percent, but no one advocated absolute free trade by abolishing all duties or by levying taxes equally upon imports and domestic products. Moreover, in some cases where steep reductions were made, in iron and steel, for example, the industry no longer needed protecting. Further minimizing the general impact on the American or the world economy, reductions tended to be for rates that had been prohibitive or only nominal to begin with. Frank Taussig, "The Tariff Act of 1913," *Quarterly Journal of Economics* 28, no. 1 (November 1913): 25. "The time has gone by when the protective system was of real consequence for the iron and steel industries," argued Taussig.

14. Burton Kaufman, *Efficiency and Expansion: Foreign Trade Organization in the Wilson Administration, 1913–1921* (Westport, CT: Greenwood Press, 1974), 234; Eliot Jones, *The Trust Problem in the United States* (New York: Macmillan, 1921), 387. The liberal ideal of free exchange of currencies and goods was far from being realized during these years. Adherence to the gold standard increased to 90 percent by 1913, but fell to 35 percent after the war; it rose again to 1913 levels by the late 1920s before collapsing to 25 percent in the 1930s. On average, world tariff barriers rose modestly from 12 percent in 1870 to 14 percent in 1914. Although tariffs fell strongly between 1900 and 1920, the reductions were undone in the 1920s, and rates would zoom to much higher levels in the 1930s.

15. Vanhanen, *The Emergence of Democracy*, 70; Vanhanen, "New Dataset for Measuring Democracy," 259.

16. John Milton Cooper, "Making a Case for Wilson," in *Reconsidering Woodrow Wilson: Progressivism, Internationalism, War, and Peace*, ed. John Milton Cooper (Baltimore: Johns Hopkins 2008), 21. But even the seriousness of the George W. Bush administration, which advocated the promotion of democracy in no uncertain terms, remains open to question.

17. The intellectual inspiration for this unembarrassed new defense of America's liaisons with authoritarian regimes came from Jeane J. Kirkpatrick, "Dictatorships and Double Standards," *Commentary* 68, no. 5 (November 1979): 34–45.

18. Hamilton Foley, comp., *Wilson's Case for the League of Nations* (Princeton, NJ: Princeton University Press, 1923), 182; remarks to the New York Press Club, June 30, 1916, in *Papers of Woodrow Wilson*, 37:334. Cf. Sondra R. Herman, *Eleven against War* (Stanford, CA: Hoover Institution Press, 1969), 179–216.

19. I have tried to trace the lineage of these ideas through the middle phase of the Cold War in *Modernity and Power: A History of the Domino Theory in the Twentieth Century* (Chicago: University of Chicago Press, 1994).

20. In *The Pity of War: Explaining World War One* (New York: Basic Books, 1999), Niall Ferguson questions whether imperial Germany constituted such a threat, suggesting that Europe might have been better off with a German victory—better the *Kaiserreich* than the Third Reich.

21. Robert S. McNamara and James G. Blight, *Wilson's Ghost: Reducing the Risk of Conflict, Killing, and Catastrophe in the 21st Century* (New York: Public Affairs, 2001).

22. Ross Kennedy, "Woodrow Wilson, World War I, and National Security," *Diplomatic History* 25, no. 11 (January 2001): 1–32; Ninkovich, *Modernity and Power*, 37–68. There remains some doubt about how seriously this more narrowly defined danger was taken by Lodge and his allies, given the defeat of Germany and the collapse of its imperial institutions. Whatever their strategic declarations, they were unwilling to make a cause célèbre of the French Treaty of Guarantee as an alternative to the League; indeed, Lodge could never get the treaty out of his committee. Louis A. R. Yates, *United States and French Security, 1917–1921: A Study in American Diplomatic History* (New York: Twayne Publishers, 1957), 116–38; William R. Widenor, *Henry Cabot Lodge and the Search for an American Foreign Policy* (Berkeley: University of California Press), 331–32.

23. On the long-term significance of Wilsonianism, see Frank Ninkovich, "Wilsonianism after the Cold War," in *Reconsidering Woodrow Wilson: Progressivism, Internationalism, and World Peace*, ed. John Milton Cooper (Baltimore: Johns Hopkins, 2008), 299–326.

24. Tucker, "The Triumph of Wilsonianism?," 83.

25. Thomas A. Bailey, *Woodrow Wilson and the Great Betrayal* (New York: Macmillan, 1945), 277. Lloyd E. Ambrosius, *Wilsonianism: Woodrow Wilson and His Legacy in American Foreign Relations* (New York: Palgrave, 2002), offers the most trenchant realist critique of Wilson and his "legacy," at the same time that some badly needed self-criticism of realist assumptions is absent.

26. David Fromkin, "What Is Wilsonianism?," *World Policy Journal* 11, no. 1 (Spring 1994): 109–10.

27. "Germany and Rome," *Nation* (September 8, 1881), 190; Herbert Tuttle, "The German Empire," *Harper's* 63 (1881): 602; "The Week," *Nation* (February 27, 1890), 169; [Carl Schurz], "Bismarck's Defeat," *Nation* (June 22, 1882), 517; [Herbert Tuttle], "The German Chancellorship," *Nation* (January 22, 1880), 55; [Herbert Tuttle], "Reaction in Germany," *Nation* (June 5, 1879), 381.

CHAPTER FIVE

1. James Truslow Adams, "Europe's Picture of Uncle Sam," *NYT*, September 6, 1931, 6. As Liz Cohen notes in *A Consumers' Republic* (New York: Vintage, 2004), 9, the inclusiveness of US consumer society at this time "was limited."

2. Warren G. Harding, second annual message, December 8, 1922.

3. Harding, 1922 State of the Union address.

4. Harding, Inaugural Address, March 4, 1921.

5. Charles Evans Hughes to the Italian ambassador (Ricci), March 8, 1922, in *FRUS, 1922*, 393.

6. Patrick O. Cohrs, *The Unfinished Peace after World War I: America, Britain and the Stabilisation of Europe, 1919–1932* (Cambridge: Cambridge University Press, 2006), 305.

7. Paul Hollander, *Political Pilgrims: Travels of Western Intellectuals to the Soviet Union, China, and Cuba, 1928–1978* (Lanham, MD: University Press of America), 1989.

8. Robert James Maddox, *William E. Borah and United States Foreign Policy* (Baton Rouge: Louisiana State University Press, 1970), 189–90; Christine A. White, *British and American Commercial Relations with Soviet Russia, 1918–1924* (Chapel Hill: University of North Carolina Press, 1992).

9. Leon Trotsky, *Stalinism and Bolshevism* (New York: Pioneer Publishers, 1937), 13.

10. *FRUS, 1922*, 331, 187.

11. "Report of the American Delegation," February 9, 1922, in ibid. 328. 376.

12. Ibid., 345.

13. In broad terms, this is what the American historian William Appleman Williams has famously argued. He was correct to do so, I believe, though I would dispute some of his associated contentions, i.e., about how Americans perceived the role of economics and of politics.

14. *FRUS, 1922*, 199; Hughes, "Some Observations on the Conduct of Our Foreign Relations," commencement address at University of Michigan, June 19, 1922, *American Journal of International Law* 16 (1922); Hughes, quoted in T. David Ochmanek and W. Anthony Lake, eds., *The Real and the Ideal: Essays on International Relations in Honor of Richard H. Ullmann* (Lanham, MD: Roman & Littlefield, 2001), 160.

15. *FRUS, 1922*, 299, 186, 210.

16. TR, special message to Congress, April 14, 1908.

17. Hoover, "Problems of Our Economic Evolution," address to Stanford University seniors, June 22, 1925, "The Bible," in Herbert Hoover Presidential Library, West Branch, Iowa. Akira Iriye, *After Imperialism: The Search for a New Order in the Far East, 1921–1931* (Cambridge, MA: Harvard University Press, 1965), is the classic account of how these expectations failed to work out in east Asia in the 1920s.

18. For these points I am indebted to the work of Robert David Johnson.

19. Harding, inaugural address, March 4, 1921; David F. Schmitz, *Thank God They're on Our Side: The United States and Right-Wing Dictatorships, 1921–1965* (Chapel Hill: University of North Carolina Press, 1999).

20. See Zasloff, "Law and the Shaping of American Foreign Policy," on the origins of legal internationalism.

21. James T. Shotwell, *War as an Instrument of National Policy and Its Renunciation in the Pact of Paris* (New York: Harcourt, Brace, 1929,) vii; John E. Stoner, *S. O. Levinson and the Pact of Paris: A Study in the Techniques of Influence* (Chicago: University of Chicago Press, 1943), 199.

22. Hoover, State of the Union message, December 3, 1929; William E. Leuchtenberg, *Herbert Hoover* (New York: Henry Holt and Company, 2009), 117.

23. Hoover, State of the Union message, December 6, 1932.

24. David F. Schmitz, *Henry L. Stimson: The First Wise Man* (Wilmington, DE: SR Books, 2001), 111; Henry L. Stimson, *The Far Eastern Crisis: Recollections and Observations* (New York: Harper & Brothers, 1936), 241, 246.

25. Hoover, State of the Union message, December 8, 1931.

26. The president's news conference, December 11, 1931. For one take on the concept of "cultural distance," see Richard J. Payne, *The Clash with Distant Cultures: Values, Interests, and Force in American Foreign Policy* (Albany: State University of New York Press, 1995).

27. Cohrs, *Unfinished Peace*, 612; Leuchtenberg, *Herbert Hoover*, 118. On world opinion as a product of the American imagination, see Robert Ferrell and Howard Quint, eds., *The Talkative President: The Off-the-Record Press Conferences of Calvin Coolidge* (Amherst: University of Massachusetts Press, 1964), 219.

28. Joan Hoff, *American Business and Foreign Policy* (Lexington: University Press of Kentucky, 1971).

CHAPTER SIX

1. On parallelisms, see John A. Garraty, "The New Deal, National Socialism, and the Great Depression," *American Historical Review* 78, no. 4 (October, 1973): 907–44.

2. FDR, wireless to the London Conference, July 3, 1933. The convoking of the conference was itself a significant development in the history of international cooperation. Previous conferences had limited themselves largely to the question of the gold standard—one of the key indicators of membership in international society and, as one banker described it, "required for the protection of civilization," though bimetallists saw it as the cause of civilization's disaster. "Gold Basis Called Vital World Need," *NYT*, February 15, 1932, 36.

3. FDR, press conference, April 15, 1939.

4. Quoted in Barbara J. Keys, *Globalizing Sport: National Rivalry and International Community in the 1930s* (Cambridge, MA: Harvard University Press, 2006), 80. The coercive power of international society is suggested by the title of the dissertation from which this book emerged: "The Dictatorship of Sport;" Frank Knox to FDR, December 15, 1937, in *Franklin D. Roosevelt and Foreign Affairs*, vol. 4, *January 1937–August 1939*, ed. Donald B. Schewe (New York: Garland Books, 1979), document 674.

5. Arthur M. Schlesinger, *Journals: 1952–2000* (New York: Penguin Press, 2007), 774.

6. Studs Terkel, *"The Good War:"An Oral History of World War II* (New York: Pantheon Books, 1984); Tom Brokaw, *The Greatest Generation* (New York: Random House, 1998);

Paul Fussell, *Wartime: Understanding and Behavior in the Second World War* (New York: Oxford University Press, 1989); Anders Stephanson, "War and Diplomatic History," *Diplomatic History* 25, no. 3 (Summer 2001): 394.

7. David Reynolds, "The Origins of Two 'Word Wars': Historical Discourse and International Politics," *Journal of Contemporary History* 38, no. 1 (January 2003): 41.

8. Melvyn Leffler, *A Preponderance of Power: National Security, the Truman Administration, and the Cold War* (Stanford, CA: Stanford University Press, 1992), 10, 525n; Basil Walker, "America's Destiny," *Current History and Forum* 53, no. 1 (June 1941): 8; FDR press conference, June 23, 1939, in *Franklin D. Roosevelt and Foreign Affairs*, vol. 4, document 314. See also the Berle diary extract in Beatrice Bishop Berle and Travis Beale Jacobs, eds., *Navigating the Rapids: From the Papers of Adolf A. Berle* (New York: Harcourt Brace Jovanovich, 1973), 223. Uwe Lübken, *Bedrohliche Nähe: Die USA und dir nationalsozialistische Herausforderung in Lateinamerika, 1937⊠1945* (Stuttgart: Franz Steiner Verlag, 2004).

9. Gregory A. Raymond, "Necessity in Foreign Policy," *Political Science Quarterly* 113, no. 4 (Winter 1998–99): 688; http://www.charleslindbergh.com/pdf/speech7.pdf. On the openness of decision making, see, e.g., Ian Kershaw, *Fateful Choices: Ten Decisions That Changed the World, 1940–1941* (New York: Penguin, 2007), 483, although he hedges a few pages earlier (473) when he says that Roosevelt's choices "appear more open in theory than in practice."

10. Hoover radio speech, "A Call to Reason," June 29, 1941, in Louis P. Lochner, *Herbert Hoover and Germany* (New York: Macmillan, 1960), 163; speech to the Forum on Current Problems, New York, October 26, 1938, *Addresses upon the American Road, 1938–1940* (New York: Scribner, 1940), 86.

11. Ralph Linton, "One Hundred Percent American," *American Mercury* (1937); Lindbergh broadcast address, September 15, 1939, http://www.charleslindbergh.com/pdf/9_15_39.pdf.

12. William C. Bullitt to FDR, December 7, 1937, in *Franklin D. Roosevelt and Foreign Affairs*, vol. 4, document 654; FDR press conference, June 23, 1939, in *Franklin D. Roosevelt and Foreign Affairs, May–June 1939*, 315; Robert J. Art, "The United States, the Balance of Power, and World War II: Was Spykman Right?," *Security Studies* 14, no. 3 (July–September 2005): 365–406.

13. FDR, radio address announcing an unlimited national emergency, May 27, 1941; FDR, fireside chat, September 11, 1941.

14. FDR, fireside chat, December 9, 1941; Acheson, undated notes, *FRUS, 1950*, 1:394. A more recent example of this kind of reasoning, as applied to global warming, comes from the writing of Nobel Prize–winning economist Paul Krugman: "It's true that scientists don't know exactly how much world temperatures will rise if we persist with business as usual," he writes. "But that uncertainty is actually what makes action so urgent. While there's a chance that we'll act against global warming only to find that the danger was overstated, there's also a chance that we'll fail to act only to find that the results of inaction were catastrophic. Which risk would you rather run?" Paul Krugman, "Can This Planet Be Saved?," *NYT*, August 1, 2008. This "precautionary principle" was also advocated by Vice President Dick Cheney in the war against al-Qaeda. See Thomas L. Friedman, "Going Cheney on Climate," *NYT*, December 8, 2009.

15. Gerhard Weinberg, *A World at Arms: A Global History of World War II* (New York: Cambridge University Press, 1995). The clearest and most convincing account of the shortcomings of geopolitical reasoning in the run-up to the Second World War is John A. Thompson, "The Geopolitical Vision: The Myth of an Outmatched USA," in *Uncertain Empire: American History and the Idea of the Cold War*, ed. Joel Isaac and Duncan Bell (New York: Oxford University Press, 2012), 91–114. But see also his "Conceptions of National Security and American Entry into World War II," *Diplomacy and Statecraft* 16 (2005): 671–97. The classic realist argument along these lines is Bruce M. Russett, *No Clear and Present Danger: A Skeptical View of the U.S. Entry into World War II* (New York: Harper Torchbooks, 1972). For a more concise presentation, see Melvin Small, *Was War Necessary? National Security and U.S. Entry into War* (Beverly Hills, CA: Sage, 1980), 215–67. Patrick J. Hearden, *Roosevelt Confronts Hitler: America's Entry into World War II* (DeKalb: Northern Illinois University Press, 1987), presents the clearest post-1960s revisionist account. For a discussion and bibliographic notes see Michaela Hoenicke Moore, *Know Your Enemy: The American Debate on Nazism, 1933–1945* (New York: Cambridge University Press, 2010), especially chap. 3. See also Robert J. Art, "The United States, the Balance of Power, and World War II: Was Spykman Right?," *Security Studies* 14, no. 3 (July–September 2005): 365–406. A still valuable historiographical survey is Justus Doenecke, "U.S. Policy and the European War, 1939–1941," *Diplomatic History* 19, no. 4 (September 1995).

16. Gabriel Gorodtetsky, *Grand Delusions: Stalin and the German Invasion of Russia* (New Haven, CT: Yale University Press, 1999). Going down this road leads to the political theory known as decisionism, most often associated with the German scholar Carl Schmitt, in which the rightness of a policy is determined solely by its having been chosen by a proper authority.

17. Maurice Matloff, *United States Naval Institute Proceedings* 79, no. 2 (1953): 744.

18. Uncertainty, it should be noted, is not inconsistent with realism. Thomas Hobbes, one of the founders of the realist tradition, wrote that danger consisted not in the certainty of being killed but in the radical uncertainty of politically unorganized life. "In such condition," he wrote movingly, "there is no place for industry; because the fruit thereof is uncertain; and consequently no Culture of the Earth; no Navigation, nor use of the commodities that may be imported by Sea; no commodious Building; no instruments of moving, and removing such things as require much Force; no Knowledge of the face of the Earth; no account of time: no Arts; no Letters; no Society; and which is worst of all, continuall feare, and danger of violent death." Thomas Hobbes, *Leviathan*, ed. A. P. Martinich and Brian Battiste (Peterborough, ON: Broadview Press, 2010), 123–24. Uncertainly also lies at the heart of the much-beloved "security dilemma" of IR theory. For his part, John Maynard Keynes argued that uncertainty lay at the core of macroeconomics. See Matthew Wilson, "The Philosophy of Keynes' Economics: Probability, Uncertainty, and Convention," *Journal of Economic Issues* 38 (2004). In economics, behavioral thinking has made inroads against the view of humans as utility maximizers in efficient markets. The locus classicus of this view is Daniel Kahneman and Amos Tversky, "Prospect Theory: An Analysis of Decision under Risk," *Econometrica* 47 (1979): 263–91. Or, more pithily, as John Kenneth Galbraith once

remarked about forecasting in his discipline: "There are two kinds of economists: those who don't know the future, and those who don't know they don't know."

19. John R. Searle, "How to Study Consciousness Scientifically," *Philosophical Transactions: Biological Sciences* 53, no. 1377 (November 29, 1998): 1937. Here I am arguing against the patronizing social scientific tradition of minimizing or ignoring what people thought on the grounds that subjective data tend to be unreliable. Although we have come a long way from the days of "black box" Watsonian behaviorism, most social scientists would still prefer to arrive at an understanding of society on the basis of objective, measurable criteria based on the supposition that whatever exists, exists in some quantity. Therefore, when in doubt, measure, and then measure some more. Typically, as Harold Garfinkel has noted, when it comes to assessing the relevance of common understandings, "models of man in society portray him as a judgmental dope." See Harold Garfinkel, *Studies in Ethnomethodology* (Malden, MA: Blackwell, 1999), 66. In foreign affairs, at any rate, we would be better served by taking more seriously what sociologist Pierre Bourdieu has called "the objectivity of the subjective." Pierre Bourdieu, *The Logic of Practice*, trans. Richard Nice (Stanford, CA: Stanford University Press, 1990), 135–41.

20. The fascist worldview was very much a regional perspective. In John Searle's usage, the status of the phenomenon in question was ontologically and epistemically subjective. John R. Searle, *The Construction of Social Reality* (New York: Free Press, 1995), 9–11.

21. Arnold Gehlen, *Man in the Age of Technology*, trans. Patricia Lipscomb (New York: Columbia University Press, 1980), 121. Gehlen's chief theoretical work is *Man: His Nature and Place in the World*, trans. Clare McMillan (New York: Columbia University Press, 1988). For a mature statement of the cultural lag theory, see William F. Ogburn, "Cultural Lag as Theory," *Sociology and Social Research* 41, no. 3 (January 1957): 167–74.

22. David Harvey, *The Condition of Postmodernity* (Oxford: Blackwell, 1990), 306, notes that under stress "time-space compression always exacts its toll on our capacity to grapple with the realities unfolding around us . . . it becomes harder and harder to react accurately to events." For the record, my emphasis on social construction and interpretation does not put me in the relativist position of denying all truth claims, nor does it marry me to the extreme skepticism that denies any knowledge of external reality. Philosophically, I am a pragmatist, a view that is perfectly consistent with science.

23. Text of Secretary of State Hull's Toronto speech, *NYT*, October 23, 1937, 5.

24. FDR to William Phillips, September 15, 1938, in *The Roosevelt Correspondence: Being the Letters of Franklin Delano Roosevelt*, ed. Elliott Roosevelt (London: George G. Harrap, 1949–1952, 3: 241; *FDR: His Personal Letters*, ed. Elliott Roosevelt (New York: Duell, Sloan and Pearce, 1947–50), 2:810.

25. Address on Armistice Day, Arlington National Cemetery, November 11, 1940.

26. FDR, speech to Pan American union, April 14, 1939; FDR, address, September 2, 1940.

27. Evan Luard, *The Globalization of Politics: The Changed Focus of Political Action in the Modern World* (New York: New York University Press, 1990), 5.

28. Nicholas John Cull, *Selling War: The British Propaganda Campaign against American "Neutrality" in World War II* (New York: Oxford University Press, 1995).

29. J. Néré, *The Foreign Policy of France from 1914 to 1945* (Boston: Routledge & Kegan Paul, 1975), 248–59; Adrienne Doris Hytier, *Two Years of French Foreign Policy: Vichy, 1940–1941* (Westport, CT: Greenwood, 1974), 214–21, 319–27.

30. FDR, inaugural address, January 20, 1945.

CHAPTER SEVEN

1. For an extended critique of this mind-set, see Walter Russell Mead, "Lucid Stars: The American Foreign Policy Tradition," *World Policy Journal* 11, no. 4 (Winter 1994): 1–17.

2. John Maynard Keynes, *The Economic Consequences of the Peace* (Los Angeles: Indo-European Publishing, 2010), 4. Address on Armistice Day, Arlington National Cemetery, November 11, 1940.

3. See John Morton Blum, *V Was for Victory: Politics and American Culture during World War II* (New York: Harcourt Brace Jovanovich, 1976), 66–67, 104–5. Ironically, with the issuance of the 1944 Beveridge report arguing for a cradle-to-grave welfare state, the war would become much more a struggle for assuring the good life for Britons than it was for Americans. FDR's program, announced in 1944, ran afoul of a growing conservative mood in the country that found political expression in the 1946 elections. But, to be fair, an International Labor Organization, with at least a nod to social justice, was created as part of the Versailles peace settlement.

4. G. John Ikenberry, "Is American Multilateralism in Decline?," *Perspectives on Politics* 1, no. 3 (September 2003); J. F. Toye and Richard Toye, *The UN and Global Political Economy: Trade, Finance, and Development* (Bloomington: Indiana University Press, 2004), 17–44.

5. Cordell Hull, *The Memoirs of Cordell Hull* (New York: Macmillan Co., 1948), 1:365; First Meeting of Commission I, in *The Bretton Woods Transcripts*, ed. Kurt Schuler and Andrew Rosenberg (New York: Center for Financial Stability, 2012) [Kindle edition]).

6. Elizabeth Borgwardt, *A New Deal for the World: America's Vision for Human Rights* (Cambridge, MA: Belknap), 6–7; Ulrich Pfister and Christian Suter, "International Relations as Part of the World-System," *International Studies Quarterly* 31, no. 3 (September 1987): 239–72. Borgwardt's book does the best job of conveying the sense of international cooperation as something both desirable and necessary that permeated postwar planning during these years. For the relationship between US foreign economic policy and globalization, see Alfred E. Eckes Jr. and Thomas Zeiler, *Globalization and the American Century* (New York: Cambridge University Press, 2003), and D. Clayton Brown, *Globalization and America since 1945* (Wilmington, DE: Scholarly Resources, 2003). Also well worth consulting is Alfred E. Eckes Jr., "Open Door Expansionism Reconsidered: The World War II Experience," *Journal of American History* 59, no. 4 (March 1973): 923.

7. Alfred E. Eckes, *Opening America's Market: U.S. Foreign Trade Policy since 1776* (Chapel Hill: University of North Carolina Press, 1995), 177, 282. This turn of events was not based

entirely on a prioritizing of foreign policy desiderata. In response to complaints about industries and individuals devastated by this global process of creative destruction, liberal economists were always ready to make the counterintuitive case that free trade was a net benefit, appearances notwithstanding.

8. Anne-Marie Burley, "Regulating the World: Multilateralism, International Law, and the Projection of the New Deal Regulatory State," in *Multilateralism Matters, Theory and Praxis of an Institutional Form*, ed. John Gerard Ruggie (New York: Columbia University Press, 1993), 125, 152, who proposes that "the U.S. blueprint for multilateralism can be plausibly understood as the projection of a domestic regulatory revolution onto the rest of the world." If so, the blueprint was extremely fuzzy, for the international clearing union proposed by Keynes was a far more internationalist scheme that, compared to the IMF, would have come closer to performing supranational banking functions.

9. Shawn Tully, "Break Up the Euro," *Fortune* 165, no. 5 (October 8, 2012): 93.

10. Paul Johnson, *Modern Times: The World from the Twenties to the Nineties* (New York: Harper, 1992), 660; Tony Judt, *Postwar: A History of Europe since 1945* (New York: Penguin Press, 2005), 324–59.

11. Manfred J. Halpern, *The Politics of Social Change in the Middle East and North Africa* (Princeton, NJ: Princeton University Press, 1963); Morris Janowitz, *The Military in the Political Development of New Nations* (Chicago: University of Chicago Press, 1964); David Ekbladh, *The Great American Mission: Modernization and the Construction of an American World Order* (Princeton, NJ: Princeton University Press, January 2010); Douglas Macdonald, *Adventures in Chaos: American Intervention for Reform in the Third World* (Cambridge, MA: Harvard University Press, 1992); Paul Krugman, "Reckonings: The Magic Mountain," *NYT*, January 23, 2000. The best historical critique of US development policies is Michael Latham, *The Right Kind of Revolution: Modernization, Development, and U.S. Foreign Policy from the Cold War to the Present* (Ithaca, NY: Cornell University Press, 2011). For a noted economist's take, see William Easterly, *The White Man's Burden: Why the West's Efforts to Aid the Rest Have Done So Much Ill and So Little Good* (New York: Oxford University Press, 2006).

12. Dorothy V. Jones, *Toward a Just World: The Critical Years in the Search for International Justice* (Chicago: University of Chicago Press, 2002); Akira Iriye, Petra Goedde, and William I. Hitchcock, *The Human Rights Revolution: An International History* (New York: Oxford University Press, 2012). On human rights, among the best recent works are Samuel Moyn, *The Last Utopia: Human Rights in History* (Cambridge, MA: Belknap Press of Harvard University Press, 2010; Sarah Snyder, *Human Rights Activism and the End of the Cold War: A Transnational History of the Helsinki Network* (New York: Cambridge University Press, 2011); and Barbara Keys, *Reclaiming American Virtue: The Human Rights Revolution of the 1970s* (Cambridge, MA: Harvard University Press, 2014).

13. Geoffrey Crowther, "Must Capitalism and Communism Clash?," *NYT*, August 6, 1944, SM5; Pitirim Sorokin, *Russia and the United States* (E. P. Dutton, 1944; reprint New Brunswick, NJ: Transaction Publishers, 2009), 205.

14. The locus classicus for this argument is Kirkpatrick, "Dictatorships and Double Standards." The record, as one might expect, was actually mixed. In some cases, such as Spain, Portugal, Taiwan, and South Korea, authoritarian regimes did serve as bridges to democracy. In other countries, like Chile, the transition was very bumpy, while in still others, like Iraq, the very idea that authoritarianism could serve as a bridge to democracy was doubtful in the extreme. For Spain, see Neal Rosendorf, *Franco Sells Spain to America: Hollywood, Tourism and Public Relations as Postwar Spanish Soft Power* (New York: Palgrave Macmillan, 2013).

15. JFK, American University commencement address, June 10, 1963.

16. Oliver Morrissey, Dirk Willem te Velde, and Adrian Hewitt, "Defining International Public Goods: Conceptual Issues," draft of chap. 2 in *Strategies for International Public Goods*, ed. M. Ferroni and A. Mody (Dordrecht, the Netherlands: Kluwer, forthcoming). On the domestic side, it should be noted, there existed as widespread fear about the automatic revival of prosperity.

17. Despite failing in its primary mission, the UN survived thanks largely to its ability to perform secondary functions. It had some political uses: as a public relations medium to appease American internationalists; as a talking shop and as a forum for negotiations; as a site for the growing number of newly independent nations to register their concerns and blow off steam; and as a resource for peacekeeping missions. It was the go-to venue for discussions of various global problems insufficiently addressed by traditional diplomacy such as environment and climate change, women's rights, human rights, technology, development; it became an indispensible source of statistical data; its specialized agencies continued to perform indispensible work in meteorology, relief and refugees, public health, food and agriculture, postal union, population control, and so on. Not least, it became a networking site for the rapidly growing number of heterogeneous nongovernmental organizations. For a convenient brief summary, see Jussi M. Hanhimäki, *The United Nations: A Very Short Introduction* (New York: Oxford University Press, 2008). See also his essay "No Early Retirement: At 63 the United Nations Is Imperative in the 21st Century," *Internationale Politik* (Spring 2009): 88–93.

18. Evan Luard, "The Growth of the World Community," *The Annals of the American Academy of Political and Social Science*, vol. 351, *The Changing Cold War* (January 1964), 173.

19. Hugh De Santis, *The Diplomacy of Silence: The American Foreign Service, the Soviet Union, and the Cold War, 1933–1947* (Chicago: University of Chicago Press, 1980), provides the best account of optimism from within the government; M. Todd Bennett, *One World, Big Screen: Hollywood, the Allies, and World War II* (Chapel Hill: University of North Carolina Press, 2012), offers the best account of optimism in the film media. It is in part because of the understanding that an attempt to rein in a great power would be futile, Luard notes, that "the ultimate sanction of armed power implied in the provisions of the Charter never came into being." Luard, "The Growth of the World Community," 170–79.

20. David A. Baldwin, ed., *Neorealism and Neoliberalism: The Contemporary Debate* (New York: Columbia University Press, 1993); Bruce Kuklick, *Blind Oracles: Intellectuals and War from Kennan to Kissinger* (Princeton, NJ: Princeton University Press, 2006).

21. This overvaluation of the role played by military power would persist into the 1980s and 1990s, when it was widely believed that Ronald Reagan's splurge on defense spending was responsible for the collapse of the Soviet Union.

22. "X," "The Sources of Soviet Conduct," *Foreign Affairs* 25, no. 4 (July 1947): 566–82; Kennan to Secretary of State, *FRUS, 1946, Eastern Europe, The Soviet Union*, 707–8. This may seem unfair, for Kennan was quite influential in the Marshall Plan, but I doubt that anyone at the time imagined where the European economic miracle would lead. Moreover, apart from Japan, he was quite skeptical of the modernizing potential of non-Western peoples. Here I am taking issue with John Lewis Gaddis, who in his magisterial biography *George F. Kennan: An American Life* (New York: Penguin Press, 2011) attributes to Kennan prophetic powers that he did not possess. As the Cold War came to a close, Kennan reiterated his long-held belief that authority was preferable to "the total undependability of our world environment." See *The Kennan Diaries*, ed. Frank Costigliola (New York: W. W. Norton, 2014), p. 624.

23. *Life*, March 3, 1950.

24. The work of Raymond L. Garthoff, particularly *Detente and Confrontation: American-Soviet Relations from Nixon to Reagan* (Washington, DC: Brookings, 1985), 524–25, stands out for alerting readers to the constraints that limited the ability of the two superpowers to impose unilateral solutions on one another.

25. For the difficulties that nuclear war posed for realist theory, see Campbell Craig, *Glimmer of a New Leviathan: Total War in the Realism of Niebuhr, Morgenthau, and Waltz* (New York: Columbia University Press, 2003).

26. One of Kennan's most influential books—perhaps his most influential—consisted of a series of seat-of-the-pants lectures in which he assailed the "legalism" and "moralism" of American policy. By my reading, this canonical text of realism was actually a scathing critique of America's liberal faith in the benign operation of international society. George F. Kennan, *American Diplomacy, 1900–1950* (Chicago: University of Chicago Press, 1951).

27. The bluntest statement of the argument that the Cold War could have been won by commercial and cultural means is found in Walter Hixson, *Parting the Curtain: Propaganda, Culture, and the Cold War, 1945–1961* (New York: St. Martin's Press, 1997).

28. Akira Iriye, "Cultural History and International History: How They Might Connect," paper delivered at the University of Paris 7—Denis Diderot (June 3, 1999); Thomas Kuhn, *The Structure of Scientific Revolutions*, 2nd ed. enlarged (Chicago: University of Chicago Press, 1970), 117.

29. *American Foreign Policy, Basic Documents, 1950–1955* (Washington, DC: USGPO, 1957), 1:8. It is true that Aristotle, like most Greeks, was unable to envision the good life outside the polis and its foundations in friendship, and consequently had little to say about international society. Moreover, the object of the Cold War, unlike the goal of the polis, was not the promotion of virtue or excellence (*areté*). Far from it, for the individualism that is at the heart of the modern liberal creed is seriously at odds with classical ideas of civic attachment in which the good of the polis took precedence over individual self-interest. But it would be absurd to restrict Aristotle's insights to the polis, for if that were the case the

peculiarities of a bygone way of life would make it wholly alien, an object of mere curiosity without continuing relevance to modern societies.

CHAPTER EIGHT

1. Another possibility often encountered is that such assertions flowed from a deep cynicism, designed to frighten and mobilize public opinion. Scaremongering? Sure, politicians do it all the time. But in this case there is no evidence to show that they took the Cold War with anything but great seriousness—much too seriously, even, on numerous occasions.

2. Although some scholars, particularly anthropologists, have been known to conflate ideology and culture, numerous distinctions can and need to be drawn between the two. For one thing, various ideologies, competitive and mutually hostile, can exist within a culture, either at the same time or serially, as in twentieth-century Germany. While cultures serve as indispensable hosts for ideologies, the relationship of ideology to culture can change quite dramatically, as is shown in the tempestuous alternation in some countries between socialism, fascism, and liberalism. Ideologies can also mutate more rapidly than cultures, and in some amazing ways, in addition to which they possess a potential for universality that particular cultures do not because they can find homes within many quite different cultures. Ideologies can become deeply embedded within cultures to the point of being naturalized, but they can also reemerge from the depths to become consciously articulated, contested, and significantly transformed. And, of course, new ideologies can always emerge. Obviously, a comprehensive exploration of such themes would easily take up a sizable book.

3. A search of Google Ngrams shows use of the term rising slowly in the 1960s and taking off in the mid-1980s, much like references to globalization. To be sure, a cosmopolitan high culture was often a unifying element, but this was merely an overlay that different from the demotic kind of transnational culture that emerged in the Cold War.

4. On some connections between political and cultural history, see Frank Ninkovich, "Das Ende der Paradigmen: Die kulturgeschichtliche Wende und die Globalisierung der Amerikanischen Diplomatiegeschichte," in *Deutschland und die USA in der Internationalen Geschichte des 20. Jahrhunderts: Festschrift für Detlef Junker*, ed. Manfred Berg und Philipp Gassert (Stuttgart: Franz Steiner Verlag 2004), 58–79.

5. Henry Stimson to Harry S. Truman, July 2, 1945, *FRUS, 1945, The Conference of Berlin (The Potsdam Conference)*, 891. Any inventory of the differences would need to include the following. In Germany, there was no continuity of government, whereas in Japan the imperial polity persisted; Germany experienced four-power control that led to a half century of national disunity, whereas Japan, though deprived of its empire, continued territorially intact; the object of policy in Germany after 1949 was to integrate Germany into Europe-wide institutions, whereas Japan's reconciliation with its neighbors was a hesitant and often testy affair. The absence of regional institutions made the bilateral relationship between Japan and the United States even more important, for both parties and for Japan's neighbors in Asia. Denazification in Germany, though it had its absurdist aspects, was far more successful than the attempt to convey a sense of Japan's war guilt. The demilitarization of Japan was sweeping, in principle at least, but efforts to purge Japan of the exceptionalist mentality that

produced Japanese imperialism was less effective. Whereas German rearmament was difficult to manage, Japanese rearmament would have been far more explosive. Hiroshima and Nagasaki provided a sense of victimhood and attenuation of war guilt that was much more muted in Germany. Most importantly, perhaps, the United States did not need Japan in the way that it needed Germany, which is why the Cold War for a time seemed to be primarily a Euro-Atlantic affair.

6. Reinhold Wagnleitner, *Coca-Colonization and the Cold War: The Cultural Mission of the United States in Austria after the Second World War*, trans. Diana M. Wolf (Chapel Hill: University of North Carolina Press, 1994).

7. D. W. Ellwood, *Rebuilding Europe: Western Europe, America and West European Reconstruction* (New York: Longman, 1992); Ellwood, "'You Too Can Be Like Us': Selling the Marshall Plan," *History Today*, October 1998.

8. Raymond L. Garthoff, "Provocative Hypotheses," *Bulletin of the Atomic Scientists* 53, no. 6 (1997): 60. For a more recent repackaging of this theme, see John Lenczowski, *Full Spectrum Diplomacy and Grand Strategy: Reforming the Structure and Culture of U.S. Foreign Policy* (Lanham, MD: Lexington Books, 2011); Liping Bu, *Making the World Like Us: Education, Cultural Expansion, and the American Century* (Westport, CT: Praeger, 2003). Laura Belmonte, *Selling the American Way: U.S. Propaganda and the Cold War* (Philadelphia: University of Pennsylvania Press, 2008) is a good synthetic account.

9. Hixson, *Parting the Curtain*; Matthew Evangelista, *Unarmed Forces: The Transnational Movement to End the Cold War* (Ithaca, NY: Cornell University Press, 1999); Petra Goedde, *GIs and Germans: Culture, Gender and Foreign Relations, 1945–1949* (New Haven, CT: Yale University Press, 2003).

10. This condescending attitude is evident among historians of foreign relations, whose mainstream practitioners view scholarly interest in cultural relations as a divertissement.

11. Subsequent attempts to deploy culture and ideology have fared little better, though some theorists argued that it could be quite effective if properly used. Joseph Nye has pointed to the important role of "soft power"—"the ability to get what you want through attraction rather than through coercion or payments"—as an underappreciated implement in the diplomatic tool kit. Adding seduction to the standard coercive forms of power is attractive because it argues for a multidimensional understanding of how international relations play out. But, for all that, this view of culture remains reductionist. Because it continues to view culture as an instrumental form of power, it fails to provide a convincing way of explaining the significant role played by American culture in the Cold War. My guess is that its explanatory usefulness in other areas is similarly limited. Joseph S. Nye, *Soft Power: The Means to Success in World Politics* (Cambridge, MA: Perseus Books), x.

12. Yale Richmond, *Cultural Exchange and the Cold War: Raising the Iron Curtain* (University Park: Pennsylvania State University Press, 2003), argues that the programs effectively influenced Soviet elites and thus paved the way for Gorbachev and his regime-ending policy departures. In contrast to this emphasis on the targeting of elites, an energetic case for the greater influence of mass culture is made in Neal Rosendorf's "The Life and Times of Samuel Bronston, Builder of 'Hollywood in Madrid': A Study in the International

Scope and Influence of American Popular Culture" (PhD diss., Harvard University, 2000), 43–46.

13. Richard T. Arndt. *The First Resort of Kings: American Cultural Diplomacy in the Twentieth Century* (Dulles, VA: Potomac Books, Inc., 2005).

14. A. Ross Johnson, *Radio Free Europe and Radio Liberty: The CIA Years and Beyond* (Stanford, CA: Stanford University Press, 2010), 55; Anne-Chantal Lepeuple, "Radio Free Europe et Radio Liberty (1950–1994)," *Vingtième Siècle. Revue d'histoire* 48 (October–December, 1995): 31–45.

15. Nicholas Cull, *The Cold War and the United States Information Agency: American Propaganda and Public Diplomacy, 1945–1989* (New York: Cambridge University Press, 2008), 503.

16. The title of Melvyn Leffler's book, *For the Soul of Mankind: The United States, the Soviet Union, and the Cold War* (New York: Hill and Wang, 2007), is taken from a remark by President George H. W. Bush.

17. It may appear from this paragraph and the argument to come that I am denying the primacy of not only of politics, but of economics, in favor of what Roland Robertson has called "the independent dynamics of global culture." All I am saying is that culture matters more or less and in different ways at certain points in history, which also holds true for politics and economics. Roland Robertson, *Globalization: Social Theory and Global Culture* (Thousand Oaks, CA: Sage, 1992), 61. In any case, I am not sure what "primacy" and "independent dynamics" are supposed to mean. On differences between Robertson's view and more deterministic standpoints, see Anthony D. King, ed., *Culture, Globalization and the World System: Contemporary Conditions for the Representation of Identity* (Minneapolis: University of Minnesota Press, 1997), 162.

18. This is an important point that first came to my attention in reading Paul Ricoeur, *Lectures on Ideology and Utopia* (New York: Columbia University Press, 1986), who pointed out that ideology requires a medium in which to flourish, viz., culture—disquieting food for thought for those who continue to adhere to the simple Marxist base-superstructure thesis in which ideologies are unmediated reflections of material conditions.

19. Karl Polanyi, *The Great Transformation* (New York: Rinehart & Co., 1944) is still the most important work I know of that raises fundamental questions about whether economics or culture deserves priority.

20. Clifford Geertz, *The Interpretation of Cultures. Selected Essays* (New York. Basic Books, 1973), 68. Probably the best-known argument of this sort is Talcott Parsons's view of culture as the mechanism of cybernetic control and coordination of a functional social system. For a brief explanation, see Kenneth Allan, *Explorations in Classical Sociological Theory: Seeing the Social World* (Thousand Oaks, CA: Pine Grove Press, 2005), 364. See also Durkheim's preface to the second edition, *The Division of Labor in Society*, trans. George Simpson (New York: Free Press, 1964), 28. One of the central arguments of Durkheim's classic text, as I understand it, is that modern society is not characterized by an atomistic individualism of the kind that Herbert Spencer appeared to posit; on the contrary, it is distinguished by the

emergence of a different form of solidarity that is supported by a vast substructure of underlying moral sentiment that is taken for granted. To use his terminology, mere functional coherence (organic solidarity) was undergirded by something deeper (mechanical solidarity).

21. My view is that there is no single absolute meaning that is common to seemingly identical cultural behaviors. The pragmatic and relativist standard classically put forward by Willard van Orman Quine, *Word and Object* (Cambridge: Technology Press of the Massachusetts Institute of Technology, 1960), is good enough for me.

22. Seth Mydans, "Ripe Time for Soviet Students in U.S.," *NYT*, September 2, 1991, 10. Said one exchange student: "It is very hard to return to the Soviet Union when you have lived in a normal country."

23. On this point, see, e.g., the argument advanced by Edward Said, *Culture and Imperialism* (New York: Random House, 1994), 66, 96, in his discussion of Jane Austen's *Mansfield Park*; Peter L. Berger, "Four Faces of Global Culture," *National Interest* 49 (Fall 1997).

24. Fidel Castro's stratagem of periodically allowing malcontents to flee to the United States was a stroke of genius, for he realized that the overwhelming majority of Cubans remained attached to the motherland and to the regime.

25. James Burnham, *The Managerial Revolution* (New York: John Day Company, 1941); Friedrich Hayek, *The Road to Serfdom* (Chicago: University of Chicago Press, 1944). For the shift of emphasis from production to consumption in American economic thought, see Kathleen B. Donohue, *Freedom from Want: American Liberalism and the Idea of the Consumer*, New Studies in American Intellectual and Cultural History (Baltimore: Johns Hopkins University Press, 2005). Dreyfus and Rabinow, while trying to get a handle on Michel Foucault's most significant intellectual contribution, argue that he shows through various examples "how our culture attempts to normalize individuals through increasingly rationalized means, by turning them into meaningful subjects and docile objects." *Michel Foucault: Beyond Structuralism and Hermeneutics* (Chicago: University of Chicago Press, 1983), xxxvii.

26. Whether the background is social, or cultural—or for that matter, what the difference between the two might be—is not made clear in most discussions of the phenomenon. For my purposes, it is both, though in what follows I shall be emphasizing its cultural aspects, if only for the reason that it makes for a better fit with what have widely been viewed as cultural developments in the post–World War II era.

27. Charles Taylor, *A Secular Age* (Cambridge, MA: Belknap Press, 2007), 173. On the importance of "imaginaries," see Taylor, *Modern Social Imaginaries* (Durham, NC: Duke University Press, 2004), 23–30, and Taylor, "On Social Imaginaries," in *Traversing the Imaginary: Richard Kearney and the Postmodern Challenge*, ed. Peter Gratton, John Panteleimon Manoussakis, and Richard Kearney (Evanston, IL: Northwestern University Press, 2007), 29–47. The idea of background is most closely associated with John Searle, whose philosophical orientation is not to my taste. Nevertheless, what he has to say about "the Background" would appear to put him in the company of certain of his bêtes noires, i.e., German philosophers whose names begin with the letter *H*. See John R. Searle, *The Construction of*

Social Reality (New York: Free Press, 1995), 9–11. A brief discussion of the background can be found at http://philosophy.uwaterloo.ca/MindDict/thebackground.html#references. The work of Martin Heidegger about a prereflective stance to the world has been seminal for many philosophers and thinkers. The hermeneutic approach of his student Hans-Georg Gadamer and his remarks about the role of "prejudices" have been more immediately relevant to my understanding of history. The essay by Hubert Dreyfus, "Being and Power: Revisited," in *Foucault and Heidegger*, ed. Alan Milchman and Alan Rosenberg (Minneapolis: University of Minnesota Press, 2003), draws some interesting parallels between Heidegger's concept of being and Michel Foucault's theme of regimes of power. Thomas Kuhn's concept of a paradigm in his *The Structure of Scientific Revolutions* seems to operate in much the same way for the sciences.

It would complicate matters unnecessarily to discuss this cultural development by using the trendy concept of memetic evolution. In the awareness that as a layman I may well be out of my depth, it strikes me that the systematic use of cultural evolution in historical explanation is an attempt to lend scientific cachet to a field that is not even a social science. As an arranged marriage based on a bad metaphor, it is likely to end unhappily.

CHAPTER NINE

1. Robert Rydell and Rob Kroes, *Buffalo Bill in Bologna: The Americanization of the World, 1869–1922* (Chicago: University of Chicago Press, 1905); Emily Rosenberg, *Spreading the American Dream: American Economic and Cultural Expansion, 1890–1945* (New York: Hill and Wang, 1982); Reinhold Wagnleitner, "The Empire of the Fun, or Talkin' Soviet Union Blues: The Sound of Freedom and U.S. Cultural Hegemony in Europe," *Diplomatic History* 23 (Summer 1999): 519. See also Emily Rosenberg, "Consuming the American Century," in *The Short American Century*, ed. Andrew J. Bacevich (Cambridge, MA: Harvard University Press, 2012), 38–58.

2. Quoted in David Kynaston, *Modernity Britain: Opening the Box, 1957–1959* (New York: Bloomsbury, 2013 [Kindle edition]).

3. Marley, *How "American" Is Globalization?* (Baltimore: Johns Hopkins University Press, 2006) minimizes American economic contributions and emphasizes the survival of local tastes and traditions. On the other hand, Michael Hirsh, *At War with Ourselves: Why America Is Squandering Its Chance to Build a Better World* (Oxford: Oxford University Press 2003), 128–29, holds that "it was America that principally globalized [European] modernity and transmuted it into a set of universal values." Why Americanization persists as a characterization of the cultural changes that swept over the world is unclear. A combination of things account for it, probably. To some it is flattering, while to critics within the United States and outside it is a convenient term of opprobrium that testifies less to the power of American culture than to one side of American imperialism. Or perhaps its attractiveness lies in its ability to capture a significant element of truth as a convenient metonymic device. More than likely it is also partly attributable to the persistence of viewing international relations solely in terms of power.

4. Edwin O. Reischauer, *Japan: The Story of a Nation* (New York: Knopf, 1974). In the case of Germany, American influence was diluted by virtue of the fact the occupation was run by a quartet in which the American voice did not necessarily stand out.

5. Peter L. Berger, "Introduction: The Cultural Dynamics of Globalization," in *Many Globalizations: Cultural Diversity in the Contemporary World*, ed. Peter L. Berger and Samuel P. Huntington (New York: Oxford University Press, 2002), 7.

6. Richard Pells, "Double Crossings: The Reciprocal Relationship between European and American Culture in the Twentieth Century," in *Americanism and Anti-Americanism: The German Encounter with American Culture after 1945*, ed. Alexander Stephan (New York: Berghahn Books, 2005), 190.

7. Baseball, while undoubtedly international if not universal, was dropped as a sport for the 2010 Olympic games.

8. For a brief history of the uses of "globalization," and the logarithmic increase in the use of the term "globalization" in the 1980s, see Nayan Chanda, *Bound Together: How Traders, Preachers, Adventurers, and Warriors Shaped Globalization* (New Haven: Yale University Pres 2007), 245–70. Just as the founding of *National Geographic* in the 1880s was significant, it is noteworthy that the journal *Global Society* was created in 1985. For the case that the 1970s mark the decade in which postwar globalization emerged, see the essays in Niall Ferguson, Charles S. Maier, Erez Manela, and Daniel J. Sargent, eds., *The Shock of the Global: The 1970s in Perspective* (Cambridge, MA: Belknap Press, 2010).While many scholars see globalization as arriving in waves over periods of a century or longer, Bruce Mazlish is notable for arguing that it is a product of fairly recent times.

9. Samuel P. Huntington, *The Third Wave: Democratization in the Late Twentieth Century* (Norman: University of Oklahoma Press, 1991).

10. Victoria de Grazia, *Irresistible Empire: America's Advance through Twentieth-Century Europe* (Cambridge: Belknap, 2005), 113–14. It would be unfair not to note that liberalism is no more enlightening when it comes to drawing the contours of the ideal society.

11. "Elite Theory," in *Blackwell Dictionary of Modern Social Thought*, ed. William Outhwaite (Malden, MA: Blackwell, 2003), 195.

12. Bill Keller, "Russia's Restless Youth," *NYT*, July 26, 1987, 27; Flora Lewis, "Oh, For a Normal Country," *NYT*, October 12, 1988, A31; Flora Lewis, "Watershed for Gorbachev," *NYT*, July 5, 1989, A21; Robin Finn, "Fetisov and Starikov, of New Jersey, U.S.A.," *NYT*, October 11, 1989, D30; Tom Malinowski, "Poland Settles Down to Democracy," *NYT*, December 8, 1990, L25; Flora Lewis, "After Five Years," *NYT*, December 12, 1990, A23. Yale Richmond, "Cultural Exchange and the Cold War: How the West Won," speech at the Aleksanteri Institute's Ninth Annual Conference "Cold War Interactions Reconsidered," October 2009, 29–31, University of Helsinki, Finland. From time to time, people in other countries have expressed a desire to live in "a normal country," e.g., Germany and Japan, post-Soviet Russia, Israel, Italy, and even the United States. The common thread here, I would argue, is the ability of international society to estrange people from national peculiarities that otherwise would remain culturally embedded.

13. Mark Twain, *Collected Tales, Sketches, Speeches and Essays*, vol. 2, *1891–1910* (New York: Library of America, 1992), 942; Peter Singer, *Hegel: A Very Short Introduction* (New York: Oxford University Press, 2001), 38. The continuing hostility of socialism to consumerism is evident in this response by President Evo Morales to an interviewer's question about how best to end capitalism: "It's changing economic policies, ending luxury, consumerism. It's ending the struggle to—or this searching for living better. Living better is to exploit human beings. It's plundering natural resources. It's egoism and individualism. Therefore, in those promises of capitalism, there is no solidarity or complementarity. There's no reciprocity. So that's why we're trying to think about other ways of living lives and living well, not living better. Not living better. Living better is always at someone else's expense. Living better is at the expense of destroying the environment." See http://endofcapitalism.com/category/consumerism/.

14. Adam Smith, *The Theory of Moral Sentiments* (Minneapolis: Filiquarian Publishing, 1977 [1759]), especially chap. 3, 77. "Of the Corruption of our Moral Sentiments . . ." in which he argues, in a disapproving Presbyterian manner, that "it is from our disposition to admire, and consequently to imitate, the rich and the great, that they are enabled to set, or to lead what is called the fashion. Their dress is the fashionable dress; the language of their conversation, the fashionable style; their air and deportment, the fashionable behaviour. Even their vices and follies are fashionable; and the greater part of men are proud to imitate and resemble them in the very qualities which dishonour and degrade them."

15. The Olympic games featured all sorts of themes—among them nationalism, internationalism, Cold War conflict, and blatant commercialism—but the desire for host countries to be included, as well as for the international community to welcome them, is apparent from the selection of post–World War II sites for the summer games.

16. "China's President Lashes Out at Western Culture," *NYT*, January 4, 2012, A7.

17. Niall Ferguson and Moritz Schularick, *NYT*, November 16, 2009. A joke making the rounds was that the United States was obligated by treaty to come to the defense of Taiwan in the event of hostilities with China, but that it would have to borrow money from China to pay for it.

18. Manuel Castells, *The Information Age: Economy, Society and Culture*, vol. 3, *End of Millennium* (Malden, MA: Blackwell, 2010), 5–67.

19. Robert Service, "The Next Russian Revolution?," *NYT*, December 23, 1991. For arguments about the role of consumerism as a force in East Germany, see Susan E. Reid, "Cold War in the Kitchen: Gender and the De-Stalinization of Consumer Taste in the Soviet Union under Khrushchev," *Slavic Review* 61, no. 2 (Summer, 2002): 211–52.

20. Richard Nixon, "A War about Peace: The Victory of Freedom," *Vital Speeches of the Day* 57, no. 12 (April 1, 1991): 357.

21. Thomas Risse-Kappen, "Ideas Do Not Float Freely: Transnational Coalitions, Domestic Structures, and the End of the Cold War," *International Organization* 48, no. 2 (Spring 1994): 185–214; Emily Rosenberg, "Consumer Capitalism and the End of the Cold War," in *Cambridge History of the Cold War*, ed. Melvyn Leffler and Odd Arne Westad (New York: Cambridge University Press, 2010), 508–9. Gorbachev was, in my estimation, a greater and

more imaginative leader than Woodrow Wilson. While both were able to penetrate beyond everyday happenings to an understanding of the deeper meaning of events, Gorbachev was able to question his belief system, something that the proud Wilson was incapable of doing.

22. *NYT*, January 6, 1987. On the role of fundamental vs. operative ideologies, see Martin Seliger, *Ideology and Politics* (New York: Free Press, 1976) and *The Marxist Conception of Ideology* (New York: Cambridge University Press, 1977), 4–5.

23. Zdenek Mlynar, *Conversations with Gorbachev* (New York: Columbia University Press, 2002), 153.

24. Gorbachev, *On My Country and the World* (New York: Columbia University Press, 2000), 175; Gorbachev, "A Common European Home," speech to the Council of Europe, Strasbourg, July 6, 1989, *Vital Speeches* 55, no. 23 (September 15, 1989): 706. Vladislav M. Zubok, *A Failed Empire: The Soviet Union in the Cold War from Stalin to Gorbachev* (Chapel Hill: University of North Carolina Press, 2007), 303–35; Gorbachev Nobel lecture, June 15, 1991.

25. James Baker, *Spiegel* interview, September 23, 2009, Spiegel Online International.

26. Gorbachev, *On My Country and the World*, 39; Gorbachev Nobel lecture, June 15, 1991.

27. Gorbachev, *On My Country and the World*, 181; Vladislav M. Zubok, "New Evidence on the End of the Cold War," *Cold War International History Project Bulletin*, no. 12/13 (Fall/Winter 2001): 13; Clifford Geertz, "Common Sense as a Cultural System," *Local Knowledge: Further Essays in Interpretive Anthropology* (New York: Basic Books, 1983), 73–93.

28. Robert D. English, *Russia and the Idea of the West: Gorbachev, Intellectuals, and the End of the Cold War* (New York: Columbia University Press, 2000), 40; Matthew Evangelista, *Unarmed Forces: The Transnational Movement to End the Cold War* (Ithaca, NY: Cornell University Press, 1999); Mikhail Gorbachev, *On My Country and the World*, 269.

29. Mikhail Gorbachev, "International Affairs, Asia and the Pacific Region," July 28, 1986, *Vital Speeches of the Day* 52, no. 23 (September 15, 1986): 707; Andrei Grachev, *Gorbachev's Gamble: Soviet Foreign Policy and the End of the Cold War* (Cambridge, MA: Polity, 2008), 233. Gorbachev's rough treatment of the Baltic states may appear to contradict this assertion. I prefer to see it as a tactical deviation.

30. Obviously, I have no sympathy for the view that Ronald Reagan deserves chief credit for ending the Cold War, which is a parochial and simpleminded view of history.

31. One can, at least in principle, imagine a time when complex historical problems will be tackled by large teams of historians, not unlike the hundreds of scientists who collaborate in particle physics. I doubt that this will ever come to pass, and if it ever does, I doubt that the histories produced by such collaboration will amount to much.

32. Those who argue that realistic deal making would have spared the world much agony tend to neglect a very important feature of realist thinking, viz., that deals are not made for their own sake. They are expressions of the limitations placed upon states by power realities. But because, in the realist scheme of things, the state system is based on the pursuit of power, such deals are by their very nature only temporary. Hence instability and

insecurity are destined to reemerge in more menacing form as states ratchet up their power potentials.

33. Thomas Paterson, *On Every Front: The Making and Unmaking of the Cold War* (New York: W. W. Norton, 1992), 230, maintains that "the Cold War actually had no winners. Both the United States and the Soviet Union had spent themselves into weakened conditions and were in a state of decline and collapse." This accords with Gorbachev's view that "we all lost the cold war." But this way of looking at things still frames the outcome in terms of winners and losers.

CHAPTER TEN

1. Charles Krauthammer, "The Unipolar Moment," *Foreign Affairs* 70 (Winter 1990/1991): 23–33. For the argument that the unchangeable truths of realism still applied, see Kenneth N. Waltz, "Structural Realism after the Cold War," *International Security* 25, no. 1 (Summer 2000): 5–41. A more neutral characterization is Elizabeth Cobbs Hoffman, *American Umpire* (Cambridge, MA: Harvard University Press, 2013).

2. On bureaucratic pathologies, see especially the classic work by Francis E. Rourke, *Bureaucracy and Foreign Policy* (Baltimore: Johns Hopkins University Press, 1972).

3. John Mueller, *Retreat from Doomsday* (New York: Basic Books, 1990), 11, is the locus classicus of the argument that great power war is obsolete. See also Christopher J. Fettweis, "A Revolution in International Relation Theory; Or, What If Mueller Is Right?," *International Studies Review* 8, no. 4 (December 2006): 677–97.

4. Obviously, the leading nations of the world did not sing in perfect harmony. They disagreed on a host of issues—genocide in Rwanda and Sudan's Darfur region, sanctions against Iraq, action against North Korea and Iran, and policy toward the Israeli-Palestinian problem, among others. Russia was an annoyance, but the nation most often identified as a source of renewed great power competition was China, with its amazing economic growth, increasing self-confidence, and burgeoning military capability. However, the dire forecasts of a looming conflict with this new giant neglect the fact that this single-party state, with its mixed economy tilting rapidly toward the capitalist mode of production, was increasingly dependent upon the continued success of an open world economy, and in particular on its close relationship to the United States as consumer of its exports, for sustaining the economic growth upon which the legitimacy of the Communist Party depended. China's continued success, moreover, was dependent on the success of globalization.
See Kenneth Lieberthal and Wang Jisi, "Addressing U.S.-China Strategic Distrust," Brookings Center, 2012. (These comments were written before the crisis between Russia and Ukraine erupted early in 2014. Nevertheless, these events have not substantially changed my views.)

5. David L. Marcus, "The New Diplomacy," *Boston Globe Magazine*, June 1, 2007, 17; Lawrence F. Kaplan, "Dollar Diplomacy Returns," *Commentary* 105, no. 2 (February 1998); Clinton, remarks at a dinner for the Conference on Progressive Governance for the 21st Century in Florence, Italy, November 20, 1999; Clinton remarks to business and community leaders in Santiago, Chile, April 16, 1998, PPUS.

6. George W. Bush, inaugural address, January 20, 2005. At the dedication of his presidential library in Dallas on April 27, 1913, Bush repeated the sentiment: "My deepest conviction—the guiding principle of the administration—is that the United States of America must strive to expand the reach of freedom."

7. Clyde Prestowitz, *Rogue Nation: American Unilateralism and the Failure of Good Intentions* (New York: Basic Books, 2003).

8. Policy makers in the early Cold War years had anticipated and rejected a hegemonic policy based on power. In 1950, Paul Nitze, in looking forward to a post–Cold War world, argued that "Pax Americana [here read hegemony] would be contrary to the American ethos, and it would invite enmity and opposition to us on the part of other peoples and nations. Moreover, it was beyond the capacity and will of the United States to enforce." Paul Nitze, *From Hiroshima to Glasnost: At the Center of Decision; A Memoir* (New York: Grove Weidenfeld, 1989), 119.

9. Max Boot, *Wall Street Journal*, July 1, 2002. Some observers offered a structural interpretation of events in which the mere existence of such a superior military force mandated its use. Clinton's secretary of state Madeleine Albright had famously wondered, "What's the point of you saving this superb military for, Colin, if we can't use it?" Madeleine Korbel Albright, *Madam Secretary: A Memoir* (New York: Miramax Books, 2003). For one synoptic effort, see Kimberly Kagan, ed., *The Imperial Moment* (Cambridge, MA: Harvard University Press, 2010). For a review of the recurrent thorny issues that attend debates about empire, see Paul K, MacDonald, "Those Who Forget Historiography Are Doomed to Republish It: Empire, Imperialism and Contemporary Debates about American Power," *Review of International Studies* 35, no. 1 (January 2009): 45–67.

10. Though Great Britain had been a world power, it was not nearly as influential militarily as the United States. It was not the dominant power in Europe; its responsibilities came nowhere near to matching those of the United States; and it was, quite unashamedly, a colonial empire. Despite many marvelous cultural achievements to its credit, Great Britain's mass democracy never came close to creating the kind of magnetic attraction that American society would generate in the postwar years.

11. Some scholars claimed to find precedents for this action, but their procrustean arguments strained to fit a historical aberration into a pattern that was not there. See especially John Lewis Gaddis, *Surprise, Security, and the American Experience* (Cambridge, MA: Harvard University Press, 2004), and Tony Smith, "The Bush Doctrine as Wilsonianism," in *Wilsonianism in Crisis?*, ed. G. John Ikenberry (Princeton, NJ: Princeton University Press, forthcoming), posted as http://ase.tufts.edu/polsci/faculty/smith/wilsonianism.pdf. For a counterargument, see Frank Ninkovich, "Wilsonianism after the Cold War: Words, Words, Mere Words . . . ," in *Reconsidering Woodrow Wilson*, 299–326.

12. Michael Mandelbaum, *The Case for Goliath: How America Acts as the World's Government in the Twenty-First Century* (New York: Public Affairs, 2005).

13. Edward A. Kolodziej and Roger E. Kanet, eds., *From Superpower to Besieged Global Power: Restoring World Order after the Failure of the Bush Doctrine* (Athens: University of Georgia Press, 2008). For a discussion of the distinction between primacy and hegemony as

an exercise of legitimate authority, see Ian Clark, *Hegemony in International Society* (New York: Oxford University Press, 2011).

14. Michael Mandelbaum, *The Frugal Superpower: America's Global Leadership in a Cash-Strapped Era* (New York: Public Affairs, 2010); Joseph S. Nye, "The Dependent Colossus," *Foreign Policy* (2002): 74–77; Joseph S. Nye, *The Paradox of American Power: Why the World's Only Superpower Can't Go It Alone* (Oxford: Oxford University Press 2002); G. John Ikenberry, "Liberalism and Empire: Logics of Order in the American Unipolar Age," *Review of International Studies* 30 (2004): 609–30.

15. Hodgson, *The Myth of American Exceptionalism*, 128–54; "Sustainability and Equity: A Better Future for All," *UN Human Development Report 2011* (New York: Palgrave Macmillan, 2011).

16. January 30, 2012, interview on Al-Hayat TV as cited in Adam Liptak, "'We the People' Loses Appeal with People around the World," *NYT*, February 6, 1912. The US murder rate per 100,000 was actually relatively moderate, though high when compared with western Europe, China, and Japan. It ranked twenty-fourth overall worldwide in 2012.

17. Fareed Zakaria, "The Strategist," *Time* 179, no. 4 (January 30, 2012): 26, 28; G. John Ikenberry, "Liberal Internationalism 3.0: America and the Dilemmas of a Liberal World Order," *Perspectives on Politics* 6, no. 1 (March 2009): 71–87.

18. Fareed Zakaria, *The Post American World* (New York: Norton, 2009).

19. President Obama's address to the nation on Syria, September 10, 2013; Mark Feisenthal, "Economists Foretell of U.S. Decline, China's Ascension," *Reuters*, January 10, 2011. Peter Beinart, "The End of American Exceptionalism," *National Journal Magazine* (Febraury 3, 2014). National Intelligence Council, *Global Trends 2030: Alternative Worlds* (Washington, DC: 2012): "By 2030, no country—whether the US, China, or any other large country—will be a hegemonic power." See also the essays in *The Short American Century*.

20. While advocating an ambitious expansion of American influence throughout the world, Henry R. Luce's famous essay "The American Century" was notable for rejecting geopolitical justifications for American participation in the war. Henry R. Luce, *The American Century* (New York: Farrar and Rinehardt, 1941), 20–24, 32–34. See David M. Kennedy's essay in *The Short American Century*, 15–37.

21. Henry Luce, "The American Century," *Life*, February 17, 1941.

CONCLUDING THOUGHTS

1. "Normal internationalism" is a term of art that I have used for this outlook in a previous work. See Frank Ninkovich, *The Wilsonian Century* (Chicago: University of Chicago Press, 1999). I was surprised later to discover an unexpected bedfellow in Jeane Kirkpatrick, "A Normal Country in a Normal Time," *National Interest* (Fall 1990): 40–43.

2. Carole Fink, *Defending the Rights of Others: The Great Powers, the Jews, and International Minority Protection, 1878–1938* (New York: Cambridge University Press, 2004).

3. Max Weber, *Economy and Society*, ed. Guenther Roth and Claus Wittich (Berkeley: University of California Press, 1978), 63–65. In this section, Weber distinguishes between

economic action and economically oriented action, which could involve political uses of force or activities such as piracy.

4. To those who might be tempted to argue that globalization is merely is merely the idea of progress with a social makeover, I would disagree. Globalization is concrete, rather than abstract or rational; it is not likely to be comprehended or managed by instrumental reason; far from being inevitable, it is reversible or at least destructible; and its progressive qualities are balanced by a host of less admirable features that do not conform with the doctrine of an underlying harmony of interests. It is a real process that policy makers have pragmatically tried to make the best of.

5. Anders Stephanson, "Imperial Pursuits," *Diplomatic History* 38, no. 4 (September 2004): 586, describes the Cold War as "the inside projection of the counter-empire, the evil empire, or, to be more precise, Anti-Christ." The most notable example of this move to expand the framework, which I applaud even as I disagree with much else, is Antonio Negri and Michael Hardt, *Empire* (Cambridge, MA: Harvard University Press, 2000). From a macrosociological perspective, the world-system theory of Immanuel Wallerstein emphasizes the priority of the world system over the functioning of its constituent states to a degree that would make even nineteenth-century determinists blush.

6. Detlef Junker, "Ein Dämon wird gesucht," *Frankfurter Allgemeine Zeitung*, March 25, 1995.

7. This I take to be the main point of Christina Klein's extraordinary *Cold War Orientalism: Asia in the Middlebrow Imagination, 1945–1961* (Berkeley: University of California Press, 2003). On the absence of "others": It was not clear who the enemy was until the War of 1812; the slave power does not count as an external enemy; the long stretch from 1865 to 1914, the 1920s to the late 1930s, and the 1990s are periods when an enemy was lacking.

8. John Gray, *False Dawn: The Delusions of Global Capitalism* (New York: Free Press, 1998).

APPENDIX

1. Max Lerner, *It Is Later Than You Think: The Need for a Militant Democracy* (New York: Viking Press, 1943), 83; John Kane, *Between Virtue and Power: The Persistent Moral Dilemma of U.S. Foreign Policy* (New Haven, CT, and London: Yale University Press), 2008. This sense of uniqueness is the meaning commonly derived from Alexis de Tocqueville's seminal description, in *Democracy in America* (Stilwell, KS: Digireads.com, 2007), 2:31.

From at least the time of the ancient Egyptians, intrinsic to many cultures was the belief that bona fide humanity was peculiar to them. Japan long viewed itself as a nation of divine origin descended from the sun goddess; Israel, or at least a large portion of it, continues to identify itself on the basis of its exclusive covenant with God, while at least some members of the Arab "nation" feel that they have a divinely sanctioned destiny to create a universal caliphate; Iranian Shiites entertain messianic beliefs of redemption coupled with a belief in a special racial-historical destiny; Russia long cultivated a semimystical image of itself as a nation that brought to the world unique spiritual qualities capable of elevating the lives of all human beings, a belief that found a new lease on life under Soviet communism; French national identity is heavily invested in its revolutionary enlightenment legacy of universalism and continues to embody those ideals in its current republican form; for many Germans during the Nazi era, the sense of superiority grounded in racial distinctiveness needs no elaboration; modern Turkish nationalism has been tinged by a powerful strain of racial superiority; China long viewed itself as the Middle Kingdom surrounded by the "four barbarians." And so on.

2. Nugent, *Habits of Empire*, 317; Thomas Bender, *A Nation among Nations: America's Place in World History* (New York: Hill and Wang, 2006), 296–97; Bender, "Is American History Exceptional? A Global Perspective," Washington History Seminar, December 5, 2011, Historical Perspectives on International and National Affairs; Daniel T. Rodgers, "American Exceptionalism Revisited," *Raritan* 24, no. 2 (2004): 46; Carl J. Guarneri, *America in the World: United States History in Global Context* (New York: McGraw-Hill, 2007). Another major critique of exceptionalism is Ian Tyrell, "American Exceptionalism in an Age of International History," *American Historical Review* 96 (October 1991): 1031–72. A good survey of some of the resulting literature can be found in Jay Sexton, "The Global View of the United States," *Historical Journal* 48, no. 1 (March 2005): 261–76. See also Michael Adas, "From Settler Colony to Global Hegemon: Integrating the Exceptionalist Narrative of the United States into World History," *American Historical Review* 106, no. 5 (December 2001): 1692–1720. Thomas Bender, "Introduction," in *America on the Global Stage: A Global Approach to U.S. History*, ed. Gary Reichard and Ted Dickson (Urbana: University of Illinois Press, 2008), xiii.

3. Joseph Lepgold and Timothy McKeown, "Is American Foreign Policy Exceptional?," *Political Science Quarterly* 110, no. 3 (Autumn 1995): 370; Stephen M. Walt, "The Myth of American Exceptionalism," *Foreign Policy* 189 (November 2011): 73. By another account, "the United States is—and always has been—a nation like all other nations, motivated by practical and realistic considerations and calculations and prepared to abandon principle if need be to achieve its larger policy goals." Mary Ann Heiss, "The Evolution of the Imperial Idea and U.S. National Identity" (Bernath Lecture), *Diplomatic History* 26, no. 4 (Fall 2002): 511–40.

4. Adas, "From Settler Colony to Global Hegemon," 1720; Joan Hoff, *A Faustian Foreign Policy from Woodrow Wilson to George W. Bush: Dreams of Perfectibility* (New York: Cambridge University Press, 2008); Hodgson, *The Myth of American Exceptionalism*, xvii. Most of those who write about the topic would say that the impact has been for the worse. A significant minority, meanwhile, would argue that the overall effect has been profoundly beneficial and a source of pride for all Americans. One author, for example, claims that America's global role is "the greatest gift the world has received in many, many centuries, possibly all of recorded history." Michael Hirsh, *At War with Ourselves: Why America Is Squandering Its Chance to Build a Better World* (Oxford: Oxford University Press 2003), 251. Scholarly works such as Tony Smith's *America's Mission: The United States and the Worldwide Struggle for Democracy* (Princeton, NJ: Princeton University Press, 2012) and G. John Ikenberry's *Liberal Leviathan" the Origins, Crisis, and Transformation of the American World*

Order (Princeton, NJ: Princeton University Press, 2011) emphasize America's contribution to the spread of democracy and its promotion of a supposedly liberal world order. The most muscular historical case for a persistent, ideologically and economically expansionist exceptionalism is made by Kagan, *Dangerous Nation*.

5. Deborah L. Madsen, *American Exceptionalism* (Oxford: University Press of Mississippi, 1998), 2; Herring, *From Colony to Superpower*. The National Security Strategy, March 2006, NSS 2006, www.whitehouse.gov/nsc/nss/2006.

6. David C. Hendrickson, *Union, Nation, or Empire*, 8. Kagan, *Dangerous Nation*, 38; Richard H. Ullman, "The 'Foreign World' and Ourselves: Washington, Wilson, and the Democrat's Dilemma," *Foreign Policy* 21 (Winter 1975–76): 103–4; Walter Hixson, *The Myth of American Diplomacy: National Identity and U.S. Foreign Policy* (New Haven, CT: Yale University Press, 2008), 5; Gilbert, *To the Farewell Address*, 17. For an introduction to American exceptionalism, see Alexander DeConde, Richard Dean Burns, and Fredrik Logevall, eds., *Encyclopedia of American Foreign Policy* (New York: Scribner, 2002), 2:63–80. Exceptionalism is also a "keyword" in cultural studies. For a quick overview, see Donald E. Pease, "Exceptionalism," in *Keywords for American Cultural Studies*, ed. Bruce Burgett and Glenn Hendler (New York: New York University Press,, 2007), 108–12.

7. Charles Hill, *Grand Strategies: Literature, Statecraft, and World Order* (New Haven, CT: Yale University Press, 2010), 150; Michael H. Hunt and Steven I. Levine, *The Arc of Empire: America's Wars in Asia from the Philippines to Vietnam* (Chapel Hill: University of North Carolina Press, 2012), 4; Walter Russell Mead, *Special Providence: American Foreign Policy and How It Changed the World* (New York: Routledge, 2002), 16.

8. For a good example of this kind of reasoning, see Howard Zinn, "The Power and the Glory: Myths of American Exceptionalism," *Boston Review* (Summer 2006).

9. Sometimes one encounters the term "Janus-faced" in such discussions, which is not a good metaphor because the Roman god Janus, often found at gates and doorways, showed the same face coming and going. Perhaps "two-faced" or references to a Jekyll-Hyde personality come nearer the mark. Actually, the signposts of American exceptionalism pointed in more than two foreign policy directions—from strict isolation, to politically disengaged cultural internationalism, to dollar diplomacy, and to full-fledged globalism at the other extreme. For an example of the Janus metaphor, see Donald Pease, "Re-Thinking American Studies after US Exceptionalism," *American Literary History* 21, no. 1 (Spring 2009).

10. Harold Koh, "America's Jekyll-and-Hyde Exceptionalism," in *American Exceptionalism and Human Rights*, ed. Michael Ignatieff (Princeton, NJ: Princeton University Press, 2005), 112.

11. Nugent, *Habits of Empire*, xv; Immerman, *Empire for Liberty*; McDougall, *Promised Land, Crusader State*.

12. Walter Bagehot, *Physics and Politics* (New York: D. Appleton & Co., 1906; Batoche Books: Kitchener, 2001), 214.

13. N.b., possibility, not necessity.

14. F. A. Hayek, *Law, Legislation, and Liberty*, vol. 1, *Rules and Order* (Chicago: University of Chicago Press, 1973), 52.

15. A mechanistic version of this analogy would amount to a form of secular Deism, in which the cultural clock, once wound, goes through its predetermined motions.

16. "Phenomenology and the Sciences of Man," in *The Primacy of Perception: and Other Essays on Phenomenological Psychology*, ed. Maurice Merleau-Ponty and James M. Edie (Evanston, IL: Northwestern University Press, 1964), 89. A quote from Cornelius Castoriadis, though forbiddingly cumbersome, nevertheless remains worth pondering: "For, what is given in and through history is not the determined sequence of the determinate but the emergence of radical alterity, immanent creation, nontrivial novelty. This is manifested by the history of existence in toto, as well as by the appearance of new societies (of new types of society) and the incessant self-transformation of each society." David Ames Curtis, ed., *The Castoriadis Reader* (Malden, MA: Blackwell, 1997), 214. Castoriadis's concept of "magma" (which resembles what I have been calling the background), his rant against causally explained identity across time, and his emphasis on culture as a creation are also pertinent.

17. Bender, *A Nation among Nations*, 296–97; Thomas Bender, "Introduction," in *America on the Global Stage*, xviii.

18. David Thelen "The Nation and Beyond: Transnational Perspectives on United States History," *Journal of American History* 86, no. 3 (December 1999): 965–75; Akira Iriye, *Cultural Internationalism and World Order* (Baltimore: Johns Hopkins University Press, 1997), 1; Tyrrell, "American Exceptionalism in an Age of International History," *The American Historical Review* 86 (October 1991), 1031–55; William H. McNeill, *Mythistory and Other Essays* (Chicago: University of Chicago Press,1986), 159.

INDEX

A-bomb, 156
Acheson, Dean, 154, 190, 209
Adams, Abigail, 18
Adams, Charles Francis, 42, 48, 68
Adams, John Quincy, 30, 32, 36
Afghanistan, 263
Africa, 21
Albright, Madeleine, 285
Al-Quaeda network, 260
Alstyne, Richard van, 30
Americanization, 200, 208–9, 218, 226–27;
    and consumerism, 214ff; and En-
    glish language, 230; and globalizing
    of America, 232–33; as metaphor for
    globalization, 227, 324n3; opposition to,
    227, 230–31; as response to globaliza-
    tion, 55–64
Anglo-Japanese Alliance, 126
Anglo-Saxonism, 62; and arbitration, 91,
    201
anti-imperialism, 72; in the 1920s, 131; and
    racism, 74; and Soviet strategy, 208, 238;
    and Wilsonianism, 109–10
antislavery, as British cause, 36
appeasement, 147–48, 159
Appleby, Joyce, 25
arbitration, 89–92
Aristotle, 43, 199, 223, 225, 319n29
Armstrong, Louis, 226
Asian "tigers," 179, 238
Atlantic Charter (1941), 173
atomic bomb, 156
Augustine of Hippo, 225
autocracies, 114, 132, 146–48, 151, 161,
    168, 181, 182, 309n15

Bagehot, Walter, 55, 289
Baker, James A., III, 246
barbarism, 32
Barlow, Joel, 20
Bastiat, Claude Frédéric, 53
Battle of Britain (1940), 155
Beard, Charles, 46, 149
Beatles, The, 227
Bemis, Samuel Flagg, 77
Bender, Thomas, 283–84
Berger, Peter, 219, 230
Bierce, Ambrose, 69
bin Laden, Osama, 261
Bismarck, Otto von, 117
Borah, William, 125, 141, 158
Bourdieu, Pierre, 222
Bretton Woods System, 174–75, 234
Brezhnev, Leonid, 243
BRIC nations, 180
Bright, John, 55
Bryan, William Jennings, 55
Buffalo Bill's Wild West, 50
Bullitt, William, 152
bureaucracy, 181–82, 258
Burke, Edmund, 12, 19, 108
Bush, George H. W., 246, 251, 258,
    262
Bush, George W., 108, 258; and rogue
    internationalism, 261–62; war on terror,
    260–61
business internationalism, 173

Calhoun, John, 32
Calvinism, 237–38
Canada, 228